Huebner School Series

FINANCIAL PLANNING APPLICATIONS
Twenty-Third Edition

Craig W. Lemoine

THE
AMERICAN
COLLEGE PRESS

HS332-23

This publication is designed to provide accurate and authoritative information about the subject covered. While every precaution has been taken in the preparation of this material, the authors, and The American College assume no liability for damages resulting from the use of the information contained in this publication. The American College is not engaged in rendering legal, accounting, or other professional advice. If legal or other expert advice is required, the services of an appropriate professional should be sought.

© 2012 The American College Press
270 S. Bryn Mawr Avenue
Bryn Mawr, PA 19010
(888) AMERCOL (263-7265)
theamericancollege.edu
All rights reserved
Library of Congress Control Number 2011935410
ISBN 10: 1-58293-059-7
ISBN 13: 978-1-58293-059-6
Printed in the United States of America

Individual Health Insurance Planning
Thomas P. O'Hare and Burton T. Beam, Jr.

Financial Planning: Process and Environment
Craig W. Lemoine

Fundamentals of Insurance Planning
Kevin M. Lynch and Glenn E. Stevick, Jr.

Fundamentals of Financial Planning
David M. Cordell (ed.)

Fundamentals of Income Taxation
Christopher P. Woehrle and Thomas M. Brinker, Jr. (eds.)

McGill's Life Insurance
Edward E. Graves (ed.)

McGill's Legal Aspects of Life Insurance
Edward E. Graves and Burke A. Christensen (eds.)

Group Benefits: Basic Concepts and Alternatives
Burton T. Beam, Jr.

Planning for Retirement Needs
David A. Littell and Kenn Beam Tacchino

Fundamentals of Investments for Financial Planning
Walt J. Woerheide

Fundamentals of Estate Planning
Constance J. Fontaine

Estate Planning Applications
Ted Kurlowicz

Planning for Business Owners and Professionals
Ted Kurlowicz

Financial Planning Applications
Craig W. Lemoine

Advanced Topics in Group Benefits
Juliana York and Burton T. Beam, Jr.(ed.)

Executive Compensation
Paul J. Schneider

Health and Long-Term Care Financing for Seniors
Allen C. McLellan

Financial Decisions for Retirement
David A. Littell (ed.)

To Tim—

Thank you for your constant perseverance, optimism and being the one person who always keeps me laughing.

Craig

The American College® is an independent, nonprofit, accredited institution founded in 1927 that offers professional certification and graduate-degree distance education to men and women seeking career growth in financial services.

The Center for Financial Advisor Education at The American College offers both the LUTCF and the Financial Services Specialist (FSS) professional designations to introduce students in a classroom environment to the technical side of financial services, while at the same time providing them with the requisite sales-training skills.

The Solomon S. Huebner School® of The American College administers the Chartered Life Underwriter (CLU®); the Chartered Financial Consultant (ChFC®); the Chartered Advisor for Senior Living (CASL®); the Registered Health Underwriter (RHU®); the Registered Employee Benefits Consultant (REBC®); and the Chartered Leadership Fellow® (CLF®) professional designation programs. In addition, the Huebner School also administers The College's CFP Board—registered education program for those individuals interested in pursuing CFP® certification, the CFP® Certification Curriculum.

The Richard D. Irwin Graduate School® of The American College offers the master of science in financial services (MSFS) degree, the Graduate Financial Planning Track (another CFP Board-registered education program), and several graduate-level certificates that concentrate on specific subject areas. It also offers the Chartered Advisor in Philanthropy (CAP®) and the master of science in management (MSM), a one-year program with an emphasis in leadership. The National Association of Estate Planners & Councils has named The College as the provider of the education required to earn its prestigious AEP designation.

The American College is accredited by **The Middle States Commission on Higher Education**, 3624 Market Street, Philadelphia, PA 19104 at telephone number 267.284.5000.

The Middle States Commission on Higher Education is a regional accrediting agency recognized by the U.S. Secretary of Education and the Commission on Recognition of Postsecondary Accreditation. Middle States accreditation is an expression of confidence in an institution's mission and goals, performance, and resources. It attests that in the judgment of the Commission on Higher Education, based on the results of an internal institutional self-study and an evaluation by a team of outside peer observers assigned by the Commission, an institution is guided by well-defined and appropriate goals; that it has established conditions and procedures under which its goals can be realized; that it is accomplishing them substantially; that it is so organized, staffed, and supported that it can be expected to continue to do so; and that it meets the standards of the Middle States Association. The American College has been accredited since 1978.

The American College does not discriminate on the basis of race, religion, sex, handicap, or national and ethnic origin in its admissions policies, educational programs and activities, or employment policies.

The American College is located at 270 S. Bryn Mawr Avenue, Bryn Mawr, PA 19010. The toll-free number of the Office of Professional Education is (888) AMERCOL (263-7265); the fax number is (610) 526-1465; and the home page address is theamericancollege.edu.

CONTENTS

ACKNOWLEDGMENTS

The author and The American College acknowledge the following contributors:

Dr. Walt Woerheide, PhD, CFP, Vice President of Academic Dean and the Frank M. Engle Distinguished Chair in Economic Security Research, for his support and encouragement.

Gwenda L. Cannon, JD, a former faculty member of The American College, for creating several cases that are used in this course and that have survived multiple revisions and continuous changes in the financial and tax environments.

The fantastic editing and support team at The American College. Special thanks to Todd Denton, Jane Hassinger and Emily Schu.

Current and former American College faculty members who have had authorship roles in this text, especially Thomas P. Langdon, JD, CFP, CPA; James F. Ivers III, JD, LLM, ChFC; David A. Littell, JD; ChFC, CFP; William J. Ruckstuhl, MBA, CLU, ChFC; Jeffrey B. Kelvin, JD, LLM, CLU, ChFC; and Ronald F. Duska, PhD.

We would also like to acknowledge the contributions of the numerous colleagues, students, and friends whose helpful suggestions have been incorporated into this text.

 **Craig Lemoine, CFP** is the Jarrett Davis distinguished professor of Financial Planning Technology at The American College. His primary responsibilities are developing case study course materials and maintaining the Fundamentals of Financial Planning course as well as this course. Prior to joining the faculty at the college, Craig worked for ten years in the financial services industry and attended graduate school at Texas Tech University, teaching in the Personal Financial Planning program. Craig has extensive experience in the financial software industry and has worked in the life insurance arena. He volunteers with multiple industry organizations and has written articles for numerous industry and academic publications including the *Journal of Financial Service Professionals* and the *Journal of Financial Planning*. Craig can be contacted at craig.lemoine@theamericancollege.edu.

Jarrett L. Davis Distinguished Professorship in Financial Planning Technology

The Professorship was established in the year 2000 as a Professorship in Finance and Accounting, and the initial incumbent was Charles S. DiLullo, who retired June 30, 2010. Craig Lemoine assumed the chair in August of 2010. With Jarrett Davis' approval, the chair name was changed in May of 2011 to its status. The objective of the professorship is to provide leadership to The College within the fields of comprehensive financial planning and study the impact technological change has on the financial service industry—to participate and teach in cutting edge courses within the identified expertise, and to take actions through speaking, writing or otherwise that will advance the name and reputation of The College.

Financial Planning is the overlap and intersection of finance, economics, and psychology. The discussion of personal financial planning for families addresses consumption and utility; should a dollar be consumed today or saved to be consumed tomorrow? This basic decision evolves into a conversation on resource allocation today and savings approaches for tomorrow. Financial planners, advisors, agents, bankers, or other financial professionals may practice either a modular or comprehensive approach to the discipline. Both approaches require sound grounding in the underlying areas of financial planning: tax, investment, retirement, insurance, gift and estate planning.

The purpose of this text is to introduce **practical applications** to comprehensive financial planning. The text will include a series of short cases and two more robust comprehensive cases. Each short case will be focused on one financial planning area. The long cases will be comprehensive and address multiple areas financial planning. The text assumes the reader has a fundamental knowledge of financial planning either through practice or the completion of a comprehensive course of study. Each short case will provide rationale to solutions but are not intended to be comprehensive topic area reviews.

Our objective in presenting this material is not to train you in the technical aspects of financial planning, nor convince you to become a comprehensive financial planner but rather to illustrate case study methods to the comprehensive financial planning process. Utilizing case studies in the pursuit of financial planning education helps the advisor develop comprehensive solutions and alternatives for client problems. In practice, financial planning often requires forming a team of specialists and experts and is rarely solely dependent on the advice of one person.

The case studies represent typical family and business problems that arise in actual practice. They may require retirement, tax, investment, legal, or insurance-based solutions. This book is intended to help readers develop a consistent problem solving approach to case studies and apply their approach to live situations, but not as a repository of technical information. Financial professionals of all kinds can benefit from developing an efficient and organized approach to the exciting challenges of financial planning.

This text has been designed to provide students interested in personal financial planning the opportunity to simulate the advisor client relationship through case studies. A case study approach gives students the opportunity to learn and apply practical financial planning solutions to client challenges. This book contains concentrated case studies that focus on specific financial planning topic areas.

Students are encouraged to work through topic focused case studies before moving to the comprehensive ones. Each case study will introduce the topic, facts, assumptions and goals of clients through a narrative. Client narratives include fact patterns and supporting analytical information as needed. After each case study, a series of questions will be asked to emulate questions that might be asked by the client. Answers from the case study are discussed in depth and referenced back to the students' outline.

Chapter one reviews the financial planning process and introduces an outline approach to financial planning. It is introductory in nature and includes brief discussion of financial planning topic areas including tax, retirement, insurance, investment, employee benefit, estate and gift planning. These reviews are not intended to be comprehensive in nature but are included to give students who specialize in specific topic areas a working overview of other content areas. Chapter one also includes a discussion on financial planning ethics and applications.

Chapter two presents the first financial planning case. This case contains fundamental insurance themes and is intended to give students the opportunity to apply an outline approach to financial planning without addressing complex issues. Chapter two provides a guide to outlining case studies as well as a detailed example outline of the case assumptions, facts, goals, recommendations and alternatives. After developing an in-depth outline, this chapter will analyze and make recommendations based on case facts. The format in chapter two can be used through the textbook, students are encouraged to study an outline approach before moving forward to additional chapters.

This text assumes you have sufficient command of the core subject areas of financial planning to present well-reasoned recommendations. This course is intended to be taken after a student has studied general financial planning principles, income taxation, retirement planning, insurance, investments and employee benefits. Presenting financial planning solutions requires an in-depth and fluid understanding of the financial planning process. Students without a background in financial planning may be better served with an introductory text or literature addressing core topic areas. The detailed technical information presented in case solutions is intended to be utilized in the same way it would be used in an actual financial plan, that is, to provide the client with decision-making information.

Financial planning professionals should consider using a combination of three types of software to help model cases. Financial planning software, tax projection software, and general office productivity software each offer unique contributions to practitioners. Financial planning software can be used to illustrate the consequences of retirement, education, investment, insurance, and business decisions. Tax projection software helps model detailed estate and gift tax implications of planning decisions. General office productivity software, such as word processors, spreadsheet programs, and slide show software can help show basic concepts through outlines, spreadsheets, or slide presentations. To protect relevancy of the analysis process, cases are not integrated with any one software tool. Financial planning software tools are constantly expanding in scope and services.

Over the past decade financial planning software has migrated from the office to the Internet. Programs are accessible remotely, data is stored off-site (in the cloud), and clients can often log in themselves to see advisor-generated Web pages. Software output will continue to develop as clients and advisors become more technologically savvy. Ten years ago software would generate paper reports for advisors to give to clients. These reports made sense to clients during the meeting but lost relevance days and weeks later. Today, financial planning software output tends to be dynamic and appeal to both analytical and visual learning styles. Advisors can make on-the-spot changes which are immediately reflected in presentations and reports, and these presentations can be filled with colorful illustrations, diagrams, and schedules.

Students may choose to apply some of the above software packages to cases presented in the textbook. The textbook, however, will apply an outline approach to solving cases, applying spreadsheets to determine net worth, cash flow and future cash flow as needed. Students should be cautious of using financial software before they understand the mechanics of financial planning. Financial planning software output is a direct by-product of the data and assumptions used, and developing a thorough understanding of a case is integral in making appropriate client recommendations.

Utilizing Financial Planning Software

Some computer-produced numerical illustrations have been included for the purpose of demonstrating the relative effect of particular recommendations on the client's income tax, balance sheet, cash-flow, and estate tax situations, that is, the effect a recommendation will have assuming all other assumptions are valid and remain constant. Computer projections are helpful in the practice of financial planning to illustrate the results of various planning recommendations.

Numerical projections, especially those that involve a time period extending far into the future, are particularly problematic because so many assumptions must be made to ascertain the results, and a change in those assumptions will alter the results. Three fundamental issues should be considered here:

- What assumptions should be used?

- Over how long a time period should projections be run?

- How will the illustration be presented to the client?

As a general rule it is usually better to use a set of assumptions with which the client is comfortable, as opposed to assumptions imposed by the planner. Even if the planner's assumptions turn out to be absolutely correct, it is unlikely that the client will remain a client long enough to discover that fact. In the event that the planner believes the client's assumptions are outlandish, another set of projections based on more conservative (or more liberal) assumptions can be included in the plan to demonstrate the results under different hypothetical circumstances.

Students must consider how they will present outcomes to clients. Financial software is a tool that can enhance the client presentation, but should not take precedence in a client meeting. Software and presentation outputs are not intended to supplement the role of the financial service professional.

As the chapters progress to more complicated case studies, cash flow and balance sheet schedules are extended from 1-year periods to 3-year periods. Financial planning software will generally provide more advanced graphics and analysis. Students are not expected produce exact results matching, but the schedules in the book are provided as guidelines in working through case studies.

Questions of Law

Despite the fact that the Internal Revenue Code controls all matters of federal taxation, many federal tax consequences are determined indirectly by local law. For example, the Internal Revenue Code states that if funds are used to discharge the legal support obligations of a taxpayer, those payments will be taxable income to the taxpayer whose obligation is relieved, regardless of who pays them. The determination of what constitutes a legal obligation of support, however, is determined under state law. To provide a complete case solution, it is necessary to give the clients a state of domicile in order to apply the local law of a particular state to these issues. Unless otherwise noted, the clients whose cases appear in this text are domiciled in the hypothetical state of Jefferson. In the areas in which reference is made to a point of Jefferson law, that reference should alert a planner to check that point under the law of the client's state. Obviously a difference in local law may necessitate a different planning result.

For example, Jefferson has an estate tax equal to the federal state death tax credit, and it has not changed its law since the enactment of EGTRRA 2001. It has no inheritance tax. Therefore there is no actual advantage in avoiding probate in Jefferson unless a corporate executor is being utilized, as corporate fiduciaries often base fees on the amount of assets they must deal with. In contrast, if the client is domiciled in a state that imposes an inheritance tax only on probate property, especially if there is no exemption for property transferred to a surviving spouse, the recommendation for the form of ownership in which a client owns certain property (such as a principal residence) may be altered.

If a state imposes an estate tax, it is the legal responsibility of the estate itself to pay the tax. In contrast, if the state imposes an inheritance tax, the responsibility for paying the tax generally rests with the beneficiary who receives property from the estate.

All of the cases in this text are set in Jefferson. If any cases vary from Jefferson, state rules and laws are outlined in the case study.

Note

This text was revised in 2011 and utilizes rules and laws applicable to the 2011 tax year. If you are using this textbook in 2012, 2013 or 2014 you will potentially be operating with different federal rules and laws. Your case solutions will likely be different than those presented in the text.

Professional Judgment

In financial planning there is rarely a single answer to a particular problem that will work for every client; there are always several possible alternatives. The ultimate recommendation will depend on the financial planner's professional judgment, which is based on personal knowledge of and experience with the client and the client's family. While the importance of this professional judgment makes financial planning an art rather than a science (and therefore more difficult to teach and to learn), it also makes financial planning a very personal and creative experience for both the planner and the client.

Learning Objectives

An understanding of the material in this chapter should enable the student to

1. Discuss comprehensive financial planning and team-based financial planning.

2. Discuss the financial planning process, financial planning practice standards and codes of ethics.

3. Explain ethical challenges facing financial advisers.

4. Discuss how the financial planning process impacts financial adviser recommendations.

5. Outline Tax Authority as it applies to financial planners.

6. Discuss the importance of building a strong financial planning team.

The world of financial services is very complex, extensive, and unique. Consumers and small businesses are constantly confronted with decisions about saving, insurance, investing, taxes, retirement and estate issues. Most individuals can organize their everyday lives, but struggle with the personal financial decisions. Globalization has led to a more complicated world in which people have a difficult time finding a way to deal with the enormous amount of information. It is often impossible to distinguish fact from opinion without being an expert in a given field.

The result is that most individuals have become less confident in their ability to make well-informed decisions about their personal and business affairs and have become increasingly dependent on advice from financial planners. Financial planners and professionals from diverse backgrounds can help consumers make smart financial choices that help consumers build wealth, security, and peace of mind.

The financial planning industry is unique. There is not a standardized method of becoming a financial planner. Some financial planners transition into the planning arena from other careers; others enter the industry in a sales capacity; some planners train in university settings. Financial planners come from all races, socioeconomic backgrounds and political affiliations. The diverse background of planners coupled with unique needs of consumers calls for planners to have extensive skill sets.

comprehensive financial planning
Financial planning, specifically comprehensive financial planning is a client-oriented process that attempts to discover client goals before exploring potential solutions. It is a method of problem solving that educates the client and encourages informed decision making about his or her own circumstances.

The comprehensive financial planner must possess many skills. Sensitivity to the client and an understanding of human behavior and needs as well as technical expertise in one or more of the financial services areas (such as law, accounting, insurance, investments, and banking) are required. Comprehensive financial planning is not for the faint-of-heart. The knowledge and information demands placed on the comprehensive financial planner are enormous. Financial planning is an especially challenging occupation because, as an emerging discipline, it lacks the tried-and-true guidelines on procedural, ethical, and other matters that already exist in established professions. Since the 1970s, however, the financial planning profession has successfully taken many steps to define itself.

The amount of information needed to successfully complete a comprehensive financial plan is vast. No one person can be expected to master such diverse subject areas as tax law, securities law, probate and local property law, life insurance, property and casualty insurance, and investment planning. Due to the immense background, many comprehensive financial planners coordinate a team of experts to help solve client goals. The team approach allows for the use of appropriate expertise when necessary within the overall context of the client's personal and business goals and objectives.

team-based financial planning
The team approach to financial planning helps deal with many of the failures of traditional problem-solving methods. Traditional problem-solving has too often resulted in advice that is both isolated and fragmented. Under the traditional approach, problems are presented to advisers in an isolated manner, and each is examined for the specific purpose of finding a solution to the single problem presented.

Prevention is not the goal of traditional planning methods. Too often problems are presented to advisers only after they have become troublesome. If a client is attempting to deal with a particularly troublesome problem, that problem tends to demand the client's total attention and becomes disproportionately important. When advice is sought on such a problem, most of the client's interest and energy are centered on an immediate or speedy solution. Traditional advisers have naturally attempted to accommodate the client's wishes in this regard and often focus exclusively on the problem at hand. Such narrow advice is bound to be insufficient, since it does not allow for full consideration of the impact of the advice on a client's total personal and financial situation. As long as clients delay seeking advice and allow problems to ripen into troublesome issues, they will continue to demand the isolated-solution approach to problem solving.

If problems can be anticipated before they become crises, preventive solutions to potential problems can be substituted for crisis-intervention methods. Comprehensive financial planning, the process that has been designed to meet this need for preventive solutions to potential problems, involves the gathering of sufficient data to produce a total overview of the client's financial, legal, and personal situation. This overview enables the financial planner to establish realistic and attainable personal and business financial goals with the client after a careful analysis has been made of the client's overall personal and financial situation. The comprehensive financial planning process also involves restructuring the client's current financial position to allow for maximum tax advantage and to eliminate, to the greatest possible extent, the legal and tax problems contained therein. Comprehensive financial planning is both a preventive and a remedial system of problem solving.

The net result of traditional problem-solving methods in the financial planning context is that traditional advice is often impersonal, inconclusive, and possibly even contradictory to other valid advice. The client is often confused when faced with the prospect of coordinating good advice on diverse subjects from several sources. Clients seek an adviser (or advisers) who understand the technical depth and the personal aspects of their problems, who will evaluate both technical detail and personal planning considerations, and who will present a cohesive, coordinated, well-developed, well-researched, and well-documented plan. This person is the comprehensive financial planner working with a qualified team of expert advisers. It is only the commitment of the financial services industry to *comprehensive* financial planning that will produce these results. Without such a commitment, financial planning will be prone to the errors and problems of traditional problem-solving methods.

SINGLE-PURPOSE APPROACH

Some advisors take the position that the simple selling of a single financial product constitutes financial planning. Clearly, these advisors would be incorrect if the financial planning process was not used to determine whether the problem their product solves is, in fact, the specific client's financial problem and if so, whether the products they are selling are the most appropriate for solving that client's problem. In this case, the advisor would be involved in product sales, not financial planning.

single-purpose approach

However, if an advisor sells the client a product to implement the recommendations of a plan developed according to the financial planning process and approved by the client, the service provided by the advisor constitutes financial planning. According to this specialist or *single-purpose approach*, all the following individuals would be engaged in financial planning as long as they use the financial planning process in working with their clients:

- a single-purpose planner who provides recommendations in only one financial planning topic area
- a stockbroker who advises a customer to buy shares of common stock of a particular company
- a salesperson who sells shares in a real estate limited partnership to a client
- a preparer of income tax returns who suggests that a client establish an IRA
- a banker who opens a trust account for the benefit of a customer's handicapped child
- a life insurance agent who sells key person life insurance to the owner of a small business
- a personal finance counselor who shows a client how to set up and live within a budget

Single-purpose financial planning generally leads to multiple-purpose or comprehensive planning. Operating without addressing tangent financial planning issues can be difficult.

EXAMPLE
Jarred, a CPA, meets with his client to discuss their 2011 federal income tax return. He suggests the client takes an itemized deduction on their federal income tax return. Jarred used the financial planning process to make his recommendation, and has engaged in single-purpose financial planning. However, in reviewing the client's record of stock purchases and sales, he believes the client would greatly benefit from investment recommendations. Jarred is qualified to give investment advice. If the client accepts his offer to make investment recommendations, Jarred will now be practicing multiple-purpose planning.

MULTIPLE-PURPOSE APPROACH

multiple-purpose approach

Client financial concerns and financial products and/or services are often seen as falling into one of the major planning areas: insurance planning and risk management, employee benefits planning, investment planning, income tax planning, retirement planning, and estate planning. Rather than taking a single-purpose approach of just solving a single financial problem with a single financial product or service, many financial advisors take a *multiple-purpose approach* by dealing with at least a large part of one of these planning areas, and perhaps some aspects of a second planning area. According to the multiple-purpose approach, the following individuals would be engaged in financial planning as long as they use the financial planning process in working with their clients:

- a multiline insurance agent who sells all lines of life, health, and property and liability insurance
- a tax attorney who assists clients with their income, estate, and gift tax planning
- an investment advisor who is registered as such with the Securities and Exchange Commission
- a life insurance agent who also sells a family of mutual funds to meet both the protection and wealth accumulation needs of clients

EXAMPLE
Bill is an insurance agent for BIG insurance company. He meets with a young couple and discusses disability insurance. After following the planning process Bill determines the couple also needs advice with retirement planning and possibly life insurance. Bill is practicing multiple-purpose planning.

COMPREHENSIVE APPROACH

comprehensive approach

Still other advisors take a *comprehensive approach* to providing financial planning services. Comprehensive financial planning considers all aspects of a client's financial position, which includes the client's financial goals and objectives, and utilizes several integrated and coordinated planning strategies for fulfilling those goals and objectives. The two key characteristics of comprehensive financial planning are

- comprehensive planning encompasses all the personal and financial situations of clients to the extent that these can be uncovered, clarified, and addressed through information gathering and counseling
- it integrates into its methodology all the techniques and expertise utilized in more narrowly focused approaches to solving client financial problems

Because of the wide range of expertise required to engage in comprehensive financial planning, effective performance commonly requires a team of specialists. The tasks of the advisor managing the team are to coordinate the efforts of the team and to contribute expertise in his or her own field of specialization.

In its purest form, comprehensive financial planning is a service provided by the managing advisor on an hourly fee-only basis. No part of the managing advisor's compensation comes from the sale of financial products or management of assets, thus helping to ensure complete objectivity in all aspects of the plan. Some team specialists also are compensated through fees, while others might receive commissions from the sale of products, while still others might receive both fees and commissions. In its less pure but often more practical form, comprehensive financial planning provides the managing advisor with compensation consisting of some combination of fees for service and commissions from the sale of some of the financial products. Again, other members of the team might receive fees, commissions, or both.

Furthermore, in its purest form, comprehensive financial planning is performed for a client all at once, meaning in a single engagement—not a single meeting. An engagement may span from a week to a decade. A single planning engagement conducted by the managing advisor and his or her team of specialists creates the one plan that addresses all the client's financial concerns and utilizes several planning strategies. This plan is then updated with the client periodically and modified as appropriate. In its less pure form, comprehensive financial planning is performed incrementally during the course of several engagements with the client. For example, the advisor in one year might prepare a plan to treat some of the client's income tax concerns and estate and insurance planning problems. In another year, the advisor might focus on the client's retirement concerns and investment planning problems and then dovetail the strategies for dealing with them with the previously developed income tax, estate, and insurance strategies. In a third engagement, the advisor might address the remaining issues in the income tax, estate, insurance, retirement, and investment planning areas and coordinate all the recommended strategies and previously developed plans. Again, each incremental part, as well as the overall plan, is reviewed periodically and revised as appropriate.

EXAMPLE
Ted is a financial planner who specializes in helping small business owners sell their businesses. Ted encounters Linda, the owner of a wildly successful marketing firm. In working with Linda, Ted realizes she needs help with retirement planning, risk management, establishing employee benefits, estate planning and business succession planning. Ted is practicing comprehensive financial planning.

THE FINANCIAL PLANNING PROCESS

The financial planning process are steps that guide financial planners through client interactions. Comprehensive or modular planners gain value from following a formalized financial planning process. The financial planning process helps establish goals, assumptions, objectives and recommendations for a client in an ethical and consistent manner. This process does not address prospecting or growing a client base, but begins with detailing planner and client responsibility.

financial planning process

The Financial Planning Process consists of the following steps. While working through each step planning process, the planner should work towards client focused planning.

Table 1-1 Steps of the Financial Planning Process	
Steps in the Financial Planning Process	*Detail*
Establish the Client/Planner Relationship	The financial planner should outline what are the responsibilities of the planner and what are the responsibilities of the client. The planner should disclose the length and scope of the relationship as well as the method and magnitude of planner compensation. Establishing the relationship helps guide the decision making process. Financial service practitioners from all compensation models benefit from establishing boundaries and clarity with their clients.
Gather Client Data including Goals	The financial planner should gather client data, including broad and specific goals and objectives. Ask the client about risk tolerance measures. Documents such as tax returns, wills, trusts, account statements and pay stubs may need to be collected to truly establish constructive outcomes.
Analyze and Evaluate Financial Status	Data gathered in the second step must be analyzed and synthesized within the context of meeting goals. This step of the planning process accounts for significant variations among planners. Planners without expertise in a specific planning area may find a benefit in including a technical staff or teammates when analyzing and evaluating client goals.
Develop Planning Recommendations and/or Alternatives	The financial planner develops recommendations based on their evaluation (step three) of data collected (step two). Planners present recommendations and alternatives that address client goals and concerns. Presenting more than one recommendation to a client gives them alternative courses of action, and may result in additional fact finding and discovery on the part of the planner. After making recommendations, the client may provide or revise their goals (step two) which will require additional analysis (step three).
Implement Financial Planning Recommendations	After agreement is reached between the client and planner on a course of action, the planner outlines how implementation will occur. If implementation results in additional planner compensation, the form and magnitude of compensation needs to be disclosed to the client. Depending on the business model of the planner, the client may implement their own recommendations or the planner may implement recommendations on behalf of the client. Any conflict of interest of the planner through the implementation of a product should be disclosed to the client.
Monitor Financial Planning Decisions	The sixth step of the planning process is guided by the first. The client and planner need to agree on monitoring responsibilities when establishing the relationship. Planners who entered into a long term relationship with their clients have an obligation of following up and updating the plan.

Prospecting

Before employing the financial planning process, advisors need to prospect and gather clients. Most financial planning firms choose a segment of the market and concentrate their efforts on a particular group or class of clients. For example, many financial planning firms specialize in planning for the self-employed professional, while other firms rarely, if ever, accept such clients and concentrate instead on closely held business owners, middle or upper management personnel, or other groups. Defining market segments help guide financial professionals towards building their books of business.

After narrowing down a "type" of client, planners are confronted with finding willing and qualified prospects, through marketing and networking. Only after generating prospects can the financial planner begin the financial planning process. Client prospecting requires perseverance, dedication and a plan of action.

prospecting   A haphazard approach to identifying prospects will most likely result in a dearth of prospects and a great deal of frustration. Therefore, it is important to create and implement a marketing plan that will generate a flow of the types of prospects a planner wants to approach. Prospecting requires a planner to:

- Define the product — Financial planning advice and recommendations, either comprehensive or modular, is the outcome of the planning process. Financial planners sometimes focus on product or physical plan delivery. While products are used and bound plans are often delivered to clients, the client is paying the advisor for their financial planning knowledge and ability.
- Create an ideal client profile — Financial planners may find an ideal client profile by looking in the mirror, their family or in their community. Planners working with larger firms have less flexibility than independent advisors, but may benefit from a stronger name recognition.
- Identify target markets — Target markets are slightly different than client profiles. A client profile establishes a type of client the planner wants to work with, while target markets are economic or geographic boundaries to help focus the prospecting search.
- Position your practice — Even comprehensive financial planning practices are not all encompassing for any type of client. Planners who position themselves as an expert in particular fields can focus their skill set and add additional value to their clients.
- Build prestige and create awareness — Hanging a shingle outside of an office does not guarantee business. Financial planners may have a business card full of credentials, but community recognition and prestige with individual clients is crucial to building a practice. Legitimate credentials (CPA, CFP®, CLU, ChFC) help clients know that a planner has achieved educational, ethical and experience requirements.

- Select prospecting methods — After building a prospecting model, planners must implement the model to achieve success when prospecting. Consistent marketing themes and methods help build planner reputation and grow a planner's client base.

The Data Gathering Session

staging meetings   After successfully prospecting clients, planners tend to break the financial planning process into a series of meetings. The first meeting encompasses the first and second steps of the process, establishing the relationship and gathering client data. Clients are generally asked to bring supporting documents, and possibly a fact finder to the first planning meeting.

data-gathering session   This data-gathering session with the client is one of the most important steps in the financial planning process. It is in this interview that the financial planner begins to establish credibility and rapport with the client. The meeting allows the planner to learn as much as possible about the client and the client's spouse and family. The financial planner should listen carefully to what the client and spouse have to say, watch their body language, and pay careful attention to subjects the clients seem uncomfortable with or try to avoid entirely. These subtle signals often convey important information about the client's personality and relationships with others—factors that can significantly affect the financial plan.

Data-gathering sessions are usually intense and can be very fatiguing to a client who may be dealing with difficult and painful subjects, and to the financial planner whose total concentration must be on the client. During these sessions important subjective data should be carefully noted. Many planning decisions are based on subjective information rather than on hard data.

The initial data-gathering session should be a counseling session in the truest sense of the word. The financial planner should attempt to suspend any inherent biases and put himself or herself in the client's position. The planner should attempt to see the world and the client's problems through the client's eyes. This does not mean that the financial planner will or should always agree with a client's point of view. The planner must, however, see the problem from the client's viewpoint in order to understand precisely what the problem means to the client. It is not the place of the financial planner to rearrange the client's affairs to meet the planner's goals, objectives, or values.

The planner's mission is to plan for the client's goals and objectives based on the client's perception of his or her problems and according to the client's value system—provided, however, that no impropriety or illegality is involved.

The data-gathering session should be an in-depth opportunity for the financial planner and the client to begin their personal relationship. It should leave the client with a feeling of confidence and trust, since it will sometimes be necessary for the financial planner to probe sensitive personal areas of the client's life and to ask painful questions. Well-considered and truthful answers to sensitive inquiries will be forthcoming only in an atmosphere of trust. To create that atmosphere of trust it is helpful to preface the session by explaining a few ground rules to the client. These ground rules should at least include comments on protecting the client's confidentiality, the necessity for full disclosure of facts and feelings, and the specific tasks the planner will perform for the client. In this situation it is helpful to be especially candid about the fact that the planner is not sitting in judgment of the client's attitudes, values, or the previous management of personal or business affairs. In order to make appropriate decisions about planning recommendations, the planner should strive to understand the client and the client's present situation and to ascertain what basic motivations are at work in the client's life. Honesty and a down-to-earth attitude are important.

Define the Scope of Engagement

define the scope of engagement
A strong positive relationship between the client and the planner usually results in a better plan for the client and more self-satisfaction for the planner. It is axiomatic that satisfied clients are an excellent source of future business.

If the planner encounters a client with whom there is a personality conflict or with whom the communication or rapport so necessary for the development of a satisfactory financial plan cannot be established, it is often counterproductive to pursue the relationship. Neither the planner nor the client is likely to be happy with the end product. If there is another available planner in the firm, it is often a good idea to assign him or her to the client as soon as the difficulties become apparent. In this way the client has a better chance of having a satisfactory relationship with the firm.

A formal agreement to proceed with the financial planning process is often entered into after the first data-gathering interview. It is rare that prior to this in-depth discussion either the client or the financial planner has sufficient information about the other to make the required commitment to the financial planning relationship. After the formal agreement for planning is entered into, an appropriate channel of communication for follow-up questions or additional information must be established. The financial planner must define the scope of the engagement between planner and client. Many times, communication will be directly with the client. In other cases, particularly when the client owns a business, others may be able to facilitate the gathering of additional data as necessary without taking the client's time. However this is to be handled, communication channels must be established because the need to clarify a point or to obtain other information is virtually inevitable.

Define Client Goals and Objectives

develop client goals and objectives

Once the client and the financial planner agree on the scope of the relationship, the financial planner takes charge of the client's data and begins the process of writing, analyzing and producing the financial plan. By this time the financial planner usually has some idea of the parts of the financial plan that require significant work and possibly are beyond his or her expertise. At this point an analysis of the client's data must be completed. It is often helpful to organize the client file into related or logically coherent pieces to aid in this analysis and to create an outline of the planning process. Many approaches can be used in this organization and outline, but basic divisions or headings, such as lifetime and death planning or personal and business planning, are good starting points.

Once a thorough analysis is completed, client goals and objectives are relatively easy to test for consistency. For example, suppose a client expresses the desire to treat his children equally when he dies, but the client's will leaves his closely held business interest to his daughter. If both items are noted under the death planning section of the file, it is apparent that there is a possible conflict, since the client may be leaving a disproportionately large portion of the potential estate to his daughter. The planner must clarify whether the client wants the children treated *equally* (all to inherit exactly the same) or *equitably* (all to be treated fairly and to inherit roughly the same value of assets). This is a subtle but important distinction. If the estate is large enough, it may be possible for the client's children to inherit equitably while preserving the business interest for the daughter. However, if the bulk of the estate consists of the family business, the planner may have to plan for a partial disposition of the business interest that will provide an equitable inheritance for the other children while leaving the daughter with control of the business.

Develop and Present Recommendations and Alternatives

develop and present recommendations and alternatives

Financial planning recommendations should be consistent with the client's lifetime objectives and wishes for postmortem disposition of property. There is nothing inherently contradictory in lifetime and postmortem planning, although the client's wishes concerning these planning alternatives may expose some inherent conflicts. One of the tasks of financial planning is to expose those conflicts so the client can make informed decisions to resolve the conflict. Prior to the emergence of comprehensive financial planning as a discipline, lifetime transactions were not considered in view of postmortem objectives, and the results were often shocking.

After analyzing and organizing the data and noting any conflicting information or objectives, the financial planner summarizes the client's objectives that are to be addressed in the financial plan. This is the foundation on which the plan is built. In addition to specific objectives that the client may have identified, the planner may be able to determine additional objectives from the subjective information collected about the client. These additional objectives should be confirmed with the client to assure that they are in fact the client's—and not the financial planner's—objectives.

At this stage of the planning process it is very helpful to review the objectives listed under the outline headings and to expand that preliminary outline to include the tax planning techniques that may be used to accomplish those objectives. It is too early to be definitive about which techniques will be implemented, so all viable alternatives should be noted at this point.

If the client has expressed a particular interest in a strategy or technique, the planner cannot ignore it even if it appears inappropriate for the client's situation. The technique or strategy should be explained so that the client feels that his or her concerns have been acknowledged and that the relevant information has been given due consideration.

critically analyze goals and objectives

Keep in mind that the function of the financial planner is not to rubber-stamp the client's choice of techniques and strategies. On the contrary, the financial planner, aided by other members of the financial planning team, should independently and objectively explore the various techniques and strategies available to accomplish each client objective and then recommend the technique that in his or her professional judgment is best suited to this client's overall situation. Many times, members of the financial planning team will need to conduct research to ascertain techniques that may be available and to understand the operation and constraints, if any, applicable to their use. The choice of the best planning technique for the client cannot be made until both the client's situation and the available planning techniques are fully understood by the planner after consultation with appropriate team members.

Whenever one of the primary areas (tax, insurance, or investment planning) in the financial planning process is outside the financial planner's area of expertise, the assistance of a technical expert must be sought. For example, a financial planner with a primary background in law will need to enlist an insurance specialist to analyze the client's insurance needs and to compare them with the client's present insurance coverage. As additional issues are uncovered, additional experts will be added to the team, and each member will provide information and analysis, including recommendations, related to his or her area of technical expertise. The primary planner must coordinate and organize input from these other technical experts into a comprehensive plan after making sure that the recommendations will not adversely affect each other or impede the achievement of the client's overall objectives.

Once all information about various techniques and strategies has been reviewed in light of the client's circumstances and objectives, definitive recommendations that meet the client's objectives can be formulated. It is often helpful from an organizational viewpoint to divide the final plan into business and personal planning sections and to further divide each section into tax, insurance, and investment planning. Under each of these sections lifetime planning and planning for dispositions at death can be considered. It is also helpful to further organize the plan into subsections, each of which deals with a particular objective. Thus the objective of funding for children's education could discuss various techniques and their related tax impacts—for example, outright gifts, Sec. 2503(c) trusts, gifts made under the Uniform Gifts (or Transfers) to Minors Act, Education IRAs, and Sec. 529 plans. In this way the plan outline is not only utilized as an organizational tool by the financial planner; it is also the framework for the plan itself.

In developing the formal plan document for presentation to the client, planners may differ in the amount of documentation that should be delivered with the plan. Some may choose to list only the recommendation of choice for a particular objective. While this may be an economical way to develop plans, it is unlikely to meet the client's need to make an informed decision about his or her own life and affairs. If several alternative techniques are available, the better approach is to discuss each of them in the plan, including the strengths and weaknesses of each technique and the reasons each strategy or technique is either well suited or poorly suited for this particular client.

When alternatives are offered, the planner will want to identify the recommendation of choice for achieving the client's objective and indicate any additional reasons why the planner's recommendation should be adopted. The planner should include in any planning recommendation citations to authority or data (tax code sections, case names, numbers, assumptions, and so on) that were considered in formulating, explaining, or illustrating that recommendation. This information is particularly helpful to the client's other advisers when they review the financial plan because it allows them to follow the planner's logic without spending unnecessary time in research. Too often the client's other advisers will have little confidence in an undocumented plan because they do not have the time to conduct research on the particular subject to validate the planner's solution. If references are made available in the plan, it is much easier for other advisers to validate the planner's recommendation if they wish to do so. It is also much harder for them to dismiss the plan as trivial or superficial. A well-documented plan is a work product that the client's attorney, accountant, or other adviser can use as a reliable blueprint in preparing documents or proposals in the implementation stage of the planning process.

After the plan has been prepared in this fashion, the planner and the client meet for a second extended session to go over the recommendations. Although the planner's recommendations should carry considerable weight, they are certainly not binding on the client. While the financial planner may have based the recommendations on his or her best professional judgment and may believe strongly in their validity, the planner must not expect the client to accept any recommendation on faith. A financial planner who takes this approach is acting as a traditional problem solver and is asking the client to make a decision based on what the client believes the *planner* knows about the subject matter, not what the client knows. In other words, the client is put back in the position of having to evaluate the expert in order to evaluate the advice. While that is always true to some extent, part of the purpose of the financial planning process is to educate clients about legal, investment, insurance, and tax matters in order to allow them to function as informed decision makers, thereby giving them more control over these important decisions.

This is the humanizing aspect of financial planning. When the process is well executed, clients become participants in making decisions about their lives and their families while receiving appropriate advice and support from the financial planner and the financial planning team. The best decisions are those made by the person or persons involved after reviewing sufficient information to make an informed selection from several known alternatives. The planner must learn to function within this framework, as well as to accept and encourage clients' questioning of planning recommendations.

ongoing relationship   By its very nature comprehensive financial planning is intended to be an ongoing relationship between the financial planner, the client, and the client's family. The facts are constantly changing. While financial planners attempt to deliver plans that are current and up-to-date, this is not always possible. Continuous additions and changes in data and the need for updating the plan are simply a part of the process. Consequently the last stage in the financial planning process is the monitoring and updating of the client's plan at regular intervals. Changes in the client's circumstances must also be recorded and dealt with during the plan's preparation and implementation.

Many times, making a particular strategy work for a client is like having a suit tailored. If the measurements were taken several weeks ago, circumstances may have occurred in the meantime that will affect the final fit. At the final presentation of a comprehensive financial plan, it may be necessary to change the recommendations entirely based on new facts or circumstances facing the client. On the other hand a slight modification—a tuck here or there—may be sufficient to adapt the existing recommendation to the new situation.

Implementing the Financial Plan

Once the client has received an explanation of the alternatives and recommendations for achieving each of his or her objectives and has discussed them with the planner, the client may immediately make decisions on some recommendations, ask for additional clarification on other recommendations, and reserve others for future consideration. This is a typical and appropriate response. If there are serious matters that require immediate attention, it is appropriate to list those items for the client on a proposed priority list. The financial adviser should remind the client that the plan must be implemented to be effective, and should suggest a proposal for implementing all or a part of the plan while the client and the planner are together.

Once the implementation of the plan has been agreed to, the client is likely to take all or part of the financial plan to other advisers for actual implementation. It is often a good idea to prepare an additional copy of the plan for the client to give to his or her attorney, accountant, life insurance agent, or investment adviser. If the client's existing advisers can review the planning recommendations from the plan itself rather than depending on the client to explain the planning concepts, the chances for misunderstanding are diminished. In addition, a well-prepared, well-documented plan often reduces the amount of possible resistance from the client's existing advisers and promotes its quick implementation.

The financial planner should arrange to review documents or proposals in draft form with the client's advisers to ensure that the planning recommendations have been correctly embodied. Draft copies should always be reviewed since it is easier to change them than the final work product. Furthermore, if there is a misunderstanding about a recommendation, it is better to discover and correct it as quickly as possible.

implementation   Implementation can be accomplished in a relatively short time for a decisive, well-organized client, or it can last for months for clients with large holdings who have many documents and agreements to execute. The planner can assist in the implementation of the plan by keeping in touch with the client's advisers and checking on the progress of various projects if they seem to be lagging. The implementation portion of the plan is completed when all the necessary documents and agreements have been signed and all necessary products are purchased and titled correctly. Note, however, that it would be a violation of securities laws for the client to be led to the conclusion that implementation must be accomplished by the same planner who provided the advice.

The final stage of the comprehensive financial planning process is the ongoing monitoring and updating of the client's plan to take into account both new developments and changes in financial or family circumstances. Changes are inevitable, and the failure to update the plan to take these changes into account results in a plan that is no longer suited to the client's needs and is potentially disadvantageous to his or her interests. In fact, failure to keep the plan adjusted for changes in the client's personal or business affairs for more than a year or two will often necessitate a new data-gathering interview and the development of an entirely new plan.

Clients who appreciate the benefits of comprehensive financial planning and the necessity of keeping the plan updated are very reliable in notifying their financial planner of major changes in their situation. Other clients may be less forthcoming with up to date information.

In either case the planner engaged in a long term relationship should arrange a personal meeting with a client at least annually. This meeting is helpful in dealing with less communicative clients, as it presents a structured opportunity for requesting updated information. With more communicative clients a good deal of quantitative information may already have been furnished, but the meeting gives the planner an opportunity to confirm or clarify it. A major benefit of the annual meeting is the opportunity to renew the relationship between the client and the financial planner and the opportunity for the planner to reevaluate the client's conversation for changes in subjective information.

Implementation may best be addressed by a formal implementation schedule. An implementation schedule outlines exactly which actions will be taken by the client, adviser, and potentially third parties. A structured implementation schedule helps assure the success of the financial plan. The schedule should contain deadlines, assigned responsibilities, and follow-up actions.

Monitor Financial Planning Decisions

monitoring After implementing financial planning decisions financial planners typically monitor the client and plan. Monitoring can take on many phases. Annual updating, semiannual phone calls and quarterly updates are all examples of monitoring the client plan. Monitoring client investments provides opportunities for financial professionals to update the other stages of the planning process. Monitoring the client's financial situation may take different forms: calling, e-mailing, using social network sites, and face-to-face meetings. Through the monitoring process advisers may find opportunities to revisit the other five steps of the planning process.

Clients have different goals, objectives and needs through their life cycle. The life-cycle process is a method of helping quantify client goals and objectives.

CFP BOARD'S FINANCIAL PLANNING PRACTICE STANDARDS

Statement of Purpose for Financial Planning Practice Standards

Financial Planning Practice Standards are developed and promulgated by Certified Financial Planner Board of Standards Inc. (CFP Board) for the ultimate benefit of consumers of financial planning services. These *Practice Standards* are intended to:

1. Assure that the practice of financial planning by CERTIFIED FINANCIAL PLANNER™ professionals is based on established norms of practice;
2. Advance professionalism in financial planning; and
3. Enhance the value of the financial planning process.

CFP Board is a professional regulatory organization founded in 1985 to benefit the public by establishing and enforcing education, examination, experience and ethics requirements for CFP® professionals. Through its certification process, CFP Board established fundamental criteria necessary for competency in the financial planning profession.

In 1995, CFP Board established its Board of Practice Standards, composed exclusively of CFP® practitioners, to draft standards of practice for financial planning. The Board of Practice Standards drafted and revised the standards considering input from CFP® certificants, consumers, regulators and other organizations. CFP Board adopted the revised standards.

Description of Practice Standards

A *Practice Standard* establishes the level of professional practice that is expected of certificants engaged in financial planning.

The *Practice Standards* apply to certificants in performing the tasks of financial planning regardless of the person's title, job position, type of employment or method of compensation. Compliance with the *Practice Standards* is mandatory for certificants whose services include financial planning or material elements of the financial planning process, but all financial planning professionals are encouraged to use the *Practice Standards* when performing financial planning tasks or activities addressed by a *Practice Standard*.

The *Practice Standards* are designed to provide certificants with a framework for the professional practice of financial planning. Similar to the *Rules of Conduct*, the *Practice Standards* are not designed to be a basis for legal liability to any third party.

Format of the Practice Standards

Each *Practice Standard* is a statement regarding an element of the financial planning process. It is followed by an explanation of the Standard, its relationship to the *Code of Ethics* and *Rules of Conduct*, and its expected impact on the public, the profession and the practitioner.

The Explanation accompanying each *Practice Standard* explains and illustrates the meaning and purpose of the *Practice Standard*. The text of each *Practice Standard* is authoritative and directive. The related Explanation is a guide to interpretation and application of the *Practice Standard* based, where indicated, on a standard of reasonableness, a recurring theme throughout the *Practice Standards*. The Explanation is not intended to establish a professional standard or duty beyond what is contained in the *Practice Standard* itself.

Compliance With the Practice Standards

The practice of financial planning consistent with these *Practice Standards* is required for certificants who are financial planning practitioners. The *Practice Standards* are used by CFP Board's Disciplinary and Ethics Commission and Appeals Committee in evaluating the certificant's conduct to determine if the *Rules of Conduct* have been violated, based on the *Disciplinary Rules* established by CFP Board.

100-1: Defining the Scope of the Engagement

The financial planning practitioner and the client shall mutually define the scope of the engagement before any financial planning service is provided.

Explanation of This Practice Standard

Prior to providing any financial planning service, the financial planning practitioner and the client shall mutually define the scope of the engagement.

The process of "mutually-defining" is essential in determining what activities may be necessary to proceed with the engagement.

This process is accomplished in financial planning engagements by:

- Identifying the service(s) to be provided;
- Disclosing the practitioner's material conflict(s) of interest;
- Disclosing the practitioner's compensation arrangement(s);
- Determining the client's and the practitioner's responsibilities;
- Establishing the duration of the engagement; and
- Providing any additional information necessary to define or limit the scope.

The scope of the engagement may include one or more financial planning subject areas. It is acceptable to mutually define engagements in which the scope is limited to specific activities. Mutually defining the scope of the engagement serves to establish realistic expectations for both the client and the practitioner.

As the relationship proceeds, the scope may change by mutual agreement.

This *Practice Standard* shall not be considered alone, but in conjunction with all other *Practice Standards*.

Anticipated Impact of This Practice Standard Upon the Public

The public is served when the relationship is based upon a mutual understanding of the engagement. Clarity of the scope of the engagement enhances the likelihood of achieving client expectations.

Upon the Financial Planning Profession

The profession benefits when clients are satisfied. This is more likely to take place when clients have expectations of the process, which are both realistic and clear, before services are provided.

Upon the Financial Planning Practitioner

A mutually defined scope of the engagement provides a framework for the financial planning process by focusing both the client and the practitioner on the agreed upon tasks. This *Practice Standard* enhances the potential for positive results.

200-1: Determining a Client's Personal and Financial Goals, Needs and Priorities

The financial planning practitioner and the client shall mutually define the client's personal and financial goals, needs and priorities that are relevant to the scope of the engagement before any recommendation is made and/or implemented.

Explanation of This Practice Standard

Prior to making recommendations to the client, the financial planning practitioner and the client shall mutually define the client's personal and financial goals, needs and priorities. In order to arrive at such a definition, the practitioner will need to explore the client's values, attitudes, expectations, and time horizons as they affect the client's goals, needs and priorities. The process of "mutually-defining" is essential in determining what activities may be necessary to proceed with the client engagement. Personal values and attitudes shape the client's goals and objectives and the priority placed on them. Accordingly, these goals and objectives must be consistent with the client's values and attitudes in order for the client to make the commitment necessary to accomplish them.

Goals and objectives provide focus, purpose, vision and direction for the financial planning process. It is important to determine clear and measurable objectives that are relevant to the scope of the engagement. The role of the practitioner is to facilitate the goal-setting process in order to clarify, with the client, goals and objectives. When appropriate, the practitioner shall try to assist clients in recognizing the implications of unrealistic goals and objectives.

This *Practice Standard* addresses only the tasks of determining the client's personal and financial goals, needs and priorities; assessing the client's values, attitudes and expectations; and determining the client's time horizons. These areas are subjective and the practitioner's interpretation is limited by what the client reveals.

This *Practice Standard* shall not be considered alone, but in conjunction with all other *Practice Standards*.

Anticipated Impact of This Practice Standard Upon the Public

The public is served when the relationship is based upon mutually defined goals, needs and priorities. This *Practice Standard* reinforces the practice of putting the client's interests first which is intended to increase the likelihood of achieving the client's goals and objectives.

Upon the Financial Planning Profession

Compliance with this *Practice Standard* emphasizes to the public that the client's goals, needs and priorities are the focus of the financial planning process. This encourages the public to seek out the services of a financial planning practitioner who uses such an approach.

Upon the Financial Planning Practitioner

The client's goals, needs and priorities help determine the direction of the financial planning process. This focuses the practitioner on the specific tasks that need to be accomplished. Ultimately, this will facilitate the development of appropriate recommendations.

200-2: Obtaining Quantitative Information and Documents

The financial planning practitioner shall obtain sufficient quantitative information and documents about a client relevant to the scope of the engagement before any recommendation is made and/or implemented.

Explanation of This Practice Standard

Prior to making recommendations to the client and depending on the scope of the engagement, the financial planning practitioner shall determine what quantitative information and documents are sufficient and relevant.

The practitioner shall obtain sufficient and relevant quantitative information and documents pertaining to the client's financial resources, obligations and personal situation. This information may be obtained directly from the client or other sources such as interview(s), questionnaire(s), client records and documents.

The practitioner shall communicate to the client a reliance on the completeness and accuracy of the information provided and that incomplete or inaccurate information will impact conclusions and recommendations.

If the practitioner is unable to obtain sufficient and relevant quantitative information and documents to form a basis for recommendations, the practitioner shall either:

1. Restrict the scope of the engagement to those matters for which sufficient and relevant information is available; or

2. Terminate the engagement.

The practitioner shall communicate to the client any limitations on the scope of the engagement, as well as the fact that this limitation could affect the conclusions and recommendations.

This *Practice Standard* shall not be considered alone, but in conjunction with all other *Practice Standards*.

Anticipated Impact of This Practice Standard Upon the Public

The public is served when financial planning recommendations are based upon sufficient and relevant quantitative information and documents. This *Practice Standard* is intended to increase the likelihood of achieving the client's goals and objectives.

Upon the Financial Planning Profession

The financial planning process requires that recommendations be made based on sufficient and relevant quantitative data. Therefore, compliance with this *Practice Standard* encourages the public to seek financial planning practitioners who use the financial planning process.

Upon the Financial Planning Practitioner

Sufficient and relevant quantitative information and documents provide the foundation for analysis. Ultimately, this will facilitate the development of appropriate recommendations.

300-1: Analyzing and Evaluating the Client's Information

A financial planning practitioner shall analyze the information to gain an understanding of the client's financial situation and then evaluate to what extent the client's goals, needs and priorities can be met by the client's resources and current course of action.

Explanation of This Practice Standard

Prior to making recommendations to a client, it is necessary for the financial planning practitioner to assess the client's financial situation and to determine the likelihood of reaching the stated objectives by continuing present activities.

The practitioner will utilize client-specified, mutually agreed upon, and/or other reasonable assumptions. Both personal and economic assumptions must be considered in this step of the process. These assumptions may include, but are not limited to, the following:

- Personal assumptions, such as: retirement age(s), life expectancy(ies), income needs, risk factors, time horizon and special needs; and

- Economic assumptions, such as: inflation rates, tax rates and investment returns.

Analysis and evaluation are critical to the financial planning process. These activities form the foundation for determining strengths and weaknesses of the client's financial situation and current course of action. These activities may also identify other issues that should be addressed. As a result, it may be appropriate to amend the scope of the engagement and/or to obtain additional information.

Anticipated Impact of This Practice Standard Upon the Public

The public is served when objective analysis and evaluation by a financial planning practitioner results in the client's heightened awareness of specific financial planning issues. This *Practice Standard* is intended to increase the likelihood of achieving the client's goals and objectives.

Upon the Financial Planning Profession

Objective analysis and evaluation enhances the public's recognition of and appreciation for the financial planning process and increases the confidence in financial planning practitioners who provide this service.

Upon the Financial Planning Practitioner

Analysis and evaluation helps the practitioner establish the foundation from which recommendations can be made that are specific to the client's financial planning goals, needs and priorities.

Preface to the 400 Series

The 400 Series, "Developing and Presenting the Financial Planning Recommendation(s)," represents the very heart of the financial planning process. It is at this point that the financial planning practitioner, using both science and art, formulates the recommendations designed to achieve the client's goals, needs and priorities. Experienced financial planning practitioners may view this process as one action or task. However, in reality, it is a series of distinct but interrelated tasks.

These three *Practice Standards* emphasize the distinction among the several tasks which are part of this process. These *Practice Standards* can be described as, "What is Possible?," "What is Recommended?" and "How is it Presented?" The first two *Practice Standards* involve the creative thought, the analysis, and the professional judgment of the practitioner, which are often performed outside the presence of the client. First, the practitioner identifies and considers the various alternatives, including continuing the present course of action (*Practice Standard* 400-1). Second, the practitioner develops the recommendation(s) from among the selected alternatives (*Practice Standard* 400-2). Once the practitioner has determined what to recommend, the final task is to communicate the recommendation(s) to the client (*Practice Standard* 400-3).

The three *Practice Standards* that comprise the 400 series should not be considered alone, but in conjunction with all other *Practice Standards*.

400-1: Identifying and Evaluating Financial Planning Alternative(s)

The financial planning practitioner shall consider sufficient and relevant alternatives to the client's current course of action in an effort to reasonably meet the client's goals, needs and priorities.

Explanation of This Practice Standard

After analyzing the client's current situation (*Practice Standard* 300-1) and prior to developing and presenting the recommendation(s) (*Practice Standards* 400-2 and 400-3) the financial planning practitioner shall identify alternative actions. The practitioner shall evaluate the effectiveness of such actions in reasonably meeting the client's goals, needs and priorities.

This evaluation may involve, but is not limited to, considering multiple assumptions, conducting research or consulting with other professionals. This process may result in a single alternative, multiple alternatives or no alternative to the client's current course of action.

In considering alternative actions, the practitioner shall recognize and, as appropriate, take into account his or her legal and/or regulatory limitations and level of competency in properly addressing each of the client's financial planning issues.

More than one alternative may reasonably meet the client's goals, needs and priorities. Alternatives identified by the practitioner may differ from those of other practitioners or advisers, illustrating the subjective nature of exercising professional judgment.

400-2: Developing the Financial Planning Recommendation(s)

The financial planning practitioner shall develop the recommendation(s) based on the selected alternative(s) and the current course of action in an effort to reasonably meet the client's goals, needs and priorities.

Explanation of This Practice Standard

After identifying and evaluating the alternative(s) and the client's current course of action, the practitioner shall develop the recommendation(s) expected to reasonably meet the client's goals, needs and priorities. A recommendation may be an independent action or a combination of actions which may need to be implemented collectively.

The recommendation(s) shall be consistent with and will be directly affected by the following:

- Mutually defined scope of the engagement;
- Mutually defined client goals, needs and priorities;
- Quantitative data provided by the client;
- Personal and economic assumptions;
- Practitioner's analysis and evaluation of client's current situation; and
- Alternative(s) selected by the practitioner.

A recommendation may be to continue the current course of action. If a change is recommended, it may be specific and/or detailed or provide a general direction. In some instances, it may be necessary for the practitioner to recommend that the client modify a goal.

The recommendations developed by the practitioner may differ from those of other practitioners or advisers, yet each may reasonably meet the client's goals, needs and priorities.

400-3: Presenting the Financial Planning Recommendation(s)

The financial planning practitioner shall communicate the recommendation(s) in a manner and to an extent reasonably necessary to assist the client in making an informed decision.

Explanation of This Practice Standard

When presenting a recommendation, the practitioner shall make a reasonable effort to assist the client in understanding the client's current situation, the recommendation itself, and its impact on the ability to meet the client's goals, needs and priorities. In doing so, the practitioner shall avoid presenting the practitioner's opinion as fact.

The practitioner shall communicate the factors critical to the client's understanding of the recommendations. These factors may include but are not limited to material:

- Personal and economic assumptions;
- Interdependence of recommendations;
- Advantages and disadvantages;
- Risks; and/or
- Time sensitivity.

The practitioner should indicate that even though the recommendations may meet the client's goals, needs and priorities, changes in personal and economic conditions could alter the intended outcome. Changes may include, but are not limited to: legislative, family status, career, investment performance and/or health.

If there are conflicts of interest that have not been previously disclosed, such conflicts and how they may impact the recommendations should be addressed at this time.

Presenting recommendations provides the practitioner an opportunity to further assess whether the recommendations meet client expectations, whether the client is willing to act on the recommendations, and whether modifications are necessary.

Anticipated Impact of These Practice Standards Upon the Public

The public is served when strategies and objective recommendations are developed and are communicated clearly to specifically meet each client's individual financial planning goals, needs and priorities.

Upon the Financial Planning Profession

A commitment to a systematic process for the development and presentation of the financial planning recommendations advances the financial planning profession. Development of customized strategies and recommendations enhances the public's perception of the objectivity and value of the financial planning process. The public will seek out those professionals who embrace these *Practice Standards*.

Upon the Financial Planning Practitioner

Customizing strategies and recommendations forms a foundation to communicate meaningful and responsive solutions. This increases the likelihood that a client will accept the recommendations and act upon them. These actions will contribute to client satisfaction.

500-1: Agreeing on Implementation Responsibilities

The financial planning practitioner and the client shall mutually agree on the implementation responsibilities consistent with the scope of the engagement.

Explanation of This Practice Standard

The client is responsible for accepting or rejecting recommendations and for retaining and/or delegating implementation responsibilities. The financial planning practitioner and the client shall mutually agree on the services, if any, to be provided by the practitioner. The scope of the engagement, as originally defined, may need to be modified.

The practitioner's responsibilities may include, but are not limited to the following:

- Identifying activities necessary for implementation;
- Determining division of activities between the practitioner and the client;
- Referring to other professionals;
- Coordinating with other professionals;
- Sharing of information as authorized; and

- Selecting and securing products and/or services.

If there are conflicts of interest, sources of compensation or material relationships with other professionals or advisers that have not been previously disclosed, such conflicts, sources or relationships shall be disclosed at this time.

When referring the client to other professionals or advisers, the financial planning practitioner shall indicate the basis on which the practitioner believes the other professional or adviser may be qualified. If the practitioner is engaged by the client to provide only implementation activities, the scope of the engagement shall be mutually defined in accordance with *Practice Standard* 100-1. This scope may include such matters as the extent to which the practitioner will rely on information, analysis or recommendations provided by others.

500-2: Selecting Products and Services for Implementation

The financial planning practitioner shall select appropriate products and services that are consistent with the client's goals, needs and priorities.

Explanation of This Practice Standard

The financial planning practitioner shall investigate products or services that reasonably address the client's needs. The products or services selected to implement the recommendation(s) must be suitable to the client's financial situation and consistent with the client's goals, needs and priorities.

The financial planning practitioner uses professional judgment in selecting the products and services that are in the client's interest. Professional judgment incorporates both qualitative and quantitative information.

Products and services selected by the practitioner may differ from those of other practitioners or advisers. More than one product or service may exist that can reasonably meet the client's goals, needs and priorities.

The practitioner shall make all disclosures required by applicable regulations.

Anticipated Impact of These Practice Standards Upon the Public

The public is served when the appropriate products and services are used to implement recommendations; thus increasing the likelihood that the client's goals will be achieved.

Upon the Financial Planning Profession

Over time, implementing recommendations using appropriate products and services for the client increases the credibility of the profession in the eyes of the public.

Upon the Financial Planning Practitioner

In the selection of products and services, putting the interest of the client first benefits the practitioner over the long-term.

600-1: Defining Monitoring Responsibilities

The financial planning practitioner and client shall mutually define monitoring responsibilities.

Explanation of This Practice Standard

The purpose of this *Practice Standard* is to clarify the role, if any, of the practitioner in the monitoring process. By clarifying this responsibility, the client's expectations are more likely to be in alignment with the level of monitoring services which the practitioner intends to provide.

If engaged for monitoring services, the practitioner shall make a reasonable effort to define and communicate to the client those monitoring activities the practitioner is able and willing to provide. By explaining what is to be monitored, the frequency of monitoring and the communication method, the client is more likely to understand the monitoring service to be provided by the practitioner.

The monitoring process may reveal the need to re-initiate steps of the financial planning process. The current scope of the engagement may need to be modified.

Anticipated Impact of This Practice Standard Upon the Public

The public is served when the practitioner and client have similar perceptions and a mutual understanding about the responsibilities for monitoring the recommendation(s).

Upon the Financial Planning Profession

The profession benefits when clients are satisfied. Clients are more likely to be satisfied when expectations of the monitoring process are both realistic and clear. This *Practice Standard* promotes awareness that financial planning is a dynamic process rather than a single action.

Upon the Financial Planning Practitioner

A mutually defined agreement of the monitoring responsibilities increases the potential for client satisfaction and clarifies the practitioner's responsibilities.

LIFE-CYCLE PLANNING

Financial Life Cycle

There are five distinct phases in an individual's *financial life cycle*. Starting at a relatively young age (age 25 or younger), a career-minded person typically will pass through four phases en route to phase five, retirement. These five phases and their corresponding age ranges are as follows:

1. early career (age 25 or younger to age 35)
2. career development (age 35 to 50)
3. peak accumulation (age 50 to ages 58–62)
4. preretirement (3 to 6 years prior to planned retirement)
5. retirement (ages 62–66 and older)

Together these five phases span a person's entire financial life. Although some people will not experience all of the phases or will spend more or less time in any one, the vast majority of career-minded people will go through all five.

A young client in the early career phase typically has several accumulation goals. A majority of these accumulation goals will have short time horizons (1–5 years) although some will have fairly long time horizons. For example, the typical client who is in the early career phase has only been married for a few years and has young children. He or she probably has a short time horizon for accumulating a cash reserve, pay off student loan debts or build emergency fund to meet unexpected contingencies. His or her time horizon for accumulating a down payment on a home generally is generally less than five years, while the time horizon for accumulating funds for the children's college educations is longer. However, this client probably has not given much thought to accumulating a retirement fund because of the numerous accumulation goals with shorter time horizons and higher priorities that he or she is facing. Balancing consumption, insurance premium, debt repayment, short term accumulation needs, and long-term savings needs are the challenges of working with clients in the early career life cycle phase.

The career development phase is often a time of career enhancement, upward mobility, and rapid growth in income. It usually includes some additional accumulation in the first few years for the children's college educations and has accumulation for retirement as a top priority throughout the period. For the most successful clients, this phase may be the time to begin general wealth building beyond basic accumulation goals, to fund extensive travel, or to plan for the lake house. Resource conservation is less important during the career development phase; developing investment discipline becomes more important.

sandwich generation
As the typical client moves into the peak accumulation phase, he or she is headed toward maximum earnings and the greatest opportunity for wealth accumulation. This phase may include accumulating funds for special purposes, but it usually continues the accumulation for retirement as a top priority. In the peak accumulation phase clients may find themselves pressured with caring for both dependent children and dependent parents. Those who struggle to support three generations (parents, self, and children) with one pool of resources are called the sandwich generation. Pressure is put on income, cash flow and resources of the primary wage earner. Additional time may need to be spent with aging parents, adding additional stress to an already difficult time. Advisers working with clients in the sandwich generation must familiarize themselves with community, social and government assistance programs for additional client support.

The preretirement phase often involves winding down both the career and income potential, and restructuring the portfolio to reduce risk and enhance income. Throughout this phase, the advisor should be actively involved in keeping the client's financial plan on target to meet all remaining accumulation goals, including the now top priority of accumulating for retirement.

The final phase in the client's financial life cycle is retirement. If the advisor has periodically reviewed and revised the client's financial plan and its corresponding portfolio, the client should have sufficient income to enjoy retirement. A financial plan and portfolio that are developed for a relatively young client need to be reviewed and revised/restructured periodically as the client ages and passes through the phases of his or her financial life cycle. As time marches on and life's circumstances change, some of the client's longer term accumulation goals may need adjusting. Restructuring the portfolio to accommodate these goals is critical if the financial plan is to be successful.

DEALING WITH ETHICAL ISSUES

Financial planners operate in an atmosphere full of ethical quandary. The nature of financial planning lends itself to ethical challenges. Financial planners add value, strategies and solutions to consumers that are intended to help clients meet goals. Consumers provide advisors either directly (through fees) or indirectly (through commissions) or both, and compensation paid to financial advisors impacts the overall return and goal making capability of clients. Financial planners find themselves along a spectrum.

At one end of the spectrum falls pro bono planning and altruistic motives. A planner can choose to work with clients for little or no compensation. Working pro bono maximizes consumer resources but minimizes planner compensation. On the other end of the spectrum financial advisors may charge excessively for services and negatively impact a consumer's ability to meet planning goals. The consumer, or client and financial planner must find a relationship that provides revenue to the financial professional while allowing clients to reach their planning goals.

guiding ethical principles   The Certified Financial Planner® Board of Standards has adopted seven ethical principles to help financial planners navigate through potential ethical struggles. On May 31, 2007, the Board of Directors of Certified Financial Planner Board of Standards, Inc. (CFP Board) announced the adoption of an updated Standards of Professional Conduct, which sets forth the ethical standards for CFP® professionals. The updated Standards have an effective date of July 1, 2008 and an enforcement date of January 1, 2009. Students may receive a copy of this code directly from the board. The Standards are based around seven driving principles, and can be found on page 6 of the Code of Ethics and Professional Responsibility.

1. **Integrity**—Provide professional services with integrity. Integrity demands honesty and candor which must not be subordinated to personal gain and advantage. Certificants are placed in positions of trust by clients, and the ultimate source of that trust is the certificant's personal integrity. Allowance can be made for innocent error and legitimate differences of opinion, but integrity cannot coexist with deceit or subordination of one's principles.

2. **Objectivity**—Provide professional services objectively. Objectivity requires intellectual honesty and impartiality. Regardless of the particular service rendered or the capacity in which a certificant functions, certificants should protect the integrity of their work, maintain objectivity and avoid subordination of their judgment.

3. **Competence**—Maintain the knowledge and skill necessary to provide professional services competently. Competence means attaining and maintaining an adequate level of knowledge and skill, and application of that knowledge and skill in providing services to clients. Competence also includes the wisdom to recognize the limitations of that knowledge and when consultation with other professionals is appropriate or referral to other professionals necessary. Certificants make a continuing commitment to learning and professional improvement.

4. **Fairness**—Be fair and reasonable in all professional relationships. Disclose conflicts of interest. Fairness requires impartiality, intellectual honesty and disclosure of material conflicts of interest. It involves a subordination of one's own feelings, prejudices and desires so as to achieve a proper balance of conflicting interests. Fairness is treating others in the same fashion that you would want to be treated.

5. **Confidentiality**—Protect the confidentiality of all client information. Confidentiality means ensuring that information is accessible only to those authorized to have access. A relationship of trust and confidence with the client can only be built upon the understanding that the client's information will remain confidential.

6. **Professionalism**—Act in a manner that demonstrates exemplary professional conduct. Professionalism requires behaving with dignity and courtesy to clients, fellow professionals, and others in business-related activities. Certificants cooperate with fellow certificants to enhance and maintain the profession's public image and improve the quality of services.

7. **Diligence**—Provide professional services diligently. Diligence is the provision of services in a reasonably prompt and thorough manner, including the proper planning for, and supervision of, the rendering of professional services.

The CFP® board sets forward rules regarding each of these principles. These seven guiding principles provide a barometer for any financial professional to consider, regardless of their view or consideration of the CFP® designation. These principles help financial advisors navigate through client situations.

Financial advisors may see the above ethical principles as a minimum standard of ethical behavior. Every advisor follows their own ethical compass both personally and in business settings. Even with a strong moral compass, financial services presents grey ethical areas from time to time.

ethical quandaries across business models

Suppose you sold a good client, and old friend, a long term care policy. After the insured was approved but before the policy was delivered learn that the friend has been diagnosed with the early stages of dementia. The insurer asks if there is any new information regarding the policy. Should dementia be reported to the company?

This situation puts the financial professional in an ethical quandary. Lying to the insurance company is wrong, but at the same time the financial professional may feel a stronger obligation towards their client's family. The legally correct outcome is to report the dementia to the insurer, but this action may have a catastrophic event on the client. Financial professionals are faced with this type of decision on a regular basis.

Fee-only financial planners also face similar situations. Clients may not have the resources to pay an annual fee. Does the planner continue working with them?

EXAMPLE
An 88-year-old widow of a client loses a lawsuit and is forced to pay most of her wealth to satisfy the judgement. An advisor charges a flat planning fee of $5,000 annually, and the widow can no longer afford the planning. The advisor can probably continue to offer pro bono planning for a certain time period, but for how long? Does the advisor abandon the widow? What if additional clients find themselves in the same situation?

Ronald F. Duska, Ph.D., former C. L. Post Chair of Ethics and the Professions at The American College, suggests steps that help determine more complicated ethical decisions.

resolving ethical problems

1. **Ascertain as many facts as possible.** Any rational analysis of a situation is helped immensely by getting clear about the facts. If one basis one's action on who is getting hurt and to what extent, those are important facts to consider. How much harm will

actually be done? How culpable are the people for their behavior? Financial advisors are constantly faced with dynamic client facts and situations. Understanding client details is integral to providing ethical advice and helping planners guide themselves through ethical challenges.

2. **Examine existing options and/or determine new options.** Often we portray ethical issues in exclusive either/or terms. Often dilemmas may appear only having two possible outcomes, but upon reflection may yield additional possibilities. If you haven't come up with a third option, you probably haven't thought about the issue hard enough. Financial planners become most valuable to their clients when they think outside the box. Creative thinking about client problems helps clients and also advances the field of financial planning.

3. **Evaluate options.** Since the primary task for ethics is the rational analysis and evaluation of human actions, past or future, the evaluation process is the heart of the ethical enterprise. But in terms of what standards should we evaluate actions? We would like to suggest several standards in the form of questions. Does the action do benefit or harm? Is the action fair? Does the action meet one's commitments? And finally, is the action legal? Does the advisor have a fiduciary responsibility or suitability responsibility towards their client? Answering these important legal questions helps guide planners through the process of making ethical decisions.

Ethical considerations occur in all of the case studies presented in the text. Students need to be aware of potential ethical developments and develop a moral compass for the road ahead.

USE OF INSURANCE AND RISK MANAGEMENT IN THE FINANCIAL PLANNING PROCESS

Financial planners most often focus on the core disciplines of risk management, investment and tax strategies when working with personal clients towards financial success. The following two sections are not intended to be comprehensive in nature, but are included as a review of financial planning fundamental knowledge.

Note

Before attempting more advanced case studies, students are encouraged to develop an in depth understanding of general insurance, investment, estate and tax planning principles.

Financial planners must help their clients identify risks and alternatives for managing those risks. Risk management requires an in depth understanding of risks, but can be distilled to a four step process:

- **Identifying risks**. The process begins with the recognition and classification of various risks.

- **Measuring risks.** The next step is the analysis and evaluation of risks in terms of frequency, severity, and variability.

- **Choosing methods to treat risks**. After measuring risk, planners can help choose and use of methods to treat each identified risk. Some risks can be avoided, some controlled, some retained under planned programs, and some transferred by a method such as insurance.

- **Risk administration**. Once the methods of treatment are chosen, plans for administration of the program must be instituted. This last step includes both implementing the methods selected and monitoring the choices to see that they are effective.

insurance in the planning process   Insurance is the principal method of treating the pure risks of many businesses and households. But without careful study of all the risk management alternatives in a coordinated decision-making process, insurance may be used inappropriately, or not used where it is appropriate.

After the client's current holdings have been analyzed for improved tax efficiency and appropriate recommendations have been made in the area of tax planning, the emphasis turns to an analysis of the client's exposure to potential loss of income or assets. There are three basic ways to deal with such exposures:

- The client bears the risk of the entire loss himself or herself (self-insurance or retention).

- The client pays another to assume the risk for him or her (shifting the risk through insurance).

- The client utilizes some combination of these strategies.

While insurance planning is as personal as the individual client, some general rules are applicable:

- Although life insurance is not the solution for all situations, current tax law does give permanent insurance products certain advantages that provide additional benefits to clients who need risk protection.

- Catastrophic risks should be insured against even when the probability of the occurrence of the loss is slight. Premium rates are usually low in these circumstances because rates are tied to the probability and magnitude of the loss.

- Small risks should generally not be insured against, especially when the probability of the occurrence of loss is high. Premium rates are usually relatively high and insurance is not cost effective.

- If the client has sufficient liquid assets to meet his or her stated objectives, it may be appropriate to fund these objectives from accumulated assets rather than from insurance proceeds.

- Insurance is a device for shifting the risks of loss from the client to an insurance company. Although many modern insurance products have substantial investment features, the primary function of insurance is still this risk-shifting function.

- Before the sale of additional (or replacement) insurance is recommended, the financial planner must be able to demonstrate to the client that it (a) meets a genuine need or objective of the client and (b) is a more cost-effective means of achieving that end than other planning techniques.

- Client objectives that will be met by the purchase of appropriate types and amounts of insurance coverage change over time. Insurance planning must be carefully reviewed and monitored along with the rest of the financial plan to assure that insurance coverage is adjusted as circumstances change.

- The need for insurance coverage does not always increase over time. Effective financial and estate planning techniques may result in a decreasing need for insurance.

- Insurance planning must always be coordinated with tax planning so that coverage is purchased in a tax-efficient manner and takes into account the tax impact of ownership and beneficiary designations.

Insurance, properly utilized, meets the client's need to minimize exposure to many types of serious losses as nothing else can. If it is improperly used, it drains the client's cash flow and consequently prevents the achievement of other objectives. Unless the coverage is positioned properly, it may needlessly aggravate estate tax problems and cost the client's family thousands of dollars in unnecessary estate tax liabilities. Judicious recommendations to purchase insurance contracts to insure against loss of income or assets can be a boon to the financial planning client. However, if recommendations are made by financial planners seeking only the planner's personal enrichment, the entire financial planning discipline suffers.

INVESTMENT RECOMMENDATIONS IN THE FINANCIAL PLANNING PROCESS

investments in the planning process

Investment analysis and recommendations are the final areas addressed in the development of the client's financial plan. The purpose of investing falls into two categories. The first category includes the prefunding of anticipated expenditures for retirement and education costs. The second category is discretionary in the sense that investments are made with the more general goal of adding to the stock of the client's assets rather than funding a specific need. Because investments are normally made from cash available after living expenditures, the appropriate time to ascertain the amount to be invested is after tax and insurance planning have been done. By assuring there is no cash drain due to poor tax or insurance planning, the maximum dollar amount will be available for investment.

Investment planning is intimately tied to the life cycle process. While accumulating assets, advisers may value equity based instruments with lower costs. Early Career, Career Development, and Peak Accumulation stages typically focus on the art of accumulating assets and wealth. Investment advisers helping clients acquire wealth will often use different strategies and techniques than those advisers working with clients in the Pre-Retirement and Retirement phases. Investment goals when decumulating a portfolio focus on tackling the client's risk of outliving their resources.

Needless to say, the choice of appropriate investment vehicles can vary widely from client to client. Recommendations on investments must be based on the planner's assessment of the client's attitude toward risk and return. For example, it would not generally be appropriate to recommend trading in commodities futures to a risk-averse client whose previous investment choices have been federally insured savings deposits or CDs.

Within the limits of a particular client's risk/return tolerances, however, there may be considerable latitude in the choice of investment vehicles. To a great extent the choice among these vehicles will depend on the client's objectives.

As with insurance planning, investment planning should be carefully coordinated with the other aspects of the client's plan, and care should be taken to ensure that the investment recommendations made are those best suited to achieve the client's objectives.

USE OF TAX PLANNING IN THE FINANCIAL PLANNING PROCESS

tax in the planning process   Because tax planning is a fundamental part of the comprehensive planning process, an understanding of the tax laws is necessary for financial planning to be effective. Without effective tax planning, comprehensive financial planning simply cannot be accomplished.

Nobody (not even a tax attorney) is an expert in all areas of taxation. In fact, tax attorneys are almost always highly specialized, most practicing in various subspecialities of tax law. This does not mean that a great deal cannot be learned about a particular area of taxation regardless of whether one has a legal or accounting background. It is a rare occasion, however, when anything other than the most simplistic tax planning can be done without the involvement of a competent tax attorney. Even if the financial planner has a legal and tax background, many planning cases will involve such sophisticated tax techniques that it will be necessary to obtain assistance and additional legal counsel from a practicing tax attorney.

Appropriate tax planning involves consideration of many planning techniques. Federal and state tax laws, as well as the different types of taxation within each system, must be considered. Unfortunately it is not unusual for clients (and many advisers) to lump all tax planning together into one broad category—taxes. This is an error that can leave clients confused and angry. For example, many clients are startled when they are told that the proceeds of their insurance policies are subject to federal estate taxes. "But my insurance agent told me that insurance proceeds were tax free," they say angrily. What the agent meant was that, as a general rule, the proceeds of life insurance are excluded from income taxation (IRC Sec. 101). Insurance proceeds, however, are not excluded from estate taxation if the decedent held any incidents of ownership in the insurance policy at death or if the life insurance policy had named the estate of the insured as the beneficiary (IRC Sec. 2042).

The Internal Revenue Code covers all forms of federal taxes. The primary types of taxes that financial planners deal with are income, gift, estate, and generation-skipping taxes, but the Code also deals with employment taxes and excise taxes that may be applicable in some planning cases.

precision   The financial planner must learn to be precise in dealing with issues of taxation, and to do so requires spending sufficient time and study to recognize the existing systems of taxation and to understand that the rules for the imposition of the various types of taxes are often very different. Specific rules have been established by statute or case law to determine when taxation occurs and when tax liabilities arise. A taxable event occurs when there is some transfer of property unless the Internal Revenue Code specifically provides otherwise. As noted in the above example concerning the federal taxation of life insurance proceeds, the income and estate tax rules are not always consistent. It is the task of the financial planner to understand the tax rules and to explain to the client the rules that are applicable to his or her situation.

After data gathering is complete, the planner analyzes the information for opportunities that would save the client income, estate, and gift taxes (and other taxes, if applicable). If the financial plan is being delivered for a fee, tax planning is a substantial portion of what the financial planner is being paid to do. Even when products are being offered for sale, it is the obligation of the financial planner to take a comprehensive and objective look at the client's situation and to save the client from costly tax blunders whenever possible. The time for product recommendations is after the client's affairs have been rearranged to maximize the benefits of the client's present holdings. For example, the best funding vehicle available for a stock-redemption agreement is of very little assistance if the agreement itself will have disastrous tax consequences or is legally unenforceable. The sale of a risky investment under the guise of comprehensive financial planning, without previous attention to the analysis and rearrangement of the client's current assets for maximum personal tax benefits, is not ethical.

One of the most important benefits of financial planning is educating the client to consider the tax benefits and costs of every transaction *before* engaging in it. Only before the transaction is consummated can the tax results be fully controlled through negotiation between the parties. Although it may be possible in some cases to restructure agreements to be more advantageous to the client, later repairs of completed transactions often are not feasible, as they are too expensive or would require the agreement of an adverse party. Each transaction should be structured in light of the client's tax, income, and cash-flow situation.

In most tax planning the timing and form of the transaction can mean everything. That is, by appropriately structuring the documents to control the form and the timing of the transaction, the drafter generally controls the tax result. Assume a client approaches the financial planner with a large potential taxable gain in a contemplated transaction. The first question in a discussion of the proposed transaction with a buyer will be how to structure the transaction so that the maximum amount of net proceeds from the sale will remain in the client's hands. The financial planner must be able to respond accurately to that question without unduly delaying negotiations. This may involve negotiating an agreement that allows reporting of the income on the installment method over 2 or more tax years. In reaching a conclusion on this issue, the factors that must be considered are the potential interest or other investment income or gain that will be forgone by stretching out the payments and the amount of taxes that will be saved by this technique. In some cases the savings are substantial. This is a simple example of how income tax planning is used in the comprehensive financial planning process.

Other taxes that are routinely considered in the financial planning process are federal estate and gift taxes. Estate planning is an important part of financial planning, but it is only one part. Financial planning deals with all current assets of the client and all proposed acquisitions or dispositions of those assets during the client's life. It then seeks at the client's death to effect the transition of those assets through an orderly plan that is not only consistent with the owner's wishes but that is tax advantageous as well.

It is not unusual for a competent financial planner to save a client thousands of dollars in potential estate tax liabilities by effective utilization of the federal estate, gift, and generation-skipping tax laws. Generally it is not sufficient to save potential estate tax dollars only at the death of the first spouse. Unless there is some compelling family planning reason for not doing so, the financial planner should consider the projected estate tax costs in the estates of both spouses and plan to minimize total taxes. The ultimate strategy is to transmit as much of the client's accumulated wealth as possible to the children or grandchildren at the death of the client and spouse. Most clients, of course, want a surviving spouse to continue to have most of the marital assets available in case of need but may want to assure that these assets cannot be squandered or diverted from their children. By utilizing appropriate estate planning techniques, marital assets can be made readily available to a surviving spouse, yet avoid inclusion in the surviving spouse's estate while ensuring that any assets that are unconsumed by the surviving spouse will be disposed of according to the client's wishes.

Although the comprehensive financial planner must know a great deal about tax issues and the tax laws to identify potential problem areas, most financial planners are not attorneys. For these financial planners the specter of a charge of unauthorized practice of law can be troubling.

Neither the American Bar Association's Model Rules of Professional Conduct nor its predecessor, the Code of Professional Responsibility, is helpful in this specific area. It is quite clear that no one other than a lawyer is permitted to engage in the practice of law. What constitutes the practice of law, however, is not clearly defined. The Model Rules of Professional Conduct takes the position that the definition of the practice of law is established by the law of the different jurisdictions and can therefore vary from jurisdiction to jurisdiction. The Code of Professional Responsibility stated that "It is neither necessary nor desirable to attempt the formulation of a single, specific definition of what constitutes the practice of law. Functionally the practice of law relates to the rendition of services for others that call for the professional judgment of a lawyer. The essence of the professional judgment of the lawyer is his or her educated ability to relate the general body and philosophy of law to a specific legal problem of a client."

Despite the American Bar Association's ambiguous definitions of what constitutes the practice of law, there are some activities that are universally regarded as the practice of law and as such are to be engaged in only by lawyers. One such activity is the drafting of legal documents.

The line between the unauthorized practice of law and the permissible giving of advice is much more difficult to ascertain, especially in fields such as accounting and financial planning. The pivotal question revolves around when the giving of tax advice or information about a particular proposed transaction or tax technique by a CPA or financial planner becomes "legal advice" and as such becomes the exclusive right of the lawyer. There is no absolute way to answer this question.

There is, however, some guidance available to assist the nonlawyer in avoiding potential problems in the unauthorized practice area. If the advice given is couched in general terms-for example, if the general principles of a technique are explained for the client's information, this should not be viewed as the unauthorized practice of law. Moreover, even advice that is specifically related to a client's situation should not constitute an unauthorized-practice violation as long as the subject matter of the advice is settled in the law and is a matter of common knowledge in the adviser's field.

The safest way to deal with the unauthorized-practice issue is to immediately involve an attorney as a member of the financial planning team. The attorney's involvement should continue throughout the planning process in those areas in which it is difficult to distinguish legal advice from advice or information that can be legitimately offered by someone who is not a lawyer.

ASCERTAINING THE VALUE OF TAX AUTHORITY

To engage in effective tax planning, a financial planner needs to understand the sources of tax authority. In evaluating a potential recommendation, as well as in dealing with other members of the financial planning team or with the client's outside advisers, the planner must know both the source and the weight of the authority on which he or she is relying. There are three interrelated sources from which tax authority is derived:

- legislative tax authority
- administrative tax authority
- judicial tax authority

Legislative authority to enact a federal income tax law was granted to Congress by the Sixteenth Amendment to the Constitution of the United States in 1913. Under this authority Congress has enacted statutes that are the primary tax authority, subject only to a successful challenge of the constitutionality of the particular statute, an issue that is ultimately decided by the United States Supreme Court. The tax statutes enacted by Congress are codified in the Internal Revenue Code. Tax statutes (Code provisions) are cited in the following way: 26 U.S.C. 351, or more commonly IRC Sec. 351, that is, the 26th title of the United States Code, Sec. 351, or Internal Revenue Code, Sec. 351. All section references in this book are to the Internal Revenue Code of 1986, as amended, and to the regulations thereunder unless otherwise noted.

After enactment, tax laws are subject to interpretation and explanation by both administrative bodies and the judicial system. The Internal Revenue Service (under delegated authority from the President of the United States or the Congress through the Treasury Department) has responsibility for the actual formulation of the next tier of tax authority, the regulations. The Treasury Regulations are subject to final approval by the Treasury Department.

The purpose of the Treasury regulations is to explain how the tax laws are to be applied. In fact, the regulations may explain, exemplify, define, or even attempt to expand the Code provision. The regulations express the official Treasury (and thereby the Internal Revenue Service) interpretation of the Code provisions. After Treasury regulations are formulated, they are issued in proposed form to allow interested parties, such as representatives of the affected group or industry as well as tax attorneys and accountants, to file comments or objections and to participate in public hearings before the regulations are adopted in final form. Once adopted, the final regulations become the official position of the Internal Revenue Service and are binding on IRS personnel. The general rule is that to the extent that the regulation is not inconsistent with the Code, it has the force and effect of law, unless and until it is overturned by a court of competent jurisdiction.

Regulations can be invalidated by courts on several grounds. A court may invalidate a Treasury regulation if (a) the regulation has incorrectly construed the Congressional intent of the statute or (b) the regulation exceeds the scope of the Code provision. Courts give substantial weight to the regulations and are generally reluctant to invalidate them. This approach is good for taxpayers and tax advisers because it means that the regulations will not undergo constant change and can therefore be relied on for planning purposes.

One note of caution: Even if a court has ruled a regulation invalid, the Internal Revenue Service can still attempt to enforce the regulation against other taxpayers in other federal jurisdictions unless and until the decision to invalidate it has been upheld by the U.S. Supreme Court. Therefore a planner must be certain to clearly inform the client that the IRS could continue to enforce the regulation despite a contrary decision by the District Court or Circuit Court of Appeals in another jurisdiction. In fact, the IRS frequently attempts to get different results on the same issue from different Circuit Courts of Appeals, thereby creating a "conflict among the circuits" in an attempt to get the Supreme Court to hear the case and resolve the conflict.

Regulations are numbered in a manner consistent with the Internal Revenue Code sections that they explain. For example, the income tax regulations for IRC Sec. 351 are cited as Treas. Regs. Sec. 1.351; estate tax regulations are cited as Treas. Regs. Sec. 20.2001; gift tax regulations are cited as Treas. Regs. Sec. 25.2501; and so on.

The next tier of tax authority consists of revenue rulings that are issued and published in response to a taxpayer's request for the Internal Revenue Service's interpretation of a particular point of law applied to a specific fact situation. When the request for interpretation is one involving an issue that is likely to affect a significant number of taxpayers, the IRS often issues a revenue ruling on the subject. The revenue ruling is a public announcement of the IRS's present position on the issue in question, and IRS personnel will act in accordance with that position.

The taxpayer, however, is not necessarily bound by the ruling. If his or her situation is substantially the same as that described in the revenue ruling and the result is favorable to the taxpayer, the ruling can be relied on in dealings with the IRS. If the facts of the case are substantially the same as those in the revenue ruling and the ruling is adverse to the taxpayer, the ruling can be challenged in the courts. Revenue rulings, unlike the regulations, are given no particular weight by the courts; that is, they are not necessarily presumed to be correct.

Unlike the regulations, revenue rulings are more often changed or modified by later revenue rulings. One should be especially careful when relying on revenue rulings to ensure that the benefits they promise have not been diminished or eliminated by subsequent rulings.

Revenue rulings are cited in two ways. Those published recently are cited to the weekly publication in which they appear, the *Internal Revenue Bulletin*. For example, the 109th Revenue Ruling of 2003 appearing in the 36th weekly *Internal Revenue Bulletin* at page 14 would be cited as follows: Rev. Rul. 2003-109, I.R.B. 36,14. Revenue rulings (and other administrative rulings by the IRS) are continuously collected by the U.S. Government Printing Office into bound volumes called *Cumulative Bulletins*. Each of these is compiled for a particular calendar year and may contain two or three volumes. If the revenue ruling has been printed in the *Cumulative Bulletin,* the citation is usually to that source and is slightly different in appearance. For example, the 50th Revenue Ruling of 2003 appears in volume two of the 2003 *Cumulative Bulletin* at page 205. The appropriate citation is Rev. Rul. 2003-50, 2003-2 C.B. 205. Whether the citation is to the *Internal Revenue Bulletin* or to the *Cumulative Bulletin,* the degree of authority of an unsuperseded revenue ruling is the same.

Revenue rulings should not be confused with revenue procedures (Rev. Procs.), which are also published in the *Internal Revenue Bulletin* and collected in the *Cumulative Bulletin*. Revenue procedures usually relate to changes in procedures within the IRS. These changes include such items as limitations or additions in the areas in which the IRS will issue rulings, as well as changes in other internal techniques.

The following diagram shows the hierarchy of legislative and administrative authority.

Figure 1-1
Hierarchy of Legislative and Administrative Authority

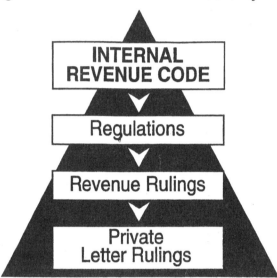

The final administrative tier of tax authority concerns the issuance of private letter rulings. Taxpayers can request a private ruling from the IRS that approves or interprets a transaction that has either not been consummated or for which a return has not been filed. The IRS will honor such requests if the transaction involves an issue on which the IRS has decided to rule. (This decision is purely an administrative one, and the areas in which the IRS will rule have become much less numerous in recent years.) The private letter ruling is a personal response to a particular taxpayer and as such is determinative only in regard to the transaction it describes. Until recently private letter rulings were mailed directly to the taxpayer or an authorized representative, and public access to them was limited. However, they are now being released under the Freedom of Information Act and are published by private publishers after all confidential and identifying information has been deleted. While private letter rulings cannot be cited as authority by taxpayers other than the taxpayer obtaining the ruling, they are often helpful to tax practitioners as an indication of the IRS position on various issues. An example of how private letter rulings are cited is as follows: PLR 200201004. The first four numbers in the citation indicate the year in which the private ruling was issued.

The ultimate judicial authority for the interpretation of the law including tax law is the U.S. Supreme Court. Once the Supreme Court has decided an issue, the decision is binding on all taxpayers and the Internal Revenue Service and therefore must be adhered to unless Congress changes the relevant Code section or unless the Supreme Court later reverses its own decision. It is not possible, however, to take tax cases directly to the Supreme Court for determination. Tax cases must originate in lower courts and work their way up to the Supreme Court level. Even then, the Supreme Court has the discretion to hear or refuse to hear a tax case presented to it.

The choice of the lowest court in which tax cases are heard depends on whether the taxpayer, after exhausting the administrative appeal procedures of the IRS, can or will pay the tax and sue for a refund or seeks a judicial determination of the contested issues before the tax is paid. If the taxpayer wishes the court to rule on the correctness of the issue before paying the tax, the case will be tried in the Tax Court (known prior to 1942 as the United States Board of Tax Appeals). Cases in the Tax Court are tried without juries. Tax Court judges decide issues of law and fact. The party against whom the decision is made can appeal a Tax Court decision to the United States Court of Appeals in the circuit where the Tax Court decision was made. If the decision is adverse to the IRS, the Service may choose not to appeal the case but may also wish not to abandon the issue. The Service will usually indicate whether it will continue to litigate the particular issue involved by acquiescing or not acquiescing in the decision. Nonacquiescence indicates that the Service disagrees with the decision and will continue to litigate the issue in future cases it believes are favorable to its position.

The Tax Court generally follows its own decisions as precedents; that is, a Tax Court in California is likely to consider the finding of a Tax Court in Massachusetts on a substantially similar issue extremely persuasive authority in determining the issue before it. This is true even if the Court of Appeals that reviewed the Massachusetts decision reversed the original Tax Court result.

Tax Court decisions that the court considers important or that express a new issue not previously dealt with in a published Tax Court opinion are collected and published by the Government Printing Office as Tax Court reports. These decisions are cited with volume number first, followed by T.C., and then page number. For example, a case appearing in the 72nd volume of the Tax Court reports at page 88 would be cited 72 T.C. 88. Other Tax Court decisions are called Tax Court Memorandum decisions and are presently available through private publishers. They are also cited by volume number, T.C.M., and page—for example, 49 T.C.M. 66. Tax Court decisions, published as either regular or memorandum decisions, carry the same degree of authority.

If the taxpayer pays the tax the IRS has assessed, the Tax Court will not determine whether the IRS acted correctly in assessing the tax. Instead, the taxpayer must take his or her case to a court that has jurisdiction over claims for refund. The taxpayer can choose either a United States District Court or the United States Claims Court. In a U.S. District Court the taxpayer can have a jury trial; in the U.S. Claims Court all trials are nonjury. Decisions from both the District Courts and the U.S. Claims Court are reported in a series called the *Federal Supplement,* which is cited as follows: 36 F. Supp. 103, meaning a particular case can be found in the 36th volume of the *Federal Supplement* beginning at page 103. However, the routes of appeal from the two courts are different—appeals from the U.S. District Courts are to the U.S. Courts of Appeals; appeals from the U.S. Claims Court are to the Court of Appeals for the Federal Circuit.

As already indicated, the party who loses in the Tax Court or the District Court can appeal the decision to the United States Court of Appeals in the circuit in which the Tax Court or District Court decision was rendered. The decision of the Court of Appeals is determinative of the issue before it (unless overturned by the Supreme Court), and therefore a Court of Appeals decision is higher authority than that of the Tax Court or a U.S. District Court. Cases from the U.S. Court of Appeals are reported in the *Federal Reporter* and are cited as follows: 72 F.2d 823 (7th Cir.), meaning that the 72d volume of the second series of the *Federal Reporter* at page 823 contains a decision by the 7th Circuit Court of Appeals.

The party who loses a case at the U.S. Court of Appeals or the Court of Appeals for the Federal Circuit can appeal the case to the U.S. Supreme Court. There is no guarantee, however, that the Supreme Court will grant a writ of certiorari (accept the case for a decision). If the Supreme Court refuses to hear the case, the decision of the Court of Appeals is determinative. If the Supreme Court hears the case, the Supreme Court's findings are the ultimate decision, and the issue is settled as a matter of law for all courts. Supreme Court decisions are officially cited as follows: 267 U.S. 972, meaning the 267th volume of the *Supreme Court Reports* at page 972.

The following diagram depicts the system of judicial authority for tax cases:

Figure 1-2
Judicial Authority for Tax Cases

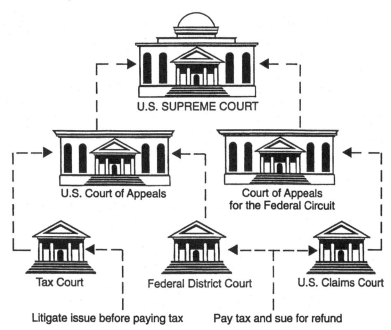

CHAPTER REVIEW

Key Terms and Concepts

comprehensive financial planning
team-based financial planning
single-purpose approach
multiple-purpose approach
comprehensive approach
financial planning process
prospecting
staging meetings
data-gathering session
define the scope of engagement
develop client goals and objectives
develop and present
   recommendations and alternatives
critically analyze goals and objectives

ongoing relationship
implementation
monitoring
Financial Life Cycle
sandwich generation
guiding ethical principles
ethical quandaries across business
   models
resolving ethical problems
insurance in the planning process
investments in the planning process
tax in the planning process
precision

Review Questions

These questions are included to help students master the material contained in chapter one. Suggested answers can be found in the accompanying study supplement.

1. What are the drawbacks of a single individual practicing financial planning? [2]

2. What are the six steps of the financial planning process? [2]

3. Which step of the planning process requires working as a team? [2]

4. What are some steps financial planners can use to identify target markets? [2]

5. Elias contacts your office to meet about his retirement. He is not sure what to bring or what your process is, but he is very eager to discuss retiring. How would you prepare Elias for your first meeting? Assume your firm utilizes the six steps in the financial planning process. [4]

6. You meet with Elias and he discloses that he is leaving his employer because they suspect he has embezzled corporate funds. What are some steps you can take to limit your exposure? Elias claims he did not engage in any embezzling activity. [4]

7. Elias turns out to be a wonderful client. Through your second or third meeting you begin to realize Elias has trouble repeating information previous consultations. He is intellectually competent but appears to have trouble focusing. What are some methods you would employ in the fourth step of the planning process? [4]

8. You believe that Elias is great candidate for a limited partnership. You own shares in the same limited partnership and will receive a 15 percent commission for every dollar that Elias invests. After following the steps of the financial planning process in earnest you derive that 10 percent of his portfolio should be invested in this instrument. What potential conflicts of interest may arise and how would you address them in the planner/client relationship? [4]

9. If Elias had met with you while he was in the peak of his career, how might your strategies and interview methods be different than working with a retiree? [4]

10. What are the seven driving principles in the Code of Ethics and Professional Responsibility? Write a brief discussion of each ethical principle, and apply it to a client situation you have encountered. [3]

11. How should financial advisers tackle ethical challenges presented by clients? [3]

12. What are two steps should insurance agents take before replacing an insurance policy? [3]

13.   What are the interrelated sources from which tax authority is derived? [5]

14.   Which judicial authority allows a client to litigate an issue before paying tax? Which court in the United States has ultimate tax authority? [5]

15.   Risk Management, Investment, Tax and Estate Planning are all valuable components of a client's financial situation. How should a financial service professional develop a financial planning team capable and competent to service the clients' needs in a comprehensive financial planning situation? [6]

Additional Considerations when Working with Live Clients

Learning Objectives

An understanding of the material in this chapter should enable the student to

1. Distinguish strengths and limitations of written case studies.
2. Analyze and critique fact finders and data gathering instruments.
3. Review assumptions, including inflation.
4. Discuss the unique aspects of personal and business planning.

case study approach

Case studies provide the opportunity to practice financial planning in an organized and open environment. They are an important learning tool that give students the chance to apply financial planning topic knowledge and integrate subject matter areas. Professional exams often include case study-type questions, which test a student's ability to process higher order cognitive topics.

The case study approach does have one compelling drawback. Clients are dynamic and constantly shifting goals, priorities and activities. Case studies cannot completely capture changes in the human condition, family situation and individual preferences. Case studies should be written with enough facts and circumstances for students to discern an answer. Live clients offer challenges in setting goals, gathering information, making assumptions and delivering information. Each case will have different characteristics and solutions. The breadth of case studies and solution approaches provide students a comprehensive and holistic approach to the planning process.

The first case study presented focuses on resource allocation for younger financial planning clients. This case requires a broad level of knowledge in core financial planning disciplines, particularly risk management areas. Students will be forced to allocate scarce resources between financial planning goals. While students may differ in their final recommendations and alternatives, utilizing an outline approach to financial planning should create consistency within planning techniques. Additional cases in the text will have different focuses, from home purchase and refinance to advanced business succession planning. Students will benefit from using an outline approach in solving each of these cases.

INITIAL DOCUMENTATION

gathering client data

In practice, a financial adviser would have to gather documents and data to complete a financial planning outline. The client would rarely provide a complete history, budget and balance sheet to an adviser without being prompted. Financial advisers gather client information using a combination of three methods:

1. Ask that the client complete a fact finder (also called a client questionnaire) before the initial meeting. The fact finder contains fields and boxes. This technique of gathering data provides asset, liability and tax information. A strength of using fact finders is incorporating the client in the financial planning process and providing them with a sense of ownership. Drawbacks of using a fact finder include relying on clients to understand their financial positions and statements, as well as having reliable penmanship.

2. Interview the client in person or over the phone. Planner and client interviews allow the adviser to follow up on questions, discover client goals, and potentially discover additional information about the client. The nature of client interviews lends them to be qualitative, and may require adviser vigilance to stick to an interview outline.

3. Fill in information gaps using documents provided by the client. Advisers may ask for standard documentation from each client before beginning the planning process and maintain a list of required documents. Financial professionals may also ask for more detailed client information as needed.

Financial professionals may perform comprehensive or modular financial planning. Even if performing modular planning, a financial planner may need to know information and review documents from tangent disciplines. An adviser hired primarily to manage investments may want to review client tax returns before making recommendations. From the return an investment adviser could glean information about the alternative minimum tax (AMT), tax rate treatment, carryforward gains and losses. AMT information might limit an investment adviser's ability to use some types of municipal bonds with a client. The tax paid by a client and the any carryforward short- or long-term losses can drastically influence a client's holdings.

information needed for financial planning by type of client

The following table gives examples of documents needed for the planning process by type of client or financial planner function. Advisers should ask for more information as needed to successfully serve their client base.

Table 2-1 Information Needed by Client Type	
Cash Flow	Credit card statements, bank and debit card records, pay stubs, filing documents (W2, K1 and 1099 forms), employer retirement plan statements and plan documents, client-generated budget, cash receipts, mortgage statement, lease or rental agreement, state and local tax returns, contact information for bankers, and insurance premium notices
Financial Position	Brokerage, bank, insurance, money market account, mutual fund, other financial statements, personal loans, state and local tax returns, mortgage statements, statement of personal property including purchase price and value, list of real estate by county and value, Social Security statements, pay stubs, contact information for brokers or agents, and retirement plan documents
Business Owners	In addition to the above documents, ask for an employee census, copy of accounting books, all tax returns, appraisal valuations, business plan, forecasted earnings and expenses
Estate Planning	Current wills, trusts, medical directives, powers of attorney (financial and medical) record of gifting, previous gift and estate tax returns, land surveying and titling, property appraisals, and letter of last instructions
Tax Planning	All of the above, including the last 5 to 7 years of tax returns, electronic tax files such as QuickBooks or Quicken, and contact information for accountants used in the past

Today's financial planning technology allows planners to prepare planning documents while in initial client meetings. Financial planners should consider the technology level of their clients when integrating active planning with data gathering meetings. Clients who are comfortable with computers and presentations may find the experience efficient and exciting, while older clients who are not as familiar with computers and live simulation may be more comfortable with a traditional approach.

IMPORTANCE OF COMMUNICATING EFFECTIVELY WITH CLIENTS

Many people take communication for granted. After all, it is an activity that most of us have engaged in since our childhood years, so why not take it for granted? The sad truth is that many of us are ineffective communicators simply because we make that very assumption.

Communication is far too important a skill to treat lightly. This is especially true in the field of financial planning. It is the single most critical skill that an advisor brings to a financial planning session. Ineffective communication is an obstacle to a strong advisor-client relationship. The failure of clients and advisors to communicate fully and clearly with each other can result in improperly identified financial goals and the formulation of inappropriate planning strategies. The result for the client is not being able to achieve his or her financial goals. The communication process is the starting point from which the advisor helps the client to establish financial goals and then designs a plan to achieve those goals. Simply put, effective communication between the advisor and client is crucial to the financial planning process.

The purpose of this chapter is to examine the communication process as it typically exists in an advisor-client relationship. Our goal is to help financial advisors become better communicators. Perhaps you already consider yourself an effective communicator; however, there are probably aspects of the communication process in which you can improve. This chapter will attempt to bring these aspects into sharper focus and provide you with techniques for becoming the very best communicator/advisor that you are able to be.

TYPES OF STRUCTURED COMMUNICATION USED IN FINANCIAL PLANNING

The three primary forms of structured communication are interviewing, counseling and advising. Laypersons often use these terms interchangeably. Yet each of these forms of structured communication has characteristics that are uniquely its own and that differentiate it from the other two. We will describe these three forms of structured communication and discuss how advisors use them in the financial planning process.

Interviewing

interviewing

Interviewing is one of the most common forms of structured communication. Interviewing can be defined as a process of communication, most often between two people, with a predetermined and specific purpose, usually involving the asking and answering of questions designed to gather meaningful information. To gather this information, the financial advisor provides the client with a fact-finder form to fill out. When the form is returned, the advisor typically schedules a fact-finder session in which he or she interviews the client by asking a series of questions designed to help in reviewing the answers, clarifying any confusion, and filling in the blank spaces. There is a specific purpose to the interview: to gather relevant information through a question-and-answer dialogue.

directive interview

Stewart and Cash in their book, *Interviewing: Principles and Practices*, refer to two basic types of interviews: directive and nondirective.[1] In a *directive interview*, the financial advisor directs and controls both the pace and the content to be covered. This is a formal and structured style of interaction. The advisor completes a fact-finder form as the client answers pointed questions. Many of the questions are asked and answered rapidly in an almost staccato fashion. What is your date of birth? Where do you live? What is your occupation? What is the highest level of education you completed? The advantages of the directive interview are its brevity and its organized collection of data. Its disadvantages are its inflexibility and the limited opportunity for the client to expound on any of the questions being asked. The planner does not give financial advice during a structured interview. The interview process is aimed at uncovering and identifying client goals, objectives and needs.

nondirective interview

In a *nondirective interview*, both the financial advisor and the client can discuss a wider range of subject areas, and the client usually controls the pacing of the interview through the depth of his or her responses. Thus, the advantages of the nondirective interview include greater flexibility, more in-depth analysis, and the potential for a closer relationship between the advisor and client. Its disadvantages are that it consumes more time and often generates data that are subjective in nature.

---

1. Charles J. Stewart and William B. Cash, *Interviewing: Principles and Practices*, seventh edition. (Dubuque, IA: Brown & Benchmark, 1993).

Both types of interviews are commonly used in the financial planning process. In fact, both types often take place in the same fact-finding session. Moreover, all interviews, whether directive or nondirective, share common characteristics. They typically take place in a formal and structured setting. The question-and-answer format is the primary method of communication. The subject matter discussed is specific to the overall purpose of the interview, and digressions from the subject are usually not encouraged. Finally, the interview by itself usually requires only a relatively short meeting of the parties. However, as used in the financial planning process, the initial interview typically starts the beginning of what is expected to be a lasting advisor-client relationship.

Counseling

counseling   The second term, *counseling*, connotes an offer of help. A financial advisor's job is to provide assistance to clients as they explore their present financial situations, begin to understand where they are in relation to where they would like to be, and then act to get from where they are to where they want to be. Counseling, as used in financial planning, usually takes time and is typified by discussion, reflection, and eventually insights that help the client select a financial plan from among the suggested or recommended alternatives. Counseling can take place within a financial planning relationship or may be entered into by a third party. Financial advisors specialize on personal finance topics, and may not be equipped to tackle psychological and behavioral issues. Building a network with access to therapists, psychologists and an addiction specialist can be strong tools that help clients achieve financial goals.

While the financial advisor's role as a counselor takes place over a period of time, the interview, as a form of structured communication, is usually of relatively short duration. In counseling, the advisor and client develop an interpersonal relationship, something that generally does not occur in a solitary interview. When we discussed interviewing, we stated that the question-and-answer format was the primary method of communication. While the advisor also asks questions in counseling, they are not his or her primary method of communication. In counseling, the advisor may paraphrase what the client has said, reflect a feeling, share feedback or perceptions, clarify, summarize, interpret, provide information, and confront. In short, counseling is not as stylized as interviewing because it is less formal and less structured. The humanness of both the advisor and the client comes into focus, all with the purpose of providing help to the client.

Advising

advising   The third type of structured communication is *advising*, which involves giving specific guidance or suggestions to clients. Advising is often confused with counseling. In fact, many clients who are unfamiliar with counseling think that what they will receive is advice. Perhaps one reason for this misconception stems from the journalistic proliferation of advice such as is offered in the "Dear Abby" type of newspaper columns. This is not to say that advice is never offered by financial advisors who are counseling their clients because it is; but most financial advisors believe that the very best kind of advice for their clients is self-advice rather than advice from an expert.

A distinction must be drawn between a financial advisor and the act of advising. A financial advisor (or other financial professional) works with clients to achieve goals. Financial advisors are generally registered with the Securities and Exchange commission (SEC) and may have attained professional designations. Registered investment advisors are a type of financial advisor. Financial advice, on the other hand, is the actual suggestions and recommendations resulting in action. Financial advice may come from family, friends, the internet or a myriad of sources. Financial advisors help deliver and mitigate financial advice to clients.

Several situations might require that financial advisors give advice. For example, a tax advisor might provide advice on tax shelters, capital gains, tax deferral, and so on. Or an investment advisor might recommend a particular stock or mutual fund because he or she believes that it is consistent with both the client's risk tolerance level and financial ability to handle risk. In each of these instances, the advisor knows much more about his or her field of expertise than do the clients, and the clients use this knowledge to help them make their decisions.

To reiterate, there are several occasions when financial advisors are called on to give advice. After all, financial advisors are the experts, and thus their advice has value. However, there is a danger for advisors in offering advice too soon in the advisor-client relationship. This danger is that the client's ability to make decisions becomes discounted in favor of the expert's opinion. In fact, offering advice has been criticized by some counseling experts who maintain that it fosters dependency and robs clients of the right to make decisions for themselves. Moreover, they believe that advisors who provide quick answers to somewhat complex financial problems are often guilty of projecting their own needs, problems, and/or values into the advice. So how do financial advisors give advice to clients without assuming responsibility for their clients' financial lives?

FOCUS ON ETHICS: How Ethical Behavior Improves Communication

Many clients misunderstand the specifics of the plans suggested or recommended by their financial advisors. This problem is compounded when complex financial instruments are required to implement the plans. It is much like drivers and automobiles. Most drivers really need transportation, and cars solve this problem. However, that does not mean that drivers understand how their cars operate.

A financial advisor once stated that there are two essential rules for effectively dealing with clients. The first is to earn their trust because trust breaks down communication barriers. Different advisors may accomplish this in different ways, but the goal is for advisors to feel free to ask challenging questions and continue probing until a satisfactory level of understanding is achieved. When there are limits to what clients can understand, earned trust is essential.

The second rule is to maintain trust, a critical factor in the advisor-client relationship. Although clients may not fully understand, they should not fail to act. Indeed, if clients understood every aspect of financial planning, they would not need their advisors. Clients often make decisions based solely on their trust in their advisors.

There is no better way to earn and maintain trust than to develop an unassailable reputation for ethical and professional behavior. A valuable side benefit is improved communication.

Perhaps the best way for financial advisors to give advice to clients is by using the six-step financial planning process to address client concerns. Advisors who adhere to the financial planning process systematically analyze their client's financial situations. They work alongside their clients as partners to help them take control of their financial lives. While the role of advisors in the financial planning process is geared more toward counseling clients than advising them, advising is still an important form of structured communication. The inherent danger of advising clients is minimized when the advice is given within the confines of the financial planning process. In that case, any advice given to a client is the result of a thorough analysis of the client's financial situation. Advisors generally give advice to clients in the form of suggestions or recommendations, but the clients are encouraged to make decisions for themselves and assume responsibility for their own financial lives.

Because there is frequent interaction between advisors and clients in the financial planning process, the distinction between interviewing, counseling, and advising is often blurred. As the discussion about the three types of structured communication indicates, financial advisors use all three types in the financial planning process, and those advisors who routinely use the financial planning process are performing their jobs in a wholly professional and ethical manner.

Types of Structured Communication
• Interviewing • Counseling • Advising

CONSIDERATIONS IN COMMUNICATING WITH CLIENTS

In the preceding section, we differentiated the three types of planned and purposeful communication: interviewing, counseling, and advising. Each one is used in the financial planning process. For instance, step 2 of the financial planning process utilizes interviewing to facilitate the completion of fact-finder forms. Counseling occurs in several steps of the financial planning process including step 2 where clients set their financial goals. Advising frequently takes place in step 4 of the process where advisors recommend or suggest several alternative strategies for their clients to consider. In other words, financial advisors generally rely on all three types of structured communication with each type being more or less appropriate for particular tasks. Let us now examine some specific communication issues that advisors confront in their everyday practices.

Structuring Communications With Clients

In any kind of planned and purposeful communication setting, the first element that needs to be attended to is structuring. Structuring serves to determine both the format, frequency and the subject matter of the interaction that is to follow. The financial advisor's task is to make the purpose of the sessions clear to the client at the outset. This would include introductions, an explanation of the process involved, a discussion of forms that are used and the amount of time that will be required to complete them, a discussion of the confidential nature of the relationship, and some prediction of what kinds of outcomes the client might reasonably expect. This structuring need not be lengthy and cumbersome; in fact, it is far better to structure in a clear, straightforward, and succinct fashion.

Consider the following example of structuring in which the advisor's approach is friendly and promises cooperation. The client is made to feel important, that he or she is the focal point of the sessions. The statement offers hope to the client that the results of the financial planning process will help him or her achieve the desired goals.

EXAMPLE
Advisor: "In order for me to provide the best possible service for you, we'll probably need to see each other on three or four separate occasions, although I want you to know that I'm available to meet with you as often as you need me. Today, I thought we'd start by discussing the financial planning process. To put this in proper perspective, I'll explain the products and services that we provide and how they might help you. In the next session, we'll gather some information about your financial situation. To do this, I'll fill out a fact-finder form, which will remain confidential between the two of us. As we go about our business together, I will develop and present to you some alternatives that will be sensible and help you meet your goals. Do you have any questions?"

In step 1 of the financial planning process, the client may be apprehensive or uncertain about how to begin. A good guide for the advisor to follow is to begin where the client is. If the client is, in fact, anxious at the outset, the advisor should take the time to discuss the difficulty of merely getting started. Talking about this will not only alleviate most of the client's anxieties, it will also help to build rapport with the client. It is important to keep in mind that whenever feelings emerge, it is best to focus on those feelings rather than ignore them. If, for example, in the middle of a session a client appears distressed over some aspect of his or her financial situation (for example, an impending divorce), some time should be spent discussing these feelings. Until feelings are addressed and dealt with, a further discussion of content is unproductive and meaningless.

Developing Rapport With Clients

rapport

Financial advisors should seek to develop *rapport* with their clients. Rapport, another way of describing a comfortable and harmonious relationship, is best developed through actions initiated by the financial advisor. The most important step in developing rapport is the advisor's acceptance of the client and the client's awareness of this acceptance. This attitude stems from a sincere desire on the advisor's part to respect the uniqueness of each client and a genuine wish to help. Clients are drawn to professionals who build meaningful relationships with them and listen to what they want to accomplish. If rapport and credibility are developed in step 1 of the financial planning process, the products and/or services the advisor recommends will more likely be reflective of the clients' real needs and values. In order for clients to implement planning recommendations, they must first trust the advisor. The advisor must prove that he or she is there to help clients, not simply to sell them something. To do this, the advisor must create an environment that promotes openness by

- alleviating the concerns of clients
- responding to the social style of clients
- communicating effectively with clients
- structuring communications with clients (as previously discussed)

Alleviating the Concerns of Clients

Various barriers that can create tension between the advisor and his or her clients during an initial session as well as throughout the financial planning process must be removed if rapport is to be developed. These barriers can be divided into four categories:

- Distrust of Salespeople—Many people have a negative image of people who sell products and/or services and avoid meeting with them for fear of being talked into buying something they do not want or need.
- Fear of Making a Decision—Decisions involve risk, and many people avoid risk especially when money is involved. Also, fear of making the wrong purchase decision (that is, buyer's remorse) can cause avoidance of stressful decision-making situations.
- Need for Stability—Many people are complacent and resist change because they prefer familiarity.
- Time Constraints—At today's increasingly hectic pace of life, busy people are reluctant to commit their time.
- Fear of Fraud—Today's financial markets have experienced fraud, Ponzi schemes, identity theft, and investment firm failure. Consumers strive to find reliable and honest advice.

Being aware of client stress can help the advisor identify opportunities to alleviate it and build rapport. Here are some tips.

- The advisor should not impose on clients. He or she should schedule the initial session (as well as future ones) at times that are convenient for clients.

- The advisor should watch his or her verbal pace. He or she should talk in an unhurried, businesslike manner and should never interrupt when clients are speaking. He or she should listen carefully to what clients are saying because listening is a necessary component in good communication.

- The advisor should remember nonverbal behaviors. He or she might be surprised to learn that as little as 7 percent of a first impression is based on what is actually said. The remaining 93 percent is based on nonverbal behaviors, such as body positions, gestures, eye contact, and tone of voice.[2]

- The advisor should encourage clients to talk. Having clients talk is not only a great tool for getting feedback, it is also a common way to relieve stress. Encourage clients to do most of the talking.

- The advisor should control his or her anxiety. Several studies have shown that a person who is already anxious becomes even more so when talking with someone who displays nervousness or anxiety.

- Advisors benefit from transparency. Disclosing compensation and product details can help alleviate client concerns.

Responding to the Social Style of Clients

Building rapport is the advisor's responsibility. This means that the advisor should be able to detect what each client wants from an advisor-client relationship and to use his or her communication skills to shape the discussion in order to satisfy those wants. Identifying the client's needs in the relationship is easier if the advisor can identify the client's social style.

social styles   Psychologist David W. Merrill described the following four *social styles:*

- driving
- expressive
- amiable
- analytical

The American population is evenly divided among the four social styles. Each person has a dominant social style that influences the way he or she works. According to David W. Merrill and Roger H. Reid, "We all say and do things as a result of certain habit patterns, and people make predictions about us

---

2.   Mehrabian, Albert, and Ferris, Susan R. "Inference of Attitudes From Nonverbal Communication in Two Channels," *Journal of Consulting Psychology ,* Vol. 31, No. 3, June 1967, pp. 248–258.

because they come to expect us to behave in a particular way—the fact is that even though each of us is unique, we tend to act in fairly consistent, describable ways. All of us use habits that have worked well for us, habits that make us comfortable, and these habits become the social style that others can observe."[3]

People are like thermostats; they are constantly seeking to reach a state of equilibrium or comfort. They seek out social situations that reinforce their behavior and avoid situations that cause discomfort. As soon as another person enters the picture, tension is produced, and each one must reestablish his or her balance and comfort zone. The challenge for each of us is to determine the proper amount of tension and stress that will provide the proper balance.

Better communication can be achieved when the advisor understands the client and treats the client the way the client wants to be treated. More effective communications and a better advisor-client relationship can be established by adapting to the client's social style in order to make him or her feel at home and less threatened. By listening to and observing the client during step 1 of the financial planning process, the advisor can learn how to communicate with the client. summarizes the characteristics of each social style and how best to respond to a person who engages that style. By communicating with the client in a manner appropriate for the client's social style, the advisor is able to build rapport with the client more quickly and thus facilitate the financial planning process.

Communicating Effectively With Clients

Financial advisors must build rapport with clients in order to help them solve their problems. One aspect of rapport building is communicating effectively, the focus of this chapter. Some advisors, however, think effective communication only means they have to explain their products and/or services to clients. In fact, effective communication involves much more. At a minimum, it requires the advisor to learn how to listen. Failing to hear what the client is really saying can cost the advisor dearly. Developing good listening skills will result not only in increased sales and the sense of a job well done, but clients are more likely to accept the advisor's suggestions or recommendations if he or she demonstrates an interest in the clients

---

3.   David W. Merrill and Roger H. Reid, *Personal Styles and Effective Performance* (CRC Press LLC, 1999). Source: The TRACOM Group. Visit www.socialstyle.com for more information.

by listening to what they have to say. Basic communication principles are discussed more fully later in this chapter.

SETTING FINANCIAL PLANNING GOALS

resource allocation

Fundamentally, personal financial planning is an economic discussion of household utility and budget constraints. Consumers can either spend their time working in the marketplace, creating goods and services in the household, or participating in leisure time. Consumers have a finite amount of resources (income & wealth) and time. Financial planning is a process by which individuals and families help resolve these conflicts.

Setting financial planning goals and the prioritization of those goals helps clients to determine how, where and when they will accumulate and divest themselves of resources. Client goals are often overlapping and pull from the same pool of money. Financial planners help clients prioritize, formalize and organize their goals. Even clients with exorbitant amounts of money are faced with resource allocation decisions.

qualitative and quantitative goals

Financial planners help clients formalize goals. A goal must be well defined, achievable and clear to the client. Goals may be quantitative or qualitative in nature. Quantitative goals are more concrete while qualitative goals have more abstract qualities:

- **quantitative goal** – I want to pay off my $13,000 credit card balance in 12 months.
- **qualitative goal** – I want to spend money more wisely.

general and specific goals

Qualitative goals may need to be broken out into more measurable quantitative steps. Spending money wisely may require sticking to a budget over a period of time, changing consumption patterns or saving behavior. Planners are well served by clarifying definitions of terms "wisely" and magnitude "more" of client intentions. Financial planners utilize fact finders and risk assessment tools to help clients identify their goals. When preparing financial plans and calculations, goals need to be specific rather than general.

- **general goal** – I want to retire in the next 5 years.

- **specific goal** – I want to retire in 2012, able to draw $50,000 inflation adjusted after tax dollars out of my portfolio each year through my lifetime.

As well as defining terms and magnitudes, the financial adviser must consider defining success in a goal statement. Success may be a win or loose outcome, or could be gauged on a scale. Savings goals targeting a specific dollar amount over a set time period are either met or not met. A client who wants to save $100,000 in 10 years will have met or failed at their goal in a decade. More complex goals may have varying degrees of success or failure.

Retirement planning is an example of a financial planning discipline that requires distinctly defining success. For some clients early retirement may be possible, but require the retiree to work part time. Some clients would consider working 10 hours a week and retiring at 62 a successful outcome, while others would consider it a failure. Planners need to understand success on a client by client basis.

ADDITIONAL INFORMATION AND ASSUMPTIONS

Written case studies are limited by obvious constraints. Client goals and objectives are stagnant and information is static. Advisers who have experience working in the field may have additional questions that they are unable to ask a client created on paper. The case studies presented in the text have the necessary information to answer chapter questions but, more importantly, are intended to give students an opportunity to recognize opportunities and practice delivering financial planning solutions. Students entering case studies into software programs may need to create additional assumptions.

Financial advisers often make assumptions through the course of financial planning. Inflation, rates of return and cost-of-living measures are common assumptions made when working with the public. Assumptions are generally based on historical precedents. Quality assumptions must have a historical perspective and reference point and be appropriate as well as defensible. Taking inflation as an example, an adviser is faced with a variety of questions.

Consumer Price Index

Primarily, what index should an adviser use to measure inflation? The Consumer Price Index (CPI) is often cited by advisers as an inflation measure. The CPI is a measure of the average change over time in the prices paid by urban consumers for a market basket of consumer goods and services. Financial advisers use this measure as a means of adjusting dollar values over time. The consumer price index (CPI) is often used as a standard measure of inflation among financial planners when working with retirement and goal planning assumptions.

The CPI is a term used to describe two separate inflation index measures.

- CPI-U (Consumer Price Index for all Urban Consumers) The CPI-U measures costs that impact around 87 percent of consumers, and is intended to measure all families living in an urban area.

- CPI-W (Consumer Price Index for Wage Earners and Clerical Workers) The CPI-W is a subset of the CPI-U. The CPI-W is based on the expenditures of families living in urban areas. These families must meet additional requirements: more than one-half of the family's income has to be earned from clerical or hourly-wage occupations. The CPI-W represents about 10 percent of the American population.

The lowest inflation rate of the CPI-U since 1913 occurred in 1921 (−10.8 percent) while the highest occurred in 1979 (13.3 percent). Given the discrepancy in range, what assumption should a financial professional use in their calculations?

Historical inflation rates vary based on indexes, but from 1920 through 2009 historical rates settled around 3.4 percent. This number is a smoothed average of past period inflation rates. A historical inflation rate provides a base guideline when preparing financial plans. However, an adviser may choose to modify this assumption to be more accurately based on a client's situation. If a client has significant ongoing medical cost and will likely continue those costs through his/her lifetime, the adviser might consider blending a medication cost inflation rate (CPI-M) with the client's regional CPI to derive a more appropriate inflation assumption. The following example addresses the importance and blending of client assumptions.

EXAMPLE
Mary and Tom Smith spend $5,000 per month; $3,000 on medical costs and $2,000 on other expenses, including all taxes. They are both 72 and retired. They each receive $1,000 a month from social security. Mary and Tom also have $200,000 invested in municipal bonds and live in a house valued at $400,000. How long can Mary and Tom remain in their home before needing to take a reverse mortgage or pursue another housing arrangement?

assumptions The brief mini-case above requires a planner to make seven key assumptions. Each assumption has a direct influence on the answer given to their client.

- *What is the rate of inflation on the $3,000 per month medical costs?*
- *What inflation rate exists on the remaining $2,000 per month?*
- *What are Mary and Tom's life expectancies?*
- *What is an accurate Social Security growth rate?*
- *How should the bonds be illustrated? What is their rate of return?*
- *Should the house value be inflated?*
- *What is the interest rate on the reverse mortgage?*

Mary and Tom want to know how long they can continue living on their current income and investable assets before they need to access some or all of their home equity. The following assumed rates are applied to the case study:

- *What is the rate of inflation on the $3,000 per month medical costs?* — **5.0%**
- *What inflation rate exists on the remaining $2,000 per month?* — **3.5%**
- *What are Mary and Tom's life expectancies?* — **85**
- *What is an accurate Social Security growth rate?* — **2.5%**
- *How should the bonds be illustrated? What is their rate of return?* — **7.5%**
- *Should the house value be inflated?* — **Yes, 4.0%**
- *What is the interest rate on the reverse mortgage?* — **8.5%**

This problem can be solved in four steps and lends itself to a worksheet environment. This problem will be solved on a monthly basis. Cash flows will be taken out of bonds at the beginning of the month. The following three steps can be applied each month to determine a payment stream and show the eventual liquidation of client assets.

1. Calculate the monthly difference between income and cash flow.
2. Subtract the difference (withdrawal amount) from the bond portfolio.
3. Grow the bond portfolio.

To calculate the monthly difference between income and cash flow, an appropriate inflation rate must be calculated. The case study utilizes $5,000 of total living expenses. $2,000 are inflated at a historical CPI-U (3.5 percent). The remaining $3,000 of living expenses is comprised of medical costs. The adviser must select an appropriate assumption with regard to medical costs. For this example, use 5.0 percent as the medical inflation rate.

The rates can then be blended to determine a more accurate overall inflation rate. A blended inflation rate can be found by taking a weighted average of rates:

Blended inflation rate = ((3/5 x Medical inflation rate) + (2/5 x CPI-U))
Blended inflation rate = (0.6 x .05) + (0.4 x 0.035)
Blended inflation rate = 4.4%

accurately gauging assumptions

After finding a blended inflation rate, the adviser can proceed to step 1, calculating the monthly difference between income and cash flow. For each month, beginning in month one, solve for cash flows.

($5,000)	Month One — Cash Flows Out
$2,000	Month One — Social Security Received
($3,000)	Month One — Cash Flow Needed from Portfolio

After calculating the first month's cash flow need, determine the impact of withdrawals on Mary and Todd's bond portfolio.

$200,000	Bond Value — Beginning of Month One
($3,000)	Month One — Portfolio Withdrawal
$197,000	Portfolio Value after Withdrawal
x (1.00625)	Average Monthly Growth of 7.5% = (1 + (.075/12))
$198,231	**Portfolio Value after the end of month one**

The above process is repeated for the second month. However, in the second month inflation begins to impact client cash needs as well as Social Security. Costs and income are inflated monthly to maintain modeling consistency. For the second month, cash flows and Social Security are slightly inflated.

($5,018)	Month Two — Cash Flows Out
$2,004	Month Two — Social Security Received
($3,014)	Month Two — Cash Flow Needed from Portfolio

After calculating the second month's cash flow need, determine the impact of withdrawals on Mary and Tom's bond portfolio.

$198,231	Bond Portfolio Value — Beginning of Month
($3,014)	Month One — Portfolio Withdrawal
$195,217	Portfolio Value after Withdrawal
x (1.00625)	Average Monthly Growth of 7.5% = (1 + (.075/12))
$196,437	**Portfolio Value after the end of month**

Two concepts are at work within this example. The first is that this problem is soon beyond the scope of using a calculator or handwritten worksheet. Once understanding the formula and function, students are encouraged to use a spreadsheet or software program to continue the calculation. Secondly, the portfolio is not growing at a rate that sustains withdrawals perpetually. Solving out the above calculation using the current set of assumptions, Mary and Tom have **71 months** (just short of six years) before they exhaust their pool of money. Given life expectancies of 85, Tom and Mary will most likely have to make a housing decision in their lifetime.

Changing one assumption in the above set (for example, raising health care inflation to 7.0 percent) causes the above problem's answer to change to **67 months.** By raising health care inflation, the blended inflation rate increases. This increase creates a larger monthly differential between living expenses and cash flow need which depletes the portfolio at a more rapid rate. The portfolio earns less compounding interest and exhausts 4 months earlier than the original example. The practical impact of this difference is about 120 days. 120 days could allow Tom and Mary time to list their house or go through the mortgage process. Lowering bond return rates or raising general inflation rates also shaves precious time from the housing decision.

assumptions   The above example illustrates the importance of accurately gauging assumptions. Realistically, Tom and Mary would visit with their financial planner on at least an annual basis. Even with annual updates, their course of action, planning and expectations are set indirectly by initial plan assumptions.

Financial advisers are surrounded by assumptions in their practice. Output from financial calculations is only as solid as the calculation's underlying assumptions, and assumptions need to be made well before any planning takes place. Occasions arise in financial planning where changing underlying assumptions will make one product or technique more favorable than its alternative, even if the probability of the underlying assumptions that have been changed occurring remains low.

Advisers should also consider short term trends when addressing inflation rates. An adviser working with a client in 1979 struggled with annual inflation rates much higher than the prevailing 20-year average at the time. While history held that high domestic inflation rates experienced in the 1970s and 1980s reverted to a lower level, advisers at the time factored slightly higher rates into their planning assumptions.

EXAMPLE

Jim is a mortgage broker who is compensated with larger commissions for the sale of adjustable rate mortgages than fixed mortgages. Jim knows that current interest rates are at historically low points. Based on historical economic conditions, interest rates will probably rise over the next 10 years. However, interest rates have fallen over the last 10-year period.

Jim has an ethical dilemma that begins with his assumptions. If he bases his assumptions on 30-year interest rates, clients purchasing adjustable rate mortgages would most likely have higher payments in the future (because interest rates are likely to increase), then he will sell fewer adjustable rate mortgages. If he shows clients a 10-year historical rate as an assumption, his illustrations show that his clients are better off with adjustable loans than fixed ones. Ideally, Jim will pursue a course of action that is in the best interest of the client and use more accurate longer-term inflation rates.

Financial planning calculations are only as strong as their underlying assumptions, and advisers should carefully and thoughtfully design the numbers they will use. Financial planning outputs from a spreadsheet or calculator are only as strong as their underlying assumptions.

DEVELOPING THE OUTLINE FOR A CLIENT'S PLAN

After reviewing case data, proceed to develop preliminary outlines for their business (if applicable) and personal plans. The outlines should identify as many applicable techniques as possible for achieving the client's objectives, since the outlines form the basis for the planner's review of the client's case. Techniques that are undesirable will be eliminated when the preliminary outline is further refined. As a planner gains experience, clearly undesirable techniques usually can be eliminated mentally, possibly during the data-gathering interview, so that an actual written preliminary outline may not be necessary.

Financial planning is generally first organized into two broad categories:

- *Personal planning*—lifetime and estate planning for the client's family and its individual members

    - Personal planning concerns will generally involve items such as personal income tax deferral or reduction; insurance needs; investment planning and strategies; effective retirement planning; educational objectives for children or grandchildren; the present titling and advice on correctly titling property; personal estate planning, including a review and analysis of the client's current plan, if any; and other personal topics raised by an examination of the client's interests or objectives.

- *Business planning*—planning for maximum income production as well as any business-ownership interest over which the client can exert sufficient control to effect a change in the business's operations or strategic direction

    - Business planning can take into consideration many business and income-production areas. It may deal with employee benefit planning including qualified and nonqualified deferred compensation; executive compensation packages; personal use of corporate assets; and the tax cost of corporate payments of certain quasi-personal expenses. Business planning may also deal with planning business transactions, such as lease transactions where the client's personal assets are leased to the business to provide personal income tax benefits and structuring legally enforceable buy-sell agreements to transfer a business at the death or disability of the owner. Business planning may also involve transferring an interest in a family-owned corporation to allow children to take over or to convert the value of the business interest into cash.

In cases where the bulk of the client's income or net worth is tied up in a business, particularly a closely held business, it is prudent to do a separate business plan and to prepare and present the business plan first. The personal planning can be prepared and presented as an ancillary plan, referring to the business plan as necessary for explanatory detail. This approach is preferable because the business and its success or failure largely control what is possible for the client to accomplish on the personal side.

In cases in which the client is a salaried person without significant control of the business, the plan may be viewed primarily as a personal plan with the "business planning" being limited to an investigation of existing salary and employee benefits. In a case like this a separate business plan will be unnecessary.

The outline method helps to ensure a complete plan design. The outline begins with a working, standard or generic outline. The working outline is then adapted to the specific clients as a master outline focusing on client recommendations and solutions.

- *Preliminary Outline* —This outline (also referred to as an operating outline) is a standard comprehensive financial planning template. It incorporates the major areas of a financial plan into a step by step process, helping the adviser ensure topics are not missed or glossed over. The operating outline presented in the text is limited in scope, and advisers specializing in a specific area of financial planning may add additional depth.

- *Master Outline* —The master outline emphasizes recommendations and is written for the client, not the adviser. Items from the master outline are loosely based on the preliminary outline and can be used in preparing a written financial plan. In practice, some type of financial planning software or analysis tool would be applied between the Working and Master Outlines. Preliminary analysis and ideas are drafted in a working outline, and developed further through the use of tools to construct a Master Outline.

preliminary outline   To begin the process, prepare a written preliminary outline to recognize and consider the widest possible array of planning techniques available for achieving a particular objective. For example, the settled tax planning techniques for achieving a particular objective, such as income shifting for educating children, are finite in number. The astute planner should become acquainted with these methods and with their basic technical requirements. Once these have become familiar, it may be apparent at an early point in the relationship with the client that a particular technique will not meet the client's objective. At this point the preliminary outline has become a mental checklist for eliminating clearly unsuitable techniques, and many planners will dispense with the actual written form. The preliminary outline, however, whether a mental checklist or a written outline, continues to be a crucial part of the financial planning process.

Figure 2-1
Financial Planning Process

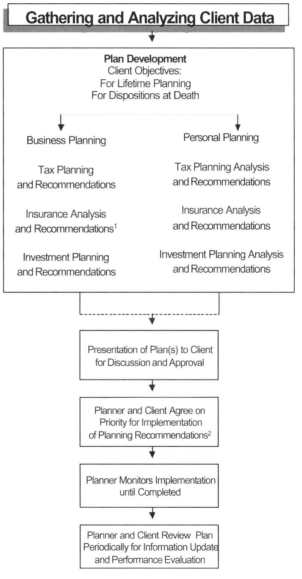

1. Investment planning may or may not be appropriate for a business interest, as many businesses reinvest profits in the business operation; that is, they invest primarily in themselves.

2. The client should be advised that he or she may enter the implementation phase with any planner of his or her choosing.

In preparing the case outline use as a model the plan development portion of the flowchart for the financial planning process. Initially the client's objectives for lifetime planning and dispositions at death should be identified and listed. Then the financial plan should be outlined with respect to tax planning analysis with recommendations and insurance analysis with recommendations. Finally the client's personal plan should be outlined with respect to tax, insurance, and investment planning analyst recommendations. Working through a client's data thoroughly and systematically in accordance with the financial planning process is the essence of comprehensive financial planning.

In the techniques selected for the model outlines and case solutions, alternatives have been chosen that are settled as a matter of law or for which substantial authority exists, even though there may be a legal issue or issues that have not been ultimately resolved. In each instance in which a technique contains legal issues that are not presently resolved, this fact should be noted in the plan solution, and such information should always be disclosed to the client. The recommendation of highly speculative techniques has been avoided in this text.

Note

This text utilizes multiple approaches to addressing client cases. Some cases are solved using one, two or three outlines. More complex cases typically have more information and data; they may require more in-depth analysis. Students are encouraged to prepare their own master outlines and compare them to the ones presented in the text.

master outline   After preparing a master outline, copy and elaborate the material into a written financial planning document suitable to give clients. Alternatively, use the master outline as a starting point for answering quiz and test questions. On timed certification exams, students may find the outline method particularly helpful. Memorizing an operating outline helps ensure case studies are met with a comprehensive approach. Case studies found on the CFP® exam, as well as the final exam for this course are generally two to three pages of material and often have pre-generated cash flow and net worth statements and corresponding multiple choice questions after the case study. Creating an outline with material facts can help students master the multiple choice questions.

CHAPTER REVIEW

Key Terms and Concepts

case study approach
gathering client data
information needed for financial
    planning by type of client
interviewing
directive interview
nondirective interview
counseling
advising
rapport

social styles
resource allocation
qualitative and quantitative goals
general and specific goals
Consumer Price Index
assumptions
accurately gauging assumptions
assumptions
preliminary outline
master outline

Review Questions

These questions are intended to help students answer questions about case studies, goals and assumptions. Answers to these questions can be found in the study supplement.

1. What is the compelling drawback of working with financial planning case studies instead of live clients? [1]

2. What documents should a financial service professional ask for when working with a young couple? What additional documents does the planner need when working with an older executive? [2]

3. Fundamentally, personal financial planning is an economic discussion of _____ and _____? [2]

4. What are the characteristics of a qualitative goal? How can adviser help a client transform a qualitative goal into an achievable success? [2]

5. How should financial service professionals model inflation when creating financial plans? [3]

6. Jan owns a small engine repair store. She wants to begin saving for retirement, and has come to you for help. She is 40 and wants to save enough to live on $50,000 (after taxes) in today's dollars for the rest of her life; she wants to retire at 60. What planning assumptions will you have to make to answer Jan's question: How much does she need to save every month towards her retirement? [3]

7. What are the three types of structured communications? [2]

8. How should financial service professionals modify data gathering and presentation strategies when working with clients of different personalities? [4]

9. What are four techniques financial service professionals can use to alleviate client concerns through the financial planning process? [4]

10. Are speaking or listening skills more important for financial advisers? How can financial advisers develop speaking and listening skills? [4]

Learning Objectives

An understanding of the material in this chapter should enable the student to

1. Learn about financial planning software and its impact on financial planning today.

2. Develop a written case for James and Elizabeth Black.

3. Discuss the challenges of working with a newly married couple

James and Elizabeth Black have come to visit with you, the financial adviser, wanting help with risk management, debt and savings goals. James and Elizabeth have specific questions about risk management including their life, disability, property casualty and automobile insurance needs. This case will focus on risk management, but James and Elizabeth also have questions about debt management and wealth building. More specifically, should they pay off debts with extra money, save extra dollars or build wealth while they pay off debt? How much could they accelerate debt payments, especially in the face of new insurance costs?

A challenge of working with Elizabeth and James is to help them design a financial plan that adds new costs through insurance premiums and begins to decrease debt load. Ideally Elizabeth and James would be able to meet all of their goals with money to spare. However, planners working in middle class and less affluent markets will often meet with clients who have more goals than resources, more hopes and dreams than cash.

James and Elizabeth have income constraints, especially when considering the goal of Elizabeth leaving the workforce sometime in the next few years. Elizabeth will have fewer costs when she becomes a home maker, but family income will also be reduced. Students need to consider an eventual decrease in income before designing any plan recommendations.

resource allocation

We will utilize the outline method to prepare an analysis of James and Elizabeth's financial plan. This case focuses on resource allocation. Challenging questions face Elizabeth and James. How much should be allocated towards insurance? Savings? Future college needs? Retirement? Paying down debt? Increasing spending? Developing a plan requires an in depth understanding the interaction between cash flow, implementation cost and time.

The first step in developing a written financial plan is to create a master outline for the family. As part of completing this master outline students will restate case objectives and assumptions and develop financial statements. After laying the groundwork for the case students can begin to form recommendations and assumptions. Keep in mind that family income will diminish when Elizabeth has children.

working with newly married clients

In this case, James and Elizabeth have a common front towards achieving their goals. A unified front towards financial planning gives both spouses synergy in meeting their unique needs. A financial planner can confidently represent the best interest of both Elizabeth and James without much concern about favoring one client's objectives over the other. Couples who are more independent may have conflicting or contradicting financial objectives.

Being newlyweds, James and Elizabeth are in the "early career" life cycle, and the planner should be ready to address their goals appropriately.

compensation models

Students should endeavor to develop recommendations and alternatives **without** a bias towards compensation strategies. Financial planning recommendations should not depend on a fee- or commission-based compensation structure. Working in the best interest of the client may require advisers to develop recommendations that are not optimal for generating adviser income. Paying off debt may be a strategy James and Elizabeth could benefit from, but making that recommendation would not provide any fee-based or commission revenue for the adviser. Conflicts of interest span the compensation models, and financial advisers need to be constantly vigilant of working towards their client's best interests. Compensation preferences will impact the implementation phase of the planning process. Fee-only advisers may recommend no-load life insurance, while commission-based advisers might recommend a reputable policy that will pay them a commission. Advisers are encouraged to disclose compensation sources to their clients. Students should disclose their business model when making implementation decisions in the case.

financial planning software

In practice, financial software would be used as a tool in developing and presenting recommendations and alternatives. Students are encouraged to work through the case using equations and worksheets before consulting software solutions. The process of working through this case will help to develop in-depth understanding of the case facts. Using software prematurely will limit critical analysis and financial planning technique retention. Students should feel free to use financial planning software to verify and validate their initial analysis.

FINANCIAL PLANNING SOFTWARE

Financial planning software is critical in today's marketplace. Financial advisers should consider using a combination of three types of software to address client goals and help model the planning process:

1. financial planning software
2. tax projection software
3. general office productivity software

Financial planning software can be used to illustrate the consequences of retirement, education, investment, insurance and business planning on a client's estate. Tax projection software helps model detailed estate and gift tax implications of planning decisions. General office productivity software, such as word processors, spreadsheet programs and slide show software, can help show basic concepts through outlines, spreadsheets or slide presentations. Our discussion focuses on financial planning software, specifically the differences between goal and cash flow based platforms.

Financial planning software programs are either goal-based or cash flow-based. Goal-based financial planning software model client goals independent of one another. It requires less comprehensive income and expense inputs and provides concise answers to client questions than cash flow-based modeling. The outcomes from goal-based tools can be prioritized and integrated, but their solutions are calculated autonomously.

Cash flow-based financial planning solves client goals in an environment that considers client income and expenses. Cash flow-based financial planning software operates funds goals with finite resources, and outcomes are limited by the scarcity of free cash flow. The following is a practical example of the differences in goal-based and cash flow-based financial planning software systems:

EXAMPLE

Jack and Leticia have met with you to discuss their estate plan. They have two large assets (a small business and residence) and are concerned about the impact of estate taxes. Jack's business is currently valued at $10,000,000 and generates revenue to Jack and Leticia of $600,000 annually. Their residence is valued at $3,000,000.

Broadly speaking, goal-based financial planning software would calculate the above estate tax looking at the asset base ($13,000,000). A growth rate could be entered for the business and residence, and future projections would be determined. Assuming a competent software package, estate taxes could be shown in 2009, 2010, and so on, based on growth assumptions. A financial advisor could suggest a life insurance strategy to provide liquidity at death based on the output from the goal-based program. Assuming a 5 percent growth rate on the above assets goal-based financial planning software would show a gross estate of $13,650,000 in 2010 ($13,000,000 × 1.05%).

A cash flow-based software system would also solve for estate taxes. In addition the cash flow-based software forces the annual revenue to be either consumed (with an offsetting expense) or saved as an asset. Insurance premiums would be deducted from cash flow and any excess business revenue would be included in the future year's estate planning calculation. Assuming a 5 percent growth rate and $100,000 of annual expenses cash flow-based financial planning software would show a gross estate of $14,150,000 in 2010 ($13,000,000 × 1.05% + $500,000 of excess cash flow). The differences in calculation techniques are broadly stated, and some software systems will allow additional modifications.

For retirement, accumulation and education planning, goal-based software systems benefit from their independence and flexibility. Goal-based planning systems may not fully encompass the complicated nature of estate planning and the impact variables have on one another. Cash flow-based financial planning software programs tend to offer a more comprehensive approach for estate planning professionals than goal-based alternatives.

In the past decade financial planning software has migrated from the office to the internet. Programs are accessible remotely, data is stored off-site and clients can often login themselves to see advisor generated Web pages. Software output will continue to develop as clients and advisors become more technologically savvy.

Ten years ago software would generate paper reports for advisors to give to clients. These reports made sense to clients during the meeting but lost relevance days and weeks later. Today financial planning software output tends to be dynamic and appeal to both analytical and visual learning styles. Advisors can make on the spot changes which are immediately reflected in presentations and reports, and these presentations can be filled with colorful illustrations, diagrams and schedules.

Life insurance software must be viewed with an appropriate lens. When working with younger clients (like those in the case study in chapter 3) advisers may find some problems integrating insurance illustrations and financial planning software. Consider the following five questions when integrating both insurance and software in a financial plan:

- Do insurance-company generated policy illustration values match those on cash flow statements and balance sheets generated by financial planning software?

  Quite often life insurance illustration tools operate independently from comprehensive financial planning systems. Agents must be cognizant of presenting realistic insurance outcomes. If a "current" and "proposed" financial planning scenario are provided to a client, financial planning software should correctly illustrate the premiums, cash value growth, and death benefit fluctuations of any permanent insurance used in financial plans.

- Are loans modeled accurately from an income and gift tax perspective?

  Loans from a cash value life insurance policy are not subject to income tax at the time of the loan; an exception exists for modified endowment contracts. Modeling gift tax implications may be more difficult. The donor is responsible for paying federal gift taxes. As an example, a policy owned by a parent may generate cash flow in the form of policy loans paid to an adult child. By directing the loans, the parent is potentially making taxable gifts to the child. The extent of those gifts should be considered by a tax professional. Any assessed taxes should be built into the modeling of future projections.

- Are withdrawals from cash values and dividends treated as unearned income to the extent they exceed basis in the policy?

  Modeling life insurance dividends in forward projecting financial plans is ethically difficult. While a mutual life insurance company may have paid policy dividends over the past two decades, dividends are not guaranteed and should be modeled sparingly. When they are included in a forward looking financial plan, remember that policy dividends are income taxable as unearned ordinary income to the extent they exceed cost basis in an insurance policy. A tax liability may occur as the result of dividends.

- When utilizing the policy for retirement or education planning needs, does the death benefit remain available for survivor needs and legacy planning?

  Cash value life insurance policies are often used for multiple purposes. Ensure that borrowing or surrendering a portion of the cash value does not cause the policy to lapse. Modeling withdrawals or loans will require updating cash flow statements, while changes in death benefit are best reflected on estate planning projections.

- How are policy guarantees and promises (such as guaranteed interest rates and waiver of premium riders) reflected in software projections?

  If not integrated with illustration tools, financial planning software programs require attention to detail when modeling complicated cash value insurance strategies. Universal or variable universal life insurance policies with shifting death benefits may require customized modeling to accurately illustrate goal funding or estate tax consequences.

Answering these five questions will help agents and advisers model insurance accurately, but accurate analysis does not market and sell life insurance. The presentation and delivery of software and analytical outputs sells life insurance.

INSTRUCTIONS

Develop a written plan that could be presented to James and Elizabeth Black. The plan should explain the problems, available techniques, technical requirements for each technique, and the strengths and weaknesses of each technique in terms of achieving the client's objectives. Focus the plan on the client's stated goals. Once the planning solution has been formulated, it can be compared with the following comprehensive plan presented in this chapter.

CLIENT GOALS AND OBJECTIVES

1. Client's Goals and Objectives for James and Elizabeth Black

    a. Maintain current lifestyle for Elizabeth and James in the event of either spouse's death or disability.

    b. Review auto and homeowners insurance policies.

    c. Determine whether James and Elizabeth should use extra income to accelerate debt payments or save towards other goals.

James and Elizabeth have come to you to evaluate three goals, which can be distilled down to two concrete statements and one open-ended question. The two goals addresses specific risk management concerns, while the third asks us to evaluate the relationship between income, debt payments and savings goals. The first two goals have simple outcomes: recommendations about future coverage. A financial adviser can calculate a concrete amount of death benefit and disability insurance required to meet future needs. Homeowners and auto insurance policies can be evaluated as sufficient or insufficient.

The third goal presents complex outcomes. Should the James and Elizabeth use extra income to accelerate debt payments or save towards other goals? A broadly phrased goal provides financial advisers with open-ended alternatives. Selecting between dozens of possibilities (such as retirement savings, education savings, emergency fund savings, paying off student loans, auto loans, and/or accelerating mortgage payments) requires a sound understanding of the dynamics and financial planning techniques that apply to each possibility. Financial advisers may even adopt a combination approach, fulfilling multiple goals simultaneously. Open-ended answers are almost always subjective and students are encouraged to expound upon strategies found in the text.

CASE STUDY FOR JAMES AND ELIZABETH BLACK

James and Elizabeth have met with you through a mutual friend. They are newlyweds and have a positive outlook on life. They want to have children in the next five years and have come to you to help them make insurance decisions. James' brother is their broker, but he does not have expertise working with insurance markets.

James and Elizabeth do not plan on moving in the next five years. They have two dogs: one Standard Poodle and one American Bulldog.

Note

The analysis for this case occurs in 2011. Students using the case in 2012 and 2013 may find different results in their analysis.

Case and Employment Facts

James was born January 1, 1985. He works as a systems analyst for a small IT firm, Golden Circle Systems. James played football in high school, is 5'10" tall and weighs 240 pounds. He has moderately high blood pressure but is working to get it under control. James has a B.S. in Electrical Engineering from Jefferson State. He earns $55,000 annually through his employer and another $5,000 from computer work for friends and family. His job is stable and James expects to receive 5-percent raises over the next decade but does not want to count on his freelance computer income.

Elizabeth was born June 15, 1986. Elizabeth has a Masters degree in Biology from Jefferson State. She is currently working, but wants to stay at home after she has children sometime in the next 5 years. Elizabeth is 5'10" tall and weighs 200 pounds. She is in good health, but has a family history of heart disease. Elizabeth earns $24,000 as a lab technician and another $5,000 from a part time job. She plans on continuing the part time job after she has children but will stop working at the lab.

Employer Benefits

James contributes 6 percent of his gross pay to a 401(k) plan and his employer matches the contribution $0.50 on the dollar. The matches immediately vest. James occasionally receives quarterly bonuses but does not count on them as a significant income source. James' employer pays 70 percent of his health care premium and a portion of Elizabeth's. James' out of pocket premium for himself and spouse is $250 per month.

This premium would increase to $325 per month for a family. The health coverage is a PPO with $50 in-network copayments with a $1,500 deductible per insured and a $2,500 family deductible. James and Elizabeth use doctors who are on the plan and have been happy with the level of service provided.

James has group life insurance coverage equal to his salary; the policy is not portable. He also participates in the employer disability program, which provides him with 50 percent of his monthly income for 5 years. This policy has a 12-month waiting period. Elizabeth does not receive any employer benefits through either of her jobs.

Financial Position

James and Elizabeth Black own a home they purchased 2 years ago. The home was originally valued at $150,000 and their initial mortgage was a $125,000 5-year ARM at 5.75 percent amortized over 30 years. They missed multiple payments along the way, and after penalties and interest the current balance remains $125,000. The ARM adjusts to the LIBOR plus 5.0 percent. The current 12-month LIBOR rate is 2.50 percent. Property taxes are 2.5 percent of the value of the home and are paid annually. The home has been assessed at a tax value of $160,000; James and Elizabeth feel this is excessive and a better fair market value is $150,000.

James' 401(k) is valued at $5,000. His account is allocated 70 percent in an S&P 500 Index fund and 30 percent in a U.S. Corporate Bond Index fund. New contributions to the account are 60 percent in the index fund and 40 percent in the bond fund. James has been pleased with the performance.

Elizabeth and James own a paid-off 1998 Honda Accord and a 2009 Ford F250. They took out a car loan for $20,000 two years ago. The loan has a 3.99 percent interest rate and at inception was a 5-year note. The Blacks have rebuilt their credit and have 670 FICO scores. James and Elizabeth own personal property (not including their cars) of around $50,000. Included in the property are Elizabeth's early American antique dining room set, appraised at over $30,000 and James' three guns, each valued at $1,500. Their other home furnishings are typical of a young couple recently out of college. Elizabeth's wedding ring set is valued at $4,000.

The Blacks each have student loans. James currently owes $24,800 and Elizabeth owes $11,000. They consolidated their loans at 6.0 percent last month, and are making combined payments of $397.45 per month. James and Elizabeth both have Roth IRAs with balances of $11,000. These accounts were established 2 years ago and are housed with James' brother. They are invested in a diverse portfolio of loaded mutual funds, but the Blacks have not provided you with statements. James and Elizabeth will fund the Roth IRAs only if they have cash available at the end of the year.

Aside from debt payments, the Blacks typically spend $2,000 per month on groceries, entertainment and travel expenses. The Blacks have a joint checking account of $3,000 and savings account of $4,000, both earning minimal interest.

Income Taxation

The Blacks had an effective tax rate of around 7 percent last year on gross income. For the purposes of this case, assume they do not have a state income tax. They estimate they will pay about the same amount of federal income taxes this year.

Auto and Homeowners Insurance

Elizabeth and James carry auto and homeowners insurance, both comprehensive and collision (non comprehensive) insurance policies on both vehicles. They have $250 deductibles on the policies. Additionally, they carry $40,000 (per person), $80,000 (all persons), $40,000 (property damage) of liability coverage. Their policies have uninsured motorist provisions but do not carry personal injury protection elements. Their monthly premium for the new truck is $100 and the older car is $58.

Elizabeth has an outstanding driving record, while James occasionally receives speeding tickets.

They are insured with an HO-3 policy. The policy insures their house up to $140,000 and contents up to $80,000. They have an additional rider for mold insurance protection (up to $30,000) and an endorsement for Elizabeth's wedding rings. Elizabeth and James purchased a window repair endorsement, lowering their deductible from 1 percent of the insured limit to $250 if windows are damaged. This policy replaces the actual cash value for any personal property losses. The annual premium of $1,400 is paid from an escrow account through their mortgage lender. They have not informed their homeowners insurance company about the pet dogs.

Goals and Objectives

Elizabeth and James have the following goals and objectives:

1. Maintain the surviving spouse's current lifestyle in the event of death or disability.
2. Review auto and homeowners insurance.
3. Determine if they should accelerate debt payments or save towards other goals.

Rate Tables and Case Assumptions

The following tables are monthly insurance rates available to James and Elizabeth in Jefferson. These rates are a pricing approximation but are intended to provide students with resource allocation decisions.

Automobile Insurance Collision Coverage Options		
	$250 Deductible	**$500 Deductible**
2009 Ford F250	$70	$60
1998 Honda Accord	$38	$18

Automobile Insurance Liability Options for James and Elizabeth			
	$25,000/ $50,000/ $20,000*	**$40,000/ $80,000/ $40,000**	**$80,000/ $160,000/ $80,000**
First Car	$25.00	$30.00	$55.00
Additional Car	$12.50	$20.00	$26.50
* = State Minimum Coverage			

Monthly Life Insurance Rates by Gender and Rating Per $1,000 of Coverage			
Male Born in 1985			
	Preferred	**Standard**	**Rated (A)**
10-Year Term	$.08	$.10	$.15
10-Year Term with Waiver of Premium (WOP)	$.09	$.12	$.17
20-Year Term	$.09	$.13	$.19
20-Year WOP	$.10	$.14	$.21
30-Year Term	$.11	$.15	$.25
30-Year WOP	$.12	$.16	$.28

Monthly Life Insurance Rates by Gender and Rating Per $1,000 of Coverage			
Female Born in 1986			
	Preferred	**Standard**	**Rated (A)**
10-Year Term	$.07	$.09	$.14
10-Year Term with Waiver of Premium (WOP)	$.08	$.10	$.16
20-Year Term	$.08	$.11	$.18
20-Year WOP	$.09	$.12	$.20
30-Year Term	$.10	$.14	$.23
30-Year WOP	$.11	$.15	$.24

Alternative Monthly Premiums per $1,000 of Coverage — Male Born in 1985			
	Preferred	Standard	Rated (A)
Variable Universal Life and Universal Life	$.22	$.28	$.39
Whole Life Policy	$.35	$.40	$.51

Alternative Monthly Premiums per $1,000 of Coverage — Female Born in 1986			
	Preferred	Standard	Rated (A)
Variable Universal Life and Universal Life	$.17	$.23	$.31
Whole Life Policy	$.31	$.38	$.40

The premiums listed above for cash value life insurance products include insurance costs, fees and expenses as well as subaccount funding components.

Disability Coverage

James could buy supplemental long-term disability coverage for $35 per month. This coverage would pay the difference between 70 percent of his earnings and his group coverage, has a 6-month waiting period, an own-occupation definition of disability and would pay through age 65.

Elizabeth could buy long-term disability coverage for $65 per month. This coverage would pay up to $1,800 per month, has a 6-month waiting period, an own-occupation definition of disability and would pay through her age 65. James or Elizabeth could purchase short-term disability coverage for $20 per month. It would pay 70 percent of either of their pre-disability benefits for up to 6 months. This coverage has a 60-day waiting period.

Homeowners Endorsement and Rider Costs

Homeowners Insurance — Premium Options for James and Elizabeth's HO-3 Policy			
	$140,000/$80,000	$150,000/$85,000	$160,000/$90,000
1% deductible	$83.33	$87.50	$95.00
2% deductible	$63.33	$67.50	$75.00

Homeowners endorsement and rider costs include:

- Mold insurance ($30,000)—$12.50/month
- Jewelry endorsement up to $5,000—$12.50/month

- Window endorsement—$8.33/month
- Antique furniture coverage—$20.00/month
- Gun endorsement up to $5,000–$12.50/month

James and Elizabeth could purchase a catastrophic health care insurance supplement with a $10,000 deductible and 90-percent coinsurance up to $20,000 out of pocket costs for $25 per month per insured. This coverage has no lifetime maximum coverage limit per insured.

Inflation and Interest Rates

- CPI-U is assumed to be 3.25 percent
- James and Elizabeth feel they could earn 6 percent on their money after taxes over long periods of time.
- Refinancing costs would be 1.0 percent of the mortgage balance plus $1,000 of fixed costs.
- Assume life expectancies of 85 for James and 90 for Elizabeth.
- James and Elizabeth do not believe social security will be in place when they retire.
- James wants to retire before he is 65.
- Students are encouraged to use current market rates if they vary from those in the text.

PRELIMINARY OUTLINE [SUGGESTED SOLUTION]

A preliminary outline discusses client goals and can be used as a master checklist for a financial planner when developing a client relationship. The preliminary outline should be broad in scope and coverage. This outline may be structured by financial planning topic area or by global planning objective. An outline structured by financial planning topic areas will have a bullet point for every topic the planner is attempting to address. A comprehensive financial planner will develop a very detailed outline while a topic oriented adviser may chose to focus on one or two planning areas.

Preliminary outlines are intended to give planners a starting point in developing a written plan document. The preliminary outline can act as a tool pointing planners towards software implementation, choosing team members, and setting meeting schedules. The broad nature of a preliminary outline allows it to be used and developed for all clients that fit a class or niche. A topic oriented preliminary outline's wide reach gives a planner the ability to take detailed notes and approaches when preparing client financial plans. A global planning outline will take an integrated approach to a client's financial plan. A global outline will focus on personal and business issues instead of financial planning topic areas. A global outline will take a comprehensive scope of personal planning, a comprehensive scope within business planning, and deliver two plans that will have a global interaction.

The preliminary outline used for James and Elizabeth Black is developed in a topic-oriented fashion. Students are free to develop unique styles of outlines that fit their business models and individual preferences.

1. Definition of client's objectives
   a. risk management evaluation
      (1) life insurance
      (2) health
      (3) disability
      (4) long-term care
      (5) automobile
      (6) property casualty insurance
      (7) other insurance needs
   b. retirement planning
      (1) integrate retirement planning with risk management needs
      (2) ensure retirement funds for a surviving spouse at death of the first spouse
   c. investment planning
      (1) discuss global investment plan
      (2) ensure retirement funds for a surviving spouse at death of the first spouse
   d. estate distribution
   e. income tax planning
   f. business planning
   g. other short-term objectives
   h. other long-term objectives
2. Assumptions

- a. inflation
- b. rates of return and expectations
- c. important dates and life expectancies
- d. health
- e. insurance costs

3. Financial statements
   - a. cash flow
   - b. net worth
   - c. other

4. Recommendations and alternatives
   - a. risk management evaluation
     - (1) life insurance
     - (2) health
     - (3) disability
     - (4) long-term care
     - (5) automobile
     - (6) property casualty insurance
     - (7) other insurance needs
   - b. retirement planning
   - c. investment planning
   - d. estate distribution
   - e. income tax planning
   - f. business planning
   - g. other short-term objectives
   - h. other long-term objectives
   - i. insurance planning

5. Implementation and monitoring
   - a. delineate responsibilities
   - b. specific product recommendations
   - c. develop a time line
   - d. retirement planning

INSTRUCTIONS

The next step in the planning process is to expand the preliminary outline to include specific case considerations. Use an expanded and detailed case summary to define case details, specific objectives, assumptions, recommendations, and an implementation schedule.

ASSUMPTIONS FOR JAMES AND ELIZABETH BLACK

Elizabeth and James will need to make many assumptions while engaging in the planning process. Some assumptions are quantitative such as rate of return, inflation and life expectancy. Other assumptions have more qualitative aspects including overall health and goal prioritization. Financial planning tools and techniques are only as sound as the assumptions behind them. As plan assumptions change, planners need to monitor and update their analysis and impact on James and Elizabeth's overall financial health.

Inflation Assumptions

The case states that students should use 3.25 percent for long-term inflation. This rate is used to provide uniform discussion of techniques and answers. Students are encouraged to use alternative inflation rates as they solve the case. James stated that he expects to average 5.00 percent raises over his career. These raises will also increase the amount he saves towards his retirement plan.

Rate of Return Assumptions

The case states that students should assume a 6.00 percent rate of return on investment assets. More complicated cases may have students solve weighted rates of return, standard deviations or design asset allocations. Risk management calculations utilize two primary rates; the inflation rate (3.25 percent) and discount rate (6.00 percent). In the case context the discount rate is a rate of return James and Elizabeth could earn on their investments over a long period of time. Students should also solve for the inflation-adjusted rate of return. This rate is used to calculate annuity payment streams.

$$\text{Inflation Adjusted Rate} = ((1 + r) / (1 + i)) - 1$$

The inflation-adjusted rate = 2.66 percent. Rates are rounded to two decimal places through the text to achieve a constant convention. While refinancing rates are not implicitly considered rates of return, they are a case assumption and are discussed in this topic area.

The Blacks' adjustable rate mortgage (ARM) interest rate is currently 5.75 percent. This rate is less than the ARM reset rate of 7.50 percent (5.00 percent + LIBOR 2.50 percent) and equal to a 30-year fixed refinance rate today. James and Elizabeth have held their mortgage for 2 years. The note is a 5-year adjustable note and the note has 3 years remaining before resetting to a new adjustable rate. Refinancing costs would be 1.00 percent of the mortgage balance plus $1,000 of fixed costs. .

Important Dates and Assumptions

James' birthday—01/01/1985

Elizabeth's birthday—06/15/1986

life expectancy   James and Elizabeth have set approximate life expectancy dates: James believes he can live until 85 and Elizabeth thinks 90. These dates are approximations; they are probably based on family histories and include an assumption of the quality of medical care continuing to increase over time. This assumption also proposes that both James and Elizabeth adopt healthier lifestyles.

Life expectancy is typically overstated through the financial planning process. In August of 2010, the CDC reported that the average life expectancy of a child born in American in 2010—not adjusting for gender, race, or economic status—has a life expectancy of slightly under 78 years (77.8). Put more simply, an infant born in August of 2008 has a 50 percent chance of living to age 78 and a 50 percent chance of dying before age 78.

Life expectancy increases over time as it adjusts for attrition. A 30-year-old has a life expectancy slightly over 78 years (78.2). The discrepancy between an infant's life expectancy and the 30-year-old expectancy is attrition. A fraction of the population will die before they reach 30. Mortality for the surviving population is reassessed. The life expectancy of centurions is more pronounced. A 100-year-old female has a life expectancy of 102.84. This means half of 100-year-olds will die before reaching the last quarter of their 102nd year.

James and Elizabeth were born in 1984 and 1985. In 2010 they would turn 26 and 27 respectively. Using gender-specific CDC charts, their life expectancies would be 77 for James and 81 for Elizabeth. They have overstated their expectancies by about a decade.

Financial planners constantly struggle with life expectancy issues. Financial plans are generally structured around the conservative assumption that less harm will come to clients by overstating life expectancy than by understating expectancy. Annual meetings and corresponding changes in a client's financial plan help keep life expectancy assumptions focused and on track. Planners should also consider contributing factors when establishing client life expectancy:

- marital status
- gender
- socioeconomic status
- family histories of longevity
- good health and BMI (body mass index)
- socioeconomic background
- medical history

Monte Carlo and bootstrapping software can provide additional techniques when working with life expectancy. These software programs can run thousands of calculations, each with a different annual life expectancy, to show clients the probability of succeeding at a financial planning goal. These types of software programs offer an additional financial planning dynamic (probability of success and failure) over static time-value-of-money calculations.

These programs should be used with a sound understanding of how life expectancy is modeled. Does the program adjust for family history? Health concerns? Gender and ethnic background? Planners need to ask questions and understand the life expectancy dynamics of software packages before presenting plans to their clients.

Health Assumptions

health concerns   James and Elizabeth have provided height and weight. Height and weight can be used to derive body mass index (BMI) which is a predictor of insurability and other risks.

BMI = (weight in pounds/(height in inches)^2) x 703

Elizabeth's BMI is 28.69

James BMI is 34.43

Client BMI impacts insurability for life, disability and health insurance. Insurance companies refer to the following federal guidelines:

Table 3-1 Body Mass Index and Weight Status	
BMI	**Weight Status**
Below 18.5	Underweight
18.5 – 24.9	Normal
25.0 – 29.9	Overweight
30.0 and Above	Obese

James might be considered obese and Elizabeth overweight. Their Body Mass Index will impact premium costs and possibly cap the amount of insurance they can receive. The National Institutes of Health (NIH) as well as many insurers link height and weight to increased risk of disease and death. Overweight and obese individuals are at increased risk for many diseases and health conditions, including the following:

- hypertension
- dyslipidemia (for example, high LDL cholesterol, low HDL cholesterol, or high levels of triglycerides)
- type 2 diabetes
- coronary heart disease
- stroke
- gallbladder disease
- osteoarthritis
- some cancers

James and Elizabeth have not indicated that they drink alcohol in excess, smoke, take drugs recreationally, or participate in other risky behavior. Clients may be hesitant to disclose this type of personal information to financial planners. Asking direct questions is prudent, as omitting this type of material information on insurance applications may be cause to void the policy at a later date.

Clients can benefit from direct discussions about health. Measuring the financial impacts of health may provide clients with additional motivation to better their quality of life.

FINANCIAL STATEMENTS FOR JAMES AND ELIZABETH BLACK

In a personal financial planning context, financial statements always include a cash flow statement and statement of financial position, or net worth statement. Other statements are included as needed. Elizabeth and James do not require in-depth portfolio analysis, business cash flow management or retirement plan census analysis at this time. Students may also want to include statements showing future projections in this analysis.

Cash Flow Statement

cash flow statement The cash flow statement is the backbone of a financial plan. The statement shows income and expenses. In this context, the cash flow statement is similar to a corporate cash flow but aimed at the individual client. Students are encouraged to use a spreadsheet program to calculate the current cash flow for the case. Students should also prepare a cash flow statement with Elizabeth no longer working full time.

effective tax rate Projected cash flow statements will be prepared for the current situation. The current situation is defined as the case study without any changes or revisions. Remember to apply appropriate inflation rates to expenses and income. This case study assumes an effective tax rate for income tax. The effective tax is applied to gross income. An effective rate is determined by taking the actual tax paid and dividing by client gross income. Basically, it is the actual tax impact. This method of calculating taxation is appropriate for a middle-income risk-management-focused case study, but would be inappropriate for a case with higher incomes or more dynamic tax implications. Using an effective tax rate on gross income creates a "net" environment. Estimating taxation on a gross income figure is only appropriate for estimating. Tax planning software should be applied to client cases to determine more accurate tax results.

After deciding on how to represent cash flows, the planner should create a cash flow statement.

Note

The cash flow below assumes full (6.2 percent and 12.4 percent respectively) employee and employer social security tax rates. Federal stimulus programs may temporarily reduce this rate in 2012 and 2013. Please use an appropriate rate for the year you are working on this case.

Cash Flow: Both James and Elizabeth Working

Table 3-2 Cash Flow Statement: Both Spouses Working			
Income			
James Salary	$55,000.00		
Elizabeth Working	$24,000.00		
Elizabeth Part Time	$5,000.00		
James SE	$ 5,000.00		
Gross Income			**$ 89,000.00**
Expenses			
Payroll Taxes			
Soc. Sec. on Wages (6.2% of Wages)	($5,208.00)		
Medicare on Wages (1.45% of Wages)	($1,218.00)		
Soc. Sec. on SE Income (12.4% of SE income)	($620.00)		
Medicare on SE Income (2.9% of SE income)	($140.00)	($7,186.00)	
Federal Income Tax			
Taxes Due (7% EFF RT)	($6,230.00)	($6,230.00)	
Property Taxes			
2.5% of Home Value (160,000)	($4,000.00)	($4,000.00)	
Debt Payments			
Payments on Mortgage (125,000 original note)	($8,753.64)		
Car Note	($3,976.99)		
Student Loans	($4,769.40)	($17,500.03)	
Living Expenses			
General Expenses	($24,000.00)		
Homeowners	($1,400.00)		
Auto Insurance	($1,896.00)		
Healthcare Premiums	($3,000.00)	($30,296.00)	
Voluntary Savings			
401(k) Contribution	($3,300.00)		
Roth Contributions (planned but not guaranteed)	($10,000.00)	($13,300.00)	
Expenses			**($78,512.03)**
Net Available Cash Flow			$10,487.97
Monthly Available Cash Flow			**$874.00**

Cash Flow Discussion: Both James and Elizabeth Working

The principal and income payments, as well as car note payments need to be calculated by students and are based on case facts.

The initial cash flow analysis brings some questions into light. Is this an accurate accounting of their expenses? Has any credit card debt been omitted? The student is limited to the facts presented in the case study but is encouraged to present additional questions they would ask the client.

After preparing an initial cash flow, a cash flow with Elizabeth exiting the workplace and having children should be created. All primary fields that have changed are outlined. Elizabeth's income is removed. Elizabeth not working will dramatically lower the client's tax rate, and the effective rate has been lowered to compensate. Students should also consider the potential issues surrounding an unchanged mortgage balance from two years ago. This issue is likely contentious for the clients, potentially a great source of frustration. How many payments were actually missed by the client? Are they embarrassed to tell the financial adviser? Rarely are clients straightforward with potentially embarrassing information. The financial adviser should ask additional follow-up questions to better flush out the mortgage situation.

Cash Flow Statement: James Working and Elizabeth at Home

Table 3-3 Cash Flow Statement: James Working				
Income				
	James Salary	$ 55,000.00		
	Elizabeth Working Full Time	$ —		
	Elizabeth Part Time	$ 5,000.00		
			$60,000.00	
	James SE	$ 5,000.00		
			$ 5,000.00	
Gross Income				$ 65,000.00
Expenses				
Payroll Taxes	Soc. Sec. on Wages	$ (3,720.00)		
	Medicare on Wages	$ (870.00)		
	Soc. Sec. on SE Income	$ (620.00)		
	Medicare on SE Income	$ (140.00)		
			$ (5,350.00)	
Federal Income Tax	Taxes Due (4% EFF RT)	$ (2,600.00)		
			$ (2,600.00)	
Property Taxes	2.5% of Home Value	$ (4,000.00)		
			$ (4,000.00)	
Debt Payments	Payments on Mortgage	$ (8,753.64)		
	Car Note	$ (3,976.99)		
	Student Loans	$ (4,769.40)		
			$(17,500.03)	
Living Expenses	General Expenses	$ (24,000.00)		
	Homeowners	$ (1,400.00)		
	Auto Insurance	$ (1,896.00)		
	Healthcare Premiums	$ (3,000.00)		
			$(30,296.00)	
Voluntary Savings	401(k) Contribution	$ (3,300.00)		
	Roth Contributions (all excess income)	$ (1,953.97)		
			$(5,253.97)	
Expenses				$ (65,000.00)
Net Available Cash Flow				$ (0.00)

Cash Flow Discussion: James Working

This revised cash flow shows the family is unable to maintain voluntary savings if Elizabeth stops working. The client will begin to change priorities. Roth contributions are a form of savings, and the $10,000 a year currently funding Roth IRAs are needed to supplement living expenses. This family may not be able to fully fund retirement, education and insurance costs. A financial planner will need to address shortfalls and when designing the plan. Monthly spending may increase when Elizabeth and James have children ($2,000 per month), which would cause further decreases to discretionary items. When Elizabeth has children, health care premiums will increase from $3,000 per year ($250 per month) to $3,900 per year ($325 per month).

The initial cash flow analysis shows that James and Elizabeth have a surplus while both of them are working but may not be able to meet their goals and objectives when Elizabeth leaves the workforce. The couple will be faced with resource allocation decisions as they move forward with the planning process. Purchasing insurance will require premium dollars. These premium dollars will take away from voluntary savings elements. If Elizabeth is not interested in working full time after she has children create solutions to this case study should be entertained.

Projected Cash Flow Discussion

Projected cash flows will also be prepared for case revisions and implementation. Projected cash flows ensure the client is in a position to achieve recommended goals moving forward. Projections will not be accurate over long periods of time and should be updated on an annual basis.

Net Worth Statement for James and Elizabeth Black

A net worth statement captures a snapshot in time of James and Elizabeth's assets and liabilities. The net worth statement of James and Elizabeth is atypical of college graduates who financed their education.

Table 3-4 Net Worth Statement for James and Elizabeth Black		
Assets		
Home (appraised value 2 years ago)	$150,000	
James 401(k)	$5,000	
Roth IRA Balances	$11,000	
Honda Accord	$2,000	
Ford F250	$15,000	
Personal Property	$50,000	
Wedding Set	$4,000	
Checking Account	$3,000	
Savings Account	$4,000	
Total Assets		$244,000
Liabilities		
Mortgage	$125,000	
Student Loan James	$24,800	
Student Loan Elizabeth	$11,000	
Car Loan	$18,000	
Total Liabilities	**$178,800**	
Net Worth		$65,200

The net worth statement shows that Elizabeth and James are on their way, but could they sustain themselves if James lost his job? Initial analysis of the net worth statement may be overinflated by personal property (a majority of which is Elizabeth's furniture). After developing cash flow and net worth statements, advisers can perform basic ratio analysis to give a more in-depth perspective of the client.

solvency ratio

A solvency ratio calculation takes client net worth and divides by asset. This ratio provides consumers with a relative idea of the robustness of their overall financial health, with ideal solvency ratios falling between 0.5 and 0.9. In the case of James and Elizabeth, the solvency ratio is $65,200 / $244,000 or 0.27. This ratio is positive but implies less debt would create a healthier financial picture.

RECOMMENDATIONS AND ALTERNATIVES FOR JAMES AND ELIZABETH BLACK

The risk management section should contain any life, disability, long-term care, health and property casualty recommendations. This section may also contain sections for business liability or commercial insurance. The rationale for recommendations is included in their discussion. In practice, rationale and analysis would be performed internally and may be presented independently of client assumptions. For the purposes of this course, analysis is presented along with client recommendations.

Risk Management Topics

Life Insurance Needs for James Black

A primary goal in this case study is to evaluate life insurance needs. After analyzing their cash flow and net worth statement, Elizabeth would be unable to sustain herself and children if James were to die.

Determining the life insurance death benefit for James and Elizabeth is a complex decision.

life insurance modeling
There are five primary ways of calculating the insurance need. Many different approaches are used to determine the amount of life insurance appropriate for any given client. Some of these approaches include the following:

- **human life value approach**—an approach that measures a person's human life value in terms of the present value of that portion of estimated future earnings which, if he or she lives long enough to achieve all the earnings, will be used to support dependents.

- **multiple of income approach**—a simplistic approach that determines life insurance needs based on the client's current annual income

- **financial needs analysis approach**—an approach that determines how much life insurance is needed to provide a principal sum that will be liquidated to meet survivors' lump-sum and ongoing income needs

- **capital needs analysis approach**—an approach that determines how much life insurance is needed to provide a principal sum adequate to fund survivors' needs while preserving the principal

Lump Sum Needs for James. An additional method of determining insurance need is the survivor needs approach. The survivor needs approach projects future needs of the surviving family members, which may be more than the human life value approach. The text will utilize the survivor needs approach to determine life insurance needs.

lump sum needs　　　Lump sum needs include all liabilities except any of James' student loan proceeds (which would be paid off at his death):

Table 3-5 Lump Sum Needs at James' Death	
Liabilities	
Mortgage	$125,000
Student Loan James	$24,800
Student Loan Elizabeth	$11,000
Car Loan	$18,000
Total Liabilities	**$178,800**

Additionally, Elizabeth will need proceeds to provide funeral costs and final expenses ($15,000–$25,000). She may want to take some time off from work to grieve. Six months of Elizabeth's income would be $12,000 from her full-time job and $2,500 from part-time work. Assume these ancillary survivor needs will total $34,500.

Total Lump Sum Needs at James' Death = ($178,800 + 34,500) = $213,300

Cash Flow Needs for James. What will change from a cash flow perspective if James were to pass away? Family income will decrease. James' salary and part-time income would drop to zero. The effective tax rate would drop dramatically (2–3 percent) and some expenses would also change. Elizabeth would be eligible for health care through COBRA for a limited period of time but would eventually need to purchase her own coverage. If death benefits paid off family debts, Elizabeth would no longer make car, mortgage, or student loan payments.

Table 3-6 Cash Flow Statement at James' Death			
Income			
	James Salary	$ —	
	Elizabeth Working	$24,000.00	
	Elizabeth Part Time	$5,000.00	
			$29,000.00
			$ —
	Gross Income		$29,000.00
Expenses			
Payroll Taxes	Soc. Sec. on Wages	$(1,798.00)	
	Medicare on Wages	$(420.50)	
			$(2,218.50)
Federal Income Tax	Taxes Due (2% EFF RT)	$ (580.00)	
			$ (580.00)
Property Taxes	2.5% of Home Value	$ (4,000.00)	
			$ (4,000.00)
Debt Payments	Payments on Mortgage	$ —	
	Car Note	$ —	
	Student Loans	$ —	
			$ —
Living Expenses	General Expenses	$ (24,000.00)	
	Homeowners	$ (1,400.00)	
	Auto Insurance	$ (1,896.00)	
	Health Care Premiums	$ (3,000.00)	
			$(30,296.00)
Voluntary Savings	Mutual Fund Ret. Savings	$ (8,300.00)	
	Roth Contributions	$ (5,000.00)	
			$(13,300.00)
Expenses			$(50,394.50)
Net Available Cash Flow			$(21,394.50)
Monthly			$ (1,782.88)

The survivor needs method of solving life insurance needs values begins with calculating Elizabeth's projected cash flow shortage. The survivor needs method then calculates the present value needed today to provide Elizabeth with supplemental cash flow through the remainder of her working years.

Note

Elizabeth's age will vary if you are completing the case before June of 2011 (24) or after June of 2011 (25). We have chosen to use 25. You may use 25, 26 or 27 based on which year you complete the case.

Elizabeth's Age = 25

Proposed Retirement Age = 65

Years to Fund = 40

PV = Solve

PMT = –$21,394.50 (Elizabeth's additional annual cash flow need, assuming she contributes to a Roth IRA)

FV = 0

N = 40

I = 2.66% (inflation-adjusted rate)

Set Calculator to BGN Mode and make one payment per year (withdrawals will begin immediately)

The inflation-adjusted interest rate is used because it accounts for inflating payments. This rate was solved in the assumption discussion of the text. PV is calculated at **$536,783.16**

This number is the amount of money Elizabeth would need today to sustain her standard of living and save $13,300 per year through her age 65.

Retirement **must** be considered when using the survivor needs model. Elizabeth was counting on James' income to help provide for her retirement. Had James lived, retirement savings amounts would be continued through Elizabeth's working years. Currently the clients are saving $10,000 annually in two Roth IRA accounts and $3,300 into James' 401(k).

Retirement planning needs can be calculated independently and their present value added to the survivor needs model, or annual savings amounts can be included as part of the survivor needs analysis. This case study assumes that if James dies Elizabeth will make Roth contributions through her working years. Roth IRAs have contribution limits, and Elizabeth would be unable to "prefund" her entire retirement planning need into a Roth IRA if James died. She will have to make annual contributions into the Roth IRA to maximize future tax-free distributions.

With those caveats, three calculations can be employed to verify the survivor needs retirement planning assumptions made in the above paragraph.

- How much will Elizabeth need annually when she retires?

  Living Expenses of $30,000 today should be inflated at 3.25% for 40 years.

  PV = 30,000

  I = 3.25%

  PMT = 0

  FV = SOLVE = $107,826

Elizabeth will need $107,826 a year to maintain her lifestyle at age 65. Another way of stating the answer to this step of retirement savings would be to state that $30,000 in today's dollars will be equivalent to $107,826 in 40 years—a fairly staggering 359 percent increase!!

- How much money will Elizabeth need at retirement to maintain $107,826 inflation adjusted withdrawals from her portfolio? (Assume immediate withdrawals, and set your calculator to begin mode.)

  I = 2.66% (inflation-adjusted rate)

  PMT = –$107,826

  FV = 0

  N = 25 (Elizabeth's life expectancy at retirement)

  PV = SOLVE = $2,002,638.95.

Elizabeth will need around $2,002,638.95 when she retires at age 65 to sustain her level of living. Elizabeth stated she does not want to assume any Social Security will be available to her in the future. Realistically, some social security will be paid to Elizabeth in 2051. However, the client desires a plan presented to her that does not consider this amount.

- How much will her retirement portfolio be at retirement, assuming she has $16,000 today (Roth IRA assets + James' 401(k)) and will add $13,300 every year to her savings goals through retirement (40 years). She is using a Roth IRA and brokerage mutual fund accounts. For the purposes of consistency, assume that the 6.0 percent long-term rate used in this equation is net of any capital gains taxes or taxes on dividends. Assume that Elizabeth will be making retirement contributions at the end of each year. Set your financial calculator to END mode for this equation.

  I = 6.0% (long-term rate)

  PMT = $13,300 (these cash flow streams are negative; Elizabeth will be saving money)

PV = – $16,000 (this is coded in as negative; Elizabeth will be depositing the money)

N = 40 (years until retirement)

FV = SOLVE = $2,222,905.63

If Elizabeth maintains retirement savings of $13,300 annually, she should have $2,222,905.63 available at retirement. This slightly exceeds her need; and would fulfill her current standard of living. Any change to this model (interest rate, years to retirement, living expenses, inflation rate) dramatically changes this outcome. Students are encouraged to solve this problem using numerous rates and measures to determine optimal outcomes.

Total Life Insurance Need for James. James total life insurance need is the sum of his assets, needs, and existing life insurance policies.

- Cash Flow Needs = $536,783.16
- Lump Sum Needs = $213,300
- Liquid Assets = ($7,000)
- Existing Life Insurance ($50,000)
- The Total Life Insurance Needs for James is $693,083.16

life insurance needs   Using the survivor needs method, James needs to purchase at least $693,083 of life insurance. In practice, this amount would be rounded up to $700,000.

Life Insurance Needs for Elizabeth

Lump Sum Needs for Elizabeth

If Elizabeth were to die, James would have similar lump-sum costs.

Table 3-7 Lump Sum Needs at Death	
Liabilities	
Mortgage	$125,000
Student Loan James	$24,800
Student Loan Elizabeth	$11,000
Car Loan	$18,000
Total Liabilities	**$178,800**

Lump Sum Needs include all liabilities.

Additionally, James will need proceeds to provide funeral costs ($25,000) and may want to take some time off from work to grieve. Six months of his income would be $25,000 from his full-time job and $2,500 from part-time work. Total miscellaneous lump sum costs would be $52,500.

Total Lump Sum Needs = ($178,800 + $52,500) = $231,300

James would not need any assistance from ongoing cash flow needs if Elizabeth were to pass away. His earnings in concert with removing debt obligations show that James does not have a cash flow deficit. James can apply the $7,000 of liquid assets towards Elizabeth's lump sum need.

Total Life Insurance Need for Elizabeth = $224,300

In practice, this amount would be rounded up to $225,000

What type of insurance policies should be purchased for James and Elizabeth? Their need at this stage in life is largely temporary, and their estate is currently well under estate tax levels.

Types of Life Insurance

Elizabeth and James should consider using one of the following types of policies to provide the additional survivor protection needed:

- Ordinary Whole Life Insurance—This form of insurance is based on the assumption that premiums will be paid on a level annual basis throughout the lifetime of the insured (or, in some variations, a term of years). In the early years of the policy the premium exceeds the cost of protection, providing the basis for cash values within the policy. The cash values of a policy depend on the size of the policy, the insured's age at the time of issue, and whether the policy is rated. Cash values are guaranteed by the contract and can be borrowed at a rate explicitly stated in the policy or based on a specified index. The increase in cash value each year is not taxable to the policyowner. Even though the policy is priced with the assumption that the premium will be paid over the life of the insured, many owners often convert their policies to either a reduced paid-up policy when the need for protection decreases (such as when children become self-supporting) or to an annuity when the insured retires.

- Variable Life Insurance—This is also a fixed, level premium policy for the lifetime of the insured. With variable life the insured selects the investment medium used within the policy, usually with a choice restricted to specific funds managed by the insurer. This policy differs from the ordinary whole life policy in that the face amount of the policy changes with the investment performance of the investment instrument chosen by the insured. Often a minimum guaranteed floor below which the policy's face value will not fall is an integral part of the policy.

  In a variable policy, all investment risk, except for the minimum death benefit floor, shifts to the policyowner. Since the investment risk is transferred to the owner, the policy cash value is not guaranteed. If the policy has cash value, borrowing the cash value is permissible. Some policies specify a variable interest rate on the loan that fluctuates with changes in some previously established standard interest-rate index. Other policies have fixed borrowing rates. However, these policies generally have a substantial surrender charge during their early years. Therefore the client should realize that a long-term commitment is being made if this type of policy is chosen.

  In addition, the insured needs to monitor carefully the performance of the investment instrument(s) selected. If the initial choice is incorrect, or if the insured fails to shift funds when economic conditions change, the amount of protection can fall substantially. This form of fluctuating death benefit might not be suitable to the client when the primary reason for acquiring additional insurance at this time is protection for survivors.

- Universal Life Insurance—This policy differs from the previous two policies in that it has a flexible premium. In addition, universal life may feature either a level or an increasing death benefit. (Certain increasing death benefits may cause the policy to be treated as a MEC, however.) The insured has the option to either increase or decrease, or even fail to pay, the premium. All premiums paid are added to the policy's cash value account, and mortality charges are deducted from the same account. Interest is credited to this account with a minimum guarantee. Interest in excess of the guarantee depends on investment performance and insurer discretion. In a universal life insurance policy some mortality risk is shifted to the insured due to the mortality charge deduction from the cash value account. Although loans can be made from the cash values, the insured can also make withdrawals of basis from the cash values that are not considered a loan by the insurance company. Therefore no interest need be paid to the insurer for the funds, and the funds need not be repaid to the insurer. However, there will be income tax consequences associated with basis withdrawals if the policy is a MEC, or if the withdrawals are associated with a reduction in the death benefit. As with the variable life policy, there are often significant surrender charges during the early years.

- Variable Universal Life Insurance—A variable universal life insurance policy is a universal life insurance policy that gives the insured the ability to direct the investment of cash values. Like a variable life policy, cash values are not guaranteed. Variable universal life insurance policies are often useful for healthy, young insureds who plan on using a maximum premium funding approach.

- Term Insurance—This policy type has an increasing premium over the lifetime of the insured. Important features of this policy are its guaranteed renewability, convertibility of the policy to permanent insurance up to age 65, and no cash value buildup over the life of the insured.

  Term insurance is initially lower priced than alternatives, but the annual premium on the term insurance will rise significantly as James gets older.

James should keep in mind that even though the investment features and tax advantages of permanent insurance are attractive, the primary function of insurance is to protect survivors. Permanent insurance is almost always the best choice for providing estate liquidity or funding the eventual payment of estate taxes.

Term insurance is an appropriate type of coverage for both James and Elizabeth. The family has a limited need for coverage, does not have a foreboding estate tax situation. They are in a relatively low tax bracket and James could maximize additional tax-deferral by increasing his 401(k) contributions. Health may be a factor in attaining coverage. Given James height, weight and blood pressure he will likely be rated for health concerns. Elizabeth would probably be considered in a standard non-preferred underwriting class. Long-term policies should be considered. This coverage will carry both James and Elizabeth through their childbearing years and would provide almost to retirement. James and Elizabeth should both price 30- and 20-year term policies. Consult the case study premium charts for policy pricing. If James and Elizabeth adopt healthier lifestyles, they will be able to acquire more reasonably priced coverage.

Universal life insurance may also be appropriate for James and Elizabeth. Universal life insurance would allow the clients to build up a cash value that could be used for retirement and estate planning needs while protecting themselves with a death benefit. They may even consider a blended approach, with underlying $100,000 universal life policies and remaining coverage in term policies. This textbook has assumed a term life purchase for modeling the case study. Students tend to have very strong opinions of which type of insurance should be purchased. Consider the insurance purchase decision outside the scope of your compensation model.

Health Insurance

health insurance
James and Elizabeth have access to a group plan available through James' employer. The coverage has $50 copayments, and the Blacks are happy with the coverage. This policy seems to meet the needs of James and Elizabeth. Recommend purchasing additional catastrophic coverage if their budget allows.

Disability Insurance

disability insurance
James is covered with a limited group disability insurance policy. His existing policy would provide 50 percent of his salary of coverage for a 5-year period if he became disabled. This 50 percent would be taxable and would not provide enough benefit for Elizabeth to stay home with children. Recommend purchasing additional coverage for James and look into waiver-of-premium benefits on other types of insurance coverage.

Elizabeth may consider disability insurance as well. She could purchase individual coverage while working. When she leaves the workforce she can consider reducing coverage.

Short-term disability coverage is available for both James and Elizabeth. The Blacks' savings account contains around $4,000. This account is not large enough to provide 6 months of income if James or Elizabeth suffered a short-term disability. Purchase this coverage temporarily and drop it when an emergency fund has grown.

Long Term Care Insurance

long term care   James and Elizabeth are a young middle-class family. With sound disability coverage long-term care insurance may not be an efficient use of resources at this time, but may be in the future. Revisit this coverage from meeting to meeting.

Automobile Insurance

auto insurance   Increase the deductible on their collision and comprehensive coverage from $250 to $500. This change will save around $360 per year. James and Elizabeth have $7,000 in their checking and savings accounts which could be used to pay an increased deductible. Liability coverage is adequate. Elizabeth and James have little property that could be seized by creditors.

Property Insurance

Raising James and Elizabeth's homeowners deductible from 1 to 2 percent will provide $240 per year in savings. This savings can be used to offset additional property costs. The Blacks state their home has increased in assessed tax value to $160,000 and should consult with a qualified property casualty expert to possibly adjust their policy to include an increased home value.

Jewelry endorsements protect Elizabeth's wedding ring above HO-3 coverage jewelry limitations. Mold insurance may not be appropriate, but students are limited by this case study and are unable to ask about specific climate conditions. This limitation prevents us from recommending a reduction in mold coverage.

A window endorsement may prove essential with children, but may not be important today. Do James and Elizabeth live in an area with small children as neighbors? This question can not be answered by the case study, and advisers may be wary to recommend a reduction in window protection.

Elizabeth's antique furniture is not covered under the current policy. This furniture has emotional and financial value to the family and should be protected. James' guns fall under the same light, and additional riders should be purchased to insure these items. Total homeowners costs will be $75 per month for property protection and an additional $65.83 for additional riders totaling $140.83 monthly or $1,689.96 on an annual basis.

Other Risk Management Concerns

Elizabeth and James do not have boats, rental property or other insurance needs at this time. When they have children their health care costs will increase and life insurance needs should be reevaluated. Property insurance may require additional underwriting, especially with both dogs. Elizabeth and James may find themselves paying a premium to insure a dangerous dog breed.

As James continues to earn more he will need to revisit disability coverage. Any life event (changing jobs, disability, inheritance, family members needing care, divorce) will require revisiting the risk management plan.

Retirement Planning for James and Elizabeth Black

retirement planning

While this case study presents an in-depth risk management analysis, the retirement planning element is not as complicated. James and Elizabeth are not comfortable assuming Social Security will be available to them at retirement.

Do James and Elizabeth need to increase their retirement savings? A similar approach to determining survivor funding can be employed to solve a basic retirement calculation.

How Much Will Retirement Cost?

How much will be needed at retirement?

All debt is projected to be paid off over James and Elizabeth's working lives. Living Expenses of $30,000 today should be inflated at 3.25 percent for 40 years.

Living Expenses of $30,000 today should be inflated at 3.25% for 40 years.
PV = 30,000
I = 3.25%
PMT = 0
FV = SOLVE = $107,826

How Much Will Elizabeth and James Need at Retirement?

How much money will Elizabeth and James need to maintain $107,826-per-year withdrawals from their portfolios? (assume withdrawals will begin immediately upon reaching retirement).

I = 2.66% (inflation-adjusted rate)

PMT = –$107,826
FV = 0
N = 25 (Elizabeth's life expectancy at retirement)
PV = SOLVE = $2,002,638.95.

Elizabeth and James will need around $2,000,000 when James retires at age 65. This amount does not include the impact of any Social Security benefits.

Are Elizabeth and James on Road to Retirement?

How much will her retirement portfolio be at retirement, assuming $16,000 today (Roth IRA assets + James' 401(k)) and adding $14,950 every year through retirement. $10,000 will be added to Roth IRAs (if a recommendation is made to continue funding), $3,300 through James' 401(k) employee contribution, and $1,650 through an employer match. The employer match causes this equation to be different than the above survivor needs analysis.

I = 6.0% (long-term rate)
PMT = $14,950 (keyed in negative as this is annual savings)
PV = $16,000 (keyed in negative as this money will be deposited)
N = 40 (years until retirement)
FV = Solve = $2,478,262.88

Current assumptions project a surplus of around $478,000 at retirement. These calculations will need to be revised annually. Some advisers may suggest reducing retirement calculations in favor of funding other goals. If both Elizabeth and James were planning on working indefinitely, this may be a positive outcome. However Elizabeth is considering leaving the workforce and accelerating retirement funding today will give Elizabeth and James a head start.

Home Refinancing

The client's third goal is to evaluate the use of extra income. Should extra income be used to pay off existing goals or to accelerate savings? The cash flow model prepared with all insurance recommendations shows excess monthly cash of around $500 per month. This money could be consumed, saved, used towards a goal, or used to pay down debt.

James and Elizabeth's mortgage is an adjustable rate loan, which will reset in 3 years. As of September 2011, they can lock in a 5.75 percent fixed rate on a 30-year note or 5.25 percent on a fixed 15-year note today. The lock in will cost them $1,000 in fixed costs and 1.0 percent of the loan balance. Locking in a fixed-rate loan protects James and Elizabeth from interest rate risk. Refinancing 2 years into a note will not lower monthly payments significantly but will offer stability. Interest rates may rise over the next 3 years and at the ARM reset date their debt could become unmanageable. Locking in while Elizabeth is still in the workforce will help with loan underwriting and provide cash flow for the refinance.

Investment Planning

investment planning   James and Elizabeth are using a family member to manage investment decisions. While they did not volunteer investment information, consider asking them for specific Roth IRA and 401(k) statements. A trusted family member may or may not be giving competent investment advice. As the financial adviser relationship evolves and trust dynamics grow with James and Elizabeth, revisit the investment plan.

If Elizabeth leaves the workforce, the Blacks will be faced with a resource allocation decision. They will either be able to meet risk management goals or continue fully funding Roth IRA accounts. A potential conflict exists between the Blacks' current investment adviser and pursuing adequate insurance protection. Consider meeting as a group to discuss insurance goals, or, with Elizabeth and James' permission, call their investment adviser to discuss specific goals.

Estate Planning

Elizabeth and James do not currently have wills and are considered intestate. All property not passing by contract, will, or operation of law passes under the laws of intestate succession (called *laws of descent and distribution* in some states). Intestate means "without making a will." A person who dies without a will or with a will that has been revoked, annulled, or in some other way declared invalid is said to die intestate. A decedent can also die partially intestate. Partial intestacy occurs when a testator has a valid will but the document does not dispose of all of the testator's property. There are intestate laws of each jurisdiction that prescribe the way an intestate's (the word as used frequently signifies the decedent) property is to be distributed. The law of the state where the person is domiciled controls the distribution of all the person's property located within the state. The intestate distribution of the decedent's real property, or tangible personal property, located outside of the state of domicile, is determined by the laws of the state where the property is located.

No distinction is usually made between real and personal property with respect to distribution under the laws of intestate descent. To provide for all property not otherwise transferred, each state has established laws of intestate succession. There is a prescribed order for disposition to the heirs of the deceased person. Intestate succession refers to the specified order of distribution by the state of the property of persons who die without leaving a valid will.

There are variations among the states with respect to the descent and distribution of an intestate's property. Usually, the person given primary consideration is the surviving spouse.

That is not to say that the surviving spouse takes all. Generally, a surviving spouse receives from one-third to one-half of the decedent's estate if there are living children or parents of the decedent. One scheme of intestate succession provides that a share first be set aside for the surviving spouse. An example is a provision for the first (some stated amount) dollars plus half of the estate to go to the surviving spouse. The remaining half is then divided equally among all children of the decedent. If there is no surviving spouse, surviving children may inherit the entire estate in equal shares. Next in line of lineal heirs are parents of the decedent. If a spouse survives but there are no children, the parents generally share the probate estate with the surviving spouse. Brothers and sisters usually come next in line, and so on. The order is rigid.

State intestacy statutes do not provide for inheritances for friends, business associates, or charities. Nor do they always make adequate provision for surviving spouses. Relatives of an individual who died intestate are frequently shocked, angered, and financially hurt by the controls put on the decedent's assets by the court. No amount of persuasion can alter the statutory scheme or convince the court that the decedent intended the property to pass to other persons.

If there are no living relatives, the property *escheats* to the state. Escheat means that property reverts to the state for lack of any individual competent to inherit the property. In other words, there are no heirs or next of kin to whom the property can pass by way of intestate succession. The state is the ultimate owner and taker of the estate and usually designates some state institution to receive the property.

Elizabeth and James do not have any estate planning documents. If they died today, they would have to rely on state laws to determine estate distribution.

Most people do not realize that even if they have not created an estate plan and executed the appropriate documents to implement their plans, a plan has been created and imposed on them by the state in which they reside. Everyone, no matter how poor, has an estate plan. Each state has drafted its own statutory scheme for the disposition of its citizens' property at death in the event that the resident dies either without a valid will or having made an incomplete disposition of property.

Elizabeth and James need to execute a will, the most basic legal instrument of all estate plans. A will is a legal instrument whereby a person makes disposition of his or her property to take effect after death. Once a valid will has been executed, the statutes of intestate succession are largely displaced by the provisions of the will. While the intestate-succession statutes may be largely displaced by a will or other personal disposition by the decedent, they may not be totally displaced. The state is concerned with the support of a spouse and minor children since these individuals may become a financial burden to the state. Therefore all states either have common-law rules or have enacted statutory provisions that protect a portion of the decedent's property for a surviving spouse under laws that are labeled variously as dower, curtesy, and homestead rights, or other statutory provisions, such as a spouse's right of election. These provisions may be operative only if the spouse and children have not been provided for by the will, or they may be absolute rights regardless of the will's provisions, such as forced heirship. The specific provisions of such laws vary from state to state, but they are a form of intestate succession. Individuals should understand what form these provisions take in their states and whether or not they can be displaced by the provisions in a will. The surviving spouse's rights can often be enforced only by an election to take against the provisions in a valid will.

It is also prudent for young families, prior to advanced age, to have arrangements in place for health care decision making. Fundamental to the decision-making system is a statement declaring the owner's intent for the medical treatment he or she wants should incapacity arise. Durable powers of attorney for health care and living wills are referred to as advance medical directives. Although a relatively small percentage of the American public currently have some type of advance medical directive, these documents are receiving more attention due to new legislation, court decisions, practical experience, and a growing recognition that *health* planning is as important as *wealth* planning. Advances in medical technology that prolong life have increased fears of lengthy artificial life support and family financial disaster. Modern medicine can keep a person alive by artificial mechanisms even though the individual is unconscious and essentially nonfunctional. Life-sustaining procedures are used in cases of accident or terminal illness where death is imminent and recovery highly improbable. Advance medical directives have evolved in response to these situations. By executing an advance medical directive such as a living will and/or a durable power of attorney for health care (medical power of attorney), individuals may make arrangements and give authority to others to carry out their health care instructions.

James and Elizabeth should also consider writing a durable power of attorney because it offers many advantages. First, proper execution of this document can help to avoid the costs, delays, and emotional upsets of competency proceedings. Second, a court-appointed conservator or guardian may not be a person the principal would have chosen. Third, the activities transacted by an attorney-in-fact are private. In contrast, court supervision of a conservator's or guardian's actions on behalf of an incompetent involves records open to public scrutiny. A power of attorney can be advantageous in community-property states if one spouse becomes disabled and both spouses' signatures are necessary for community-property transactions.

Executing a power of attorney is relatively inexpensive and not time consuming due to the simplicity and availability of standard forms. Furthermore, a competent principal may revoke the instrument at any time. Assets do not have to be retitled or transferred. In most cases, it is not necessary to file or record a power of attorney with any governmental authority, although some states require recordation and other formalities for real estate transactions.

Income Tax Planning

tax planning   Tax planning may provide James and Elizabeth with cash flow savings. This case does not require advanced income tax planning, but is an opportunity to stress tax fundamentals for young families. James and Elizabeth benefit from taking advantage of James 401(k) plan. Increased deferrals would create lower actual taxes paid.

Student loan interest is deductible for James and Elizabeth. While the case does not specify if James can contribute to a flexible spending account through his employer, he might be able to defer a portion of his salary to pay for deductible, copayments, or other health care expenses.

Encourage record keeping with the intent of itemizing deductions in upcoming years. They will be able to take an itemized deduction on mortgage interest and property taxes. Unreimbursed employer expenses or charitable deductions can be used to achieve additional itemized deductions.

The tax environment is dynamic; rates and thresholds change and are difficult to predict. James and Elizabeth will not need to access retirement funds for 20 to 30 years. The long time frame between initial retirement contributions may lead students to alternative retirement funding options, such as traditional IRAs, annuity or life products.

Business Planning

James does occasional computer work for friends and family. He has not indicated any business incorporation or affiliation. While James has not expressed an interest in growing a business of his own, his volume and income may continue to increase over time. Financial planners may ask James some basic business planning questions.

- Does James engage in written formal contracts when working with clients?
- Will he continue to build his client base over the next 3–5 years?
- What start-up costs are associated with pursuing a business?

James and Elizabeth have not entered into the financial planning engagement with the express purpose of evaluating part time business income. However, James may be exposing himself to tax and liability risk, and these risks are detrimental to his financial plan. James' homeowners liability coverage will not provide any protection if he is negligent when engaging in a business relationship by working on a friend or family member's computer. James should talk with a business lines property/casualty insurance agent or company about insuring a small business.

He may decide not to purchase coverage, but a comprehensive financial plan requires analyzing and evaluating client risk. James faces additional liability exposure if he is avoiding or omitting this part-time income on his tax return. Tax evasion or omission can create significant problems towards successful long- term financial planning, and if James' business grows, implementing accounting systems early on will save him time and expense.

Other Planning Objectives

Thc Blacks have expressed an interest in having children. Education savings can begin using excess dollars while Elizabeth is working. A brokerage account or savings account can be funded today with periodic contributions. This account could be used at a later date to jump-start the college savings process.

After implementing recommended risk management and cash flow strategies James and Elizabeth have around $500 per month. Dedicating these funds towards a saving plan can lay a strong foundation for reaching tomorrow's goals.

While not explicitly mentioned, the Blacks should consider notifying their homeowners coverage about their dogs. Some dog breeds are considered dangerous and insurers may not pay liability claims that result from a dangerous breed animal.

CASH FLOW RESTATED WITH RISK MANAGEMENT RECOMMENDATIONS IN PLACE

Table 3-8 Cash Flow Statement with Risk Management Recommendations			
Income			
	James Salary	$ 55,000.00	
	Elizabeth Working	$ 24,000.00	
	Elizabeth Part Time	$ 5,000.00	
			$84,000.00
	James SE	$ 5,000.00	
			$ 5,000.00
Gross Income			$89,000.00
Expenses			
Payroll Taxes	Soc. Sec. on Wages	$ (5,208.00)	
	Medicare on Wages	$ (1,218.00)	
	Soc. Sec. on SE Income	$ (620.00)	
	Medicare on SE Income	$ (140.00)	
			$ (7,186.00)
Federal Income Tax	Taxes Due (7% EFF RT)	$ (6,230.00)	
			$ (6,230.00)
Property Taxes	2.5% of Home Value	$ (4,000.00)	
			$ (4,000.00)
Debt Payments	Payments on Mortgage	$ (8,753.64)	
	Car Note	$ (3,976.99)	
	Student Loans	$ (4,769.40)	
			$(17,500.03)
Living Expenses	General Expenses	$ (24,000.00)	
	Homeowners Insurance	$ (1,689.96)	
	Auto Insurance	$ (1,536.00)	
	Healthcare Premiums	$ (3,000.00)	
	Life Insurance Premiums	$ (2,544.00)	
	Optional LT Disability Coverage	$ (1,200.00)	
	Optional ST Disability Coverage	$ (480.00)	
	Catastrophic Health	$ (600.00)	
			$ (35,049.96)
Voluntary Savings	401(k) Contribution	$ (3,300.00)	
	Roth Contributions	$ (10,000.00)	
			$(13,300.00)
Expenses			$ (83,265.99)
Net Available Cash Flow			$5,734.01
Monthly			$477.83

CASH FLOW RESTATED WITH REFINANCING RECOMMENDATIONS

Table 3-9 Cash Flow with All Recommendations in Place			
Income			
	James Salary	$ 55,000.00	
	Elizabeth Working	$ 24,000.00	
	Elizabeth Part Time	$ 5,000.00	
			$84,000.00
	James SE	$ 5,000.00	
			$ 5,000.00
Gross Income			$89,000.00
Expenses			
Payroll Taxes	Soc. Sec. on Wages	$ (5,208.00)	
	Medicare on Wages	$ (1,218.00)	
	Soc. Sec. on SE Income	$ (620.00)	
	Medicare on SE Income	$ (140.00)	
			$ (7,186.00)
Federal Income Tax	Taxes Due (7% EFF RT)	$ (6,230.00)	
			$ (6,230.00)
Property Taxes	2.5% of Home Value	$ (4,000.00)	
			$ (4,000.00)
Debt Payments	Payments on Mortgage	$ (8,521.68)	
	Car Note	$ (3,976.99)	
	Student Loans	$ (4,769.40)	
			$(17,268.07)
Living Expenses	General Expenses	$ (24,000.00)	
	Homeowners Insurance	$ (1,689.96)	
	Auto Insurance	$ (1,536.00)	
	Healthcare Premiums	$ (3,000.00)	
	Life Insurance Premiums	$ (2,544.00)	
	Optional LT Disability Coverage	$ (1,200.00)	
	Optional ST Disability Coverage	$ (480.00)	
	Catastrophic Health	$ (600.00)	
			$(35,049.96)
Voluntary Savings	401(k) Contribution	$ (3,300.00)	
	Roth Contributions	$ (10,000.00)	
			$(13,300.00)
Expenses			$(83,034.03)
Net Available Cash Flow			$5,965.97
Monthly			$497.16

After locking in payments, Elizabeth and James can consider utilizing monthly excess cash flow. As long as Elizabeth continues to work the Blacks will have ample resources to meet their current standard of living and debt obligations. Once she leaves the workforce the family becomes more susceptible to financial strains and cash flow shocks. Building an adequate savings fund can help smooth out months when James or Elizabeth earn less part-time income.

One month of debt payments and living expenses including risk management recommendations is slightly under $4,400. James and Elizabeth will have around $4,800 in their checking and savings accounts after refinancing. This cash would sustain them for one month if they both lost their jobs. Increasing liquid assets to a minimum of $13,000 would give James and Elizabeth 3 months of living expenses.

Three months provides a cushion to hunt for new jobs and maintain current level of living. A written case study limits gauging James and Elizabeth's propensity to endure risk. If they were risk averse a larger emergency fund should be considered, if the clients were risk tolerant a 3-month fund would be appropriate.

A 3-month emergency fund will need to be at least $13,200. James and Elizabeth have $4,800 in liquid assets today and can save $500 per month.

How many months will they need to save to accumulate an emergency fund?

Set Calculator to Beginning

PV = $4,800

FV = $–13,200

PMT = –$500

I = (2.50%/12) (The 12-month LIBOR rate can be used as a gauge for savings account and money market interest rates)

N = 16.21

If James and Elizabeth save $500 per month they will be able to fill an emergency fund in a year and a half. Students may have a different philosophy towards debt management and savings, and are encouraged to provide case solutions with alternative recommendations.

IMPLEMENTATION CONSIDERATIONS

implementation

Financial planner business models vary and have different expectations on client responsibilities. Comprehensive financial planning firms may offer multiple business lines; investment, life insurance, home and property insurance and tax services. Other firms have a single purpose such as asset management or investment services. Comprehensive or single purpose, most planners are limited in products and services they can implement for clients by professional competency, registration, or licensing issues.

Financial planners may face challenges with implementation in comprehensive planning situations:

- Planners must determine what areas of planning they are competent to perform and which areas require other team members. Competency can be defined by business model or limitations set on a broker-dealer or registered investment adviser level.

- Advisers must discern how to work with other team members and experts in the best interest of the client. The planner needs to consider if the client's current trusted advisers are able and willing to implement recommendations. If the adviser recommends new team members due diligence should be performed to ensure every team member is working together towards client goals.

- Financial professionals need to set service level expectations. Planners will generally help clients with account applications, but what about buying a new car or refinancing a house? Will health care insurance be evaluated? Does the planner help clients with employer rollover paperwork? Client expectations and limitations help establish relationship boundaries and can limit adviser liability.

Implementation Chart for James and Elizabeth Black

Create an implementation schedule between planner and client. For James and Elizabeth an implementation list would include home refinancing, insurance acquisition, and building savings. Students should delineate what items are responsibilities of Elizabeth and James and which items will be handled by the financial planner. Some implementation items will require both the client and adviser to participate. The implementation schedule developed below assumes a moderate level of adviser participation, but does not rely on the adviser for all implementation decisions. Students may choose to develop more detailed or more involved implementation plans.

Implementation	Description	Responsibility
Purchase life insurance for James	Fill out applications, arrange any medical exams, collect first month's premium payment	Adviser
Purchase life insurance for James	Attend medical exam, provide checking information for direct premium payments, finalize contingent beneficiaries	James
Purchase life insurance for Elizabeth	Fill out applications, arrange any medical exams, collect first month's premium payment	Adviser
Purchase life insurance for Elizabeth	Attend medical exam, provide checking information for direct premium payments, finalize contingent beneficiaries	Elizabeth
Purchase catastrophic health coverage for both James & Elizabeth	Review policy terms, confirm coverage, assist with applications	Adviser
Purchase catastrophic health coverage for both James & Elizabeth	Submit to underwriting as needed, pay first month's premium, sign all applications	James & Elizabeth
Purchase group short-term disability coverage for James & Elizabeth	Sign up for short-term disability policy through employers. Revisit policy when emergency fund exceeds $4,000.	James & Elizabeth
Purchase individual disability coverage for Elizabeth	Submit to underwriting as needed, pay first month's premium, sign all applications	James & Elizabeth
Purchase supplemental disability coverage for James	Submit to underwriting as needed, pay first month's premium, sign all applications	James & Elizabeth
Refinance mortgage	Meet with banker to discuss refinancing options and interest rates. Pending confirmation of case facts, proceed with refinancing process.	James & Elizabeth
Estate planning	Arrange a meeting with a trusted estate planning attorney, give James and Elizabeth a template to fill out listing potential guardians, beneficiaries, trustees and power of attorney.	Adviser
Estate planning	Fill out template paperwork, meet with attorney to draft planning documents	James & Elizabeth
Work towards a health lifestyle	Meet with a physician to discuss healthier lifestyle options and consider local health clubs.	James & Elizabeth
Build emergency savings	Save excess dollars every month with a goal of $500. Visit with local bank about savings and checking account options.	James & Elizabeth

Discussion of Product Selection

This case had product costs predetermined in the case study. In practice, planners shop marketplaces to find appropriate products for their clients. Product selections are influenced by market conditions and dynamics and easily become dated in case studies. Advisers should seek out multiple insurers when appropriate to cost coverage. Auto and homeowners insurance will vary dramatically across the 20–30 age group. Additionally some policies may more easily incorporate pricing for a dangerous animal than others. The Roth IRA accounts need to be analyzed in more depth. While the Blacks have a family tie to their broker, those resources and assets may be better used in the development of another goal.

FOLLOW-UP AND MONITORING

Financial planners must develop a follow up schedule with their clients. Plans are generally revisited on an annual basis, but more often as circumstances may dictate. Elizabeth and James are a young couple and will have challenges ahead. This plan should be updated on an annual basis, possibly more frequently when they are expecting children.

Students are encouraged to utilize the outline and methodology introduced in this case towards live clients, especially young couples. As Elizabeth and James progress through the lifecycle process, their goals and needs will change. These changes are best addressed by monitoring the client's situation, periodically evaluating their insurance and investments.

ADVANCED PLANNING APPLICATIONS FOR ELIZABETH AND JAMES

As students complete their cases for Elizabeth and James; some additional financial planning considerations should be discussed. Fundamentally, this case revolved around giving James and Elizabeth a "check up"; encourage them to continue saving, but the proper insurance, have wills and trusts developed and keep their property casualty insurance up to date. This case presents traditional financial planning challenges facing clients early in their career and marriage.

Modeling survivor needs with an outline method forces students to use static return estimates. In this situation, we assumed a long term rate of return net of taxes to be 6.00 percent and inflation 3.25 percent. Utilizing Monte Carlo software might allow for a more robust analysis of survivor needs. Additionally, students might utilize a more sophisticated asset allocation for the Blacks, perhaps creating a more aggressive portfolio that trends to be more conservative over time. The maxim generally holds; young couples with children need more life insurance for survivor needs protection than couples with older children.

Retirement planning for 25 year old clients is extremely vague. Younger clients rarely have an accurate image of what their long term earnings will be, spending will be or what life challenges may come their way. Advisers working with younger clients should stress that saving today opens more options for tomorrow. A simple time value of money calculation captures the cost of waiting to save for retirement. Assume a 25 year old client saves $5,000 annually today until their age 65. At an 8.00 percent interest rate; the client will have slightly under 1.4 Million ($1,398,905). The same client who waits until 35 to begin saving will need to sock away more than twice that amount annually ($11,434) in order to have the same amount set aside at retirement. Younger clients have costs, pressures and stress on their money, advisers encouraging them to save for retirement, even without concrete goals, open more opportunities for the client later in life.

CHAPTER REVIEW

Key Terms and Concepts

resource allocation	lump sum needs
working with newly married clients	life insurance needs
compensation models	health insurance
financial planning software	disability insurance
life expectancy	long term care
health concerns	auto insurance
cash flow statement	retirement planning
effective tax rate	investment planning
solvency ratio	tax planning
life insurance modeling	implementation

Review Questions

These questions are intended to help students answer questions about case studies, goals and assumptions. Answers to these questions can be found in the study supplement.

1. When might newly married clients need separate representation from financial advisers? When should newly married clients use the same financial adviser? [3]

2. How does goal based financial planning software differ from cash flow based software? [1]

3. What are some potential hazards of utilizing unassociated life insurance illustrations with financial planning software? [1]

4. Why is a goal that requires resource allocation more complicated to analyze than a goal to review an insurance policy? [2]

5. How do credit scores impact the financial analysis of a case study? [2]

6. Assume your client considers borrowing $300,000 to buy a home. What would their monthly payments be on a 30 year loan? On a 20 year note? Assume a 6.0 percent interest rate. [1]

7. Why should financial adviser outline cases before entering information into financial planning software? [1]

8. Assume a client wants to retire on $50,000 in today's dollars. They are 40 today and plan on retiring at 60, making their first portfolio withdrawal on their 60th birthday. The client assumes an inflation rate of 4.0 percent, and a market rate of return of 7.0 percent annually. They estimate a life expectancy of 90. How much does the client need to save annually, starting today, to meet this goal? [1]

9. Find the present value of cash needed to generate annuity payments of $10,000, beginning at the end of the year. Assume the payments inflate at 6.0 percent annually and the client can invest and earn a 10 percent annual market rate. [1]

10. What are some risks associated with health and lifestyle for young clients? What are some strategies advisers can employ to help clients manage health risks? [3]

11. What are some drawbacks to dying without a valid will? What are the key documents a young couple should consider drafting? [3]

12. What are arguments for and against using an effective tax rate when working with a young couple? [3]

13. Why do a standard poodle and American bulldog (Pitbull) present problems for clients? What steps can the clients take to mitigate personal risks? [2]

14. What are common elements of lump sum insurance needs? [2]

15. What are common elements when calculating cash flow insurance needs? [2]

Learning Objectives

An understanding of the material in this chapter should enable the student to

1. Review planning for the younger client.
2. Discuss home buying and financing alternatives.
3. Apply time-value-of-money calculations.

Comprehensive financial planning for a client without a significant asset base is more difficult than it appears. In most of these cases there is little discretionary cash, and not all personal and financial objectives can be pursued at one time. In almost every instance there will be hard choices for the client to make, particularly in regard to the priority of objectives to be pursued given the available resources. The financial planner must be especially sensitive to the client's concerns and intentions to assist the client in setting realistic and achievable goals as well as in establishing priorities.

This case study has similar elements to the previous one, but introduces students to a more advanced discussion of home ownership. This case also focuses on home purchase decisions and mortgage financing.

planning for young couples
Planning for those with few assets may be necessary for persons other than young couples. The concerns and objectives of these different clients will necessarily be different, and the planning recommendations will be markedly different. Despite differing concerns and objectives, the problems of asset allocation to achieve client objectives are generally similar. All planning is a process concerning the allocation of scarce resources. Few, if any, clients have sufficient resources to pursue all their objectives at one time, but the greater the resources, the fewer the objectives that must be deferred. The converse is also true: the fewer the resources, the greater the number of objectives that must be deferred, in whole or in part, until resources are available.

Students should note that this case study is presented with a different focus than the previous one they encountered. This style of case study encourages students to create a master outline, design an initial cash flow statement and then explore additional client goals and strategies. Building a solid and strong initial cash flow statement will allow students to build their plan around a strong foundation. Review the cash flow statement using a spreadsheet program, and after solving the case manually utilize financial planning software for additional perspective.

CASE NARRATIVE

Dick Johnson is now 26 years old and Jane is 25. They have been married for 4 years. Dick completed college just before their wedding, and Jane completed her last year of college after their marriage.

Jane is an assistant manager for a major hotel chain and earns approximately $35,000 per year. Dick is a new-to-the-industry paralegal and earns $30,000 annually. They both expect annual salary increases of at least 5 percent through their working careers.

They live in a comfortable but not luxurious two-bedroom apartment for which they pay $800 per month in rent plus utilities. Since Jane recently had to have a new car, they purchased a small sedan for $10,700 last November, financing $9,000 at 6 percent for 4 years. They estimate that the car is now worth about $8,600 and they owe $8,800 on the note. Dick's car, which is 3 years old and paid for, is presently worth approximately $4,000 in Dick's estimation.

Shortly after they were married, Dick and Jane bought furniture, which is now fully paid for. No major appliance purchases were necessary, since the apartment supplied these items. The Johnsons estimate the replacement value of their household furnishings at $14,000.

Jane borrowed $4,000 under the government-guaranteed student loan program to help her complete her undergraduate education. The deferred subsidized Stafford loans were made at a 9 percent simple interest rate and became payable over a period of 10 years the year following her graduation. Jane currently owes $3,150 on her student loan. As is common with loans of this type, no interest accrued until repayment began.

Note

Quite often case studies state interest rates or assumptions that may be slightly outside current market conventions. These types of case studies encourage the student to think outside of the box and plan for future economic or political changes. As always, students are encouraged to adjust rates and assumptions in their solutions to be more in line with current political and economic conditions.

Dick and Jane have saved almost $16,000 since their marriage. These savings are presently invested in a money market fund that has earned a high of 7 percent and a low of 3 percent over the past 3 years. Its annualized yield for last year was approximately 4 percent. In addition to their money market funds, they have approximately $4,500 in a joint checking account and $24,000 available in a savings account. The savings account earned $623 of interest last year.

They feel their next investment should be a house and wonder if they can afford a mortgage. They are also concerned about how to support their lifestyle when they start having children if either Dick or Jane stays home with their child(ren), particularly if they have purchased a home by then.

Both like the idea of owning a house. They are aware of the escalation in prices for houses over the last decade and feel that they should invest in a house now. However, they are also concerned about the debt involved in buying a house. Jane's upbringing instilled in her a distrust of owing money, a practice her father still preaches. She recognizes that the purchase of a home is usually a young person's or a young couple's first significant investment but has a difficult time overcoming her fear of indebtedness. After looking at houses for some time, Dick and Jane are most attracted to those in the $90,000 to $120,000 range but wonder if they will be able to afford a house of this price.

Dick and Jane realize they must give due consideration to their long-term financial well being by owning more than a home and money market accounts. However, they do not have any investment experience. Each grew up in a family of modest means, and neither studied the subject of investments in college. Jane was an English major and Dick majored in history/political science. Since they feel they are working hard to accumulate money, at this time they are apprehensive about placing their savings at any great degree of risk and describe themselves as risk averse. They have furnished the following information about their annual expenditures:

Table 4-1 Estimate of Johnsons' Current Annual Expenditures and Anticipated Annual Increase		
Estimate of Annual Expenditures		**Anticipated Annual Increase in Next 3–5 Years**
Food	$4,800	4%
Rent	9,600	5
Utility/phone	2,100	6
Car payment	2,383	0
Clothing	1,800	4
Student loans	608	0
Entertainment	1,500	6
Auto insurance	800	8
Gas, oil, repair (automobile)	600	6
Medical insurance (Dick)	240	8
Medical and dental care	1,100	8
Tenant's insurance	250	8
Charitable contributions	200	5
Savings	2,000	0
Total	$27,981	Blended Inflation Rate 4.27%

Dick and Jane would like to start their family during the next 2 or 3 years. They would like to have at least two children and would not object to having as many as four. Both are from large families and enjoyed warm family relationships. However, they are concerned about whether they will be able to afford children and give them more than just the basic necessities, a fact they feel will probably keep their family smaller than if they had greater resources.

At present Dick's and Jane's parents are all living. In fact, both families still have younger children at home. Their family backgrounds are economically modest, and they receive no continuing support from their families, nor does either expect a significant inheritance from his or her parents. Their families have occasionally helped them with small gifts of cash, some of which have been used to purchase furniture and some of which they have saved.

Neither Dick nor Jane has any health problems, but an investigation into the health of their parents reveals that Dick's mother has severe allergies that have been life threatening on occasion. Both Dick and Jane are insurable and would qualify for "preferred" status through underwriting. While they do not anticipate any significant assistance or inheritances from their parents, neither Dick nor Jane can foresee the necessity of assisting them financially at the present time. They do recognize, however, that such a possibility exists as their parents grow older.

The Johnsons have never seen a lawyer about estate planning. Neither has a will. Jane has named Dick the beneficiary of her group life insurance, and she has named her estate the beneficiary of her pension plan proceeds. Dick has named his estate the beneficiary of his group life insurance policy and of his profit-sharing plan. Both Dick and Jane say they would like to plan to preserve the lifestyle of the other should one predecease. If there are children, they would want them provided for. Both say they would expect the other to remarry if one died.

Dick and Jane have medical insurance and some disability insurance through their respective employers. They do not carry additional life insurance or additional medical or disability protection.

Jane's employee benefit plan is very generous and includes the following coverages:

- *Group term life insurance equal to 2½ times salary*. Dick is the beneficiary.

- *Short-term disability benefits under a salary continuation plan*. During the first 4 months of disability her salary will be continued in full; during the next 2 months 50 percent of her salary will be paid. However, after 6 years of service, her salary will be continued in full for the entire 6 months.

- *Group long-term disability insurance*. Benefits commence after a 6-month elimination period and are paid until age 65 as long as Jane is unable to perform her regular job. Benefits are equal to 60 percent of salary reduced by her primary disability benefit under Social Security.

- *Group comprehensive major medical insurance*. Unlimited medical benefits are provided subject to a $100 calendar-year deductible and copayments of 20 percent for most medical expenses (some expenses are covered in full). The plan contains a stop-loss limit so that all expenses are paid in full for the remainder of a calendar year in which Jane has had out-of-pocket medical expenses of $2,000.

- *Group scheduled dental insurance*. The maximum annual benefit is limited to $1,000.

- *Maternity leave*. Jane will be paid for up to 4 months' maternity leave.

Jane is a participant in a defined-benefit pension plan, under which she can retire at age 65 with benefits equal to 70 percent of the average of her high 3 of the last 5 years' salary.

All Jane's plans are noncontributory for the employee's coverage. Dependent coverage is available for the medical and dental coverage. The cost is $65 per month, which reflects a 50 percent employer contribution. Jane has not elected dependent coverage, but she and Dick have considered the possibility because of his more limited coverage.

Dick's employer provides him with the following benefits, all of which are noncontributory except the major medical coverage, which costs him $20 per month:

- *group term life insurance in a flat amount of $10,000.* His estate is the beneficiary.

- *10 days of sick pay annually at full pay.* Unused sick pay can be carried over, up to a maximum of 100 days. Currently Dick has 9 unused days from previous years.

- *group major medical insurance.* A lifetime benefit of $250,000 is provided subject to a $200 annual deductible and 20 percent copayments for all expenses. There is no stop-loss limit.

INSTRUCTIONS

After considering all these facts, prepare a working outline and a financial plan for the Johnsons. After you have completed your answers, you can compare them with the suggested working outline and the completed financial plan for the Johnsons that follow.

WORKING OUTLINE [SUGGESTED SOLUTION]

1. Clients' objectives

    a. For lifetime planning

        (1) Purchase an affordable first home.

        (2) Plan for Jane or Dick to stay home if possible after children are born.

    b. For dispositions at death: provide for the orderly continuation of lifestyle of a surviving spouse and children, if any.

2. Personal planning

a. Tax planning

   (1) Present situation

   (2) Purchasing a house with tax-deductible dollars

   (3) Tax implications of home ownership

   (4) Mortgage considerations

   (5) Other factors to consider when purchasing a home

   (6) Choosing the appropriate financing for the purchase of a residence

      (a) Creative financing

      (b) Conventional financing

      (c) Subsidized or guaranteed financing

      (d) Financing major appliances and fixtures with the house

      (e) Purchasing a house for rehabilitation

   (7) Financing recommendations

      (a) 15-year mortgage with balloon payment

      (b) Fully amortized 30-year mortgage

   (8) Extent to which purchase of a home will preclude Jane or Dick staying at home with children

   (9) Estate planning

b. Insurance planning

   (1) Disability income insurance

   (2) Medical insurance

   (3) Life insurance

   (4) Property and liability insurance

c. Investment planning

   (1) Purchasing a home

   (2) Emergency fund

   (3) Investable funds

   (4) Client characteristics

   (5) Recommendations

PERSONAL FINANCIAL PLAN FOR DICK AND JANE JOHNSON [SUGGESTED SOLUTION] CLIENTS' OBJECTIVES

1. For lifetime planning

    a. Purchase an affordable first home.

    b. Plan for Jane or Dick to stay home if possible after children are born.

2. For dispositions at death: provide for the orderly continuation of lifestyle of a surviving spouse and children, if any.

3. Start an investment program.

BASE CASE

Dick and Jane Johnson have provided you with an in depth perspective of their financial situation. The first step of preparing a base financial case is to restate assumptions and review them with the client. After restating assumptions, develop a cash flow and net worth statement. A primary goal of Dick and Jane is to buy a home, which will have significant property and income tax implications. Students should prepare tax projections for the Johnson family to model renting. The tax projections will be updated as the case progresses to show the impact of buying property. Using an effective tax rate is inappropriate when demonstrating the tax implications of a home purchase.

Tax rates, credits and exemptions are likely to change on an annual basis. Student answers may be different than the answer presented in the book, which utilizes the 2008 tax code. Students may also want to model Dick and Jane Johnson in a home state with state income tax. Either modeling scenario will enhance understanding of federal and state income tax projections.

Financial planners may not be tax accountants. In practice, the case would contain a disclaimer that tax projections should be reviewed by a Certified Public Accountant or other tax specialist and are not for use in a tax return or in an audited financial statement.

Assumptions

- The checking account balance is maintained at $4,500; the account is non-interest-bearing.

- Dick's and Jane's salaries are increased at 5 percent annually.

- Money market funds earn 4 percent interest annually.

- Investable cash earns 5.25 percent annually.

- Expenditures for food and clothing will increase annually at 4 percent.

- Expenditures for rent and charitable contributions will increase 5 percent annually.

- Expenditures for utilities, telephone, entertainment, and automobile gas and repairs will increase 6 percent annually.

- Expenditures for medical insurance and other medical care, as well as both automobile and tenant's insurance, will increase by 8 percent annually.

- Decreases in value of furniture have been ignored.

- Automobiles decrease in value at a rate of 15 percent annually.

- The inflation rate for taxes is 3.5 percent annually.

Income Tax Projection for Dick and Jane Johnson

Table 4-2 Tax Projections for Dick and Jane Johnson			
Earned Income			
Jane's Salary	$30,000.00		
Dick's Salary	$35,000.00		
		$65,000.00	
Interest & Dividends			
Money Market Fund	$640.00		
Cash	$623.00		
		$1,263.00	
Adjusted Gross Income			**$66,263.00**
Potential Itemized Deductions			
4% State Income Tax (on AGI)	$2,650.52		
Charitable Contributions	$200.00		
Property Tax	$0.00		
Mortgage Interest	$0.00		
		$2,850.52	
Current Year MFJ Standard Deduction		$10,900.00	
Current Year 2 Personal Exemptions		$7,000.00	
Total Deductions and Exemptions			$17,900.00
Taxable Income			**$48,363.00**
Current Year Projected Income Tax Due			$6,451.95
Highest Marginal Rate			15%

When preparing cash flow, income tax, or net worth statements, phantom columns can help clients understand future recommendations. In this situation, the phantom column shows $0.00 for property tax and $0.00 for mortgage interest. In later case iterations, values will be generated from a home purchase. Dick and Jane will be able to visualize changes and future purchases more effectively by comparing similar statements than they would comparing statements with different rows.

Balance Sheet for Dick and Jane Johnson

Table 4-3 Balance Sheet for Dick and Jane Johnson		
Assets		
Home	$0	
Checking Account	$4,500	
Money Market	$16,000	
Savings Account	$24,000	
Dick's Car	$3,400	
Jane's Car	$9,000	
Furniture	$14,000	
Total Assets		$70,900
Liabilities		
Jane's Student Loan	$3,150	
Jane's Car Loan	$8,800	
Total Liabilities		$11,950
Net Worth		$58,950

Cash Flow Statement for Dick and Jane Johnson

Table 4-4 Cash Flow for Dick and Jane Johnson			
Income			
Jane's Salary	$ 30,000.00		
Dick's Salary	$ 35,000.00		
		$ 65,000.00	
Interest & Dividends	$ 1,263.00		
		$ 1,263.00	
Gross Income			**$ 66,263.00**
Expenses			
Payroll Taxes			
Soc. Sec. on Wages	$ (4,030.00)		
Medicare on Wages	$ (942.50)		
		$ (4,972.50)	
Federal Income Tax			
From Tax Schedule	$ (6,451.90)		
		$ (6,451.90)	
State Income Taxes			
4% of AGI	$ (2,650.52)		
		$ (2,650.52)	
Property Taxes			
2.5% of Home Value	$ —		
		$ —	
Debt Payments			
Payments on Mortgage	$ —		
Car Note	$ (2,383.00)		
Student Loans	$ (608.00)		
		$ (2,991.00)	
Other Planned Expenses			
Rent	$ (9,600.00)		
Tenant Insurance	$ (250.00)		
Auto Costs	$ (1,400.00)		
Charitable Giving	$ (200.00)		
Medical Costs	$ (1,340.00)		
Other Expenses	$ (10,200.00)		
		$(22,990.00)	
Voluntary Savings			
Planned Savings	$ (2,000.00)		
IRA Savings	$ —		
		$ (2,000.00)	
Expenses			**$(42,055.92)**
Net Available Cash Flow			$24,207.08
Monthly Available Cash Flow			$ 2,017.26

PERSONAL PLANNING: INCOME TAXES

Present Situation

Dick and Jane are 26 and 25 years old respectively and have been married for 4 years. Jane is an assistant manager for a major hotel chain and currently earns $35,000 a year. Dick is a paralegal earning $30,000 per year. They anticipate that their salaries will increase approximately 5 percent annually in the foreseeable future. At present they rent an apartment for $800 a month plus utilities. They feel that the apartment rent will increase at least 5 percent annually.

Their major assets are approximately $16,000 in a money market fund, about $24,000 of net investable cash flow, approximately $4,500 in a joint checking account, and their household furnishings that are fully paid for and whose replacement value they project at $14,000. The household furnishings do not include any major appliances since they are furnished with the apartment.

Their other major assets are two cars, one of which Jane purchased for $10,700 in November of last year. They made a $1,700 down payment and financed $9,000 at 6 percent for 4 years. They estimate its present value at $8,600. Dick's car, which is paid for, is 3 years old and is worth approximately $4,000.

The Johnsons' primary financial planning objectives at present are to ascertain whether they can realistically afford the purchase of a home and, if so, what would be the best way to accomplish their goal. One of their most pressing concerns is that it will probably require both their salaries to purchase and maintain a home, but there is the possibility, even the likelihood, that either Jane or Dick would prefer to stay home with their children. They would like to start their family within the next 2 years.

As already noted, since their marriage 4 years ago the Johnsons have accumulated approximately $16,000 in savings, presently invested in money market funds that are paying about 4 percent, and over $23,700 of investable cash flow moving forward. Other than the car loan their only significant liabilities are Jane's two government-guaranteed student loans totaling less than $4,000. The loans could easily be paid off completely out of current cash flow.

The tax, cash-flow, and net worth projections in the base case illustrate the Johnsons' financial position.

Tax Implications of Home Ownership

Clients such as the Johnsons who are contemplating the ownership of their first home often need information on the tax benefits of home ownership. All too frequently they view their mortgage and property tax payments as rent—that is, a personal expense without income tax ramifications. However, ownership of a primary or principal residence provides significant tax advantages, some of which also apply to the ownership of a second home.

Once clients decide that home ownership is desirable, then their concern should focus on its financial feasibility. A paramount consideration should be the advantage of leverage gained from financing and the beneficial effect the tax law accords home ownership.

Rarely does someone acquire a first (or subsequent) principal or secondary residence by paying the entire purchase price from savings. Rather, the down payment and the closing costs frequently consume much of the buyer's available assets, and borrowing the balance is the only feasible alternative.

Benefit of Leverage

Since home mortgages do not have an equity-kicker clause benefiting the lender, the full benefit of any increase in home prices accrues to the debtor/owner. Borrowing a portion of the acquisition price results in financial leverage that enables the homeowner to reap sizable returns on his or her equity in the home should its price rise. This gain realized on the amount invested (that is, on the equity in the property) exceeds the percentage increase in the property's market price. If the owner invests $20,000 and borrows $80,000 to acquire a $100,000 residence that then increases in net value (net of buying and selling expense) by 5 percent, or $5,000 ($100,000 × .05), the owner reaps a 25 percent gain ($5,000 & divide; $20,000) on the equity investment.

Tax Advantages

tax advantages of home ownership

Homeowners also benefit from various tax advantages found in the Internal Revenue Code. Some of the tax advantages associated with owning a home are the following:

- deductibility of interest paid on a home mortgage
- deductibility of state and local property taxes assessed on the home

- tax exemption of the realized gain when a principal residence is sold (subject to limitations discussed below)
- step up in basis for ownership interest of a deceased homeowner
- possible $8,000 first time home buyer tax credit or other local tax incentives

Deductibility of Interest Paid on a Home Mortgage

As a general rule, an individual who itemizes deductions in lieu of using the standard deduction may deduct against adjusted gross income the interest paid on the mortgage of their principal residence in the year when payment is made. Likewise, interest payments for a mortgage on a second home (a vacation home whose owner is the sole user) also qualify as an itemized deduction against adjusted gross income.

In addition, if at the time of the initial acquisition the buyer pays points (one point being one percent of the face amount of the loan) to the lender to facilitate granting the mortgage for either a primary or a second home, the points are deemed to be interest and are deductible. Exceptions to the general rule of deductibility of interest and points include:

- *a limit on the acquisition indebtedness that may be deducted as qualified residence interest.* For any tax period, the amount of qualified residence interest that may be deducted as acquisition indebtedness may not exceed the interest paid on a maximum of $1 million of home acquisition indebtedness (or $500,000 each for a married couple filing separate returns). The limit is the total indebtedness of both the primary and other qualified residences.

- *a limit on the home equity indebtedness interest that may be deducted as qualified residence interest.* For any tax period, the amount of qualified residence interest that may be deducted as home equity indebtedness (other than acquisition indebtedness) may not exceed the interest paid on the fair market value of the qualified residence less the amount of the property's acquisition indebtedness. Further, the maximum amount of home equity loan interest that may be deducted as qualified residence interest may not exceed the interest paid on a home equity loan of $100,000 ($50,000 in the case of separate returns by a married couple).

- *nondeductibility of points paid to refinance a qualified residence.* Although the dollar amount of any points paid to acquire the initial mortgage on a qualified residence is fully deductible in the year paid, the dollar amount of points paid to refinance existing indebtedness on a residence must be allocated ratably over the life of the new mortgage. Should the indebtedness be paid off prior to its full term, any points not so allocated are deductible at the time of payoff.

- *the manner in which the taxpayer uses the property.* The deductibility of interest applies only to properties that qualify as residences. For property to qualify as a residence in any given year the taxpayer (or a qualifying member of the taxpayer's family) must use it for personal purposes for a number of days exceeding the greater of 14 days or 10 percent of the days during the year that the property is rented at a fair rental. If the taxpayer (or a member of the taxpayer's family) uses the property during any part of any day that the unit was rented, that day is considered a personal use, not a rental, day.

For the taxpayer who uses the property as his or her principal place of business, the interest allocable to the portion of the dwelling used exclusively for business purposes is not deductible as acquisition or home equity interest. (If other requirements are met, it would qualify as a deductible business expense.)

Deductibility of State and Local Property Taxes

State and local property taxes generally qualify as a deduction in the year paid. Deductibility of taxes on a second home is restricted in a manner similar to limitations on interest deductibility.

Step Up in Basis at Death of Homeowner

A residence, like other assets owned by individuals, qualifies for a step up in basis upon the taxpayer's death. Thus any capital gain resulting from ownership of one or more qualified residences may escape income taxation.

The proportion of the residence owned by the deceased receives the step up in basis. When a residence is owned jointly with the spouse, the deceased (spouse) is assumed to own one-half. The surviving spouse will then own the property, with a basis in his or her hands equal to the sum of his or her original basis plus the stepped-up value transferred through the estate of the deceased spouse.

Note that the step up in basis provision provides no benefit for individuals or married couples whose home has not appreciated more than the exclusion amount allowed for personal residences as discussed above.

Keep in mind that this discussion focuses on the general rules concerning the deductibility of expenditures associated with home ownership and the income tax exclusion applicable to personal residence sales. Each of these elements must be examined for every client.

Tax Disadvantages

As detailed in the previous section, the Internal Revenue Code provides homeowners with numerous federal income tax advantages. But two major tax disadvantages exist. The tax code treats the personal residence(s) as it does other personal property when it is sold at a loss; that is, the loss is not deductible against any of the taxpayer's income to the extent it exceeds $3,000.

Another tax disadvantage occurs from the fact that not all state income tax laws treat the sale of residences in the same manner as the federal government. Some states permit rollover of capital gains and others do not. Some states allow a one-time exclusion of $250,000 of any realized gain for taxpayers aged 55 or older and others either do not have an exclusion or have a different dollar amount exclusion. The result of these differences requires the homeowner to keep two sets of financial records for determining the basis in the property for federal and state income tax purposes. This record keeping becomes more complex if the client changes his or her state of domicile.

NONTAX CONSIDERATIONS

nontax considerations of home ownership

Although the tax advantages of owning a personal residence are numerous, for many individuals nontax reasons are the primary consideration in determining whether to purchase a home:

- *privacy*. Most non-homeowners live in some form of multiple dwelling such as apartment houses or converted single family homes where common walls, ceilings, or floors do not guarantee privacy. (Some owner-occupied homes, such as townhouses and condominium apartments, have similar privacy constraints.)
- *security*. Owning one's residence, even if subject to a mortgage, can provide financial security as well as psychological benefits. Economic well-being is enhanced since a part of each payment decreases the homeowner's debt and increases the equity. There

is psychological security from the fact that the property belongs to its owner and that the law protects this ownership interest.

- *preference*. Many individuals realize benefits by making both the interior and exterior reflect their own tastes (within limits of zoning requirements). They also enjoy being able to make redecorating decisions themselves.

- *space*. Owner-occupied homes generally are larger than all but the most elegant rental units. The additional interior space, as well as the exterior grounds, enable individuals to develop and enjoy their lifestyle activities.

OTHER FACTORS TO CONSIDER WHEN PURCHASING A HOME

Young clients like the Johnsons who have not been homeowners need information in addition to tax factors in order to make an informed decision. Given Jane's job, it is quite likely that she will be transferred by the hotel chain during her career. Because of this possibility, the Johnsons should consider the potential salability of any home they purchase in the near future. (Note: Most hotel chains provide the hotel manager with an apartment in the hotel so that the person is available "around the clock" to cater to unexpected customer needs. This does not appear to be a factor the Johnsons must consider at this time.) Some features that affect the marketability of a residence are the following:

- *location*. According to real estate experts, "location, location, and location" are the three important variables in determining the value of a particular parcel of real estate. Particularly if resale at some not-too- distant time is highly likely, the location of residential property is especially important. A secluded home down a long country road or one that has a bridge over a stream could be difficult to sell. Location also includes the general ambiance of the community, the quality of its schools and other municipal services, the level of local taxes relative to other nearby communities, and its proximity to work, public transportation, and highway networks. These are some of the more important features that the Johnsons should consider when making their selection.

- *lifestyle features*. For ease of marketability, the home chosen should have appeal to a wide spectrum of potential buyers. Housing styles and consumer preferences change, and any home the Johnsons acquire should be within the mainstream of homebuyers' preferences. Likewise the property should have "eye" or "curb appeal," since prospective buyers' first impressions are highly important. Amenities of the property, such as decks and attractive gardens and shrubs as well as the interior design and rooms that most purchasers desire, also facilitate its resale.

CHOOSING APPROPRIATE FINANCING FOR PURCHASE OF A RESIDENCE

Creative Financing

mortgage financing
In seeking out a house to purchase, it may be advantageous for the Johnsons to consider various means of both conventional mortgages and creative financing. For example, home loans have traditionally been made with a down payment of 20 percent and the balance financed by a fixed-rate mortgage usually for a term of 20, 25, or 30 years. However, two changes have resulted in a rather major difference in the financing of residences.

1. The first change has been the securitization of home mortgages, which developed as more and more banks and savings and loans desire to sell their acquired home mortgages shortly after they are generated. The buyers of these mortgages want somewhat standardized terms, particularly regarding mortgage duration. Consequently in many parts of the country potential homebuyers can only choose between a 15-year and a 30-year mortgage. The mortgage crisis of 2008 may give pause to continued trends in the collateralizing and securing of mortgage notes. The collateralizing of mortgage notes is one of the primary culprits in bank irresponsibility in lending practices.

2. The second change is a result of changes in interest rates. During periods of high interest rates, various other types of mortgages have become available, such as variable- or adjustable-rate mortgages in which the interest rate either floats continuously or is set for a period of years and then reset based on a specified index at the time of the adjustment. This type of financing does not lock in a fixed-dollar amount for a house payment that a young couple can depend on for the entire term of the mortgage. Variable rate mortgages have become more common place over the past ten years, and continue to be an alternative lending mechanism.

To make variable-rate mortgages more appealing to consumers, some financial institutions have introduced the convertible residential mortgage. This vehicle typically permits the borrower on any one of the first 5 years' anniversary dates of the loan to convert the variable-rate mortgage to a fixed-rate mortgage at the then-prevailing rate for home mortgages (although it could be linked to some other measurable market interest rate). If not converted, the mortgage retains its variable-interest-rate feature. When mortgage rates are high, the borrower can probably expect to see lower market interest rates at one of those first 5 anniversary dates, thereby making conversion worthwhile. In addition, the typical interest-rate changes as specified in the contract on a year-to-year basis are often tied to the Treasury bill index and can have an annual cap of 2 percent and a life-of-the-loan cap of 6 percent.

A further attractive feature is that, as with other variable-rate mortgages, the initial interest charged the borrower is about 2 percent less than that for a fixed-rate mortgage at the time the contract is initiated. Finally, the cost of converting the mortgage is specified in the mortgage and is currently about $750, an amount far less than the cost of refinancing. Despite the attractiveness of this set of features, some disadvantages do exist. First, the interest rate will be slightly higher than that charged on a nonconvertible, variable-rate mortgage. In addition, interest rates could rise steadily over the 5 years, and the borrower would have to either convert to a higher fixed rate than was available at the inception of the mortgage or continue to face the uncertain variable-rate provisions for the duration of the mortgage unless refinanced. Also the maximum 6 percent increase in the rate over the life of the mortgage could significantly raise the monthly payment needed to amortize the loan, placing a heavy strain on the borrower's budget. Other drawbacks include conversion issues such as inadvertent nonexercise of the option or converting just before a significant decline in interest rates.

For these and many other reasons, specifically the inability to assure the level of payments required for retiring the mortgage indebtedness, variable- or adjustable-rate mortgages are not recommended for the Johnsons if there are other alternatives available. If these alternatives are not available, a variable- or adjustable-rate mortgage that has reasonable limits on interest-rate increases could be considered.

Some sellers of homes will either finance the entire purchase or take back a second mortgage at less than the market rate of interest. If a suitable property can be found, especially one with an assumable loan at an advantageous interest rate, and the seller is willing to take back a second mortgage for most or all of the remaining balance of the purchase price, this type of arrangement can result in a significantly less expensive interest rate and a net saving to the buyer. One disadvantage of this type of financing is that the term on the second mortgage is frequently short, usually no more than 5 to 7 years, requiring substantial cash outflows in the initial years of the home purchase. While this financing technique should not be ignored, any creative financing arrangement should be carefully explored in detail with a competent attorney prior to the signing of a purchase agreement.

Where possible, the typical home purchaser will reject the variable- or adjustable-rate mortgage, preferring to have the certainty of a fixed payment during the period of indebtedness. Lenders, on the other hand, do not like to be locked into a fixed-rate loan for a period as long as 25 or 30 years. One compromise some financial planners recommend is a 15-year, fully amortized loan. If the client can afford the higher monthly payments, this can be a viable approach. However, not all clients can afford the larger payments, and many who could might prefer not to make larger payments. Another alternative attracting some home-purchaser acceptance is the 15-year, fixed-rate mortgage with a predetermined balloon payment. The full amount of such a loan is not paid off during its term, and the borrower must seek refinancing some time before the end of the loan. This creates an uncertainty for the borrower as to the level of interest to be paid to refinance the balloon payment, thereby increasing the risk to the borrower. But since the lender accepts a slightly lower interest rate due to the shorter term of the loan, this form of loan arrangement can have attractive features for the borrower.

The first attractive feature of this type of mortgage arrangement is that the borrower does have the benefit of a fixed payment during the life of the loan. A second feature is that the interest rate is slightly lower because of the shorter duration. Third, the loan can be structured to result in a manageable monthly payment, perhaps only slightly higher than would be the case with a conventional 30-year loan. These factors will result in a significantly larger portion of the total indebtedness being paid off during the initial 15-year period. A fourth advantage is that the shorter structure meshes with the fact that the typical mortgage is paid off before 15 years because homeowners tend to either trade up to a larger home or move to another geographic location. Fifth, it could be possible to arrange terms permitting additional principal payments without penalty on an irregular basis that will result in a further reduction of the balloon payment due at the end of the 15-year term. Sixth, in this particular situation, 15 years from now Jane and Dick will most likely have received salary increases, thereby making refinancing of the amount required to meet the balloon payment feasible even if mortgage interest rates are significantly higher at that time.

Conventional Financing

Other more conventional avenues of financing are still generally available. These financing techniques include so-called conventional mortgages or 80, 90, and 95 percent loans. These loans, especially those of 90 and 95 percent of the purchase price, may require the payment of discount points by the buyer and the purchase of personal mortgage insurance for the protection of the lending institution. Paying these points to the lender results in a higher effective interest rate being charged to the borrower. Private mortgage insurance is required because lending institutions are fearful that borrowers with minimal equity invested in a residence might simply walk away from the property and forfeit the equity if it becomes difficult to meet the mortgage payments, requiring the lending institution to foreclose on the loan. Mortgage insurance is usually paid for as part of the monthly mortgage payment and insures lenders against a loss should they encounter a foreclosure situation and be unable to recover the balance of the mortgage amount.

Subsidized or Guaranteed Financing

A most attractive option, especially for the Johnsons and people who are similarly situated—that is, first-time homebuyers or homebuyers who have limited cash to invest in a home—exists in the form of subsidized or guaranteed mortgages, most familiarly known as VA (Veterans Administration) and FHA (Federal Housing Administration) loans. In addition, locally subsidized mortgage loans are periodically made available for first-time buyers in many areas.

The VA loan requires no down payment and is available to persons who have served in the U.S. military. Our facts indicate that neither Dick nor Jane has any military service, so a VA loan would not be an option. FHA loans, on the other hand, are available without regard to military service and require down payments of approximately 3 percent of the purchase price of the residence up to $25,000 and 5 percent for any remaining amount. There is a maximum amount available for FHA loans, as they are designed primarily to assist low- and middle-income families in acquiring homes. These maximum amounts are set by geographical region based on the prevailing cost of moderate-priced housing. Housing in the price range that the Johnsons are discussing would not exceed the maximum amount available under an FHA loan.

Since the financing arrangements for a home purchase can be so critical, the Johnsons should be aware that some sellers do not choose to offer their homes for sale under an FHA contract, because for purchases with FHA financing the seller is obligated to make necessary repairs to meet the FHA's standards before the loan will be approved. In selecting houses to consider for purchase, the Johnsons will want to alert their real estate agent or broker or both to the fact that they prefer FHA financing for their purchase. Of course it is possible to offer an FHA contract to a seller who has not indicated that he or she will accept FHA financing; however, this type of contract may be rejected purely on the basis of the additional costs to the seller. It is frequently more time efficient to ask the real estate agent or broker to ascertain whether FHA financing is available for a specific house.

A third form of government-subsidized mortgage that might be available to the Johnsons is state-or city-subsidized mortgage financing. Those qualifying for the subsidized program receive mortgages at 2 or 3 percentage points below the market rate. To qualify, the home buyer typically must be a resident of the state (or city), be a first-time purchaser, be willing to live in a renovated area, and have an income at or below a specified level. These mortgage loans are generally of the fixed-rate form and are of relatively long duration (25 to 30 years). Depending on where the Johnsons reside, they might qualify for this form of loan. The case study process limits discussion of locally subsidized loan programs.

Financing Major Appliances and Fixtures with the House

Another advantage in financing and furnishing a home can be obtained if items such as lighting fixtures, window treatments (curtains, drapes, and blinds), and particularly major appliances are being sold with the property. This is especially true of decorative items such as lighting fixtures and window treatments if the purchaser thinks they are attractive or, at the very least, would be content to live with them temporarily. Acquiring basic appliances such as a refrigerator, washer, dryer, and dishwasher can run well over $5,000. If these appliances are purchased as separate items from retail sources, there is a further cash drain at a time when most young couples with limited assets are least able to afford it. Even if the house is being offered for sale without appliances, it may be possible to negotiate with the owner so that for an additional amount included in the contract-offering price, all or certain specified appliances are left with the property. Any items such as appliances or window treatments that are included in the offering price must be specified in the offering contract.

If the owner agrees to include appliances in the purchase price, at the very least an immediate and significant cash outflow is avoided. If cash to pay for the appliances is lacking, retail finance charges that may be considerably higher than the effective mortgage rate can also be avoided. If the cost of the appliances is added to the purchase price of the residence, mortgage costs will increase by a nominal amount. While this approach may result in overall higher costs over the term of the mortgage, it prevents a severe cash outflow in the year the house is purchased. Furthermore, the cost of used appliances, even though relatively new and quite serviceable, is significantly less than the cost of new appliances of the same type. Such a plan may also save in delivery charges and time away from work, as delivery and installation are required on new purchases.

The same approach can be used for the purchase of lawnmowers, yard tools, and any other equipment necessary to maintain the residence if the seller is willing to negotiate on these items. If yard equipment or tools are not included in the mortgage amount as a part of the residential purchase package, a separate offer can be made to the seller to purchase these items, provided they are serviceable, for a nominal sum. Frequently these offers are accepted, especially if the seller is making a long-distance move and the transportation costs of packing and moving the items exceed their value or if the present owner is moving to a different type of residence, such as a move from a single-family house with a substantial yard into a condominium or an apartment.

In short, young couples such as the Johnsons should be alert to the most advantageous methods of financing, from a cash-flow standpoint, and the opportunity to acquire the appliances, decorative fixtures, and equipment necessary to furnish and maintain the property that they are purchasing. These items may be less than perfect for their purposes but can be replaced one by one as their usefulness deteriorates or their maintenance becomes a problem. This gives the first-time home purchaser the opportunity to spread the acquisition of new major appliances over a number of years rather than making all purchases at once.

PURCHASING A HOUSE FOR REHABILITATION

**purchasing an
older home**

An additional option for the Johnsons could be to look for a house that has not been maintained and/or redecorated and to rehabilitate that house into a residence they would enjoy. The Johnsons may also consider purchasing a home in the foreclosure process. This is particularly appealing to some first-time home purchasers, since these dwellings frequently lack the visual appeal to command a premium price and consequently can be acquired at considerable savings. It is not unusual for a house that sells in the $90,000 to $100,000 range to sell unrenovated in the high $60,000 to low $70,000 range or even less, depending on the renovation required.

Unless the purchaser has some experience in rehabilitating a house, the project can become quite a chore. In choosing a house for renovation, the first step is to select one whose space and basic layout meet the family's needs and whose appearance appeals to the family. Individuals undertaking a renovation project for the first time should probably restrict their purchase to buildings requiring only cosmetic changes, unless one or both of the purchasers are exceptionally adept at or interested in home repair. Even if the Johnsons are interested in rehabilitation, it would probably be best to avoid a total rehabilitation that includes a number of structural changes in the proposed dwelling. These types of changes can actually be quite expensive while appearing deceptively inexpensive to an amateur. For the present, if the Johnsons choose to consider the rehabilitation of an existing dwelling, they should limit their choices to those dwellings that are structurally sound, in which all major systems are functional, and that require only paint, wallpaper, and some redecorating.

To assure the structural soundness of an existing dwelling, the services of a building engineer should be utilized to provide a written report covering structural soundness and the soundness of all major systems (plumbing, heating, cooling, and electrical). Frequently the charges for an inspection report are surprisingly nominal, usually not exceeding a few hundred dollars, while the information provided can be invaluable.

There are generally two ways to accomplish a rehabilitation project. The first is to engage a contractor or decorator to make the necessary or desired improvements, and the second is to attempt many or most of the improvements oneself. For those with limited resources, the latter may be the only viable alternative. As long as the dwelling has been carefully chosen, and the purchaser understands the types of necessary improvements, it is not uncommon for the purchaser to successfully redo a dwelling to a great monetary advantage. Basic redecorating such as painting and wallpapering is achievable even by the inexperienced person if he or she is diligent and patient.

A person considering the purchase of a dwelling to rehabilitate should be aware that the availability of financing, specifically FHA financing, may be contingent on the building's being in a certain state of functional repair. Although the precise standards that the structure must meet to be eligible for financing can vary according to the area of the country, at a minimum the acquisition of FHA financing requires that the building is structurally sound and that all major systems are functional. Since these are the minimum criteria that have already been recommended in the event that a dwelling is purchased for rehabilitation, no problems should arise if the Johnsons decide to attempt a rehabilitation project. However, purchasing a home for rehabilitation is a major project involving a substantial time commitment. The Johnsons may want to consider this alternative but have not specifically expressed interest in this type of project.

Properties in foreclosure would require Dick and Jane to procure financing and purchase property in an auction format. If Dick and Jane were willing to wait a year or two before purchasing a home, they may be able to save enough to buy a foreclosed home with cash. Foreclosed home buying requires research, patience and an inventory of foreclosures in the area.

FINANCING RECOMMENDATIONS

The following analysis presumes the Johnsons purchase a $90,000 home with a down payment of $18,000.

Fully Amortized 30-Year Mortgage

Based largely on the economics of the financing, the 15-year mortgage is very attractive. However, the planner must consider the clients' total situation. The Johnsons are inexperienced in financial matters, and they describe themselves as having an aversion to any risk. The Johnsons should look into obtaining an FHA loan if possible. The uncertainty associated with the 15-year mortgage with balloon payment may not provide the requisite peace of mind for Dick and Jane. To relieve Jane's concern about debt, the mortgage terms should permit prepayment of principal without penalty on an irregular or regular basis. This permits excess cash to be channeled toward debt reduction. Therefore in light of the total situation the 30-year, fixed-rate, fully amortized mortgage is the recommended choice.

The following projections of the Johnsons' tax, cash-flow, and net worth positions represent an assumption that the Johnsons buy a residence for a purchase price of $90,000 this year and make a down payment of $18,000 on the purchase from savings and money market proceeds. The balance will be fully amortized financing at a fixed rate of 8.75 percent over a period of 30 years. These projections assume that the Johnsons are able to purchase major appliances with the property.

CASE II

$90,000 Residence Purchased

New Assumptions

1. The Johnsons purchase a house for $90,000, making an $18,000 down payment and financing the balance of $72,000 with an 8.75 percent fixed-rate mortgage with a term of 30 years.

2. Closing costs for the home purchase are 5 percent of the amount of the mortgage.

3. Property taxes on the home are 2.5 percent of the home value, or $2,250 and increase 5 percent annually.

4. The residence increases in value at 5 percent annually.

5. Homeowners insurance will replace the existing tenants insurance and will cost $900 a year.

6. Closing costs are paid out of cash flow.

Income Tax Projections with Home Purchase

Table 4-5 Income Tax Projections with Home Purchase			
Earned Income			
Jane's Salary	$30,000.00		
Dick's Salary	$35,000.00		
		$65,000.00	
Interest & Dividends			
Money Market Fund	$640.00		
Cash	$623.00		
		$1,263.00	
Adjusted Gross Income			$66,263.00
Potential Itemized Deductions			
4% State Income Tax (on AGI)	$2,650.52		
Charitable Contributions	$200.00		
Property Tax	$2,250.00		
Mortgage Interest	$6,279.57		
		$11,380.09	
Current Year MFJ Standard Deduction		$10,900.00	
Current Year 2 Personal Exemptions		$7,000.00	
Total Deductions and Exemptions			$18,380.09
Taxable Income			$47,882.91
Current Year Projected Income Tax Due			$6,379.94
Highest Marginal Rate			15%

Balance Sheet with Home Purchase Dick and Jane Johnson

Table 4-6 Dick and Jane Johnson Balance Sheet with Home Purchase		
Assets		
Home	$90,000	
Checking Account	$4,500	
Money Market	$16,000	
Savings Account	$6,000	
Dick's Car	$3,400	
Jane's Car	$9,000	
Furniture	$14,000	
Total Assets		**$142,900**
Liabilities		
Jane's Student Loan	$3,150	
Jane's Car Loan	$8,800	
Mortgage	$72,000	
Total Liabilities		**$83,950**
Net Worth		**$58,950**

Cash Flow with Home Purchase Dick and Jane Johnson

Table 4-7 Dick and Jane Johnson Cash Flow with Home Purchase			
Income			
Jane's Salary	$ 30,000.00		
Dick's Salary	$ 35,000.00		
		$ 65,000.00	
Interest & Dividends	$ 1,263.00		
		$ 1,263.00	
Gross Income			**$ 66,263.00**
Expenses			
Payroll Taxes			
Soc. Sec. on Wages	$ (4,030.00)		
Medicare on Wages	$ (942.50)		
		$ (4,972.50)	
Federal Income Tax			
From Tax Schedule	**$ (6,379.94)**		
		$ (6,379.94)	
State Income Taxes			
4% of AGI	$ (2,650.52)		
		$ (2,650.52)	
Property Taxes			
2.5% of Home Value	**$ (2,250.00)**		
		$ (2,250.00)	
Debt Payments			
Payments on Mortgage	**$ (6,707.09)**		
Car Note	$ (2,383.00)		
Student Loans	$ (608.00)		
		$ (9,698.09)	
Other Planned Expenses			
Rent	**$ —**		
Mortgage Insurance	**$ (900.00)**		
Auto Costs	$ (1,400.00)		
Charitable Giving	$ (200.00)		
Medical Costs	$ (1,340.00)		
Other Expenses	$ (10,200.00)		
		$(14,040.00)	
Voluntary Savings			
Planned Savings	$ (2,000.00)		
IRA Savings	$ —		
		$ (2,000.00)	
Expenses			**$(41,991.05)**
Net Available Cash Flow			**$24,271.95**
Monthly Available Cash Flow			**$ 2,022.66**

EFFECT OF HOME PURCHASE ON STAYING HOME WITH CHILD(REN)

having children   Dick and Jane will easily be able to purchase a home if they both remain in the work place. Their free cash flow remains fairly constant if they continue renting or purchase a home. Interest and dividends remain unchanged in the previous cash flow statement because Dick and Jane are considering purchasing a home later in the year, and they may receive interest and dividend income through the current period.

Both Dick and Jane believe that, if at all financially feasible, a parent should be the care-provider for their offspring until enrollment in primary school. They have discussed how best to achieve this result in light of their situation. Jane's career would probably come to a halt if she were to resign her position to care for their child(ren). In addition, she has a higher level of income than Dick does and has a bright career potential.

Dick, on the other hand, holds a position that has little upward potential. He lacks any interest in studying law but would like to prepare for a career teaching history and other social science courses at the high-school level. To achieve this goal he needs the requisite education courses at the college/university level since he did not take them in college. In addition, he would like to earn a master's degree in history. They have agreed that he should start obtaining the necessary education credits as soon as feasible. They expect that he will complete these courses, at night and on Saturdays, prior to the birth of their first child. At some later time, he can begin graduate studies for the master's degree.

Under the Family Medical Leave Act, both Dick and Jane would qualify for time away from their work to care for a newborn. This law specifies that employees are entitled to 12 weeks of unpaid leave for this purpose. Since they are employed by different firms, each is eligible for this leave during the 12-month period following the child's birth. The 12 weeks must be taken all at one time. During the leave, benefits must continue, but the employee is responsible for paying the cost of any contributory benefit plans. Usually a request for this parental leave must be submitted in writing a reasonable time in advance of the starting date.

In the Johnsons' case it would be possible for Jane to take a 3-month maternity leave while Dick continues to work. When Jane returns to work at the end of her leave, Dick could start his unpaid 12-week leave. Afterward he can begin studying for the master's degree, they hope with a tuition scholarship from the university. Dick's conversation with the university indicates a good possibility for the scholarship. He also learned that the university maintains a day-care center, at nominal charge, for the children of graduate students. This appeals to the Johnsons. Dick could arrange his schedule generally around Jane's, relying on the day care as a backup.

After completing the requisite education courses, Dick might be able to occasionally substitute-teach at nearby high schools. No estimate of his potential income from this source is made at this time. The Johnsons would also incur childcare expenses when Dick is teaching. When their child starts kindergarten, Dick will seek a full-time high-school teaching position.

On the following pages tax, cash-flow and net worth projections of the Johnsons' position have been run under two sets assumptions. The first set of projections assumed that Dick and Jane purchased a house in September and finance it with a mortgage of $72,000 at a fixed rate of 8.75 percent for 30 years. The second assumption models cash flow for with a child next year, and that Jane returns to work after her maternity leave and Dick stays home with the child. Dick will be covered under Jane's health insurance.

This model will show the impact of Dick leaving the workforce. Integrating the cash flow and balance sheets will help Dick and Jane project the amount of time Dick can dedicate to school and staying at home with a child.

CASE III

$90,000 Residence Purchased; Dick Leaves Work

New Assumptions

1. The Johnsons will have their first child next year, and Dick will not return to work until he exhausts savings and money market assets.
2. Living expenses will increase by $4,800 a year to represent additional costs towards a child.
3. Dick will be covered under Jane's health insurance at a cost of $780 annually, which will increase at 8 percent annually.
4. Planned savings will stop while Dick is in school.
5. Dick's nonscholarship education costs will be $3,000 annually. This costs includes books, commuting and supply expenses.

Cash Flow Statement Dick Stays at Home with a Child

Table 4-8 Cash Flow—Dick and Jane Johnson with a Child			
Income			
Jane's Salary	$ 30,000.00		
Dick's Salary	$ —		
		$ 30,000.00	
Interest & Dividends	**$ 820.00**		
		$ 820.00	
Gross Income			**$ 30,820.00**
Expenses			
Payroll Taxes			
Soc. Sec. on Wages	$ (1,860.00)		
Medicare on Wages	$ (435.00)		
		$ (2,295.00)	
Federal Income Tax			
From Tax Schedule	**$ (1,385.76)**		
		$ (1,385.76)	
State Income Taxes			
4% of AGI	**$ (1,232.80)**		
		$ (1,232.80)	
Property Taxes			
2.5% of Home Value	**$ (2,250.00)**		
		$ (3,482.80)	
Debt Payments			
Payments on Mortgage	**$ (6,707.09)**		
Car Note	**$ (2,383.00)**		
Student Loans	**$ (608.00)**		
		$ (9,698.09)	
Other Planned Expenses			
Rent	**$ —**		
Mortgage Insurance	**$ (900.00)**		
Auto Costs	$ (1,400.00)		
Charitable Giving	$ (200.00)		
Medical Costs	**$ (2,120.00)**		
Other Expenses	**$ (15,000.00)**		
College Expenses	**$ (3,000.00)**		
		$(22,620.00)	
Voluntary Savings			
Planned Savings	**$ —**		
IRA Savings	$ —		
		$ —	
Expenses			**$(40,714.45)**
Net Available Cash Flow			**$ (9,894.45)**
Monthly Available Cash Flow			**$ (824.54)**
Liquid Assets After Home Purchase			
Checking Account	**$4,500**		
Money Market	**$16,000**		
Savings Account	**$6,000**		
			$26,500.00

This case illustrates that Dick and Jane will be operating in a deficit of $824.54 a month while Dick is in college and out of the workforce. To solve how many years they can sustain this sort of spending, students can perform a time value of money calculation solving for number of periods. The following NPER will show how many years the Johnsons can sustain an income deficit.

Dick in college   NPER = Solve

PV = $26,500 (Liquid assets comprised of checking, money market and savings accounts)

FV = $0 (The amount Dick and Jane are willing to have their savings drop to. A minimum level of comfort. Students may want to increase this number to three or six months of living expenses. Dick may begin working a part time job or acquire student loans if his additional college grew in length in scope).

Int = (−0.238%) Effective Interest Rate assuming conservative blended inflation of 5.0% and liquid asset blended growth of 2.5%

NPER = 2.63. Dick will have between two and two and a half years to complete his education before he needs to reenter the workforce. Financial planners might advise Dick to complete more rapidly, or work part time around his wife's schedule Students are encouraged to solve this case study using different college costs, inflation measures and emergency fund limitations.

ESTATE PLANNING

Neither of the Johnsons has ever made a formal estate plan nor has either executed a valid will. As a result, if either dies, most of his or her property will pass under the statutory scheme for intestate succession. Under the local law of the state of Jefferson the surviving spouse of a couple with no children will take all the property as the heir-at-law. However, if the decedent had children, the surviving spouse generally takes a child's portion, but a surviving wife takes no less than one-fifth of the estate, regardless of the number of children. This rule applies regardless of whether the child is a minor or legally an adult. If either Dick or Jane died before executing a valid will but after the birth of their first child, intestate succession could result in a minor child or children taking an interest in property as well. Needless to say, this can be problematic in this case and should be avoided. The failure to execute a will also makes it impossible to leave property to friends or even family members who are outside the statutory scheme of intestate distribution. The Johnsons' present estate plan is inadequate in that it attempts to allow beneficiary designations and settlement options to substitute for appropriate estate planning documents such as wills. In addition, it utilizes the government's estate plan, intestate distribution, rather than a plan reflecting the Johnsons' wishes. Such a plan inherently lacks the flexibility that proper estate planning documents can provide.

The Johnsons do not need a complicated estate plan at this time. Although they do not have enough assets to be concerned with federal estate taxes, each should execute a will that clearly states his or her wishes concerning their property. This type of estate plan is very feasible in Jefferson because Jefferson is a state where the estate tax is based on the federal credit for state death taxes, and the emphasis on avoiding probate is much less important than in estate or inheritance tax states that impose these taxes only on probate property. This may simply mean that each leaves his or her property to the other, or that the bulk of property is left to the surviving spouse, but that certain items, such as family heirlooms or collectibles, are returned to a member of that particular family.

At present an estate plan in which both Dick and Jane have wills leaving the property each owns to the other would be sufficient for their needs. Each will should convey the testator's interest in his or her principal residence owned at the time of death to the surviving spouse, subject to the indebtedness secured thereby. This provision makes it clear that estate assets need not be unnecessarily depleted by paying off the entire mortgage indebtedness. Although it is recommended that the Johnsons take title to the home as joint tenants, this provision can still be included as a safeguard in the event of a different titling arrangement.

The Johnsons should make the bequests of their property to the spouse conditional on the survival of the spouse and provide that in the event the spouse fails to survive, the property will go into a trust for their living children, if any. If there are no living children and no surviving spouse, Dick and Jane may want to designate members of their families as ultimate beneficiaries under their wills.

One note of caution: A valid will is automatically revoked in Jefferson by the marriage or divorce of the testator or by the birth of a child that is not contemplated by the will. Therefore, the will should state that the term *children* is intended to include after-born children, to avoid an unintended revocation when a child is born.

In addition, the Johnsons' wills should name a guardian for the child(ren). Either one of their siblings or parents on whom they can agree could be appropriate. In addition, a trustee or guardian of the property left to each child needs to be identified.

As additional life insurance is acquired, consideration should be given to having a life insurance trust own the policies and be designated as the beneficiary. This method can provide flexibility in the distribution scheme as well as professional management for the assets.

PERSONAL PLANNING: INSURANCE

Disability Income Insurance

disability insurance

Since it appears that both Dick and Jane must continue to work to support their present lifestyle, an analysis of the disability insurance available to both of them through their employer plans indicates that there could be a material problem even though Jane has relatively generous benefits under a long-term disability plan.

In Jane's case short-term disability does not seem to be a problem as her salary would be continued in full for the first 4 months of any disability but would drop after 4 months to 50 percent of her salary for 60 days (unless she had completed 6 years of employment, in which case her salary would be continued in full for 6 months). The long-term disability plan would then begin to pay benefits, which are equal to 60 percent of her salary reduced by her primary disability benefit under Social Security, if applicable. Under the definition of disability provided in the description of Jane's long-term disability plan, it is not necessary that she qualify for a Social Security disability benefit in order to collect from her disability insurance plan. Nonetheless, full disability benefits under Jane's plan would result in a 40 percent reduction in her gross income, which could adversely affect the family's lifestyle.

Unfortunately many disability income insurers will not provide additional coverage when existing benefits are in excess of approximately 70 percent of current salary. Jane should be aware, however, that a good disability income plan is crucial to her family, particularly in view of Dick's mother's problems with allergies, which tend to be familial, although not necessarily hereditary. If she should wish to change employment, she should carefully review both the dollar amounts and the definition of disability in her prospective employer's plan. If the plan is materially less generous than the one under which she is presently covered, she should investigate the cost of supplementing the plan by the purchase of an individual policy of disability income protection.

While Dick remains employed, his benefits, on the other hand, are extremely limited. At best if Dick were to become seriously ill and had accumulated the maximum unused sick days permitted under his plan, he would have his salary continued for only about 3 months.

It is recommended that the Johnsons look into the cost-effectiveness of personal disability income insurance for Dick, especially when they purchase a residence or start a family. The personal disability insurance should have at least a 90-day elimination period so it will not be prohibitively expensive.

Medical Insurance

medical insurance   As indicated, Jane has a good comprehensive major medical insurance plan through her employer. Dick, on the other hand, has a much less liberal plan. Because it is possible for Dick to be covered as a dependent under Jane's subsidized insurance plan for a cost of $65 monthly ($45 more than the amount he is already paying), it is probably appropriate that Dick withdraw from participation in his group medical insurance plan and that Dick and Jane elect to cover him under her plan, which would provide him with additional benefits such as dental insurance, which he does not have under his present plan. He would also have unlimited lifetime medical benefits that are subject to a $100 calendar-year deductible as opposed to the $200-per-year deductible that he must now satisfy. In the case of a serious injury or illness, the fact that Jane's plan contains a stop-loss limit of $2,000 for any calendar year would be very important. A change to participation under Jane's plan should certainly be implemented no later than the time the Johnsons plan to begin their family. Also, they will need dependent coverage when their first child is born.

Life Insurance

life insurance   Jane's employer presently provides her with group term life insurance in the amount of $87,500 (2½ times her annual salary). Dick's employer provides him with group term life insurance in a flat amount of $10,000. Jane has named her estate the beneficiary of her group term life insurance, and Dick has named Jane the beneficiary of his group term life. It may be preferable for Jane to name Dick as the beneficiary of her group life insurance. Since the Johnsons' lifestyle depends on both their earnings, the life insurance amounts they presently have appear inadequate.

This will be especially true if the Johnsons go ahead with the purchase of a home and begin a family. The precise amounts of additional insurance necessary will depend on whether the Johnsons wish to replace Dick's or Jane's earnings from the income on life insurance proceeds should either die prematurely, or whether they agree that the survivor should plan to invade the principal amount of such proceeds. Perhaps the most conservative approach would be to ensure that enough life insurance protection is available so that either option is possible in the case of an untimely death of either breadwinner. In that event the total amount of death benefits necessary to replace Jane's salary, assuming an 8 percent return if the proceeds were invested, would be approximately $437,500. Of that amount Jane's employer already provides insurance of $87,500. Since the amount of insurance through Jane's group term life plan will increase as her salary increases, the additional amount of insurance necessary to assure total replacement of her salary at an 8 percent rate of earnings on the proceeds is approximately $350,000.

Dick's employer provides only $10,000 of group term insurance. Based on our facts, this amount will not increase during the term of his employment. In order to assure that Dick's salary will be replaced if the proceeds of life insurance are invested at an earning rate of 8 percent, Dick will need additional insurance in an amount of approximately $365,000.

It would be our recommendation that these amounts of insurance be applied for, obtained, and carried at least for the foreseeable future, as there are few other assets to provide income in the event of the untimely death of either spouse.

If the Johnsons' had exhibited any difficulty in disciplining themselves to save toward the cash reserves of 3 to 6 months' discretionary income necessary for an emergency fund, consideration could have been given to one of the interest-sensitive whole life policies that are available. While these policies do have higher premiums, these premium levels will create cash values within the policies that are available for use as emergency funds through policy loans. If they had exhibited a present need for premium flexibility, consideration of universal life (which offers both premium flexibility and the option to withdraw part of the cash value outright without the necessity for any loan or interest implications) would also have been appropriate.

The Johnsons, however, do not appear to have these problems or needs at this time. The type of insurance that best meets their current needs appears to be available in the form of a guaranteed annual renewable convertible term product. Because of their youth the cost of this coverage would be nominal and would allow them to continue to save personally for their emergency fund and to invest for funding other personal objectives.

Of course, the insurance needs of any client should be routinely and periodically reevaluated to assure that appropriate amounts and types of insurance are being carried.

Property and Liability Insurance

property insurance

The facts indicate that the Johnsons are carrying property and liability insurance on their apartment furnishings.

When a residence is purchased, the lending institution will normally require that the building be insured for damage arising from fire and probably other perils. This protection can be combined with protection against loss or damage to the contents of the house and with liability coverage by utilizing a homeowners policy. Many types of special endorsements can be obtained and may be necessary if there are valuable assets such as jewelry, furs, art, or other collectibles. However, our facts do not indicate that the Johnsons need these endorsements at present. If they are needed later, they can be added to the existing policy.

The Johnsons should, however, choose a liability limit that will adequately protect them. It would be difficult to recommend a liability limit of under $100,000, and the Johnsons should consider a limit as high as $300,000 to assure that they could withstand a high jury award in the event that they were sued.

Furthermore, the Johnsons might prefer to have greater liability protection than is provided by their auto and homeowner's policies. A $1 million umbrella policy with a deductible equal to the upper limit of their existing liability coverage could offer sufficient peace of mind for its relatively small cost.

PERSONAL PLANNING: INVESTMENT

Purchasing a Home

Without question the Johnsons' most important immediate investment will be the purchase of a home. As already indicated, that purchase should provide not only personal satisfaction but also a good return on their money should they decide to sell. In addition, if they live in their principal residence for 2 out of the 5 years prior to sale, the first $500,000 of gain is excluded from income tax.

For all these reasons the purchase of a house is one of the best investments that Dick and Jane can make at this time.

Emergency Fund

emergency funding
The Johnsons should also be aware that most investment advisers recommend that clients maintain a relatively liquid emergency fund ranging from 3 to 6 months of disposable income (gross income less taxes). Since the Johnsons presently have few other financial assets, they should attempt to keep their emergency fund at the high end of the range (at or near 6 months' disposable income). Moreover, given the purpose of this money, it should be retained in liquid investments that provide some annual income, although safety and virtually immediate access to the money have greater priority than does income. Their money market mutual fund (MMMF) meets these criteria. However, some of the investable cash funds could be used to purchase six separate $1,000 CDs with one maturing in 30 days, one in 60 days, and so on, with the sixth CD maturing in 180 days. When the first 30-day CD matures, it can then be rolled over into a 180-day CD. The same procedure can then be followed to convert each CD to a 180-day maturity schedule. Once the initial CDs have been rolled over, a continuous 6-month period rollover can be followed. This will provide the Johnsons with $1,000 cash available monthly and without penalty for emergency purposes, in addition to the ready access of the remainder of their emergency fund in the money market mutual fund. Because of its lack of full liquidity without penalty before maturity, the yield on the CDs could be one-fourth of one percent higher than the money market mutual fund. More important, the Johnsons will establish a relationship with a bank beyond their current checking account that can provide access to other financial services the depository institution offers. This relationship could be beneficial to their overall financial planning.

Investable Funds

Except for the planned purchase of a home the Johnsons have not yet developed any plans covering objectives to be satisfied through capital accumulation. With both Dick and Jane working, they will be able to save an additional $2,000 a month. Establishing some plans for the eventual investment of this money is important. If they do purchase a home and have their first child next year this amount will be less, yet the sooner they begin learning about and implementing a plan of investing, the more long-term financial success they will enjoy.

The Johnsons would also benefit from taking advantage of retirement savings accounts, either through their employers or using Individual Retirement Accounts.

CLIENT CHARACTERISTICS

As a guide to their investment planning the Johnsons must first recognize their own personal and financial situation. Elements to analyze for this activity include the following:

- *Level and stability of their income.* For a young married couple who are both employed, their family income level is above the national average. Both are employed in fields for which a strong demand exists in the economy. Neither has earnings from employment that would be subject to fluctuations because of being on a commission system. Based on these considerations, the Johnsons' income position permits consideration of investing for long-term capital appreciation.

- *Family situation.* Since they have no family responsibilities other than to themselves, this opportunity to begin building for their financial future should not be overlooked. If and when any children become part of their responsibilities, a revision of any currently developed accumulation plans will be necessary.

- *Net worth.* Although net worth is modest at this time, the projections clearly indicate growth over the next few years as a result of the annual saving from their income flows. These annual increments, virtually all in the form of cash, require effective investment planning.

- *Age.* The Johnsons' age, as well as their current level of income, favors an investment strategy focusing on capital appreciation. As a general rule or guide, younger investors should position their investment assets in those media characterized by higher degrees of risk for several reasons. First, they are more optimistic about both the future and their own individual prospects than are older individuals. Second, the opportunity to recoup losses, should that happen, exists due to the longer time period remaining before withdrawal from active employment. Third, over any period of time inflation erodes the buying power of dollars invested unless the return on investments exceeds the inflation rate. These needed higher returns are associated with higher-risk investments. As long as the accumulation objective sought does not require a specific sum of money within a short period of time, as is the situation with Dick and Jane, the desirability of investments with long-term appreciation and correspondingly higher risk seems appropriate.

- *Experience.* Based on the facts of this case Dick and Jane have no investment experience. Lacking any experience in investment management and/or analysis, they must initially limit their investment activities to those media not requiring constant monitoring, care, and on-the-spot decision making.

- *Attitudes toward risk.* Dick and Jane stated that they are risk averse at this time. For this reason any recommendations for use of their investable cash flow must be relatively conservative in nature.

The Johnsons' current personal and financial situation indicates that they are young, have no financial responsibilities, have a good, stable income from employment, and are rapidly increasing their net worth. These are all factors that, when used as a prelude to making any investment recommendations, suggest investments focusing on long-term appreciation with some degree of risk. On the other hand, their lack of experience and their risk propensities suggest a more conservative approach.

RECOMMENDATIONS

investment recommendations

The real growth in their investable income will occur 2 or 3 years from now. These next 2 or 3 years should be a time when the Johnsons obtain some experience with modest investment activities and reexamine their risk tolerances and investment objectives.

The Johnsons should embark on a relatively conservative investment strategy. Using mutual funds enables them to achieve diversification of their portfolio to minimize business and financial risks, obtain professional management, and provide the convenience of either adding to or liquidating their holdings. The liquidation aspect is important should they be unable to live with the risk of fluctuating values of the portfolio. To achieve a relatively conservative portfolio and still provide some growth potential, they could place their investable cash flow in a family of funds divided as follows:

- *50 percent into a balanced fund.* These funds spread their portfolio among bonds, common stocks, and preferred stocks. The objectives of balanced funds, in order of priority, are to preserve capital, to generate current income, and to obtain capital gains. Hence they are the most conservative of all funds that invest in common stocks. Their performance over the last 10 years suggests a compound annual return of approximately 10 percent. These funds are of two types. The first invests about 70 percent in common stocks, with the remainder in bonds. The second type reverses the allocation and has about 30 percent in common stock.

- *40 percent in an index fund* (an exchange-traded fund or passive mutual fund). These funds own a portfolio that replicates a broad-based market index, such as the Standard & Poor's 500. Although this type of fund has more risk than the balanced fund described above, its risk equals that of the market, and its return exceeds that of the balanced fund. The compound annual return, based on past data, is around 11 percent.

- *10 percent in a growth common stock fund.* This could have the greatest risk to the Johnsons since these funds are more aggressive, having a primary objective of growth, and invest in companies that continually reinvest their earnings in research and development. The stocks held in their portfolios will have minimum dividend income. The compound annual returns over the last 10 years for a typical fund, although not the most aggressive, are about 14 percent.

The experience with this modest and conservative investment plan will provide the Johnsons with the opportunity to assess their risk propensity, gain more personal knowledge of investments, and finally earn a return higher than they are currently earning on their disposable cash.

CHAPTER REVIEW

Key Terms and Concepts

planning for young couples	Dick in college
tax advantages of home ownership	disability insurance
nontax considerations of home ownership	medical insurance
	life insurance
mortgage financing	property insurance
purchasing an older home	emergency funding
having children	investment recommendations

Review Questions

These questions are intended to help students answers questions about case studies, goals and assumptions. Answers to these questions can be found in the study supplement.

1.   What are advantages to using blended inflation rates? [1]

2.   List the tax advantages of home ownership. [1]

3.   Bob purchased a $1,300,000 home and financed 90 percent of the purchase price at a 8.0 percent interest rate. Assuming Bob's itemized deductions are not limited by his income, and he is not subject to any alternative minimum tax rules, how much of an interest deduction can he take this year? [2]

4.   Walter refinances his mortgage. Can he deduct any points he pays to refinance? Could Walter deduct points paid on a first mortgage? [2]

5.   What are the nonfinancial advantages of home ownership? [2]

6.   What are two changes that have impacted the housing market over the past decade? [2]

7.   How are government subsidized mortgages different than conventional notes?[2]

8.   How does the family medical leave act protect wage earners when they have children?[2]

9.   Assume Mary has living expenses of $5,000 a month. She has an emergency fund of $80,000 in a money market account. Assume Mary's income is cut to $2,000 a month net of taxes, inflation is 4 percent and Mary can earn 3 percent on her emergency fund. How many months will Mary be able to support herself assuming no unemployment benefits? [3]

10.   Chapter four lists six characteristics that help guide the investment process. What are the characteristics? [1]

Learning Objectives

An understanding of the material in this chapter should enable the student to

1. Review planning for the self-employed professional.
2. Discuss types of business entities.

Comprehensive financial planning for a client without a significant asset base is more difficult than it appears. In most of these cases there is little discretionary cash, and not all personal and financial objectives can be pursued at one time. In almost every instance there will be hard choices for the client to make, particularly in regard to the priority of objectives to be pursued given the available resources. The financial planner must be especially sensitive to the client's concerns and intentions to assist the client in setting realistic and achievable goals as well as in establishing priorities.Some professionals, such as physicians, dentists, and attorneys consistently earn relatively high incomes. Due to the demands of their practices they often lack the time to educate themselves about the merits of various financial planning techniques and are consequently somewhat unsophisticated in financial matters. As a result this type of client is often accumulating disposable income for investment or the achievement of personal objectives at a slower rate than he or she believes is desirable.

In addition, as high-income earners, professionals are likely to be on every sort of solicitation, mailing, and prospect list. Because of the demands on their time that limit the opportunity to compare the advantages and disadvantages of various products or to consult with several service or product providers, the services and products that professionals have purchased are likely to be poorly coordinated.

As a result professionals may be wary about becoming involved in the financial planning process and have limited time to share with financial professionals. They tend to have driving personalities and prefer a direct and efficient approach to financial planning. However, once they are convinced that comprehensive financial planning can save them substantial amounts in taxes and in the cost of other services and products and can materially decrease the amount of time spent evaluating and coordinating services and products, and once they are convinced that the comprehensive financial planner is credible as a client-oriented deliverer of services and product recommendations, professionals usually engage in the planning process enthusiastically. Because professionals are already accustomed to making major decisions, they can be very satisfying clients to work with when they are presented with appropriate information about alternative solutions and asked to adopt a planner's particular recommendations. Since the professional's time is limited, he or she should be kept adequately involved and informed throughout the planning process without being taken away from professional and personal obligations any more than is absolutely necessary.

For all these reasons planning for the professional is a highly specialized field. Many financial planning firms choose to do planning exclusively for professionals. Because professionals tend to have high discretionary incomes, there is more competition among financial planners for this type of client.

CASE NARRATIVE

Personal Information

Dave Anderson, aged 41, is an orthopedic surgeon. His wife, Diana, is 39. They have been married for 16 years. Diana is a registered nurse and was working as an emergency room nurse when they met. Diana enjoyed her career and continued to work until shortly before their first child was born. She has not worked outside her home since that time and has no immediate plans to return to her career. She does not know whether she would like to resume nursing if she did return to work. Dave and Diana have two children, Deidre, 9, and Melissa, 6, and have just discovered that they will have another child in about 7 months. Although they are somewhat concerned about Diana's health and the health of the child, they consider this development a happy surprise.

Dave and Diana own their home, which had an approximate fair market value of $615,000 at the end of last year. When they purchased the house 10 years ago, it cost $79,000. Of that sum they paid $16,000 in cash and financed the balance of $63,000 at 12 percent for 30 years. Over the years, they have made significant improvements to the residence that were paid for from current cash flow. Dave holds title to the house in his name alone.

They plan to take one major trip at least every third year and estimate the cost at $30,000 in today's dollars. In off years family vacations are estimated to cost approximately $10,000 in today's dollars. The Andersons are currently in an off year and will spend $10,000 on a vacation.

The Andersons give about $7,000 annually to various charities, and Dave also gives $3,000 to his medical school every year for its endowment fund.

The older Anderson children have done very well in school. Although Melissa is just midway through first grade, it looks as if she will also do well. None of the children appear to have any handicaps or problems that would necessitate expensive special schooling. In fact, they are quite bright. Since the children appear gifted, the Andersons ask that you project the cost of education through the undergraduate level at a higher-quality educational institution. It is too early to tell about postgraduate or professional schools for the Anderson children, but Dave and Diana would like them to be able to pursue their education as far as they wish. Presently the children attend public schools, but there is some interest in transferring them to a private school with more rigorous academic requirements as they enter high school. At present tuition and other expenses for an appropriate private school are approximately $30,000 per year per child.

Dave and Diana do not have a luxurious lifestyle. They enjoy travel and have tastefully furnished parts of their home with antiques, most of which Diana has discovered on what she calls her "treasure hunts." They do not collect museum-quality antiques because of their attitude that it is more important for them to have a comfortable home than to have a lot of material things that have to be protected from the children and their two Shetland sheepdogs. However, they have acquired a number of very fine old pieces at nominal prices due in large part to Diana's willingness to learn about antique furniture, paintings, and other accessories. Dave and Diana do not view their household furnishings as investment vehicles, whatever their value. They enjoy living with them and are not concerned about whether a particular piece is appreciating in value. They believe their furnishings are worth approximately $125,000.

In truth, Diana is much more interested in furnishing the house than is Dave, who requires only that it be comfortable and in fact is quite content with the furnishings they acquired when they were first married. Dave is more interested in accumulating funds for investment. He is also interested in reducing income taxes to the extent that is still possible under the current federal income tax laws.

In the course of furnishing their house, Diana has acquired an appreciable amount of knowledge about antique Oriental porcelain and thinks that once the children are older, she would enjoy collecting some finer pieces more seriously and perhaps trading in them in a small way. She would also like to increase her knowledge of Oriental rugs and possibly purchase some for personal use and perhaps as an investment. She has even thought that after the children are older and need less of her time at home, she might consider opening a small shop that would specialize in Oriental rugs and antique Oriental porcelain. She had hoped that she could explore this possibility seriously within the next year or two but thinks now that she would like to stay at home full-time with the new baby for at least 2 or perhaps 3 years. However, she has not decided whether she wants to remain at home full-time as long as she did with the other children. Dave has mixed feelings about her returning to work and at this time would prefer that she remain at home with the baby at least until the child has started school. He does recognize that this will require Diana to delay any possibility of starting her own business for another 6 to 8 years.

Dave's parents are still living, and as far as he knows, they are in good health and are all right financially, although they have not accumulated a large amount of material wealth. Fred Anderson, his father, is a high-school principal and is 63 years old. Amy, his mother, 61, is a violinist who has given music lessons for many years. They were able to help Dave through undergraduate school as a result of careful saving; Dave was also awarded a sizeable scholarship.

Diana's father died when she was a teenager, and although she believes that he did not leave her mother too well provided for, she does not know for certain. While Diana was growing up, her mother implied that finances were quite limited. However, she was able to provide the funds required for Diana to go to nursing school. Diana's mother, Sarah, now 59, remarried 20 years ago. Her stepfather, Alex Smythe, now 63, is retired from the U.S. Postal Service after 30 years of service (retiring at 55 years of age) and is currently employed as the clerk of the superior court for Metropolis County. Diana's mother appears to be in good health, but her stepfather had a slight heart attack last year and later had a double heart bypass. While he seems to be recovering well, Diana is concerned about her mother's financial condition and what would become of her if something should happen to Alex. Her mother worked as a secretary after Diana's father died, but she has been a housewife since she married Alex. Diana and Dave have discussed their concerns about Alex's health with Sarah but have not really discussed the matter of her financial future in any depth.

Diana inherited a coin collection from her father that he and she had accumulated during her childhood. She thought of it primarily in terms of sentimental value and was surprised to learn some years later that its estimated worth was approximately $5,000 when she inherited it 26 years ago. Dave became interested in the collection and has essentially taken over its management, adding to it from time to time, and he estimates that it is probably worth $200,000 today. They keep the collection in their safety deposit box at the bank.

Dave tells you that he made some real estate investments several years ago. As an investment he purchased a single-family house 12 years ago for $57,000, financing $47,500 at 9.5 percent for 25 years. The house is rented for $1,200 per month and is presently worth about $225,000. For depreciation purposes $5,000 of the purchase price was allocated to the land and the remaining $52,000 to the building.

Dave also purchased an undeveloped commercial lot 12 years ago for $100,000. He put $20,000 down and financed the $80,000 with an interest only loan. The loan is variable, renews every three years and is currently locked in at 10 percent. He estimates that the land is worth approximately $460,000, and he has recently been approached by a buyer who is willing to pay him $470,000 if the transaction can be closed early next year. Dave is interested because the land does require cash flow to carry the note and taxes, and it produces no income. However, he is uncertain about whether he should sell the lot to fund other goals.

Dave has a "love/hate" relationship with his current broker. Dave allocates investable funds to securities and has benefited from the overall bull market in both stocks and bonds. Dave's selections followed the recommendations of an account representative from a local brokerage firm. Initially Dave acquired individual securities, but an article in a financial planning magazine describing the mutual fund features of diversification and professional management convinced him that funds would be a better approach for his personal investment plan. Dave expressed a desire to continue the investment program at the same or greater dollar level, until such time as he plans to retire.

The Andersons own two cars, both in Dave's name. Diana's car was purchased 2 years ago in June for $12,400; $10,000 of the purchase price was financed at 10 percent for 48 months. The value of the car is approximately $10,000. Dave's car was purchased last December for $22,000. Dave paid for the car with cash.

The Andersons have no other significant personal assets or liabilities except a $5,000 joint checking account and $20,000 in a joint savings account.

Security Name	Qty.	Date Bought	Total Cost	Date Sold	Sales Price	Market Value	Annual Income	Growth	Yield
Table 5-1 Dave Anderson's Portfolio Transactions, 1991 through Today									
Clean Soap Inc.	250	12/1/1994	$1,200						
	250	4/1/1999	2 for 1 Split						
	500	7/1/2006	2 for 1 Split			$35,000	$1,000	14.00%	2.86%
Job River Textile	20	1/1/1995	$ 19,800	1/1/2005	$24,000	$ —	$ —	NA	
Moogle Options	100	1/1/2003	$5,000	3/1/2003	$85,000	$ —	$ —	NA	
High Fly Airlines	100	1/1/1996	$10,500	Out of Business		$ —	$ —	NA	
Nationwide Oil	200	6/1/1999	$9,000			$12,000	$500	5.00%	4.17%
Burp Soda	500	3/1/2002	$8,500						
	500	3/1/2009	$4,000			$8,250	$ —	–12.00%	0.00%
Shiner Mutual Fund	1,512.55	5/8/2007	$25,000			$22,000	$800	–7.50%	3.64%
Stan's Auto	1,850	1/1/2007	$198,555			$52,804	$ —	–68.00%	0.00%
Column Totals			$281,555		$109,000	$130,054	$2,300		

Dave and Diana had some estate planning done about 6 years ago. Their basic estate plan is described below.

Dave's will provides that an amount equal to one-half his adjusted gross estate, including the house, goes to Diana in a marital trust with a testamentary power of appointment if she survives him. The remainder of his estate after the payment of estate taxes is left in a residuary trust for the benefit of Diana, Keith, Deidre, and Melissa for Diana's life. The trustee of the trust is empowered to pay income or corpus to or for the benefit of Diana, Keith, Deidre, or Melissa as necessary for their health, support, maintenance, or education. Diana has a limited power of appointment over the principal of the trust, which can be exercised both during her life and at her death. She can appoint the principal only to Keith, Deidre, or Melissa, but may not exercise the power of appointment to satisfy any of her support obligations. At Diana's death the remainder of the trust principal is to be paid equally to Keith, Deidre, and Melissa, if living. If any one of them is deceased, the deceased child's portion is to go to his or her living children, per stirpes.

Diana's will leaves all her property to Dave if he survives her, otherwise equally to her living children or children of a deceased child, per stirpes. Neither will contains a provision dealing with afterborn children.

The First Trust Company is named executor and trustee under Dave's will. Dave is named executor of Diana's will, with the First Trust Company named as successor if he is unable to serve. Diana is not happy with the fact that all her property would be tied up in a trust. She says she hates the idea of having to deal with a bank officer "for every little thing I need." Dave says he is only interested in having Diana and the children taken care of and in Diana's having someone to help her manage and direct the investment of the funds. He is also anxious to avoid unnecessary estate taxes. These are subjects they have discussed at various times since their last wills were drawn, and neither has changed his or her original position. Diana is also concerned that virtually all their assets are held in Dave's name.

Dave purchased a $100,000 term life insurance policy 8 years ago. Six years ago, as part of their estate planning, the insurance policy was gifted to an irrevocable insurance trust. Diana is the trustee of the trust until Dave's death, when the First Trust Company becomes the successor trustee. The dispositive provisions of the insurance trust are identical to those of the residuary trust under Dave's will. The trust document does not give the beneficiaries the right to withdraw funds gifted to the trust. The annual premiums over the past five years have been $279, $327, $377, $443, and $521.

Dave also carries a personal disability income policy that would provide disability income coverage after a 30-day waiting period in the event of a disabling accident or illness. If an accident causes the disability, the monthly benefits are as follows:

Table 5-2 Accidental Disability Benefits Dave's Policy	
Date of disability through 30th day	$ 0
31st through 90th day	2,900
91st day through end of first year	5,400
First day of second year through age 60	4,900
After age 60 throughout life	4,700

If illness causes the disability, the monthly benefits are as follows:

Table 5-3 Disease Disability Benefits Dave's Policy	
Date of disability through 30th day	$ 0
31st through 90th day	2,900
91st day through end of first year	5,400
First day of second year through fifth year	4,900
Sixth and seventh years	2,900
Eighth year throughout life	1,400

Disability is defined under these policies as being disabled from one's own occupation for 5 years and after that being unable to perform any occupation for which one is otherwise suited by reason of education, experience, or training. The cost of the disability income coverage is $1,539 annually.

Dave has $560,000 in homeowners coverage that provides replacement-cost coverage on the family house. There is a residential rental property policy covering the rental house for 90 percent of its replacement value. Both these policies have inflation-adjustment provisions. The automobiles are new enough to warrant the collision and comprehensive coverage that is included in Dave's auto policies. The liability limits carried in these auto policies are the maximum available in the standard premium classification, and they dovetail with the Andersons' personal umbrella policy, which provides up to $1 million in protection over the homeowners and automobile policy limits.

The total homeowners and auto policy premium is $5,323 annually and is expected to inflate at 6.0 percent.

The Andersons estimate they spend $40,000 annually on other living expenses; such as entertainment, food, clothes and transportation costs.

Business Information

Dave went to medical school at Johns Hopkins University and did his internship at Johns Hopkins Hospital. He then served 2 years in the Air Force as a physician and returned to Johns Hopkins to complete his residency in orthopedic surgery. After finishing his residency, he set up his own practice in a large metropolitan area in the state of Jefferson, where he has been in practice a little over 10 years. The practice is well established and has become more profitable in recent years. Dave presently operates his practice as a sole proprietorship. He does, however, share office space with Larry Brown and Janet Cole, two other orthopedic surgeons who are also sole practitioners. They all share office overhead (rent, utilities, and the like) equally, except for direct staff costs, malpractice insurance, and some equipment, for which each physician is responsible individually. The physicians have occasionally covered each other's calls at night and on weekends, but they do not share patients or profits in any way. They sometimes refer patients to one another but have no formal partnership or professional relationship.

Dave estimates that his office equipment is worth about $45,000 and that the office furniture is worth about $20,000. Both the equipment and the furniture have been fully depreciated for tax purposes.

The total rent for the office space is $5,000 a month, and Dave's share for his office space is $2,000 a month. It is quite likely that the building in which he is located will be sold within the next 2 years. A realtor acquaintance gave Dave a casual estimate that the property (land and building) currently has a market value of $550,000 and probably would have a market value of $600,000 in 2 years. Operating expenses and property taxes, according to the realtor, would total about $10,000 annually. Dave would not like to relocate his practice because it is located conveniently near the three hospitals at which he has staff privileges.

For the past 6 years his practice has provided him with net income of over $100,000 per year, and it has increased approximately 6 to 8 percent each year. This year Dave's Net Profit (after rents, salaries and expenses) was

$250,000. His profit sharing contribution was $55,000, and net income was $195,000. He feels that he devotes the maximum possible time to his practice and that the number of patients cannot increase appreciably. Dave expects that his yearly income will continue to increase but is concerned about the effect that his participation in two HMOs and a PPO will have on his income growth. He estimates profit will level off at no more than $300,000 in today's dollars.

He could increase his income to a greater degree if he were willing to devote more of his time to the practice, but he feels that he is already committing so much of his time to it that his family obligations are barely being met, and he is unwilling to curtail further the time he can spend with Diana and their children. Diana would like him to spend more time with her and the children, particularly while they are growing up, and they indicate that this issue causes some friction between them. He is strongly committed to his career and must even spend some of his at-home hours trying to keep up with advances in his field.

Dave employs three full-time employees: Martha Ann Hammond, 23, his secretary-receptionist; Jeanne Smith, 22, a radiology technician; and Sally Evans, 31, a nurse. Martha Ann Hammond was hired in August 2006 and is paid $30,000 annually. Jeanne Smith was hired in November 2006 and is paid $45,000 annually. Sally Evans has been with Dave since shortly after he opened his practice and usually works with him in surgery as well as at the office. She is paid $60,000 annually.

When asked how he feels about his employees, Dave says that they are all hardworking and that they earn their salaries. He volunteers that he would not be interested in planning for employee benefits that unduly discriminate against them. When asked to clarify what he means by unduly discriminatory benefits, he says that he has no objection, for example, to providing retirement benefits to his employees at or near the current levels. In fact, he feels obligated to do so. However, he is interested in maximizing benefits for himself while minimizing costs.

In the second year of his practice Dave established a profit-sharing plan integrated with Social Security, under which participants become 100 percent vested in their plan benefits after the completion of 3 years of service. The plan now provides for immediate 100 percent vesting upon an employee's entry into the plan. However, employees are not eligible for entry into the plan until they have completed 2 years of service.

Dave has contributed to the profit sharing plan for the past 7 years. The plan is presently invested in annuity assets earning 8.0 percent with a 10 percent surrender fee if he withdrew dollars in the next two years. The trustee of the account is the First Bank and Trust of Jefferson. Diana is the named beneficiary of the plan. The plan has $350,000 of assets, 72 percent of the plan assets are allocated to Dave.

Dave includes his employees in his profit sharing plan when they become eligible. He also provides them with medical insurance coverage with a $1 million lifetime benefit and a $1,000 annual deductible. Eighty percent of the first $3,000 of covered expenses is paid by the insurer and 20 percent by the employee. After $3,000 of covered expenses, the plan pays 100 percent. The costs are $200 per month for employee coverage and $275 per month for employee and dependent coverage. Dave provides medical coverage but not dependent coverage for his employees. However, he participates in the plan and carries dependent coverage despite the fact that the cost is not fully tax deductible.

In the normal course of his practice, Dave usually has $25,000 in excess funds from his practice, which he deposits in a separate money market deposit account until they are needed for quarterly tax liabilities or other expenses. In addition, he says that his accounts receivable usually average $45,000 to $55,000 and that most are covered wholly or partially by insurance, so there are rarely significant uncollected receivables. They are currently $50,000.

Drs. Brown and Cole have discussed with Dave the possibility that the three of them could combine their practices and perhaps take on a younger doctor to help expand the practice. They have discussed a professional partnership or incorporating all their practices together. Dave is not too interested in this concept because he is not convinced that he would be willing to be part of a larger organization, but he is considering incorporating his own practice. He has considered incorporation in the past but has always decided it was too much trouble and expense. He is wondering whether incorporation is still as beneficial under the current tax laws. Dave does not wish to change his form of ownership unless a change would bring him significant tax or economic benefits.

Goals and Priorities for the Andersons

When asked to rank the following standardized list of general financial objectives in order of their priority, the Andersons' response was the following:

Table 5-4 List of Priorities	
Provide college educations for all their children	1
Take care of the family in the event of Dave's death	2
Maintain their standard of living	3
Reduce tax burden	4
Take care of self and family during a period of long-term disability	5
Invest and accumulate wealth	6
Enjoy a comfortable retirement	7
Review and negotiate an estate plan	8

Next the Andersons were individually asked to rate their responses to a standardized list of various investment vehicles from 0 to 5, with 0 representing an aversion and 5 representing a substantial preference. Their responses are shown below.

Table 5-5 Investment Vehicle Preferences		
Investment Vehicle	**Dave**	**Diana**
Savings account	2	3
Money market account	2	4
U.S. government bond	1	2
Corporate bond	2	3
Corporate stock (growth)	4	2
Mutual fund (growth)	4	2
Mutual fund (income)	1	3
Municipal bond	3	1
Real estate (direct ownership)	4	3
Insurance and annuities	1	2
Limited partnership units (real estate, oil & gas cattle equipment leasing)	3	1
Commodities, gold, collectibles	2	4*
*Diana says she would not be interested in commodities or gold, but she thinks collectibles can be very good investments.		

The Andersons then each responded to a list of general personal financial concerns by rating the concerns from 0 to 5, with 5 indicating a strong concern and 0 indicating no concern. Dave and Diana rated their concerns.

Table 5-6 Andersons' Personal Financial Concerns		
Area of Concern	Dave	Diana
Liquidity	2	3
Safety of principal	3	3
Capital appreciation	5	3
Current income	2	3
Inflation protection	4	4
Future income	3	4
Tax reduction/deferral	4	3

INSTRUCTIONS

Based on this information, prepare a working outline for the Andersons' financial plan. When this has been completed, it can be compared with the suggested solution that follows.

WORKING OUTLINE

1. Clients' objectives

    a. For lifetime planning

    (1) Fund special schools and college education for children.

    (2) Accumulate enough wealth to maintain their lifestyle and to be secure at retirement.

    (3) Reduce tax burden.

    (4) Investigate the possibility of the sale of the commercial lot.

    (5) Investigate the benefits of incorporating Dave's practice.

    (6) Explore the advisability of Diana's wish to start her own business.

    (7) Investigate possibility of purchasing office building.

    b. For dispositions at death

        (1) Ensure that the family will have sufficient assets to maintain their lifestyle if Dave should die prematurely.

        (2) Avoid unnecessary taxes at the deaths of both Dave and Diana.

2. Business planning

    a. Tax planning

        (1) Present situation

        (2) Choosing the appropriate business form

            (a) Continuing as a sole proprietorship

            (b) Forming a professional partnership

            (c) S corporations

            (d) C corporations

            (e) Recommendations

        (3) Qualified plans of deferred compensation

            (a) Integration with Social Security

            (b) Money-purchase pension plan

            (c) Recommendation for qualified plans for Dave

        (4) Buy-sell agreements to ensure that Dave's practice is marketable at death or disability

    b. Insurance planning

        (1) Funding the buy-sell agreement(s)

        (2) Medical, disability, and life insurance plans

            (a) Medical expense insurance

            (b) Disability income insurance

        (3) Property and liability insurance for the business

        (4) Professional liability insurance

        (5) Business overhead expense disability insurance

3. Personal planning

    a. Tax planning

        (1) Present situation

    (2) Fund private school and/or college education for children.

        (a) Gifting

- Outright gifts
- 529 Plans
- UGMA and UTMA gifts

        (b) Income shifting

- Sec. 2503(b) trusts
- Sec. 2503(c) trusts
- Family partnership
- Caveat: parental obligations

    (3) Reduce tax burden.

        (a) Achieve personal objectives through income-shifting devices to reduce cost.

        (b) Defer tax liability on a portion of Dave's income from the practice through the use of qualified plans.

        (c) Individual retirement accounts

    (4) Ensure adequate protection in the event of Dave's disability.

        (a) Design buy-sell agreement to become operative in the event of Dave's disability.

        (b) Personal disability income coverage

    (5) Ensure a comfortable retirement.

    (6) Consider various problems Diana might encounter in setting up her own business.

        (a) Preliminary general planning

        (b) Taking advantage of start-up losses

    (7) Dispositions at death

        (a) Analysis of present plans

        (b) Recommendations

        (c) Failure of present estate planning documents to contemplate the birth of Dave and Diana's fourth child

        (d) Considerations regarding Diana

        (e) Diana's dissatisfaction with leaving all assets in trust

        (f) Problems with present life insurance trust

   b. Insurance planning

     (1) Life insurance

        (a) Ordinary whole life insurance

        (b) Single-premium whole life insurance

        (c) Variable life policy

        (d) Universal life policy

        (e) Term policy

        (f) Recommendations

     (2) Disability insurance

     (3) Personal property and liability insurance

   c. Investment planning

     (1) Refinancing clients' home

     (2) Financial status of the clients

     (3) Funding the children's education

        (a) Secondary school expenses

        (b) College expenses

        (c) Investment alternatives for education funding

           • Moderately high-risk income bond funds

           • Growth-oriented no-load mutual fund

        (d) Investment media selection

           • Use of corporate bonds

           • Use of higher-risk investments

(4) Repositioning of existing assets

    (a) Earned income

    (b) Investment income

    (c) Passive income

- Concept of passive income
- Special real estate rules
- Revenue Reconciliation Act of 1993 changes

    (d) Recommendations

- The commercial lot
- Real estate investments
- Security portfolio

(5) Increasing net worth

    (a) Collectibles (coins, porcelain)

    (b) Growth-oriented no-load mutual fund

    (c) Selected issues of common stock

    (d) Preferred stock

    (e) Corporate bonds

    (f) Municipal bonds

    (g) Municipal bond fund

    (h) Leveraged, closed-end bond funds

    (i) Junk bonds

    (j) Real estate

(6) Recommendations

INSTRUCTIONS

Prepare a financial plan for the Andersons. When you have prepared your solution, it should be compared with the suggested solution that follows. Students may choose to add additional elements to the case discussion.

PERSONAL FINANCIAL PLAN FOR DAVE AND DIANA ANDERSON [SUGGESTED SOLUTION]: CLIENTS' OBJECTIVES

1. For lifetime planning

    a. Fund special schools and college education for children.
    b. Accumulate enough wealth to maintain their lifestyle and to be secure at retirement.
    c. Reduce tax burden.
    d. Investigate the possibility of the sale of the commercial lot.
    e. Investigate the benefits of incorporating Dave's practice.
    f. Explore the advisability of Diana's wish to start her own business.
    g. Investigate possibility of purchasing office building.

2. For dispositions at death

    a. Ensure that the family will have sufficient assets to maintain their lifestyle if Dave should die prematurely.
    b. Avoid unnecessary taxes at the deaths of both Dave and Diana.

Business planning is an integral part of Dave and Diana's financial plan. Dave's business is the lifeline of the Anderson family. The profit sharing plan provides wealth, client base provides income and the business structure makes insurance and health care benefits available to the Anderson family. Students should address the business needs of the Anderson family while simultaneously working with personal financial planning principles. The text will develop a business plan first and construct a personal plan using the outcomes from business planning.

BASE CASE

Assumptions

1. Assume a state income tax of 4 percent annually on all AGI.
2. The checking account balance is maintained at $5,000; the account is non-interest bearing.
3. The joint savings account balance of $20,000 earns 4 percent interest annually. Interest accumulates in the account.
4. Surplus cash is invested in the savings account and will earn 4 percent annually.
5. Dave's gross receipts and business expenses are expected to increase at 5 percent annually.
6. Diana inherited a coin collection from her father 26 years ago. The fair market value of the collection is presently $60,000 and is expected to increase annually at 6 percent.
7. Dave and Diana believe their brokerage account will grow at 6.0 percent moving forward.
8. The value of the personal residence ($615,000) will increase at 8 percent annually. The original amount of the mortgage was $63,000 at an interest rate of 12 percent for a term of 30 years. The house was purchased ten years ago.
9. The value of the commercial lot ($460,000) will increase at 4 percent annually and was purchased 12 years ago. The original amount of the mortgage was $80,000 at an interest rate of 10 percent for a term of 20 years.
10. The value of the rental property ($225,000) will increase at 6 percent annually and was also purchased 12 years ago. The rental property was purchased. Currently the property rents for $1,200 per month and has operating expenses of approximately $900 annually. All these amounts will increase at 6 percent annually.
11. Dave has office furniture valued at approximately $20,000 and office equipment valued at $45,000. No increase or decrease in value has been assumed.
12. Dave's accounts receivable average $50,000.
13. Property taxes on all nonrental home properties are 1.5 percent annually.
14. The rental home is in a different school district, where property taxes are 1.95 percent annually.

15. Nondeductible living expenses are expected to increase at 6 percent annually.

16. Charitable contributions are expected to increase at 6 percent annually.

17. Dave's profit sharing plan is presently invested in annuity assets earning 8 percent.

18. Automobiles decrease in value at a rate of 15 percent annually beginning next year.

Income Tax Schedule for Dave and Diana Anderson

Table 5-7 Anderson Income Tax 2008 Projection—Base Case			
Earned Income This Year			
Business Profit	$250,000.00		
PS Contribution	($55,000.00)		
		$195,000.00	
Interest & Dividends			
Brokerage Account	$2,300.00		
Joint Savings Interest	$800.00		
		$3,100.00	
Real Estate Investments			
Rental Home Income	$14,400.00		
* Rental Loan Interest	($3,596.84)		
Rental Home Prop Tax	($4,387.50)		
Rental Home Operating Expenses	($900.00)		
** Rental Home Depreciation	($2,080.00)		
Lot Interest	($8,000.00)		
Lot Prop Taxes	($6,900.00)		
		($11,464.34)	
Adjusted Gross Income			**$186,635.66**
Potential Itemized Deductions			
4% State Income Tax (on AGI)	($7,465.43)		
Charitable Contributions	($10,000.00)		
Home Prop Taxes	($9,225.00)		
Home Interest	($7,106.00)		
		($33,796.43)	
		—	
SE Tax Adjustment		($9,151.50)	
Current Year 4 Personal Exemptions		($14,000.00)	
Total Deductions and Exemptions			($56,947.93)
Taxable Income			**$129,687.73**
Current Year Projected Income Tax Due			**$25,109.43**
Highest Marginal Rate			25%

* Rental loan interest was calculated by using an amortization schedule, and finding the interest in year 12 of the loan. The rental property had $47,500 financed at 9.5 percent over a 25 year loan. Home Interest was calculated in the same manner.

** Rental depreciation was initially calculated at $2,080 annually and will remain flat until basis is completely depreciated. Dave has not depreciated his commercial lot.

Current Year exemptions and tax rates will likely be different than the year a student is working on this case. Solving this case using actual federal, state and local property tax rates will better prepare the student for working with actual clients.

Dave and Diane Anderson Balance Sheet

Table 5-8 Dave and Diane Anderson Balance Sheet		
Assets		
Cash Accounts		
Checking	$ 5,000.00	
Savings Account	$ 20,000.00	
		$ 25,000.00
Brokerage Account		
All positions	$130,054.00	
		$ 130,054.00
Business Assets		
Accounts Receivable	$ 50,000.00	
Furniture and Equipment	$ 65,000.00	
Accounts Receivable	$ 50,000.00	
Operating Account	$ 25,000.00	
Dave's % of PS Plan	$252,000.00	
		$ 442,000.00
Investment Properties		
Rental House	$225,000.00	
Commercial Lot	$460,000.00	
		$ 685,000.00
Personal Assets		
Home	$615,000.00	
Coin Collection	$60,000.00	
Personal Property	$125,000.00	
Diana's Car	$ 10,000.00	
Dave's Car	$ 22,000.00	
	$832,000.00	
Total Assets		**$2,114,054.00**
Liabilities		
Diana's Car Loan (after 24 months)	$ (5,496.29)	
* Rental House	$ (37,101.00)	
Commercial Lot	$ (80,000.00)	
* Mortgage	$ (57,128.00)	
Total Liabilities		$(179,725.29)
Net Worth		**$1,934,328.71**

Cash Flow Statement for Dave and Diana Anderson

Table 5-9 Anderson Projected Cash Flow Current Year			
Cash Inflow			
Net Cash Flow from Business	$ 195,000.00		
		$ 195,000.00	
Interest & Dividends	$ 3,100.00		
		$ 3,100.00	
Rental Property Income	$ 14,400.00		
		$ 14,400.00	
Gross Income			$ 212,500.00
Expenses			
Payroll Taxes			
** SE Taxes on Soc. Sec.	$ (13,242.20)		
** SE Medicare on Wages	$ (5,655.00)		
		$ (18,897.20)	
Federal Income Tax			
From Tax Schedule	$(25,109.43)		
		$(25,109.43)	
State Income Taxes			
4% of AGI $186,635	$ (7,465.43)		
		$ (7,465.43)	
Property Taxes			
Home	$(9,225.00)		
Rental House	$(4,387.50)		
Commercial Lot	$(6,900.00)		
		$(20,512.50)	
Charitable Contributions			
Charities	$ (7,000.00)		
Medical School	$ (3,000.00)		
		$ (10,000.00)	
Debt Payments			
Mortgage	$ (7,776.36)		
Rental House	$ (4,980.07)		
Commercial Lot	$ (8,000.00)		
Car Note	$ (3,043.51)		
		$ (23,799.94)	
Other Expenses			

Rental Upkeep	$ (900.00)		
Vacations	$ (10,000.00)		
Life Insurance Premium	$ (521.00)		
Disability Insurance Premium	$ (1,539.00)		
Medical Insurance Premiums	$ (5,700.00)		
Homeowners & Auto	$ (5,323.00)		
Other Expenses	$ (40,000.00)		
		$ (63,983.00)	
Voluntary Savings			
Education Savings	$ —		
		$ —	
Expenses			$(169,767.50)
Net Available Cash Flow			$42,732.50
Monthly Available Cash Flow			$3,561.04

* Debt payments include principle and interest

** The Social Security wage base is capped at $106,800 for 2011. Students using this case in 2012 and 2013 should use appropriate wage bases. Social Security was assumed to be 12.4 percent for self employed individuals and Medicare at 2.9 percent. Federal tax stimulus packages may decrease this number in 2012 or 2013.

BUSINESS PLANNING: TAXES

Present Situation

Dave has a well-established and profitable private practice as an orthopedic surgeon. The practice is conducted as a sole proprietorship, even though there is a space-sharing arrangement with two other orthopedic surgeons. The practice has produced over $100,000 in income for Dave for each of the past 6 years. Last year he earned $195,000 after his Profit Sharing contribution, and he expects to earn at least $200,000 to $300,000 in the current year.

Dave has been approached by Drs. Brown and Cole about consolidating their practices either through a professional partnership or by incorporating the three practices as one corporation.

Dave believes that bigger is not necessarily better and thinks that it would probably be a mistake to consolidate the practices. He also thinks that combining practices would greatly increase administrative problems. He has not dismissed the idea despite his reservations, but he is more interested in incorporating his own practice if he decides to incorporate at all. Prior to changing the form of his business he would like information on his options so that he can assess the changes that would be necessary in his practice under the available forms of doing business.

Dave presently provides a good medical insurance plan for each of his employees. He is also a participant in this plan, although the payments on his behalf are not tax deductible (as a business expense) for federal income tax purposes.

Choosing the Appropriate Business Form

The following discussion addresses potential problems and solutions when considering which form of corporation should be held and maintained. This text is not intended to be a complete reference on partnerships, corporations and business transition, which is covered quite competently in American College Courses HS331 and HS321. The following discussion contains excerpts from Fundamentals of Income Taxation in the form of a conversation between two professionals.

Continuing as a Sole Proprietorship

The sole proprietorship is the most informal type of business ownership because there is such a close identity between the business and the business owner. Sole proprietorships are not separate entities for tax-reporting purposes (as are partnerships) or for taxpaying purposes (as are corporations). The owner of the sole proprietorship reports business-operating results on his or her tax return and pays taxes on the business income. There is no separate income tax form to file since all business income and losses from a proprietorship are computed on Schedule C of Form 1040 and added to or subtracted from the proprietor's gross income from other sources, if any. Bona fide business losses can be used to offset other income of the proprietor without the constraints imposed by the basis rules and passive activity loss rules for partnerships and S corporations. The taxable year of the sole proprietorship must be the same as the taxable year of the owner.

In a sole proprietorship the proprietor owns all assets and therefore has total control over the business. A proprietor can retain complete control or delegate some authority to employees on his or her own terms. There is no board of directors, and there are no partners or shareholders for the proprietor to answer to or to question his or her decisions. Some business owners enjoy the informality, flexibility, control, and freedom that the sole proprietorship affords.

Sole proprietorships are not, however, without their drawbacks. The close identity between the proprietor and the business can leave the proprietor personally vulnerable to liability for acts of employees or agents. This situation does not normally exist when business is carried on in a corporate form. There is also no opportunity to take advantage of splitting income (and thereby the income tax liability) between the sole proprietor and another taxpayer, as is the case in regular (C) corporations. In addition, there are still some restrictions with regard to qualified retirement plans that apply to self-employed persons and owner-employees that are not applicable to other employees.

As a physician, Dave is personally liable for his own acts of negligence or malpractice, regardless of whether he operates as a sole proprietor, a partner, or a corporation. His relationship with Drs. Brown and Cole is not of a type that could result in Dave's being held liable for their acts. Therefore with respect to personal liability exposure, incorporation would not provide him with a significant advantage over his present situation.

Forming a Professional Partnership

Like the sole proprietorship, the partnership is a non-tax-paying entity. While the partnership is a tax-reporting entity that has taxable income or losses and must file a tax return, the partnership itself is a mere conduit, and the partnership income and losses are passed through to the partners. The characterization of income or losses as capital or ordinary is made at the partnership level and is passed on to the individual partners for reporting on their individual income tax returns. The partnership can also be used to pass through tax losses (limited to the partner's basis in his or her partnership interest) to the individual partners in order to offset income from other sources.

The Internal Revenue Code defines a partnership as any business, financial operation, or venture carried on through a syndicate, group, pool, joint venture, or other unincorporated organization other than trusts, estates, or corporations (IRC Sec. 7701(a)(2)). The definition is broad and flexible, and the partnership can in fact be a very flexible form of business ownership that allows for a significant amount of informality in business operations. A partnership is not without its potential problems, however, regarding both legal and tax issues.

One of the most troubling problems in operating a business, particularly a professional practice, in the form of a partnership is that all the general partners are responsible for all the debts of the partnership as well as the debts of other partners arising out of the partnership business. For a group of professionals such as physicians, this means that a malpractice suit resulting in a professional liability judgment is the responsibility of each of the partners to the full extent of the liability. If the person who made the professional error is unable to pay all the liability, each of the other partners is fully liable for the payment of the required amount. In strict legal terms each partner is "jointly and severally liable" for the total liabilities of the partnership and of the individual partners arising out of the partnership business. This can necessitate one partner making huge payments on behalf of another partner. The amount of each partner's liability is not limited to the assets the partner has in the partnership but extends to personal assets as well. Therefore it is possible for each partner to lose everything he or she owns in satisfying the liabilities of the partnership or the malpractice judgments of the partners. Joint and several liability extends to all obligations of the partnership and is not restricted to the area of professional liability.

Partnerships, like sole proprietorships, do not offer the opportunity to split income between a business entity and an individual. Because the partnership is not a taxpaying entity, all income is taxed to the partners. If the partnership has taxable income, each partner must pay tax on his or her portion of that amount in the year in which it is recognized by the partnership regardless of whether it is actually distributed to that partner.

Primarily because of the increased personal liability exposure, forming a professional partnership is not recommended in this case.

The Partnership in Operation. *Steve:* OK. Suppose we get a partnership in operation. Since the partners will pay the income tax on partnership income, is the partnership required to file a federal return?

Mike: Yes, the partnership must file a return—IRS Form 1065—but it is for informational purposes only. A civil penalty is now imposed on any partnership that fails to file a complete partnership information return, unless reasonable cause is shown. The penalty consists of $195 times the number of partners for each month that the failure continues, up to 12 months. This penalty is in addition to criminal penalties for willful failure to file a return, supply information, or pay tax.[4] The form is due 3½ months after the

---

4.   IRC Sec. 6698(a) and (b).

partnership fiscal year ends. Under Sec. 706, the partnership tax year must be the same as one or more majority partners who have an aggregate interest in partnership profits and capital exceeding 50 percent. If the tax year of the partner(s) owning a majority interest can not be used or does not apply, the partnership must use the tax year of the principal partners' (partners owning 5 percent of more of capital or profit interests), unless a business purpose for a different tax year can be established. Since most individuals are calendar-year taxpayers, most partnerships also will have a calendar-year reporting period and file their informational return on April 15 each year.

Steve: Let's discuss how the partner is taxed.

Jim: Each partner must include in his or her return for each taxable year his or her distributive share of the partnership income or loss items. Each partner's share of partnership income and loss is computed with regard to what was realized in the taxable year of the partnership.

Steve: Could you be more specific as to which items would be includible as distributive shares?

Jim: The partners must include in their individual tax returns their shares of the partnership income or loss. They must also take into account (and report on their 1040s) a number of separate partnership items,[5] including

- capital gains and losses
- Sec. 1231 gains and losses
- charitable contributions
- dividends received by the partnership from stock holdings

The partners would then add their share of each of the above items to their individual income and deductions. For example, one partner's share of partnership capital gains and losses would be added to his or her personal capital gains and losses. In the same way, a partner's distributive share of the firm's charitable contributions is added to his or her individual contributions, and the individual charitable contribution deduction limitations are applied to the total.

Steve: How do the partners determine who gets what, that is, how are the distributive shares of each item determined?

---

5.   IRC Sec. 702(a).

Mike: Generally speaking, the distributive shares of each item are to be determined in accordance with the partnership agreement. If the partnership doesn't cover a particular item, the partner's distributive share of that item is the same percentage as his or her percentage share of partnership income or loss.[6] If the partner would normally receive one-third of all profits and losses, he or she would receive one-third of all capital gains.

Sometimes partners, through the partnership agreement, attempt to shift an item to the taxpayer in whose hands the item will be most beneficial. This allocation of one type of item to the partner who can obtain the greatest tax benefit (such as an allocation of all depreciation deductions to the highest tax bracket partner) may be ignored by the IRS. If such a provision does not have "substantial economic effect,"[7] the partners' shares of that item will be readjusted by the IRS just as if the partnership agreement contained no provision as to the item; that is, each partner's distributive share of that item is determined in accordance with his or her share of partnership income or loss.

It's difficult to determine the distinction between an acceptable and unacceptable allocation. Generally the dollar amounts of income received by the partners must be substantially affected by any special allocations independent of tax consequences.

If the economic after-tax consequences to one partner are enhanced by an allocation, the economic after-tax consequences to some other partner or partners should be diminished if the allocation is to be treated as having substantial economic effect. Using present-value concepts, this principle is applied for calculating economic consequences over the course of a number of years. Treasury regulations state the application of these principles in detail. Those regulations need to be studied to determine the effects of any special allocations that the partnership may be considering.

If special allocations do not satisfy the requirement of substantial economic effect, they will usually be allocated in accordance with the general provisions in the partnership agreement for sharing income and loss.[8]

With respect to contributed property by the partner to the partnership, the partnership will generally be required, rather than permitted, to allocate

---

6.   IRC Sec. 704(b).

7.   IRC Sec. 704(b)(2).

8.   Treas. Reg. 1.704-1(b).

built-in gain or loss on contributed property to the contributing partner, and not in accordance with each partner's interest in the property.

Steve: Suppose that one partner feels his or her distributive share of partnership income is inadequate as compensation for the efforts provided. Can that partner obtain some type of salary from the partnership?

guaranteed payment

Jim: Yes, a partner can obtain a salary or, as previously illustrated, a *guaranteed payment*. A guaranteed payment is a sum paid to a partner, regardless of whether the partnership has income. This payment is deductible by the partnership.

Guaranteed payments are ordinary income to the recipient partner. Perhaps an additional illustration of the treatment of guaranteed payments would be helpful. Ethan, a partner in the Ethan Ward partnership, is to receive a payment of $10,000 for services, plus 40 percent of the ordinary business income or loss of the partnership. Assume that after deducting payment of the $10,000 salary to Ethan, the partnership has a loss of $8,000. Of this amount, $3,200 (40 percent of the loss) would be Ethan's distributive share of partnership loss. In addition, Ethan must report as ordinary income the guaranteed payment of $10,000 made to him by the partnership. This guaranteed payment would be reportable by Ethan in the taxable year of the partnership in which it deducted the payment and that ended with or within Ethan's own taxable year.

Steve: Suppose a partner wants to sell his or her partnership interest 2 or 3 years after the partnership is in operation. The amount received on the sale minus his or her basis in the partnership will be taxed. Is that partner's basis in the partnership interest the same as his or her original basis?

Jim: No, the partner's basis will not be the same.

A partner's basis is increased by the following three factors:

1. his or her capital contributions
2. his or her distributive share of partnership income
3. his or her share of liabilities assumed

A partner's basis is also reduced by the following three factors:

1. his or her share of losses
2. his or her distributions or draws
3. his or her share of liabilities relieved

Steve: Let's see if I understand. When a partnership is formed, the basis of a contributing partner's partnership interest is (1) the amount of money contributed plus (2) the adjusted basis of the property he or she contributes to the partnership.

This same rule applies to a new partner who contributes money or property. The initial basis of a partner who receives an interest as an inheritance is basically determined by valuing the interest at the date of the decedent's death. If an individual acquires a partnership interest by gift, the new partner's basis would be the same as the old donor-partner's basis plus any adjustment for gift tax paid on the transfer.

If a partner loans money to the partnership, that partner's basis is increased by his or her share of the partnership's liability to him or her as an outsider.

If only services are contributed, and the contributing partner receives an interest in partnership capital (i.e., an interest in the property contributed by his or her copartners), then the contributing partner realizes current ordinary income as long as there are no substantial restrictions on that partner's right to withdraw or dispose of his or her interest in partnership capital. When such income is realized, that income will be added to the partner's basis.

Abe and Benny open a delicatessen. Abe owned luncheonette equipment with an adjusted basis of $4,000 and a fair market value of $5,000. He entered into an agreement with Benny in which Abe would contribute his equipment to the partnership and Benny would contribute $5,000 in cash. By mutual agreement, each man will own a 50 percent interest.

Since the adjusted basis of Abe's property was $4,000, the basis for Abe's 50 percent interest is $4,000. On the other hand, Benny's basis is equal to the cash he contributed, which is $5,000.

Of course, the original basis is only a starting point. If we had to determine the basis of a partner's partnership interest 1 year after the formation of the partnership, we would have to adjust the original basis to reflect changes that have occurred.

We'd start with the original basis, increase that figure by any subsequent capital contributions, and also increase it by the sum of the partner's share of the partnership's ordinary income (both business and separately stated items of income, such as capital gains) as well as its tax-exempt receipts. So, for example, if the partnership received life insurance death proceeds, this cash would serve to increase each partner's basis.

Since an increase in a partner's share of liabilities is treated as if cash had been contributed, a partner's basis increases to the extent of his or her share of increased partnership obligations, such as accounts or notes payable and mortgages assumed.

Next, we'd reduce basis (but not below zero) by the amount of a partner's share of partnership losses (including separately stated items of loss, such as capital losses), distributions by the partnership to the partner, and the amount that the partner's share of liabilities was decreased.

Suppose the two of you formed a partnership. This year the firm lost $10,000. Jim's distributive share of the loss was $5,000. If the adjusted basis of his partnership interest, before considering his share of the partnership loss, was $2,000, he could claim only $2,000 of the loss this year. The adjusted basis of his interest would be reduced to zero. An individual partner's loss deduction cannot exceed his basis for his partnership interest at the end of the year for which the loss occurred. However, the partner is entitled to an unlimited carryover of nondeductible partnership losses.

If your partnership realized an $8,000 profit next year, Jim's $4,000 share of that profit would increase the adjusted basis of his interest to $4,000 (if we don't take into account the $3,000 excess loss he could not deduct last year). Next year's return should show his distributive share of partnership income to be $1,000 ($4,000 distributive share minus the $3,000 loss he was not allowed to take this year). The adjusted basis of his partnership interest at the end of next year would be $1,000.[9]

What's the purpose for those increases and reductions in basis?

Mike: When we increase a partner's basis, what we're doing in effect is shielding those amounts from a subsequent tax. For example, when you sell your partnership interest, you should not have to pay tax on income you've already paid tax on. By the same token, your share of the tax-exempt income (such as life insurance proceeds) received by the partnership should be considered an additional capital investment by you—so if you sell your partnership interest, you should not be taxed on that item, either. Likewise, if you assume a portion of the partnership's liabilities, it's the same as if you

---

9. Where a partner cannot determine the adjusted basis in the partnership interest, the adjusted basis of his or her interest may be determined by reference to the partner's proportionate share of the adjusted basis of partnership property, as long as it is reasonable that the result produced will not vary substantially from the above basis rules. IRC Sec. 705(b); Treas. Reg. Sec. 1.705-1(b).

contributed a like amount of cash. You should be able to recover that amount of cash tax free.

Reductions in basis serve just the opposite purpose. By reducing basis, you account for recoveries of basis on capital invested in the partnership resulting from losses deducted against other income, distributions of property or money from the partnership to you, and decreases in your share of partnership liabilities.

Partnership basis is important in determining the amount of loss that can be recognized. It also affects taxation upon the disposition of a partnership interest on a partner's retirement or death.

Types of Corporations

There are many different types of corporations. For example, there is the ecclesiastical corporation that is organized to hold property in connection with the advancement of a particular religious faith. An eleemosynary corporation is created to hold property for the benefit of a charity or benevolent society. The type of corporation you gentlemen are contemplating is a subsection of a third general type, the civil corporation. The civil corporation encompasses all corporations other than ecclesiastical or eleemosynary. The civil corporation can be political, quasi-public, or private.

Reebel: Would we be considered private?

Kress: Yes, political corporations are created by governments to manage public affairs. The Post Office Corporation is a good illustration. Sometimes companies are privately owned but exist to serve the public. Where the state maintains close control and supervision over the conduct of a corporation's business, it is considered quasi-public. An example would be a gas or electric company.

The organization you are considering would be organized for the benefit of its members, the three of you. Such a private corporation, operated for a profit, is called a "stock" company. This means that the capital of the business is divided into transferable portions known as shares that are evidenced by stock certificates. These certificates will entitle holders to participate in a distribution of profits. As you know, a certificate represents a stockholder's proportionate interest in the profits, the net assets, and the control of the corporation.

close corporation

**closely held
corporation**

Initially your organization will probably be a private stock corporation classified as a "close" rather than a publicly traded corporation. A *close corporation* or *closely held corporation* is one that has no shares of its stock available for purchase by or in the hands of the general public.

Someday you may want to expand the business and finance the growth with money from outside investors. In a sense, you would be "opening" such a close or private corporation by offering to issue shares of stock through a listing of the stock on a public stock exchange.

As long as a corporation remains close, however, there will likely be only a few shareholders. These same people will probably also serve as directors and working officers. Therefore ownership, management, and key employees in your organization will be identical in fact—although separate for legal and tax purposes.

S Corporations

S corporation

C corporation

Kress: What you are referring to sounds like an *S corporation*. The Internal Revenue Code allows a closely held corporation to elect not to be taxed as a regular corporation, or *C corporation*, if it meets certain requirements. Basically the result is that the corporation is not taxed as a separate entity.[10]

In other words, the corporation itself does not (with certain exceptions) pay tax.[11] Instead, corporate net income is taxed directly to its shareholders. This enables shareholders of a small, closely held corporation to obtain some of the tax and nontax advantages of corporate form without its disadvantages. The S corporation election avoids double taxation of corporate income resulting from dividend payments (even with lower dividend tax rates). It also avoids the tax penalty on accumulated earnings as well as the personal-holding-company tax. Corporate income and losses will be immediately passed through to the shareholders. However, some of the tax-advantaged fringe benefits that are available to employees of a regular corporation do not apply to shareholders of an S corporation.

All these characteristics are consistent with the underlying purpose of an S corporation, which is to promote tax neutrality when choosing the form

---

10.   IRC Secs. 1361-1363; IRC Secs. 1366-1368.

11.   IRC Sec. 1374 (tax imposed on certain built-in gains).

in which to do business (for example, a sole proprietorship, partnership, or corporation). Congress felt that, to the extent tax treatment influenced the choice of business form, the result was a potential distortion of normal business practices. Therefore provisions were made in the Code to allow for S corporation treatment.

To qualify for S corporation status, the following requirements must be met:

- An S corporation can have only one class of stock.
- An S corporation must have no more than 100 shareholders. Members of the same family are treated as one shareholder. For this purpose, "members of the family" include a common ancestor and all lineal descendants of the common ancestor (including spouses and former spouses of such descendants). However, the common ancestor cannot be more than six generations removed from the youngest generation of shareholders at the time the election is made. Different rules applied to S elections made before 2005.
- An S corporation can have no shareholder other than an individual, an estate, or certain types of trusts (except for qualified Subchapter S subsidiary corporations).
- An S corporation must be a domestic corporation—that is, incorporated in the United States.
- An S corporation may not have nonresident alien shareholders.

Types of trusts that are permitted to be S corporation shareholders include the following:[12]

- voting trusts
- grantor trusts
- trusts treated as owned by an individual other than the grantor under IRC Sec. 678
- qualified subchapter S trusts (QSSTs)
- electing small business trusts (ESBTs)

Any such trust that owns S corporation stock or trusts that receive the stock under the terms of a will may hold the stock for a 2-year period after the death of the grantor of the trust or previous owner of the stock. A QSST is a trust that, among other requirements, must distribute all of its income currently to one individual. In general, an ESBT is a trust whose beneficiaries

---

12. IRC Sec. 1361(c), (d), and (e).

are all individuals or estates. Charitable organizations may, however, hold a contingent remainder interest in an electing small business trust. No interest in an electing small business trust may be acquired by purchase.

An S corporation does not pay corporate tax on its income. The result is that the shareholders are taxed on the taxable (i.e., ordinary) income of the corporation in proportion to their stock ownership. If the corporation has a loss, it can be deducted directly by the shareholders. As I have already noted, using this type of election, the corporation and its shareholders are taxed in most (but not all) respects in a manner similar to the way they would be taxed if they were operating as a partnership.

The S corporation election is used in a number of situations. For example, if you expected high initial losses in your first year or two of business operations, you would want to pass through the corporation's losses since you are all in high individual income tax brackets, so that you could use them against your own income tax liability.[13]

An S corporation election might also be indicated where business owners want to take advantage of limited liability but do not want to incur a double taxation when income earned and taxed by the corporation is later distributed to its shareholders.

An S corporation election may also be indicated when shareholders intend to withdraw substantially all corporate earnings and (1) not all stockholders are employees who could justify their shares as salary payments, (2) the amount of earnings is so great that any attempt to pay them out as salaries would result in unreasonably high salaries, or (3) the corporation has taxable income that would be taxed at a corporate rate higher than the shareholders' individual marginal rates without an S election. The S corporation election also avoids the double tax that still occurs to both a corporation and its shareholders when an actual or constructive dividend is paid out of earnings.

By an irrevocable and unqualified gift of shares of stock, a taxpayer can arrange to split income with another family member. Thus it is possible to transfer income to lower-bracket donees. By getting stock into the hands of various family members, it is possible to shift income to other taxpayers even though the income may be used to satisfy support or other family obligations that the donor would otherwise have to pay with after-tax dollars.

---

13. IRC Sec. 1366(a) and (d).

In fact, you could even use the S corporation election to allow the corporation to continue income payments to you at retirement (or to your widow should you predecease her) without double tax consequences. You know that the IRS may question high salaries to older stockholder-employees, claiming that part of the pay is really a nondeductible, yet still taxable dividend. The election generally avoids this question since payments to shareholders are not taxed as dividends. Thus where a shareholder is inactive, less able to contribute services, or in need of retirement income, but does not want to create a double tax, the S corporation may be the answer, depending on the circumstances.

Baily: How long is the S corporation election effective?

Kress: Once made, an S election is effective indefinitely. However, the election can be terminated in any of the following ways:

First, the corporation can elect to revoke the election with the consent of the shareholders who own more than 50 percent of the stock.

Second, the election terminates if the corporation no longer qualifies as a "small business corporation"—that is, if it has more than 100 shareholders, or a nonresident alien acquires stock, or if an entity other than permitted shareholders acquires stock. Also the issuance of a second class of stock would terminate the election.

Third, if more than 25 percent of the S corporation's gross receipts for 3 successive tax years is from certain types of passive income and the corporation has accumulated earnings and profits from its days prior to the S election, the election will be terminated.[14] Certain banks, bank holding companies, and financial holding companies are exempted from this rule.

The revocation can be elected on or before the 15th day of the third month of the present taxable year and will be effective for that entire taxable year, unless the revocation specifically requests a revocation date in the future. If so, the revocation will be effective on the date selected. If no future date of revocation is specified but the revocation election is filed after the permissible period, the revocation is effective at the beginning of the following taxable year. Voluntary revocations generally result in an inability to reelect the S status for 5 years without obtaining IRS consent to the reelection. The IRS can, in appropriate circumstances, waive the 5-year waiting period and permit

---

14. IRC Sec. 1362(d).

the corporation to make a new election effective for the following taxable year. Also, if an S corporation election is invalid or late, the IRS may grant relief if the proper remedial action is taken by the corporation.

Let's get back to our discussion of regular corporations. We'll begin with a discussion of some tax issues that arise when a corporation is formed.

C Corporations and the "Small Corporation" Exemption

C corporations are generally subject to the AMT. However, certain C corporations are exempt from the application of the AMT. For tax years beginning after 1997, the AMT does not apply to C corporations that fit a specific definition of a "small corporation." To meet this exception, the corporation must meet an average annual gross receipts test. This test is applied as follows:

- For new corporations, average annual gross receipts must not exceed $5 million for the corporation's first 3 taxable years. The corporation's first year is counted under the 3-year test, but the corporation will not be subject to the AMT for its first year. The initial year's gross receipts are annualized under the test. After the initial test is passed, the corporation must not have 3-year average annual gross receipts in excess of $7.5 million or its exemption will be lost.

- For corporations in existence before 1997, a $5 million average annual gross receipts test is applied to the 3 taxable years beginning with the first taxable year ending after December 31, 1993. If the corporation was not in existence for 3 years when this test is applied, it is then applied on an average basis to the period of the corporation's existence. Note that all corporations in existence in 1997 must have passed the test for the 1997 tax year and qualified for the exemption or else the exemption was permanently lost. Once the gross receipts test is passed, the corporation must not have 3-year average annual gross receipts in excess of $7.5 million or the exemption will be lost.

C Corporations

As a general rule property can be transferred from a proprietorship or a partnership into a regular corporation, (or to an S corporation) without the recognition of gain or loss on the transfer (IRC Sec. 351). The regular or C corporation is both a tax-reporting and a taxpaying entity. The corporate tax rate for the first $50,000 of taxable income is 15 percent for C corporations (except for qualified personal service corporations). However, leaving excessive funds in the corporation to avoid taxation at the individual level can lead to additional tax problems such as the accumulated-earnings penalty tax, which is a punitive tax, with additional tax rates of 15 percent imposed on all accumulated taxable income (IRC Secs. 531–537). The accumulated-earnings tax prevents individuals from retaining funds in the corporation for purposes other than the reasonable needs of the business. However, operating businesses can maintain up to $250,000 in the corporation without subjecting themselves to the accumulated-earnings tax. Professional corporations such as a medical practice are personal service corporations and are allowed to accumulate up to $150,000 without subjecting themselves to the accumulated-earnings tax. If accumulated taxable income exceeds these amounts, the retention of earnings and profits must be to meet reasonable business needs or the corporation will be subject to the accumulated-earnings tax. This tax is imposed in addition to regular corporate tax rates. Except in unusual circumstances the accumulated-earnings tax is not a major problem in a professional corporation, since most income can be paid out in the form of salaries and tax-advantaged benefits for the shareholder-employees.

There are few intricate rules for setting up a regular corporation for tax purposes. There is no limitation on the number or type of persons or entities that can be shareholders. Any enterprise doing business in a corporate form, as defined under state law—and indeed some associations that are not technically legal corporations but possess a majority of the corporate attributes (centralized management, continuity of life, limited liability, and free transferability of interest) are treated as corporations for tax purposes. Owners of regular corporations may also be employees of the corporations and as such are entitled to reasonable salaries and certain tax-free fringe benefits.

An important nontax advantage of the corporate form, whether it is an S corporation or a regular C corporation, is the limited personal liability of the shareholders. The general rule is that in a suit or claim against the corporation a shareholder's potential liability is limited to the amount of money that he or she has invested in the corporation.

As noted earlier, the liability of a professional is not completely limited. Each professional is personally responsible for his or her own negligence regardless of whether the practice is conducted in corporate form. This risk cannot be shifted to the entity and must be insured against. Furthermore, in the state of Jefferson one shareholder in a professional corporation may be subject to liability for the actions of another shareholder. Therefore, incorporation of a medical practice does not produce a significant liability advantage in Jefferson.

There is additional expense in changing the form of any business from a sole proprietorship to a corporation. These expenses will result primarily from the necessity of filing separate tax returns. There are also significant organizational expenses involved in establishing a corporation.

Limited Liability Companies

Limited liability companies (LLCs) offer many of the advantages of the corporate form of business but still allow income to pass through to the individual shareholders. A limited liability company is treated as a partnership for federal tax purposes even though it generally offers limited liability for its members.

Like corporations, limited liability companies do not offer absolute protection for members in a professional practice. As a physician, Dave cannot protect himself against malpractice claims resulting from his own negligence by forming a business entity. He can only protect himself against the malpractice claims brought against his partners. An LLC would provide Dave with protection from malpractice claims against his partners if the medical practice was allowed to operate as an LLC. Many states, however, have laws that prohibit a professional practice from operating as an LLC. Consequently an LLC would not be a viable option in this case.

Recommendations

Due to the nature of Dave's professional relationship with Drs. Brown and Cole, he should not consider forming a professional partnership with them at this time. Dave has indicated clearly that he has no wish to be part of a larger organization.

Therefore the remaining issue is whether Dave should continue to operate as a sole proprietor or incorporate his practice either as a C or as an S corporation.

As previously stated, incorporation in this case does not present significant protection from personal liability, since Dave is personally liable for his own professional acts regardless of whether he incorporates, and he has no partners for whose acts he would be liable. As long as Dave maintains adequate professional liability insurance, his personal assets should be protected. There is no compelling reason for Dave to incorporate at this time. Moreover, a C corporation could present tax problems if Dave decided to liquidate the corporation, since *both* the shareholder and the C corporation are taxed on the distribution of appreciated assets in a liquidation.

Incorporating would provide Dave with personal asset protection and the ability to use shares of his business in the estate planning process. Dave could later use shares of his business to fund a Family Limited Partnership and gift them to his children at a discounted value. A corporation would be better positioned to sustain a lawsuit and fund a business transition. Assume incorporation costs fully deductible by the business of $3,000 in the year of incorporation and ongoing accounting costs of $1,000 if students chose to model incorporation.

An alternative recommendation is to maintain the status quo and take no action at this time. Purchasing adequate business liability protection will cover Dave, and until he knows if a potential buyer or his children will continue in the business. The decision to incorporate can be made at a later date. Students should emphasize Dave's need for adequate business liability coverage.

Dave should also consider incorporation and corporate ownership his office building if he chooses to purchase it. Additional risks are associated with owning an office building and they might be best addressed by incorporating.

Qualified Plans of Deferred Compensation

Dave's retirement plan is of the profit-sharing type. It is integrated with social security. In a profit-sharing plan, the employer may make an annual deductible contribution of up to 25 percent of covered compensation. A separate rule (Sec. 415 limits) requires that no single employee may have more than the lesser of 25 percent of pay or $49,000 (2011 limit) allocated to his or her account annually.

Note

> To avoid repetition, the technical information on defined-benefit and defined-contribution plans has been omitted from this discussion. In a complete financial plan, an analysis of qualified plan benefits would be necessary. If you are not familiar with this information, please review it before proceeding through this suggested solution.

Also note that earned income from self-employment is also reduced by the deduction for one-half of an individual's self-employment Social Security taxes. Dave is required to pay a total of $18,898 in Social Security and Medicare taxes. This is calculated as follows:

OASDI tax: 12.40% x $106,800 (for 2011; not considering a potentially temporary tax relief act) = $13,243, plus

health insurance (HI) tax: 2.9% x $195,000 = $5,655

If Dave continues to operate without other highly paid employees, he may consider a profit sharing plan that is integrated with Social Security. The actuarial calculation of plan contributions is generally outsourced to third party plan administrators and will provide Dave with a healthy allocation of retirement plan contributions skewed in his favor.

However, a third rule also has to be considered, which may reduce the maximum contribution further. The maximum amount of compensation that can be considered in determining contributions or benefits cannot exceed $245,000 (in 2011). This compensation cap is used for calculating benefits and for determining the maximum allowable deduction.

For example, in Dave's nonintegrated plan he is contributing 15 percent of compensation to the plan for each employee. This means that the contribution for Dave is 15 percent of $195,000, or $29,500. In addition, when determining the maximum deductible contribution the Sec. 415 limit also applies. Note that it would be possible for Dave to have somewhat more under this rule if other participants were receiving contributions of less than 15 percent of compensation. One way to do this would be to continue to integrate the plan with Social Security (see below).

Choosing the Right Type of Plan

When you have a full understanding of the client's objectives, you can choose the proper nonqualified plan. There are many varieties of nonqualified plans, but our focus will be primarily on deferred-compensation plans. Several terms commonly used in this field that are helpful to understand include

golden handshakes

golden handcuffs

golden parachutes

• golden handshakes—additional benefits that are intended to induce early retirement

- golden handcuffs—additional benefits that are intended to induce an executive to remain employed, rather than leaving prematurely
- golden parachutes—substantial payments made to executives who are terminated upon change of ownership or corporate control
- incentive pay—bonuses given for accomplishing short-term goals that can be used by the executive for retirement purposes

There are two major types of nonqualified plan designs: the salary reduction plan and the supplemental executive-retirement plan. Each approach is discussed below.

Choosing between a Qualified Plan and the Other Tax-Sheltered Plan

Employers in private industry can choose between qualified plans, SEPs and SIMPLEs. The nonprofit employer that is a 501(c)(3) organization can choose any of these plans and also has the option of sponsoring a 403(b) tax-sheltered annuity plan.

Establishing and maintaining a qualified plan requires a significant amount of documentation, government reporting, and employee communication. For the small business, these requirements can be quite onerous. SEPs and SIMPLEs are intended to provide the small business with some less complicated options. Plan documents are less complicated, and there are fewer IRS reporting requirements. Simplicity translates into lower administrative expenses and less time spent operating the plan. However, in exchange for simplicity is a rigidity in plan design. These plans have less flexibility than qualified plans in most regards. The important differences include

- *Coverage.* While the qualified plan rules provide significant flexibility in the number and makeup of the employees covered by the plan, the SEP and SIMPLE eligibility requirements are set in stone.
- *Vesting.* Contributions must be fully and immediately vested in the contributions to SEPs and SIMPLEs, while qualified plans can have a vesting schedule.
- *Contributions.* In some cases in a qualified plan, benefits or contributions can be different for different classes of employees. This is not the case in SEPs and SIMPLEs, where all participants must receive essentially the same level of benefits.

- *Maximum contributions.* In most regards, the limits are lower for SEPs and SIMPLEs than for qualified plans.

The SEP is the appropriate plan option when the employer is going to fund all of the plan benefits. In a SEP, as in a profit-sharing plan, the employer can make contributions annually (or more often) on a discretionary basis. When the employer wants to allow employees the opportunity to make additional contributions on a pretax basis (making it similar to a 401(k) plan), then the SIMPLE is the appropriate choice.

The 403(b) tax-sheltered annuity is a unique retirement planning vehicle. Only tax-exempt 501(c)(3) organizations and public school systems are allowed to sponsor such plans. At one time, there were relatively few rules governing these plans. However, over time, the situation has evolved, and more and more of the rules that apply to qualified plans now also apply to 403(b) plans.

Choosing Between a Defined-Benefit and a Defined-Contribution Plan

defined-benefit plan

Assuming the employer is going to choose from among the qualified plan options, the first consideration is whether the employer wants a plan of the defined-benefit or defined-contribution type. All qualified plans fall into one of those two categories and each category represents a different philosophy of retirement planning. This philosophy is reflected in the definition of each term. A defined-benefit plan specifies the benefits each employee receives at retirement. In most plans, the benefit is stated as a percentage of preretirement salary, which is payable for the participant's remaining life. Under a defined-benefit plan, the contributions required by the employer vary depending upon what is needed to pay the promised benefit, and the amount of annual funding is determined each year by the plan's actuary.

In many ways, the defined-benefit plan looks like an insurance solution to the retirement problem. The risk that is being insured is the loss of income due to the inability to work any longer. Another risk is that an individual will outlive his or her money in retirement. The traditional defined-benefit plan addresses both of these issues. The amount of the benefit is tied to what will be lost—employment income. To address the issue of longevity, in the traditional plan, the benefit is payable for the retired employee's entire life. It is interesting to note that this plan design is due in part to the fact that the first defined-benefit plans were funded with insurance products, although today many "self-fund" the promised benefits.

defined-contribution plan   In a defined-contribution plan, on the other hand, employer contributions are allocated to the accounts of individual employees. This approach is similar to a personal savings approach in which an individual opens a bank account and makes regular contributions, and the account grows based on the rate of investment return. Because of this characteristic, defined-contribution plans are sometimes called individual account plans. One way to look at these dissimilar approaches is to say that defined-benefit plans provide a fixed predetermined benefit that has an uncertain cost to the employer, whereas defined-contribution plans have a predetermined cost to the employer and provide a variable benefit to employees (based upon the rate of return).

All qualified plans fall into either the defined-benefit or the defined-contribution category. The names of the various qualified plans and the categories into which they fall are listed below. Note, however, that two types of plans are referred to as hybrid plans. First is the cash-balance plan, which is a defined-benefit plan that has some of the characteristics of a plan using the defined-contribution approach. Second is the target-benefit plan, which is a defined-contribution plan that has some of the characteristics of a defined-benefit plan. These distinctions will become more clear when the plans are discussed in more detail. Also note that the SEP, the SIMPLE, and the 403(b) tax-sheltered annuity plan all use a defined-contribution approach and share the same strengths and limitations of other defined-contribution plans (in comparison to the defined-benefit approach).

Qualified Plan Categories	
Defined-Benefit Plans	**Defined-Contribution Plans**
• Defined-benefit pension plan	• Money-purchase pension plan
• Cash-balance pension plan	• Target-benefit pension plan
	• Profit-sharing plan
	• 401(k) plan
	• Stock bonus plan
	• ESOP

Integration with Social Security

Similar to the defined-contribution plan, the defined-benefit formula can be designed to provide a greater percentage of benefits for highly paid employees than for rank-and-file employees. Even though the rules are conceptually similar to defined-contribution plans, the integration-level approach for defined-benefit plans applies somewhat differently.

The rules also allow for an integration approach in which a benefit is described and then a portion of an individual's Social Security benefit is subtracted from the total (referred to as offset integration). At one time, this was the most common integration approach in defined-benefit plans. However, because under current law this approach rarely works as well as the integration-level approach and is, therefore, not used very often, it will not be discussed here.

The integration-level approach is called excess integration. Here's how an excess plan works:

- The plan has a specified integration level, which is generally the IRS's covered compensation table.
- The benefit formula provides the participant an additional benefit for final average compensation earned above the integration level.
- The additional or "excess" benefit cannot exceed either of the following limits:
    - The excess benefit percentage for each year of service cannot be more than the lesser of 0.75 percent of final average compensation or the percentage of final average compensation based on total compensation. For example, if the plan's formula provides a benefit of .5 percent of total final average compensation, the maximum excess percentage that can be provided is only .5 percent.
    - An excess benefit can only be provided on a maximum of 35 years of service, meaning that the maximum excess benefit can not exceed 26.25 percent of compensation (.75 multiplied by 35).

covered compensation   The integration level in a defined-benefit plan is almost always covered compensation, which is the average of the taxable wages for the individual participant using the 35-year period ending with the year that the employee reaches his or her Social Security full retirement age. The table below provides a portion of a covered compensation table for 2010. The concept of covered compensation is confusing for two reasons. First, as you can see in the table, covered compensation is different for participants of different ages, because the average of taxable wage bases depends on the years worked. Older workers will have lower covered compensation levels than younger workers, because the taxable wage bases over their final 35 years of work are lower than those for younger workers using more current years. Second, every year the table for covered compensation changes as cost-of-living increases apply. This means that the covered compensation amount keeps increasing as an individual gets older. To satisfy the integration rules, the plan must define final-average compensation as at least the 3 highest years of compensation.

Table 5-10 2010 Covered Compensation		
Calendar Year of Birth	**Calendar Year of Social Security Retirement Age**	**2010 Covered Compensation ($)**
1944	2010	59,268
1945	2011	61,884
1946	2012	64,464
1947	2013	67,008
1948	2014	69,408
1949	2015	71,724
1950	2016	73,920
1951	2017	76,044
1952	2018	78,084
1953	2019	80,052
1954	2020	81,972

EXAMPLE
The ABC Corporation has a defined-benefit plan with an integrated benefit formula. The formula provides participants with an annual benefit of one percent of final-average compensation (defined as the average of the highest 3 years of compensation) plus an additional .75 percent of compensation earned in excess of an individual's covered compensation, multiplied by years of service. The additional integrated portion of the benefit is capped at 35 years of service. This benefit formula complies with the integration rules. The excess benefit does not exceed the lesser of .75 percent per year of service or 1 percent (the benefit provided on final average compensation) and the excess is only provided on the first 35 years of benefit service. Let's calculate a benefit for Joe who retires at age 65 in 2010 (born in 1945) with 30 years of benefit service and a final-average salary of $90,000. Joe's covered compensation is $61,884. Joe's annual benefit is ($90,000 × .01 x 30) + ($33,516 × .0075 x 30) = ($6,326 + $27,000) $33,326.

Integration with Social Security

Dave has indicated that he is not interested in unduly discriminating against his employees with regard to benefits in the plan, although he is interested in minimizing costs. With these two considerations in mind, Dave might consider continuing his plan's integration with Social Security. In this way, Dave can continue to make a contribution for himself while somewhat reducing the contribution for his employees. The integrated profit sharing plan contribution results in significant savings, while still providing employees with an excellent retirement plan.

Money-Purchase Pension Plan

Another option that Dave has is to add a second plan to supplement his profit-sharing plan. With a money-purchase profit-sharing combination, the maximum deductible contribution is still 25 percent of compensation.

Unlike a profit-sharing plan, a money-purchase plan must have a predetermined contribution formula. At the present time Dave is making 15 percent contributions to the profit-sharing plan. However, if at any time he wants to make a smaller contribution, he is allowed to do so. If he establishes a money-purchase pension plan, he will have less flexibility. Consequently, a money-purchase plan is not recommended in this case.

Recommendation for Qualified Plans for Dave

Adding this supplemental plan defined benefit plan is an interesting option for Dave but will require him to make annual contributions. Instead, Dave could retain complete flexibility by reserving the right to contribute up to 25 percent of compensation to the profit-sharing plan.

Dave might consider adding a 401(k) option or Roth 401(k) option to the existing plan. Dave is close to the section 415 limit with his current plan. However he may be able to hire Diana as an administrative assistant and pay her enough to maximize her 401(k) contribution and minimize her social security tax.

If Dave paid Diana $20,000 in 2009, she would owe payroll taxes of $1,530 and be able to defer $15,500 into a 401(k). Diana would actually have to be paid reasonable wages for hours worked, but could be hired as an office manager.

The $20,000 could be generated from reducing his $55,000 profit sharing contribution to $35,000. With a reduced total contribution, Dave could also make a $15,500 deferral from his taxable wages. Dave may have to make additional safe harbor contributions to his employees, but these could come from an additional reduction in the overall plan match.

Dave should seek the assistance of a pension attorney or consultant if he decides to adopt 401(k) elements in his plan. Also, if Dave decides to change his profit-sharing plan or add a money-purchase plan, he will incur additional expenses. Dave needs to fully understand these costs so that he can compare the cost savings of the plan redesign against the additional costs that he will incur.

Buy-Sell Agreements to Ensure That Dave's Practice Is Marketable at Death or Disability

One of the Andersons' most important assets is Dave's practice; in fact, it is presently their most important asset in terms of income production. Currently, there is no guarantee that the practice could be translated into cash within a reasonable time after his death or disability because Dave has never implemented a legally enforceable agreement for the sale of his practice. The failure to implement a legally enforceable and appropriately funded buy-sell agreement often results in significant losses upon the disposition of a closely held business.

In the event that Dave continues to live but becomes disabled, his business interest should be convertible to cash to provide him with additional monies throughout the period of his disability. The design and implementation of an appropriate buy-sell agreement is the most effective way to ensure the accomplishment of these objectives.

Because buy-sell agreements are usually funded wholly or partially with life insurance, they are particularly troublesome when the parties are of widely disparate ages or if one of the parties' health is impaired. The difference in ages or health conditions can result in the younger or healthier party being forced to personally pay nondeductible high premiums for insurance on the life of an older or impaired party.

We have no information that would indicate that such a problem might arise in this case. In the absence of these problems Dave should discuss the possibility of entering into a buy-sell agreement with either Dr. Cole or Dr. Brown or both, since they have expressed an interest in expanding their practices. Since Dave is not particularly interested in expanding his practice, it may be possible to interest one or both of the other physicians in agreeing to purchase his practice should he die or become disabled. On the other hand, it may be necessary for Dave to agree to a reciprocal purchase agreement if he wants the assurance that his practice can be quickly converted to cash. Based on the results of these negotiations, Dave can decide whether to proceed.

If Dave decides to proceed with buyout arrangements, the provisions and funding of the agreement should be carefully considered. At a minimum the agreement(s) should provide for the other party or parties to become obligated to purchase Dave's shares if he is deceased or becomes disabled. While death is easily ascertainable, issues may arise as to when disability should trigger a buyout.

In the event of disability, however, a definition of disability that will make the buy-sell operative must be contained in the document.

A buy-sell agreement should not be designed to provide for the immediate buyout of a disabled party. An appropriate waiting period should be adopted to balance the client's need for disability income and the time at which the client can psychologically deal with the fact that he or she will be unable to resume professional duties.

One of the most difficult aspects in designing a buy-sell agreement is deciding on a valuation for the business interest. The best way to ascertain the value of a going business is to have the business appraised by an appropriate professional. In many cases, however, closely held business owners are reluctant to engage an appraiser because of the expense. In addition, even if an appraisal is made currently and a firm dollar value is entered into the buy-sell agreement, it is likely that the agreement may not become operative for many years. In that event the appraisal figure is meaningless because it is outdated. The value of the business could have risen tenfold or fallen to half its stated value, yet if the amount stated in the buy-sell agreement has not been revised, the purchasing party is obligated to pay only the original price as stated in the agreement. This can result in a significant hardship to the estate or beneficiaries of the closely held business owner if the value of the business has increased or to the purchaser if the value of the business has decreased.

Even when a buy-sell agreement is in effect, most parties will not meet to redetermine the value of the business on a regular basis because they are preoccupied with other matters. Absolute dollar values in a buy-sell agreement are problematic and should be avoided.

In the case of a personal service business such as Dave's professional practice, an appraisal of the current value of the business can be used as the starting point for the buy-sell agreement. Furthermore, the appraisal should provide the criteria on which an appropriate ongoing valuation formula for the practice can be based. A valuation formula should be included in the buy-sell agreement in lieu of a stated dollar figure if possible. The formula approach is preferable to any other since it allows the value of the business to be determined at any given point in time.

In this case a unilateral purchase agreement between one or both of Dave's professional colleagues and Dave should be explored. It is likely that Dave's colleagues will want a reciprocal buy-sell arrangement, in which case Dave will have to reconsider his willingness to increase the size of his practice. The agreement should be funded partially or wholly by insurance to the extent that it is available. A realistic value for Dave's practice should be established, preferably by an appraisal, and maintained by a formula set forth in the buy-sell agreement.

BUSINESS PLANNING: INSURANCE

Funding the Buy-Sell Agreement(s)

Our recommendation for funding the buy-sell agreement is full or partial funding with life insurance. At this point, without further information about whether the buy-sell agreement will be a unilateral or cross-purchase agreement, specific funding recommendations for an after-death buyout would be inappropriate.

The other elements that must be considered in funding the buy-sell agreement are the appropriate amount and availability of coverage if Dave's disability triggers the buy-sell.

Insurers are generally unwilling to provide coverage with lump-sum benefits for professionals who are sole practitioners. Therefore it will be necessary for Dave to discuss with Dr. Cole or Dr. Brown or both whether one or both would be willing to enter into a buy-sell agreement that would protect him in the event of his becoming disabled without the agreement being insured. If one or both of the other physicians are interested in these terms, the business valuation price according to the formula in the buy-sell agreement may be paid in installments over the shortest possible period that Dave and his attorneys can negotiate.

The crucial issues in an uninsured disability buyout are not materially different from the issues encountered in insured agreements. They include primarily the definition of disability and the waiting period before the agreement becomes operative. The parties must agree to the definition of disability, and the length of the waiting period must be set forth in unambiguous terms in the buy-sell agreement.

There is a real danger in selecting too short a waiting period for a buyout agreement as it could result in a mandatory sale of Dave's business interest because of a relatively short-term disability that lasts longer than the waiting period specified by the agreement. It would be advisable to have a waiting period of at least 24 months before triggering the buyout agreement.

Medical and Disability Insurance Plans

If Dave decides not to incorporate his practice, there does not appear to be any significant advantage to having the existing proprietorship provide additional group insurance benefits, as proprietors are not considered employees of proprietorships, and therefore contributions on their behalf are not tax deductible as a business expense.

Medical Expense Insurance

The medical insurance plan that Dave presently provides for his employees and in which he and his family participate appears to provide excellent benefits at a competitive price. The premiums paid on behalf of the employees are deductible as a business expense. However, since Dave operates as a sole proprietorship, the tax treatment of health benefits provided for himself and his family is different. Sole proprietors can deduct the cost of purchasing health insurance coverage for themselves and their own families as an adjustment to gross income on their personal income tax return.

Disability Income Insurance

Although Dave presently has an individual disability plan, a review of the limits of its coverage makes it apparent that it is insufficient to allow him to maintain his present lifestyle. In all likelihood it will be impossible to achieve this objective solely with disability income protection, since insurers will not provide such a high ratio of coverage to total income. Generally a higher upper limit of coverage is available if an employer purchases the disability income coverage (70 percent) than if the employee individually purchases the coverage (60 percent). In this case, however, the overall limit would be approximately $6,000 per month of benefits either through an employer plan or (as in this case) if Dave purchases the coverage individually. This results from the fact that at this high level of income, maximum benefit limits tend to merge.

Employer disability policies are deductible to the employer, but any benefits would be subject to tax. If Dave establishes a proper buy-sell agreement at his death or disability, business coverage would be redundant. Maximizing and analyzing his individual policy is more effective from a tax perspective.

Property and Liability Insurance for the Business

With little information given in the case about the business assets to be covered by property and liability insurance, it is difficult to make any recommendations other than noting the necessity of having these coverages thoroughly reviewed by a professional in the field of property and liability insurance.

Professional Liability Insurance

Professional liability coverage for physicians and surgeons is often referred to as medical malpractice insurance. As a result of the significant premium increases in this type of insurance and the objections to those increases by physicians, a newer type of lower-cost policy has become popular.

The original type of coverage, known as occurrence-based coverage, protected the insured from any claims stemming from medical procedures performed while the policy was in force. This coverage would pay benefits for liability even if the incident giving rise to the liability was first discovered many years after the policy expiration date and when no further premiums were being paid. Thus the premium charged while the policy was in force had to be high enough to cover inflation and the risk associated with future claims amounts.

The newer type of policy, known as claims-made coverage, pays only for claims made during the time the policy is in force. Claims will be payable by the insurer only if the medical treatment giving rise to the claim was performed after the retroactive date specified in the policy and before the policy termination date. This type of policy necessitates continuation of coverage after the medical professional retires or otherwise discontinues practice. The extended reporting-period endorsements keep this protection in effect after the base policy terminates. Premiums must generally be paid for the first 3 years of the extended reporting-period endorsements. If the professional does not engage in any aspect of practice for the entire 3-year period, a single additional premium of less than the regular premium will extend the claims-made protection to perpetuity.

In cases where the physician changes back to an occurrence-based coverage after having a period of claims-made coverage, it will also be necessary to extend the reporting period by endorsements. Without an extension there would be a gap in coverage. The occurrence-based coverage would not cover procedures performed during the period the claims-made coverage was effective.

In terms of cost the claims-made coverage can be as low as one-quarter of the premium for occurrence-based coverage in the first year. The claims-made premiums will increase to about 85 percent of occurrence-based premiums after 5 or more years.

The potential liability for an orthopedic surgeon is quite high. In fact, there have already been single-case liability judgments in medical cases that exceeded $5 million. It is therefore suggested that professional liability coverage with policy limits of $10 million be carried. If the policy acquired is claims-made coverage, it is important to seek a retroactive date that coincides with the termination date of the most recent occurrence-based professional liability coverage. Although coverage for $1 million of liability protection is available at a cost of approximately $15,000 annually, liability coverage is scalable. Dave's sole proprietorship can obtain the recommended $10 million of protection on Dave and his nursing staff for about $30,000 a year. This cost is substantial, but the potential savings to Dave's livelihood is astronomical.

Business Overhead Expense Disability Insurance

Because of the limitations that insurers impose on the upper limits of disability income benefits, it is virtually impossible to get adequate coverage to ensure that all the usual and normal expenses of one's life are covered by insurance benefits, especially when the disabled person has continuing business overhead expenses. Business overhead expense disability coverage aims at closing this gap. In a case such as Dave's this coverage normally pays for continuing business expenses, such as office rent, utilities, nurses' salaries, postage, office equipment and supplies, and business taxes. This type of disability is usually defined as the inability to perform the duties of the insured's own occupation. Various benefit durations are available but should not exceed the effective date of the disability buyout provisions of the buy-sell agreement if Dave and Drs. Brown and/or Cole enter into such an agreement. Based on the facts of this case approximately $5,000 in monthly benefits would be the maximum available coverage, and benefits would be available for a period of 24 months. Representative annual premiums for $5,000 in monthly benefits with various elimination periods are listed below. The elimination period should be based on Dave's available cash flow. The recommendation is that a period of no less than 60 days be elected.

Elimination Period	Annual Premium
30 days	$1,025
60 days	630
90 days	385

Financial Statements Restated with Business Planning Recommendations

After reviewing business planning, four planning recommendations were considered:

- Increase business liability insurance from $1,000,000 to $10,000,000. The cost of this increase will be $15,000 and will be reflected in Dave's total profit.

- Buy business overhead insurance with a 60-day elimination period.

- Dave pays a business appraiser to value his business. While the costs were not mentioned in the case, we have assumed $2,000 for this service.

- Change retirement plans to include a 401(k) contribution.

  - Dave will pay Diana $20,000

  - Dave and Diana will make $15,500 (2008) elective contributions

  - Diana will pay Self Employment tax of the Social Security and Medicaid portion of her $20,000. The taxes will total 15.3 percent of her compensation or ($3,060). Half of these taxes can be written off ($1,530) against income.

  - Dave will maximize cash flow and make a profit sharing plan contribution up to his (415) limit ($46,000– $15,500). Dave's portion of the contribution should target $30,500. A total contribution of $35,000 should satisfy this amount. Dave will have to discuss allocation procedures with his plan actuary to ensure compliance with all IRS rules and regulations.

After implementing all proposed changes, the Anderson's will lower their federal income tax to $17,290. This savings when coupled with maximizing 401(k) deferral options will increase annual retirement savings from $49,000 (Dave's 415 limit) to at least $57,500 (Dave's 415 limit and Diana's 401(k) deferral.

The Anderson family will have around $1,600 a month remaining to fund their personal goals.

Anderson Restated Income Tax Projections

Table 5-11 Anderson Restated Income Tax Projections			
Earned Income This Year			
Business Profit	$250,000.00		
PS Contribution	($35,000.00)		
Diana's Salary	($20,000.00)		
New Costs	($17,360.00)		
		$177,640.00	
Diana's Paycheck	$20,000.00		
		$20,000.00	
Interest & Dividends			
Brokerage Account	$2,300.00		
Joint Savings Interest	$800.00		
		$3,100.00	
Real Estate Investments			
Rental Home Income	$14,400.00		
* Rental Loan Interest	($3,596.84)		
Rental Home Prop Tax	($4,387.50)		
Rental Home Operating Expenses	($900.00)		
** Rental Home Depreciation	($2,080.00)		
Lot Interest	($8,000.00)		
Lot Prop Taxes	($6,900.00)		
		($11,464.34)	
401(k) Deferrals			
Dave's 401(k)	($15,500.00)		
Diana's 401(k)	($15,500.00)		
		($31,000.00)	
Adjusted Gross Income			**$158,275.66**
Potential Itemized Deductions			
4% State Income Tax (on AGI)	($6,331.03)		
Charitable Contributions	($10,000.00)		
Home Prop Taxes	($12,000.00)		
Home Interest	($7,106.00)		
		($32,662.03)	
2011 MFJ Standard Deduction		—	
SE Tax Adjustment	**($10,654.50)**		
2011 4 Personal Exemptions	($14,800.00)		
Total Deductions and Exemptions			($58,116.53
Taxable Income			**$100,159.11**
2011 Projected Income Tax Due			**$17,290**
Highest Marginal Rate			25%

PERSONAL PLANNING: TAXES

Present Situation

Dave and Diana have been married for 16 years. They have two children: Deidre, 9, and Melissa, 6, and have just discovered that they will have another child in about 7 months. The older children are very intelligent, and the Andersons are considering sending them to a private high school with rigorous academic standards, where tuition is $30,000 per school year. Dave and Diana would also like to plan now to finance college educations for their children.

They purchased a home for $79,000 that has appreciated to its present value of $615,000. The house is furnished with some lovely antiques that Diana has acquired over the years. They own two relatively new cars.

Dave owns a single-family residential rental property and an undeveloped commercial lot. A potential buyer has made an offer for the commercial lot, and Dave is interested in a recommendation as to whether the lot should be sold. Dave has been acquiring a portfolio of stocks, bonds, and mutual fund shares.

Dave earns a substantial income from his practice as an orthopedic surgeon, and the Andersons enjoy a good life. They want to maximize their wealth accumulation, provide themselves with retirement funds sufficient to continue their lifestyle, and provide for the family if Dave should die prematurely.

Fund Private School and/or College Education for Children

Dave and Diana have asked you to prepare an estimate of projected costs for educating their children at a top-quality institution. They are immediately interested in providing money to fund private high schools and will most likely wish to fund college as well. The Andersons have high aspirations for their children, and a $30,000 private school bill will take significant resources.

Tax advantaged saving options are limited for primary and secondary education, and Dave and Diana are hovering close to the 28 percent marginal income tax bracket. The Andersons want to avoid ordinary and interest income in the pursuit of their children's educations.

The following assumptions include four years of college immediately following high school. The Andersons believe they can earn 8.0 percent on education funding assets and that education inflation will remain at 6.0 percent.

Table 5-12 Amount Needed Today to Fund Deidre's Education for 8 Years		
Diedre's Age	Future Costs of High School and College	Amount Needed Today to Fund Cost in the Future
14	$(40,146.77)	$27,323.22
15	$(42,555.57)	$26,817.23
16	$(45,108.91)	$26,320.61
17	$(47,815.44)	$25,833.20
18	$(50,684.37)	$25,354.80
19	$ (53,725.43)	$24,885.27
20	$(56,948.96)	$24,424.43
21	$(60,365.89)	$23,972.13
	Amount Needed Today to Fund Education Expenses	$204,930.89

A similar calculation can be run for Melissa:

Table 5-13 Amount Needed Today to Fund Melissa's Education for 8 Years		
Melissa's Age	Future Costs of High School and College	Amount Needed Today to Fund Cost in the Future
14	$(47,815.44)	$25,833.20
15	$(50,684.37)	$25,354.80
16	$(53,725.43)	$24,885.27
17	$(56,948.96)	$24,424.43
18	$(60,365.89)	$23,972.13
19	$(63,987.85)	$23,528.20
20	$(67,827.12)	$23,092.49
21	$(71,896.75)	$22,664.85
	Amount Needed Today to Fund Education Expenses	$193,755.37

The Andersons need to set aside around $400,000 today to secure secondary and college funding for Diedre and Melissa. Alternatively, they could save money on an annual basis. The Andersons are in a unique position to have wisely acquired a commercial lot that could be sold for at least $640,000. A portion of proceeds from the sale could be used to accrue college savings costs. At the birth of the next child, additional savings needs will arise. At this time the plan will focus on Diedre and Melissa.

A question remains of what type of instrument should be used to fund savings costs. Growing assets in a conservative tax-advantaged environment is a priority for Diedre and Melissa. The following sections outline account types that can be used for education savings. Specific recommendations about education funding will be made later in the planning process.

Gifting

Outright Gifts. Under the current federal gift tax exclusion, a person (donor) can give any other person (donee) up to $13,000 per year per donee, gift tax free (IRC Sec. 2503(b)). That amount can be doubled if the donor's spouse agrees to join in the gift, regardless of whether the spouse actually contributes any portion of the gift (IRC Sec. 2513). Use of the annual gift tax exclusion is an effective way for clients to shift assets to their children and take advantage of the children's lower tax brackets. However, outright gifting presents some problems. The person giving the gift (the donor) must part forever with the property that is gifted, including any earning capacity that it has. All but the wealthiest clients are reluctant to part with assets that they may need for their later years.

The Andersons could utilize outright gifting to supplement other accumulation techniques if actual college costs exceed those that are anticipated and funded for. If these "gifts" were made in the form of actual tuition payments to a qualified educational institution, the amount paid is exempt from federal gift taxes (IRC Sec. 2503(e)). They would, however, have to be made with after-tax dollars; therefore there are better techniques for funding the bulk of their children's educations.

UGMA and UTMA Gifts. In addition to the problems already described with outright gifting, there are problems with giving gifts to minors. The Uniform Gifts to Minors Act (UGMA) and the Uniform Transfers to Minors Act (UTMA) provide mechanisms by which a donor can give a gift to a minor without necessitating the appointment of a guardian of the minor's property. (A majority of the states have adopted the newer Uniform Transfers to Minors Act.) Instead, a custodian of the gift is designated. This custodian has full powers over the gifted property and its income on behalf of the minor child. In many cases the donor is the minor child's parent, who also functions as the custodian of the UGMA or UTMA account. Gifts under the Uniform Acts qualify under the federal gift tax provisions as present-interest gifts without the necessity of withdrawal rights or annual payments of income and as such are subject to the $13,000-per-year-per-donee gift tax exclusion (IRC Secs. 2503(b), 2503(c)).

There are some planning issues associated with UGMA and UTMA gifts:

- If the donor is the parent of the minor and also the custodian of the UGMA or UTMA account and dies while still the custodian, the total amount of the account will be included in his or her estate for federal estate tax purposes because of the control he or she can exercise over the account (IRC Sec. 2036(a)).

- The type of property that can be transferred effectively under the Uniform Acts is severely restricted in some states. The Uniform Acts are *not* uniform from state to state. When the original UGMA was being lobbied for, the most effective lobbying group consisted primarily of securities dealers attempting to facilitate gifts of stock and securities to minors. The result of this lobbying effort is that many of the UGMA statutes enacted by the various states restrict UGMA gifts to money, securities, life insurance, or annuity contracts. Other types of property, such as real estate, cannot be effectively transferred by UGMA gifts in many states. (If this is the result in the state in which a particular client is located, the UGMA transfer can be made under the UGMA statute in one of the several states that allows for transfers of almost any type of property, including real estate. This is accomplished by having the instrument specify that the transfer is being made pursuant to the Uniform Gifts to Minors Act of the more favorable state.) In states that have adopted the Uniform Transfers to Minors Act, there is more flexibility regarding the types of assets that may be transferred.

- The custodianship generally terminates when the minor reaches either age 21 or the local legal age of majority. At that time all funds in the custodial account must be distributed to the beneficiary. This gives the 18-, 19-, or 21-year-old (depending on local law) unfettered discretion over the disposition of the assets, which may result in the assets being squandered rather than being used for the purpose for which the custodianship was established.

- Income from assets in custodial accounts will be subject to the kiddie tax for minors under 14 years of age, regardless of whether the income is distributed to the minor. A custodial account, unlike a trust, is not a separate taxpayer from the minor beneficiary.

While gifts to minors under UGMA or UTMA can be utilized effectively for relatively small sums, they are generally not the technique of choice for larger sums because of the mandatory distribution at the legal age of majority, the potential kiddie tax problems, and potential federal estate tax inclusion for the donor-parent who acts as custodian.

Funding 529 Plans for College Savings. The Andersons are unable to use 529 plans for secondary education, but could reserve funds in 529 accounts today that the girls could use for college in the future.

Sec. 529 qualified tuition programs   Every state jurisdiction sponsors some type of prepaid, tax-favored savings plan designed to help parents pay for future college expenses. These are referred to as *Sec. 529 qualified tuition programs.*

Under EGTRRA 2001, the funds accumulated in a qualified tuition program grow tax deferred. Also, distributions are tax free as long as the proceeds are used for "qualified" higher education expenses, such as room, board, tuition, books, and supplies. EGTRRA allows accumulated funds to be used at any accredited institution of higher learning in the United States, as well as at many foreign institutions. If funds in the account are not used for higher education, they are subject to income tax and a 10 percent penalty upon distribution.

Some additional tax advantages exist for the donors (parents and grandparents) to the account. For example, the donor maintains full control of the funds in the account even after the child reaches age 18. (Conversely, in an UGMA account—defined below—an "adult" child takes over control at majority age.) Furthermore, donors can contribute up to 5 years' annual gift tax exclusion amounts to a child's account in one single year. This means that assuming an annual exclusion of $13,000, a grandparent can put as much as $60,000 into a child's Sec. 529 plan in a year without incurring gift tax (married parents and/or grandparents can contribute $120,000 gift tax free), as long as the donor does not make any additional gifts to that beneficiary over that 5-year period. Moreover, the total amount of deposits enjoys tax-free growth in most plans. Furthermore, tax-free withdrawals for qualified expenses can be made from Sec. 529 plans in the same year as withdrawals from other qualified accounts, provided these funds are used for different expenses.

The funding vehicles for these tax-advantaged accounts include mutual funds, which allow for professional management, portfolio diversification, and high return potential over the accumulation period prior to a child's college years. At the present time, Sec. 529 plan holders can change investment options within plans once a year, giving parents even greater flexibility and control over these funds.

   Sec. 2503(b) Trusts. A trust device that can be utilized to provide gifts to minors is the IRC Sec. 2503(b) trust, which provides certain advantages and disadvantages when compared with the Sec. 2503(c) trust, discussed later in this section. The principal advantage of the Sec. 2503(b) trust is that it need not terminate when the beneficiary attains the age of 21. A principal disadvantage is that the trust must pay the net income to the beneficiary annually or in more frequent installments. That is, it cannot accumulate income even during the minority of the beneficiary. This means that income from the trust that is paid to beneficiaries under the age of 14 will be taxed at the marginal rate of the beneficiary's parents, generally to the extent that the child's income exceeds $1,500 per year adjusted for inflation (under the kiddie tax). This substantially reduces the income shifting benefits of the 2503(b) trust.

Another disadvantage of the Sec. 2503(b) trust is that the value of the income interest and the value of the remainder interest (the property that composes the principal of the trust) are computed separately for gift tax purposes. Only the value of the income interest is eligible for the annual gift tax exclusion.

The Sec. 2503(b) trust may not allow discretionary payments to more than one beneficiary. Furthermore, there can be no postponement or delay in the payment of the net income of the trust. If there are any restrictions on distribution of trust income (for example, if the income is conditional or discretionary in any way) the annual exclusion will be unavailable.

The mandatory payment of the trust income can be a major tax and nontax disadvantage when the beneficiary is a minor. This is especially true if significant sums of money are involved, since it could necessitate the appointment of a guardian of the minor's property. This procedure is both expensive and tedious. Guardians are subject to court supervision in handling the funds of the minor and are statutorily prohibited from entering into certain investment transactions.

Because of the mandatory payment requirement and the fact that the trust beneficiaries—the Anderson children—are minors under age 14, it would not be advisable to utilize the 2503(b) trust to fund college education for the children.

Sec. 2503(c) Trusts. If a trust is structured according to the terms of IRC Sec. 2503(c), gifts to the trust qualify for the gift tax exclusion without giving the beneficiary a right to withdraw funds or without the necessity for paying the beneficiary the income at least annually. A transfer to a Sec. 2503(c) trust can be more advantageous than transfers to an UGMA custodianship because no statutory restriction on the type of property transferred is applicable in the case of 2503(c) trusts. In addition, the property can be maintained in the trust at least until the beneficiary reaches age 21, even when the age of majority under state law is less than 21. A Sec. 2503(c) trust is an irrevocable trust. Therefore the donor cannot take back the funds once they are gifted to the trust.

The Internal Revenue Code requires that both the property and the income from the property of a 2503(c) trust be available to be expended by or for the benefit of the beneficiary during the time before he or she attains the age of 21. In addition, to the extent that trust assets have not already been expended by or for the beneficiary before attaining the age of 21, the property and the income of the trust must pass to the beneficiary. If the beneficiary fails to live to the age of 21, the accumulated income and the principal must be payable to the estate of the beneficiary unless he or she can appoint it to another under a general power of appointment.

The Internal Revenue Code requires that the principal and income of the trust must be available for distribution in the time period before the donee reaches age 21. The regulations, however, go further. Treas. Reg. Sec. 25.2503–4(b)(1) prohibits "substantial restrictions" on the trustee's power to make distributions of trust income and principal. This might prohibit any specific restrictions in the trust instrument on the distributions of income and principal for certain specified purposes, such as illness or education. As a practical matter, the trustee can make distributions or accumulate income for the purposes intended by the donor in his or her discretion as trustee.

In addition, the Sec. 2503(c) trust cannot be used for the benefit of a class of beneficiaries. Trust instruments routinely describe payments to a class of beneficiaries in substantially the following language: "All the net income from the trust is to be distributed annually or at more frequent intervals to or for the benefit of the grantor's three children, as necessary, in such amounts as the trustee in his sole discretion shall deem necessary." Although under this type of provision the terms of the trust provide that all the net income of the trust is to be distributed at least annually, the amount of the income receivable by any one of the beneficiaries remains within the discretion of the trustee and is not presently ascertainable. Accordingly the use of the annual exclusion is disallowed for transfers to such a trust. It is possible to utilize Sec. 2503(c) trusts for more than one beneficiary, however, by using either a separate trust for each beneficiary or a separate-share trust. A separate-share trust divides the trust principal into definite portions with each portion having a specified beneficiary.

Another statutory requirement of the Sec. 2503(c) trust indicates that the trust cannot exist past the date of the beneficiary's 21st birthday. The Treasury regulations, however, provide that the trust will not be disqualified provided that the donee (beneficiary) has the right to extend the term of the trust upon reaching the age of 21 (Treas. Reg. Sec. 25.2503–4(b)(2)). The right to continue the trust can apparently require that the beneficiary must affirmatively compel distribution at age 21 (Rev. Rul. 74–43, 1974–1 C.B. 285). The right to compel distribution at age 21 may exist for only a limited period of time, as long as the period of time is reasonable. Thirty to 60 days have been deemed reasonable in a number of private letter rulings (PLR 7824035; PLR 7805037). If the beneficiary fails to compel the distribution from the trust during the permissible period or otherwise affirmatively allows the trust to continue, the trust will continue until it terminates under the terms of the trust instrument.

It is often undesirable to allow the trust principal and accumulated income, if any, to pass through the estate of a minor, since a minor is not legally competent to make a will. This results in the funds passing under the intestacy laws. However, the Treasury regulations provide that if the beneficiary is given a general power of appointment over the trust principal and accumulated income and fails to exercise this power of appointment, regardless of whether he or she is competent as a minor to do so under local law, the trust continues to qualify for the annual exclusion. In fact, the trust instrument may provide that in the absence of the exercise of the power of appointment there is a gift in default of the exercise of the power. This gift-over may be made to whomever the grantor of the trust desires, including his other children. This is an especially advantageous provision, the inclusion of which should be considered in any Sec. 2503(c) trust.

Family Partnership. Family partnerships are another income-splitting device that can be valuable in allowing higher-bracket taxpayers to shift income to lower-bracket family members. In order to be effective, the partnership must be a bona fide partnership and not merely an attempt to assign the income of a high-bracket taxpayer to taxpayers in a lower tax bracket. To withstand an assignment-of-income attack by the IRS, the income produced by a partnership should be attributable to the capital and/or services contributed by the partners. A general principle of income taxation requires that income be taxed to the person who earns it. An impermissible assignment of income will generally not be deemed to occur if (1) the income tax liability for income derived from personal services remains with the person who performed the services and (2) the income tax liability for income produced by utilizing capital remains with the owner of the capital. A shift in the ownership of capital under this principle would result in the shifting of the income tax liability.

For family partnerships in which "capital is a material income-producing factor," the tax status of a partner is recognized if he or she owns a capital interest in the partnership, whether the interest was acquired by purchase or by gift (IRC Sec. 704(e)(1)). The tax status of partners in a family partnership in which capital is not a material income-producing factor is much more troublesome.

The achievement of partnership status for tax purposes will not be accomplished unless the ownership of the capital interest in the partnership is bona fide. In most family planning situations a partnership interest will be gifted either directly or indirectly to a family member; that is, a capital interest in the partnership will either be a direct gift, or the funds necessary to purchase a capital interest will be gifted. The fact that the interest was acquired by gift does not necessarily make it suspect. There are, however, some other tests that are applied to ascertain the genuineness of the transfer. Transactions that are suspect include the following:

- a donor partner's retention of the right to control the distribution of the income of the partnership. This may indicate that the transfer is less than genuine unless the income is retained for the reasonable needs of the business with the other partners' consent. The donor partner can, however, retain the right to control and distribute partnership income without any negative implications provided that right is retained and exercised in a fiduciary capacity (Treas. Reg. Sec. 1.704-1(e)(2)).
- retention of control over the donee's disposition or liquidation of the donated interest beyond reasonable business restrictions
- retention of control over assets essential to the partnership's business (such as ownership of a crucial asset leased to the partnership) that would give the donor partner unusual power to affect the partnership's viability or business

Minors can be recognized as general partners for tax purposes without the minor's interest being held in trust (Treas. Reg. Sec. 1.704-1(e)(2)). The fact that a minor is very young, however, may result in the minor's losing his or her tax status as a partner, unless it can be demonstrated that the minor is competent to manage his or her own property and participate in the partnership activities in accordance with his or her interest in the property (Treas. Reg. Sec. 1.7041(e)(2)). The test is not based on the legal age of majority under the local law of the state but is a test of the minor's maturity and experience (Treas. Reg. Sec. 1.7041(e)(2)). Because of these limitations, minors in their individual capacity should not be made general partners. If a general partnership interest is to be transferred to a minor, the partnership interest should be conveyed to a trust for the minor's benefit.

Another option is to make minors limited partners in family partnerships. Gifts can be made of either the limited partnership interests or of money to purchase the partnership units. Limited partners by definition do not participate in the management of the partnership business. The Treasury Regulations state that in order for a limited partnership to be recognized for federal tax purposes it must be organized and conducted in accordance with the applicable state limited partnership law. The Treasury regulations further provide that the absence of services and participation in management by a donee partner in a limited partnership is immaterial (Treas. Reg. Sec. 1.704-1(e)(2)). This allows for a great deal of control to be retained by the donor general partner. That control cannot extend, however, to placing restrictions on the disposition of the partnership interest that would not be acceptable to unrelated limited partners.

The Andersons could form a family limited partnership and contribute the residential rental property to it; however, the cash flow and appreciation from this property are not sufficient to make it an effective mechanism for funding the children's educations. In addition, an interest in a limited partnership does not qualify for the special $25,000 real estate allowance under the passive-loss rules discussed in the investment planning section. For these reasons a family partnership is not the recommendation of choice.

Caveat: Parental Obligations

If an income-shifting device (such as the 2503(c) trust) is utilized, it is important to ensure that the resulting income is not used to satisfy the legal support obligations of the parent. If parental obligations are satisfied with these funds, the distribution is income taxable to the parent despite the fact that the income-shifting device is otherwise fully effective. The extent of parental support obligations is determined under local law. In all states the parental obligation of support extends to necessities—food, clothing, shelter, and the like. In some states the legislatures or the courts have extended the scope of these parental obligations to include such things as college educations and private schools when those are consistent with the family's lifestyle and are within their financial means.

In the state of Jefferson the parental obligation of support does not extend to providing private school or college for children. There is a case, however, that holds that a father who enters into an agreement—incorporated into a divorce decree while a child is a minor—to send a child to college is legally obligated to provide that college education even after the child's majority.

State laws vary widely in this area. Some states make parental obligations the legal responsibility of the father only, while some states extend the duty to the mother as well. The applicable state rules should be thoroughly investigated prior to implementing any income-shifting device.

Reduce Tax Burden

Achieve Personal Objectives through Income-Shifting Devices to Reduce Cost

The Andersons can meet personal financial goals by freeing up funds. Gifting money to children might reduce the overall tax burden, but the Andersons may want to retain control of assets until their children are older. 529 accounts are a solution to college funding problems, but high school funding will require either leaving assets in the parents names and paying expenses by liquidating assets, using educational IRA accounts, UGMA accounts or a blended combination of choices.

The Andersons will begin deferring in excess of $57,000 using 401(k) profit sharing plan. The design is outlined in the business planning section of the plan document. Additional IRA contributions are possible, but may take away from other planning goals. The life insurance and investment sections of the plan will address mechanisms of additional tax savings strategies.

Ensure Adequate Protection in the Event of Dave's Disability

Design Buy-Sell Agreement to Become Operative in the Event of Disability

Buy-sell agreements can be designed to become operative in the event of the disability of a shareholder, but insurers generally will not provide coverage for professional sole proprietors. The buy-sell agreement for Dave's practice could be designed to become operative in the event of disability if he can get his professional colleagues to agree to an installment payout in lieu of the availability of insurance funding.

Personal Disability Income Coverage

The primary advantage of personally acquired disability income coverage is that the proceeds are received tax free. The primary disadvantage of personal disability income coverage is that the premiums for coverage are not tax deductible. In addition, there are different limitations on coverage amounts available under personal and corporate coverage plans. Generally the amounts available under personal disability coverage are lower than those available under employer disability coverage. In Dave's case the total amount available under either personal disability income coverage or employer coverage is approximately $6,000 a month, because his high income has effectively caused the coverage limits to merge. As discussed in the business planning section, Dave should obtain the maximum amount of coverage through a personally owned policy.

Ensure a Comfortable Retirement

Dave's profit sharing plan is the Andersons' primary vehicle for accumulating funds for retirement. Dave's balance at year end is projected at $252,000 Contributions are projected to remain constant unless tax laws affecting profit sharing plans change.

Although the plan balance is presently earning 8 percent, a more conservative rate of return should be assumed beyond the 5-year plan horizon. Dave will reach age 65 in 24 years. If an inflation-adjusted rate of return of 6 percent is assumed for the plan (to express his retirement date plan balance in today's dollars), the plan balance with 401(k) and profit sharing contributions in 24 years will be approximately $3,900,000. This number was determined using a future value calculation with $57,000 contributions over 24 years and a starting balance of $252,000.

Dave and Diana will have a number of options at that point. They could take the plan proceeds in a lump-sum distribution and systematically liquidate the principal over life expectancy. They could also choose to live on the income only. Alternatively they could use the plan balance to purchase a joint and survivor annuity with an installment refund feature. This decision, of course, will be based on their circumstances at that time.

However, it does appear that the Andersons will enjoy a comfortable retirement under the assumptions given.

The Andersons' current committed and discretionary expenses (excluding taxes and investment outlays) are approximately $63,000 per year. The retirement plan assumptions include an inflation-adjusted rate of return to express the future plan balance in today's dollars. Therefore either the annuity or an alternative payout method should provide the Andersons with sufficient funds for a comfortable retirement under the assumptions.

Assuming further that the Social Security system remains intact, the Andersons would probably receive a total monthly benefit of at least $4,200 (combined benefit) in inflation-adjusted dollars, based on the retirement benefit formulas currently in place.

As discussed in the business plan, Dave can consider the implementation of a defined-benefit plan in combination with his profit-sharing plan if he wants to provide additional security for his retirement.

Consider Various Problems Diana Might Encounter in Setting Up Her Own Business

Preliminary General Planning

Since the new baby will delay the start date for Diana's proposed business specializing in antique Oriental porcelain and Oriental rugs, the detailed planning for that venture should be postponed until she is closer to the time when she will be able to commit to such an effort. This may not be for several years, depending on a family decision about how long she should stay home with the baby. However, it is appropriate to begin doing some preliminary long-range planning.

In the interim Diana can continue developing her expertise by attending classes and undertaking an independent study of the subject matter. After the baby is old enough to be left with baby-sitters or in nursery school, she might consider taking a part-time job for a few hours each week at a shop specializing in some of the items she wishes to feature in her business. This would allow her to continue developing her expertise and also to deal with some of the actual day-to-day problems that are encountered involving similar businesses.

If she finds that she is still interested in her own shop, she might consider opening it only during school hours for a few years and then expanding the shop's hours if business warrants and as her need to be home decreases. Many specialty shops have restricted hours, and their owners will see customers at other times by appointment only. The most important point is that Diana should not feel that she must delay opening her own business until she can devote 10 hours a day 6 days a week to it, since it is doubtful that she will realistically be able to do that until all her children have left home.

Taking Advantage of Start-Up Losses

When Diana does start her own business, it may not be profitable at the very beginning. It would be helpful to the Andersons' tax situation if any start-up losses could be used to offset some of Dave's income. This result can be accomplished by operating the business as a sole proprietorship, an LLC, or as an S corporation. While the operation of the business in any of these forms can pass through start-up losses, sole proprietorships, LLCs, and S corporations are subject to the hobby loss limitations under IRC Sec. 183, which should be explored prior to making a decision about the form in which to operate the business.

Dispositions at Death

Analysis of Present Plans

Dave's present will provides that an amount equal to one-half of his adjusted gross estate goes to Diana in a marital trust, with the remainder going to a residuary trust for the benefit of Diana and the children.

Dave and Diana's gross estates are well below any federal estate tax liability in 2011. However, sound planning is the key to Dave and Diana's success moving forward. Consider reviewing existing estate planning documents with a qualified estate planning attorney to take advantage of potential portability of Dave's federal estate tax credit. Also consider recommending durable power of attorneys, statements of guardianship and testamentary trusts to aid either spouse with the disposition of their property at death. Evaluate the estate plan in an ongoing basis to ensure it is tax effective and up to date.

Considerations Regarding Diana's Status

The primary tax problem with the marital trust that Dave has in his present will is that it includes the personal residence (a non-income-producing asset). This will not disqualify the trust for the federal estate tax marital deduction. One-half of the house could currently be conveyed to Diana subject to the indebtedness as a joint owner with Dave. This transfer will not result in any federal gift tax consequences, may improve creditor protection under state law, and could probably have significant psychological benefits. In addition, Diana's car could be transferred to Diana outright now. This property should not be placed in a marital trust.

Dave's new will should also contain a simultaneous death provision to protect the federal estate tax marital deduction if he and Diana were to die together in a common disaster.

Diana's present will is adequate except that it does not provide for the new child and should be redrafted in contemplation of the birth of the new baby. Also as she acquires more assets, it would be advisable to review her estate plan with respect to (1) utilization of her applicable credit if she dies first, and (2) a provision requiring that Dave survive her by 6 months in order to inherit under her will. This provision will avoid unnecessarily increasing Dave's taxable estate if Diana should die first.

Diana's Concern with Leaving All Assets in Trust

If the recommendations previously made are implemented, Diana would no longer have all her assets tied up in trust. There are joint checking and savings accounts, and she has been named the beneficiary of Dave's Keogh plan; consequently those funds will go directly to her and will not pass to the marital trust under Dave's will. The house will be held in joint ownership and Diana will hold title to her car. She will also have a special power of appointment over the irrevocable insurance trust, as discussed in the insurance planning section. If Diana is still concerned about the inaccessibility of the funds in the residuary and marital trusts, she can be given some additional powers in the trust instrument that will give her absolute access to some of these funds without triggering adverse estate tax consequences. A typical example of this type of power is an annual noncumulative right to withdraw the greater of 5 percent of the trust corpus or $5,000. Neither the exercise nor lapse of such a power will cause gift or estate tax problems. In fact, Diana could be the trustee or a cotrustee of the residuary trust with the bank as independent trustee and be a beneficiary without risking inclusion of the trust in her estate as long as her ability to distribute trust funds (income and corpus) to herself is limited by an ascertainable standard. The statutory language describing an ascertainable standard states that funds may be distributed for "health, education, support, or maintenance" without risking estate tax inclusion as a general power of appointment (IRC Sec. 2041(b)(1)(A)).

Problems with Present Life Insurance Trust

The present irrevocable life insurance trust does not contain a Crummey provision (that is, a provision allowing the beneficiaries of the trust to currently withdraw amounts gifted to the trust). For this reason the gifts to the trust fail to qualify as present-interest gifts and do not qualify for the gift tax annual exclusion (IRC Sec. 2503(b)). The result is that each time Dave makes a gift to the trust for the payment of the insurance premium, a taxable gift results. Although the amounts of the gifts are small, gift tax returns reflecting the total amount gifted annually should be filed. (Note that there will not actually be any federal gift tax liability since the applicable credit will be available to cover the imposition of any federal gift tax.)

A properly structured irrevocable insurance trust is recommended for the newly acquired insurance. The question of what to do with the present trust remains. The trust can be effectively discontinued by an immediate cessation of gifts to pay premiums; however, serious consideration should be given to maintaining this trust, even though it generates some small annual gift tax liability, at least until the new insurance is in place. It would also probably be prudent to maintain the present coverage until contestability periods under the new coverage have passed.

The dispositive provisions of the new irrevocable insurance trust can (but are not required to) be the same as the terms of the residuary trust under Dave's will. Certainly the trust should empower (but not require) the trustee to loan money to or purchase assets from either Dave's or Diana's estate.

Recommendations

Dave's estate plan should be revised to allow an amount equal to the unified credit equivalent to pass to a residuary credit shelter trust with provisions similar to his present residuary trust. The remaining assets should pass to Diana under the marital trust arrangement. This will avoid payment of federal estate taxes in Dave's estate if he predeceases Diana. Diana can subsequently take steps to reduce her estate and thereby reduce the total federal estate taxes ultimately payable.

At this time, Dave's plan should be revised so that he gifts at least half of his securities (or more if he so desires) to Diana. The purpose served by this asset transfer is to avoid having these assets included in his gross estate should Diana predecease him since he would then no longer have the benefit of a marital deduction. For the same reason Dave could consider making additional gifts of securities in the future.

To make this course of action effective, Diana's will needs immediate redrafting to include the establishment of a credit bypass trust that will use part of her applicable credit. In case Diana's securities holdings increase in value due to their appreciation or further gifts from Dave, her will should direct that her security portfolio fund the bypass trust at least up to the applicable credit exemption. Dave is to be named the income beneficiary, and their children are to be named the remainderpersons. Her will can specify that her coin collection is to pass to the children and that Dave is to hold these assets on their behalf until the youngest child attains age 21.

PERSONAL PLANNING: INSURANCE

Life Insurance

Should Dave die prematurely, the Anderson family would experience a loss of cash inflow of more than $200,000 annually. While there would also be a reduction in expenses and income taxes, the family's needs after Dave's death would still run between $90,000 and $100,000 annually to maintain their present lifestyle. There is an immediate need for additional insurance protection that could be reduced over a period of years in concert with the buildup of retirement fund balances and other investment assets.

Dave has a $100,000 term life insurance policy in an irrevocable life insurance trust. As discussed previously, a new irrevocable insurance trust with a Crummey provision has been recommended. If additional life insurance is applied for, owned, and paid for by the trust and the trust is the named beneficiary, the proceeds will not be included in Dave's estate for federal estate tax purposes. The trust will invest the life insurance proceeds and use the income for the benefit of Diana and the children.

If the trust could earn 6 percent and was funded with a $2,000,000 insurance policy, the family would have an additional income flow of $120,000. Alternatively, should the trust earn only 4 percent on the proceeds, a total of $3,000,000 would be needed to generate $120,000 per year and still preserve principal. Thus Dave needs between $1,900,000 and $2,900,000 of life insurance. Consider purchasing $2,500,000 of permanent first to die life insurance in an irrevocable insurance trust with Diana as the primary trustee and children as contingent trustees.

This additional protection should cover the family income needs if prices remain relatively stable in the future. If there is significant inflation, however, there will be a need to increase the insurance coverage. As the children reach college age, though, the funds set aside for their education will provide much of their needed support. Also the longer Dave lives, the greater will be the accumulation of investment assets and contributions to the benefit plan that can provide income to Diana. When Diana reaches the age of eligibility for Social Security benefits, her income will also increase, so the need for insurance protection should always be periodically reviewed. Should Diana predecease Dave, his continued cash flow would provide resources for the family.

Students are free to use alternative measures, such as the human life value or cash flow methods (as presented in the Elizabeth and James Black case) to solve insurance needs. The selection of life insurance products involves choices among many available designs. Dave should consider using one of the following types of policies to provide the additional survivor protection needed.

Ordinary Whole Life Insurance

This form of insurance is based on the assumption that premiums will be paid on a level annual basis throughout the insured's lifetime. In the early years of the policy the premium exceeds the cost of protection, thereby providing the basis for cash values within the policy. The cash values of a policy depend on the size of the policy, the insured's age at the time of issue, and whether the policy is rated. Cash values are guaranteed by the contract and can be borrowed at a rate either stated therein or established by an index. In addition, the increase in cash value each year is not taxable to the policyowner. Even though the assumption is that the premium will be paid over the life of the insured, many owners convert their policies to either a reduced paid-up policy when the need for this protection decreases, such as when any children become self-supporting, or to an annuity upon retirement.

Single-Premium Whole Life Insurance

This form of insurance differs from the ordinary whole life policy in that only one premium, paid at policy inception, is made. These policies enjoy the customary life insurance advantage of tax-free internal cash value increases and income-tax-free death benefits. If owned by the insured, the proceeds would be includible in the insured's estate for estate tax purposes.

In single-premium whole life policies there is typically an initial cash value equal to the premium paid to acquire the policy. These policies also have a guaranteed minimum interest rate stated in the policy, but frequently the actual return is higher than the minimum guaranteed return. The interest rate applicable to policy loans is either equal to or a given percentage above the current rate credited to the cash value. These policies also impose a surrender charge if they are terminated within a specified period of time. They enjoy tax-deferred accumulation of substantial up-front cash values.

Current tax law imposes a series of rules that has altered the traditional attractiveness of single-premium whole life insurance contracts unless the policyowner plans to leave the cash values with the insurer and looks to the death benefit as the primary purpose for purchasing the contract. IRC Sec. 7702A specifies that if a contract is a modified endowment contract (MEC), any cash withdrawals, including policy loans, will be deemed to be interest earnings first and then a withdrawal of premium. Any withdrawal treated as income is obviously subject to taxation at the policyowner's marginal tax rate. In addition, a 10 percent penalty tax applies.

A modified endowment contract exists if at any time the accumulated amount of the first 7 years' premiums paid on the contract exceeds the accumulated amount of "net level premiums" that would be payable if the contract provided for paid-up future benefits after the payment of seven level annual premiums. The first year's death benefit will be deemed to apply for the purpose of computing the "net level premium" if there is no reduction in the death benefit during the first 7 years even though such a reduction might occur in a subsequent year, such as the tenth year. If a death benefit smaller than the first year's death benefit becomes the face amount during the first 7 years of the policy, then the reduced benefit is used for calculating the amount of the net level premium. Sec. 7702A defines net level premium in such a way that the 7-pay test premium varies from one insurance product to another.

A material change automatically makes a policy subject to the 7-pay premium test. If the test is failed, the policy will be characterized as a modified endowment contract. Any increase in future benefits provided under the policy is a material change, with three exceptions: (1) an increase in benefits attributable to cost-of-living adjustments (CPI or similar index related), (2) the payment of premiums to fund the lowest death benefit payable during the first 7 years, and (3) the crediting of interest and policyholder dividends to the premium paid to meet the requirements of the second exception. Special rules apply to life insurance contracts having an initial death benefit of no more than $10,000. Recent clarifications added to the federal income tax laws specify that a material change includes (1) any increase in the death benefit under the contract or (2) any increase in, or addition of, a qualified additional benefit under the contract.

These tax limitations on the use of single-premium policies have limited the benefits and flexibility previously available with such policies.

Variable Life Policy

A variable life insurance policy is also a fixed, level-premium policy for the lifetime of the insured. With variable life the insured selects the investment medium used within the policy, usually with a choice restricted to specific funds managed by the insurer. This policy differs from the ordinary whole life policy in that the face amount of the policy changes with the investment performance of the investment instrument(s) chosen by the insured. Often a minimum guaranteed floor below which the policy's face will not fall is an integral part of the policy. However, all investment risk shifts to the policyowner. Since the investment risk is transferred to the owner, no guarantees are included as to the amount of the policy's cash values. If cash values do exist within the policy, borrowing of these values is permissible. However, borrowing from the policy can result in taxation if the policy is defined as a modified endowment contract under IRC Sec. 7702A. Some policies specify a variable interest rate on the borrowing that fluctuates with changes in some previously established standard interest rate. Other policies do have fixed borrowing rates. Since these policies have a substantial surrender charge during their early years, the client should realize that a long-term commitment is being made if this policy is chosen.

In addition, the insured needs to monitor carefully the performance of the investment instrument(s) selected. If the initial choice was incorrect, or if the insured has failed to shift funds as economic conditions change, the amount of protection could fall sizably. This form of fluctuating death benefit might not be suitable to the client when the primary reason for acquiring additional insurance at this time is protection for survivors.

Universal Life Policy

A universal life insurance policy differs from the previous policies in that it has a flexible premium. Universal life is available in two forms—either a level or an increasing death benefit. In addition, a changing face amount of any life insurance death benefit payable under universal life contracts as a consequence of changes in the amount of the annual premium being paid will result in the policy's being subject to the 7-pay test at the time of the change. The insured has the option to increase, decrease, or omit the premium. However, all premiums when paid are added to the policy's cash value account, and all mortality charges are deducted from the same account. Interest is credited to this account with a minimum guarantee. Another unique characteristic of this policy, compared to the three previous policies, is that some mortality risk is shifted to the insured by the potential for increases in the mortality rate. Also a minimum interest rate on the cash value is guaranteed, and interest in excess of the guarantee depends on investment performance and insurer discretion. Any interest buildup in the policy is currently tax free. Although the cash values can be borrowed, the insured can also make withdrawals from the cash values that are not considered a loan, so interest does not have to be paid to the insurer for the withdrawals. Furthermore these withdrawn funds do not have to be repaid to the insurer. However, there may be income tax consequences of such withdrawals. As with the variable life policy, there are significant surrender charges during the early years.

Term Policy

Over the lifetime of the insured this policy has an increasing premium used solely to provide life insurance protection. Important features of this policy are its guaranteed renewability, convertibility of the policy to permanent insurance up to age 65, and no cash value buildup over the life of the insured.

Recommendations

Dave should consider purchasing a universal life insurance policy with a guaranteed death benefit. The initial face amount of the policy should be $2,500,000. The policy is assumed to cost $10,000 annually and will be funded with gifts made to a trust. Students are encouraged to shop policies and use corresponding premiums. The policy should be structured with an emphasis on death benefit and not on building cash value.

Dave's personal insurance should be applied for and owned by a properly structured irrevocable life insurance trust that should also be the beneficiary of the insurance policies. This avoids the necessity of transferring policies to the trust, which would cause the insurance proceeds to be included in Dave's estate should he die within 3 years of the transfer (IRC Sec. 2035). The insurance trust should contain provisions similar to or identical with the terms of the residuary trust under Dave's will. It should also contain a valid Crummey provision. If the terms of the insurance trust and the residuary trust are substantially identical, a provision in either or both trusts allowing the trustee to combine them can achieve savings in administrative costs. Diana can continue to function as trustee of this trust until it is funded at Dave's death, and the trust instrument should provide that the corporate trustee should then automatically take over as the successor trustee to avoid having the trust taxed in Diana's estate at her death.

The trust might contain a special power of appointment allowing Diana to make gifts of the trust principal to individuals other than herself, her creditors, her estate, and her estate's creditors. In this way the trust can purchase cash value life insurance on Dave's life, and the Andersons can have access to the inside buildup and/or side funds through Diana's special power. This power should not result in the inclusion of the insurance proceeds in either Dave's or Diana's estate. In addition, Diana has expressed concern that virtually all the Andersons' assets are in Dave's name. A special power would provide Diana with some control over the property in the irrevocable insurance trust. However, this technique is aggressive and its tax effects are uncertain. Therefore the advice of a tax attorney must be obtained before its use is seriously considered.

Dave and Diana should keep in mind that even though the investment features and tax advantages of some of the permanent forms of insurance are attractive, the primary function of insurance is to protect survivors. However, that does not prevent them from considering or even using additional permanent life insurance as part of their planning for both investment and the protection of their survivors.

Disability Insurance

The maximum available levels of both disability income and disability business overhead coverage are recommended. As additional investments are made that could be relied on to produce income, these amounts should be reviewed to ensure that these coverage levels are still needed.

Personal Property and Liability Insurance

On the facts of our case the property and liability coverage carried by the Andersons is adequate, and additional protection is available through a personal liability umbrella policy. No changes appear necessary in this area.

PERSONAL PLANNING: INVESTMENT

The Andersons have four general financial objectives that may be met by proper investment planning, selection, and monitoring. They have stated these objectives in the following order of priority:

- to fund their children's education
- to reduce their tax burden
- to increase their net worth
- to enjoy retirement

The Andersons have also stated their desire to "maintain their lifestyle." This can be interpreted as a constraint on meeting the other objectives, three of which may be classified as wealth-accumulation objectives. The objective of reducing their tax burden can be met while achieving the other wealth-accumulation objectives.

There are several investment vehicles suitable in various degrees to achieving the Andersons' objectives. The planner must consider this entire array and advise the Andersons on the suitability of these vehicles and the proportion of investable funds the Andersons should place in each vehicle, keeping in mind the clients' stated preferences for particular investments. The planner must also be prepared to reposition assets within the portfolio as the clients' financial environment and preferences change.

Once the family and the business are established, the first financial objective is to provide protection to the family in case of Dave's premature death or disability. Insurance is also needed to protect the clients' assets, as previously discussed. After insurance needs have been met, any investable funds remaining must be used to best meet the clients' other needs. Therefore once properly insured, the Andersons should establish an emergency reserve fund to finance their everyday affairs, to handle unexpected contingencies, and to take advantage of favorable prices. This emergency fund could be kept in their savings and checking accounts, or in a money market account.

Since Dave is self-employed, owns few income-producing liquid assets, and is the breadwinner for a family of four (soon to be five), an increase in their liquid financial assets to the upper 6-month limit would be appropriate. Although Dave does have $50,000 of accounts receivable from his medical practice, he will also have continuing expenses for his medical practice. Therefore it would be inappropriate to consider these accounts receivable as his emergency reserve.

Refinancing Clients' Home

Consideration should be given to the terms and conditions of the mortgage on the Andersons' home. The mortgage for the residence was taken out when interest rates were quite high. Dave was unaware that mortgages can be paid off early and a replacement mortgage obtained that will provide substantial cash-flow savings as a result of lower market interest rates.

Because of the pooling of home mortgages to create collateralized mortgage obligation bonds, today's mortgage market conditions require that the duration of individual mortgages be standardized. With few exceptions—such as a close relationship with a lending institution that will hold, rather than sell, an individual's mortgage—the choices available to consumers are either 15- or 30-year mortgages. Because of their financial position the Andersons would not be looking at refinancing as a means of having only an additional $100 or so of disposable income to meet their expenses. In addition, they are not desirous of extending the duration of the mortgage that has about 16 years remaining, but they are interested in refinancing their home with a 15-year mortgage at the current interest rate of 7.75 percent with zero points. Dave is not interested in paying points as a means of lowering the nominal interest rate on the loan since—unlike initial financing points, which are immediately deductible—points associated with a refinancing have to be amortized over the life of the loan.

The monthly mortgage payment for the original 30-year, 12 percent mortgage is $648.03.

The new note payments are based on a balance of $60,000. The $60,000 includes the existing loan balance and all closing costs. A new 15-year, 7.75 percent mortgage would have payments of $556.21, or a reduction in the monthly payment of around $93. The new mortgage payment, with a lower interest component, will reduce the mortgage interest that the Andersons can deduct against their federal income tax. The first years interest on this loan will total around $4,423.

In light of over $1,000 reduction in the annual expenses for their home, it is recommended that they refinance. The full arrangements for the refinancing will be completed by next year.

Financial Status of the Clients

The Andersons are in a strong financial position. They can maintain their current standard of living while achieving their desired objectives. Their projected cash flows, if managed prudently, are sufficient to permit the Andersons to fund their children's education, increase their net worth, and enjoy their retirement without borrowing or cutting corners.

The planner in this situation should be concerned with how best to achieve the objectives by recommending various investment vehicles that will be effective for the Andersons in accumulating wealth and reducing the tax burden.

Funding the Children's Education

The Andersons have yet to do any funding of the education expenses for their two children. At this time, accumulating money for the expected child's education would be premature. That need can be addressed after the birth of the child next year.

They have two distinct education expenses for each of their three children: those associated with tuition for secondary (high school) education and those for a 4-year college education.

In the tax planning section of the plan, education funding calculations were provided. Selling the commercial property will result in $470,000 of gross proceeds. After paying off the note, $390,000 remains. The property has a cost basis of $100,000, and the sale would create a long term capital gain of $370,000. The Andersons are interested in reallocating Dave's security portfolio. Liquidating the portfolio altogether would generate $130,054 of proceeds and a long term taxable loss of around $116,000.

If the Andersons were to sell all portfolio positions in the same year they sold the commercial lot, they could offset a portion of the commercial lot's taxable gain, $370,000, with a capital loss of ($116,000). The resulting aggregate gain would be $254,000 and result in taxes (15 percent) of around $38,100. The Andersons need to reserve $38,100 from total proceeds from their portfolio and commercial lot sale. In 2008 and 2009 capital gains rates are at a near all time low, and the clients should be encouraged to take advantage of these low rates.

$390,000 (sale of the lot less note) + $130,054 (portfolio sale) = $520,054

$520,054 (proceeds) less $38,100 (tax withholding) = **$481,194**

Invest $100,000 into 529 plans with balanced portfolios for both Jennifer and Deidre. Utilize the remaining $281,194 in a growth oriented account that can be used for future goals. A discussion of investment alternatives for the Andersons investment portfolio follows.

Increasing Net Worth

Now that plans have been established to satisfy the Andersons' other financial objectives of funding their children's education and having an emergency reserve, they wish to invest their disposable income in such a way as to increase their net worth and maintain and improve their lifestyle. To a large extent this objective overlaps with that of reducing their tax burden. The primary concern is seeking growth while reducing the tax burden.

Collectibles (Coins, Porcelains)

One method of generating an inflation hedge while achieving growth is to invest part of one's disposable income in collectibles. Diana has already had experience in collectibles; she has a coin collection she inherited. She also has a strong interest in porcelain. Given the Andersons' age and the years until retirement, it seems appropriate to invest some portion of their disposable income in enhancing the coin collection and in porcelains. The advantages would be the growth potential of these assets, the inflationary hedge the assets might provide, the pride of ownership, and the lack of current income for tax purposes.

The disadvantages would include the illiquidity of the investment: there is an expense in terms of time and money in converting these assets to cash. A second disadvantage is the negative cash flow during the holding period: the investment has to be insured and appraised and may be warehoused. Finally, there is an opportunity cost involved.

From an income tax perspective, gains on the sale of collectibles, such as coins and porcelain, are taxed at a 28 percent capital-gains rate. Collectibles are not eligible for the lower 15 percent capital-gains rate.

Investing in collectibles requires a high degree of expertise on the part of the investor to avoid unknowingly purchasing counterfeits or being swayed by an improper appraisal. Another possible disadvantage is the loss of value that may occur from reduced demand for the collectible. Collectibles go in and out of vogue quickly. The investor must also exercise care to avoid buying at retail and later selling at wholesale, as has occurred with investments in diamonds.

If the Andersons invest in collectibles, they can potentially benefit from the inflationary hedge and capital appreciation that they desire. Despite being somewhat risky as an investment, collectibles are consistent with their risk profile. In addition, they have strong appeal to Diana. The Andersons should continue acquiring collectible coins and assets.

Growth-Oriented No-Load Mutual Fund

The Andersons could use a no-load diversified mutual fund consisting of growth-oriented blue-chip common stock. The advantages would be capital appreciation and an inflationary hedge as investment media for their children's education funds.

Mutual funds should also be attractive to this client since they provide professional management of the assets by handling the day-to-day needs for selection and timing of securities transactions. As a practicing physician, Dave may not have the time, expertise, or inclination to perform these tasks. In addition, ownership of shares in a mutual fund provides diversification of the portfolio due to the fund's ownership of securities spread over various sectors of the economy, thus reducing most of the business risk.

No-load mutual funds are purchased and redeemed at their net asset value. Immediately after dividends are declared, the net asset value of the shares falls. Consequently if the Andersons select no-load mutual funds as one of their investment choices, they should purchase shares shortly after the fund declares its periodic dividend. If shares are purchased shortly before the dividend [declaration] date, the Andersons will use after-tax savings to purchase the shares and then have taxable dividend income returned to them. In addition, the net amount of their investment working for them in the fund will be reduced by the amount of the distributed dividend.

One disadvantage of this investment vehicle is the necessity of converting the growth-oriented asset into an income-producing asset when needed for their stated objective, which would produce a taxable event. Another disadvantage of investing in a growth fund is that like any mutual fund, it cannot be expected to consistently outperform the market. Unfortunately, however, a badly managed fund can continually underperform the market.

For the education funding, the first priority of the Andersons, the trust established for each child should use relatively conservative funding instruments. However, the potential for taking some risk should not be overlooked.

High-Income Bond Funds

These bond mutual funds, sometimes referred to as junk bond funds, possess a greater degree of business and interest-rate risk since they invest in a portfolio of corporate bonds at minimum or slightly below what is deemed investment-grade quality to obtain higher yields. Other than the composition of their portfolios, they do not differ from other bond funds. Since the Andersons have a relatively high income and since Dave appears willing to take some degree of risk, these could be a viable investment medium for the education funding purposes.

U.S. Treasury Inflation-Indexed Bonds

In early 1997 the Treasury floated the first series of 10-year bonds that have inflation protection for the bondholder. This protection covers both the semiannual interest that bondholders will receive as well as the amount returned upon maturity. This issue yielded a base interest rate of approximately 3.45 percent. At the time of each semiannual interest payment, the base interest plus an inflation increase (less a deflation decrease), calculated by determining the change in the consumer price index (CPI) from the bond's date of issue to the date of the interest payment, is made (with an adjustment for the semiannual payment). Thus the interest payments will increase proportionately to increases in the CPI. This interest is subject to the federal income tax each year.

The process for determining the increase in the face (par) amount of the bond also employs the CPI. For each calendar year the relative increase in the index is determined and is applied to the value of the bond on January 1 of the year. For example, if the index were 100 on January 1 and 105 on December 31, a $1,000 face value bond would have an increase in its face value of 5 percent to $1,050. If the CPI went from 105 to 108 in the second year, the adjustment would be $1,050(108/105), for a new face value of $1,080. This annual increase in the face amount of the bond is considered income for tax purposes for that year. Therefore in the first year the bondholder has $50 of phantom income ($30 in the second year) that is part of his or her taxable income. For some, like the Andersons, who are in the 28 percent tax bracket starting in 2005, this is not a recommended investment to hold unless held in a tax-deferred manner. Even then, the return will match inflation, but after paying income taxes during the distribution period, the investor will not keep up with inflation. (*Note:* Since there is a guarantee that the bond will have a minimum value of $1,000 upon maturity regardless of the extent of any future deflation, should significant deflation occur, the bondholder could gain on an after-tax basis.)

Municipal Bonds

General obligation municipal bonds are the safest of all municipal bonds because the obligation to repay the investor is a legal obligation of the taxing authority. Thus the investor is guaranteed repayment out of the taxing power of the community or the state that issues the bonds. The public-purpose feature is important because if the bonds are so classified, the interest payments the Andersons receive will be exempt from both regular income taxation and the alternative minimum tax. Revenue bonds are riskier because the bondholders will be repaid from the revenue generated from whatever purpose the proceeds of the bond were used to finance. For instance, if a community issues revenue bonds to build mass transit facilities, the bondholders are to be repaid out of the revenues generated by the system. A risk element is that if the revenues are not forthcoming, the bondholders might not be repaid. Moreover, the interest earned on new revenue bonds, although exempt from ordinary income taxation, will be taxable to taxpayers who are subject to the alternative minimum tax.

Dave has acquired some municipal bonds during the past year due to the attractiveness of their tax-exempt interest income. He could consider further purchases of such bonds as a means of sheltering the income from taxation. These bonds have risks and limitations similar to those of corporate bonds.

Municipal Bond Funds

Selecting a no-load municipal bond fund is also a practical and desirable method for the Andersons to reduce their tax burden. The fund should invest in general obligation municipal bonds that are also "public-purpose" bonds to avoid potential AMT issues.

To minimize risk, the Andersons should invest in a fund in which 80 percent of the portfolio consists of general obligation bonds. The bond portfolio should contain only bonds rated AA or better. The AA rating, although not a guarantee of investment performance, is a strong indicator that default will not occur and that the investor will be repaid on time.

The advantages of a municipal bond fund include professional management, diversification, minimal record keeping, and a high degree of liquidity. Other benefits of the fund may include automatic reinvestment of income distributions, withdrawal plans, exchange privileges, and check-writing privileges.

Perhaps the most significant and best-known advantage of a municipal bond fund is that the interest earned on the fund is free of federal income tax if the fund invests in public-purpose bonds. To the extent that the fund invests in bonds issued by the state in which the Andersons live, interest on those bonds should also be free of state income tax.

The disadvantages of a municipal bond fund are the possibility of erosion of value in inflationary times, the possibility of a risk of default, and the possibility that the fund might produce an after-tax return less than that from a taxable bond fund of similar investment-quality rating.

In some instances an investor may also be able to avoid state and local income taxes when purchasing municipal bonds. In this case, the taxable yield calculation may be modified to take this into account. The same equation is used, but the investor's marginal tax rate is substituted with the investor's combined tax rate. To calculate the investor's combined tax rate, it is first necessary to determine the effective state tax rate. The effective state tax rate takes into account the fact that state income taxes are deductible for federal income tax purposes. Failure to factor the deductibility of state income taxes into the equation would overstate the taxable yield.

Effective state tax rate = marginal state tax rate × (1 − federal marginal tax rate)

The combined tax rate for use in the above equation is simply the sum of the effective state tax rate and the federal marginal tax rate.

Combined tax rate = effective state tax rate + federal marginal tax rate

The purpose of modifying the equation to use the combined tax rate is to take into account the additional yield that would have been required to pay state income taxes if the municipal bond interest was not exempt from this tax.

Disadvantages of the fund also include the possibility of a sales charge, a redemption fee, a high management fee, and interest-rate risk. The interest-rate risk has previously been described in the discussion of corporate bonds for the children's education funding. Briefly, interest-rate risk occurs when interest rates rise, causing the present value of bonds to decline. If the bondholders sell the bonds, they can do so only at a lower price. On the other hand, if the bondholders hold the bonds until maturity, interest risk will not have created a capital loss. However, reinvestment of interest income will be at a lower rate than anticipated and cause the fully compounded return actually earned on the investment to be less than what was anticipated.

A municipal bond fund is appropriate for the Andersons' portfolio because the fund achieves one of their major objectives: tax reduction. If they invest in a fund that owns AA- or higher-rated general obligation bonds, there is a minimal level of default risk. Given the Andersons' high tax bracket, these funds should provide a satisfactory return on their investment. The Andersons could also benefit from the possibility of capital appreciation, depending on future movements in interest rates.

Leveraged, Closed-End Bond Funds

Instead of raising the full amount of capital from the sale of equity shares in the fund, some bond funds also obtain a portion of their investable funds by issuing either short-term or intermediate-term fixed-cost instruments. One form of these fixed-cost instruments is 7- to 30-day adjustable preferred stock. When the preferred matures, new preferred is issued as a replacement. Other funds raise their fixed return by arranging 30- to 90-day adjustable bank lines of credit or issue either money market notes or fixed 5-year notes. This additional capital, along with the original capital, is used to acquire a portfolio of either taxable or tax-exempt bonds, depending on the fund's stated purpose. The leverage from the borrowed funds (typically between 25 and 45 percent of total capital, although the SEC permits as much as 50 percent), if favorable, will enhance the yield to the fund's shares if a sufficient difference exists between the cost of the borrowed funds (short-term interest rate) and what can be earned on the portfolio (intermediate- and long-term interest rates). In practice these funds set a target yield they seek to achieve. Most of the taxable funds invest in high-yield corporate bonds. The tax-exempts typically invest in investment grade municipal bonds. Other than the use of leverage, these funds possess the same characteristics, advantages, and limitations of other bond funds.

Currently the taxable leveraged bond funds yield between 9 and 10 percent as compared with the tax-exempt yields of about 6 percent. The percent of this spread is close to the Andersons' expected tax bracket. The higher-yielding taxable funds could be an attractive investment opportunity to the Andersons, who should keep in mind that the interaction of the leverage and the nature of the portfolios makes them riskier than similarly invested nonleveraged funds.

Junk Bonds

Traditionally it was the default risk of either newly formed corporations or of troubled corporations or municipalities that caused the market to label certain debt instruments as junk bonds. Since these bonds receive ratings lower than investment grade, they provide relatively high rates of return to investors willing to accept the associated high risk.

In recent years a new crop of junk bonds has come to the market as a result of the numerous leveraged buyouts instigated either by existing management of publicly traded corporations or by outside interests (raiders). In either case a controlled corporation is formed for the purpose of acquiring the stock of a target corporation. Those individuals who directly own the equity interest in this controlled corporation put up a relatively small amount of the funds needed for the acquisition. The remainder of the funds for the stock tender offer is obtained through debt financing (bonds). Since these bonds represent perhaps as much as 90 percent of the capital raised by the acquiring firm, the firm is said to be highly leveraged. Despite actual profitability, if the acquired firm is unable to spin off sufficient cash flow for the servicing of the debt, default can occur. However, in this scenario the default is due to the high degree of financial leverage (debt). Regardless of whether the bond rating services rate these bonds as low or noninvestment grade, investors perceive them as high risk and thus require a high yield. An alternate scenario would involve the acquired corporation's issuing new debt and then repurchasing most of its stock from the controlled acquisition corporation. In this case the operating (acquired) corporation must have sufficient cash flow to service its own debt. When this pattern occurs, previously issued debt of the acquired corporation will be downgraded in its investment classification.

Junk bonds typically yield between 3 and 5 percent more than investment-grade bonds. Recent events have resulted in some of these bonds being sold at discounts of 35 percent or more from their face amount. This makes those bonds even more attractive provided the issuing corporations do not default. Dave could use a portion of his investable cash flow by diversifying an investment in these junk bonds through the mechanism of a mutual fund.

Real Estate

Dave currently rents the office space used for his medical practice and he indicated that the building might be sold. Since Dave has stated that direct ownership of rental real estate is his preferred investment vehicle, he might consider the purchase of the building in which his office is located.

Should Dave purchase the building, there would be a $16,284 operating loss in the first year. This loss would decrease by about $3,000 per year, and by the sixth year of ownership operating income should become positive. If Dave owned and managed the building personally, the losses would be passive losses for tax purposes, except for the portion attributable to Dave's own business use. These losses could be deducted against any passive income since the rental real estate currently owned will have positive income. The losses for this building would be suspended.

If Dave does purchase the building, the net cash flow picture appears attractive. Except for the first year, in which a cash flow deficit of $2,688 occurs, and the second year, in which $188 is incurred, the building's cash flow—after all operating expenses, property taxes, interest expense, and principal payments—becomes positive in the third year.

Since at this time the economics of the building appear attractive, Dave could inform either the building's owner(s) or the realtor that he might be interested in purchasing it if it is placed on the market.

Ownership of the building has other beneficial considerations for the Andersons. As stated earlier, it not only meets Dave's (and to a lesser degree, Diana's) investment vehicle preference, but it can also provide a mechanism that meets two of their general personal financial goals—capital appreciation and inflation protection. Moreover, the opportunity to employ one or more of the children in a bona fide job maintaining the building as a means of shifting some income not subject to the kiddie tax is an additional plus from the Andersons' perspective.

CASE II

New Assumptions

1. An additional $10,000 cash flow to provide for life insurance premiums for $2,500,000 ILIT policy.
2. Lot and brokerage account liquidated with $38,100 withheld for taxes.
3. $481,194 available for education goals and other spending needs.
4. 529 plans set up for each daughter in the amount of $100,000 each.
5. Refinance home at 7.5 percent for 15 years. $60,000 refinanced. Payments of $556.21 and first years interest of $4,423.

Anderson Balance Sheet with Recommendations

Table 5-14 Anderson Balance Sheet with Recommendations			
Assets			
Cash Accounts	Checking	$ 5,000.00	
	Savings Account	$ 20,000.00	
			$ 25,000.00
Investment Account	Mutual Fund or Annuities	$281,194.00	
	529 Plan Jennifer	$100,000.00	
	529 Plan Deidre	$100,000.00	
			$ 481,194.00
Business Assets	Accounts Receivable	$ 50,000.00	
	Furniture and Equipment	$ 65,000.00	
	Accounts Receivable	$ 50,000.00	
	Operating Money Market	$ 25,000.00	
	Dave's % of PS Plan	$252,000.00	
			$ 442,000.00
Investment Properties	Rental House	$225,000.00	
	Commercial Lot	$ –	
			$ 225,000.00
Personal Assets	Home	$615,000.00	
	Coin Collection	$ 60,000	
	Personal Property	$125,000	
	Diana's Car	$10,000.00	
	Dave's Car	$22,000.00	
			$832,000.00
	Total Assets		$2,005,194.00
Liabilities			
	Diana's Car Loan (after 24 months)	$(5,496.29)	
	* Rental House	$ (37,101.00)	
	* Mortgage	$ (60,000.00)	
	Prop. Taxes Due	$ (38,100.00)	
	Total Liabilities		$(140,697.29)
	Net Worth		$1,864,496.71
	ILIT Funded with UL Policy and $2,500,000 DB		

Anderson Tax Projections with New Assumptions

Table 5-15 Anderson Tax Projections with New Assumptions			
Earned Income This Year			
Business Profit	$250,000.00		
PS Contribution	($35,000.00)		
Diana's Salary	($20,000.00)		
New Costs	($17,360.00)		
		$177,640.00	
Diana's Paycheck	$20,000.00		
		$20,000.00	
Interest & Dividends			
Brokerage Account	**$0.00**		
Growth Mutual Funds or Annuity	**$0.00**		
Joint Savings Interest	$800.00		
		$800.00	
Real Estate Investments			
Rental Home Income	$14,400.00		
* Rental Loan Interest	($1,383.23)		
Rental Home Prop Tax	($4,387.50)		
Rental Home Operating Expenses	($900.00)		
** Rental Home Depreciation	($2,080.00)		
Lot Interest	**$0.00**		
Lot Prop Taxes	**$0.00**		
		$5,649.27	
401(k) Deferrals			
Dave's 401(k)	($15,500.00)		
Diana's 401(k)	($15,500.00)		
		($31,000.00)	
Adjusted Gross Income			**$173,089.27**
Potential Itemized Deductions			
4% State Income Tax (on AGI)	($6,925.57)		
Charitable Contributions	($10,000.00)		
Home Prop Taxes	($6,900)		
Home Interest	**($4,423.00)**		
		(28,246.57)	
		—	
SE Tax Adjustment		($10,654.50)	
Current Year 4 Personal Exemptions		($14,800.00)	
Total Deductions and Exemptions			($53,701.07)
Taxable Income			**$119,388**
Current Year Projected Income Tax Due			**$22,097.05**
Highest Marginal Rate			**25%**

Income taxes are higher after the sale of the commercial lot. The lot provided tax advantages, such as deductible income and property taxes.

CHAPTER REVIEW

Key Terms and Concepts

guaranteed payment	golden handcuffs
close corporation	golden parachutes
closely held corporation	defined-benefit plan
S corporation	defined-contribution plan
C corporation	covered compensation
golden handshakes	Sec. 529 qualified tuition programs

Review Questions

1. What are the biggest two challenges in meeting with self employed, high income individuals? [1]

2. Jim is self employed and a 100 percent owner of Jim's Paint and Peel. Paint & Peel has ten employees and is an S Corp. Jim's revenue and profit fluctuates wildly on an annual basis; reporting a loss of $25,000 in 2008 and a profit of $80,000 in 2009. What challenges could Jim face when shopping for group or individual disability insurance policies? [2]

3. How can financial advisers navigate between spouses with different risk tolerance levels? How should joint money be allocated? [1]

4. Provide the distinguishing characteristics of the following business structures (as a student note, this question is significantly weighted on the final exam): [2]

    - Sole Proprietorship
    - Professional Corporation
    - S Corporation
    - C Corporation
    - Limited Liability Corporation (LLC)

5. Why do retirement plans integrated with social security offer a larger contribution for higher wage earners than non integrated plans? [1]

Learning Objectives

An understanding of the material in this chapter should enable the student to

1. Review planning for the small business owner.
2. Discuss challenges faced by small business owners.

Comprehensive financial plAn important and very interesting aspect of financial planning is planning for the shareholder-employees of small family-owned businesses. These businesses usually represent both the client's largest asset and the family's primary source of income. The family in this instance may include the client, spouse, and adult children who are employed by the business, and even nonactive children or other more peripheral family members who benefit from the business either directly or indirectly. In these cases it is important to recognize that the business and the client typically have distinct legal and tax identities. While the needs of the business and the objectives of the client as an individual may sometimes appear to be adverse, the survival of the business and the improvement of the client's personal situation are very closely related. It is essential in these cases to seek solutions to problems and methods to achieve the client's personal objectives that will be acceptable compromises between the business and the individual and that will allow the survival and continuing vitality of the business. Naturally owners of small family businesses would not want their lifetime work placed in jeopardy or acquired by someone outside the family group.

CASE NARRATIVE

Personal Information

Lawrence (Larry) and Anne Miller are 62 and 59 respectively and live in a small town of approximately 30,000 people. They have been married 40 years and have three children. Steve, their oldest son, is 38, is married to

Jennifer, and has two children, Alex, 10, and Tony, 7. Doug, their second son, is 32, is divorced, and has one child, Maria, 8. Lisa, their daughter, is 28, is married to Tom, and has three children, Kerry, 5, Katie, 4, and Andrew, 1. The Millers have given each grandchild on his or her first birthday a gift of $1,000 under the Uniform Gifts to Minors Act. The children's parents are designated custodians of the UGMA accounts. Larry and Anne do not plan further significant gifts to their grandchildren.

The Millers started their furniture business 37 years ago with money borrowed from Anne's father. In return for issuing the loan Anne's father owned 33 percent of the company stock until his death 12 years ago, although the indebtedness had long since been repaid. When Anne's father died, he left her 23 percent of the company stock (57.5 shares). He left Steve the remaining 10 percent of the company stock (25 shares). Because of Larry's hard work the business has grown into a profitable enterprise and has provided a good living for him and Anne and their children. Steve, the oldest son, has been involved in the business on a full-time basis since he graduated from college. He is Larry's heir apparent in the management and ownership of the business.

Larry's basis in his Millers stock is approximately $160 per share. Anne and Steve's stock, which was inherited from Anne's father, has a basis of $1,000 per share in their hands.

The younger son, Doug, also worked in Millers and in another furniture store his father owned in a town about 45 miles away. Six years ago when Larry became uneasy about dividing his time between the two stores, Doug and a business associate purchased the stock of the second store, a separate corporation. The purchase price was $230,000 for 100 percent of the stock, and it was financed with a $20,000 cash down payment and an installment note for 15 years at 10 percent interest. From the sale Larry has annual income of $27,609. This $27,609 figure is made up of the following components for tax purposes: $10,833 return of basis, $4,500 capital gain, and $12,276 of ordinary income. Doug and his business associate still own the store and seem to be doing well.

Larry and Anne's daughter, Lisa, has never been involved in the business, as she married immediately after college and her husband's career requires that they relocate frequently.

Larry says his primary concern at this point is to assure that Steve can succeed him in both the management and the ownership of the corporation.

At the same time he does not wish to deprive his other children of a part of their inheritance. He does not, however, believe that leaving the business to Steve, Doug, and Lisa equally will be the most efficient way to assure the continuity of Millers, which is very important to him. In addition, the bulk of his wealth is directly or indirectly tied up in Millers and he would like to explore ways to transform this investment into a secure retirement income for Anne and himself. Larry says he is too young to retire and has no definite plans to retire at 65. However, he would like to start cutting back on his day-to-day duties in the business and give Steve some time in a more direct management position before phasing himself out of the business. He has no idea when he would like to completely give up participation in the business and sees himself as continuing to participate at some level as long as his health permits.

He does, however, wish to be free to travel more extensively and to spend more time with Anne and their grandchildren. Larry thinks he is ready to transfer effective control of the management of the corporation to Steve. Although he is still heavily involved with Millers every day, he doesn't think it necessary or fair to wait until he dies for Steve to own a controlling interest in the business.

Anne has lived in their small town all her life. In addition to 23 percent of the stock of Millers her father also left her some other assets, most of which were blue-chip securities. She continues to manage a portfolio of these investments that she enjoys trading. Anne thinks that she has been quite successful in managing the portfolio under the supervision and with the advice of a stockbroker with whom she has been associated for many years. Larry does not share his wife's interest in stocks and bonds; instead he has kept his excess cash in money market funds for the past 5 years.

Anne liquidated a portion of her stocks and bonds several years ago in order to buy a beach condominium in a neighboring state and financed the purchase with a 20 percent down payment and a 20-year loan at 7 3/4 percent interest. After 3 years she decided she was uncomfortable with "being in debt" and paid off the mortgage. Anne's beach condominium has potential as an income-producing property and in fact is rented for brief periods during the year, producing about $6,000 of net income annually. She prefers, however, not to treat the property as a money making proposition because it requires her to give up too much of the flexibility she enjoys in taking the children and grandchildren to the beach for a week or a weekend whenever it is convenient for her to do so. Property taxes on the condominium were $1,000 last year and are expected to increase 6 percent annually.

The Millers are both uncomfortable with large amounts of debt and therefore have no significant liabilities. Their personal residence was purchased from Anne's grandfather 30 years ago for $25,000. It is an older home, dating back to the 1890s, and they believe it is currently worth about $400,000 in the local market. It would be expensive to replace; in fact, replacement cost would probably be in the $450,000 range. The house is completely paid for. Much of the furniture in the house was inherited from Anne's family. Larry considers that the remainder of the furniture has been gifted to her, as it has been acquired through the years. They estimate the value of the household furnishings at $100,000. Property taxes on their residence were $4,150 last year and are expected to increase at 3 percent annually. The Millers gave $3,000 to charity last year, and their nondeductible living expenses were $30,000. They expect these amounts to increase by about 6 percent annually.

Larry and Anne carry $300,000 of insurance coverage on their house under a homeowners form 3 that provides for replacement cost coverage. The personal liability coverage limit of the policy is $150,000. They also carry a personal auto policy on their automobiles with liability limits of $300,000 and physical damage coverage.

Larry has two personal life insurance policies, both of which are whole life policies. The face amount of the first policy is $83,500. It is owned by Larry with Anne as the beneficiary and has a present cash value of $19,293. The second policy has a face amount of $10,000 and a present cash value of $7,647. Larry is the owner, and his estate is the beneficiary.

Anne has only one insurance policy, the face amount of which is $10,000. There is $6,430 in accumulated dividends on deposit, making $16,430 the amount of death benefits available. The present cash value of the policy is $4,890. The insurance policy is owned by Anne and is payable to Larry as the beneficiary.

Both Larry and Anne realize that they are paying substantial income taxes, but they are not interested in any aggressive tax-planning techniques that might cause the IRS to audit them. They have never been audited and would rather pay the taxes than worry about any involvement with the IRS.

The following is a statement of net worth for Larry and Anne as of December 31 of last year.

Table 6-1 LARRY AND ANNE MILLER Statement of Net Worth December 31, last year		
Assets	**Owner**	**Value**
Checking account	Joint	$3,000
Savings accounts	Anne	12,000
Money market fund	Larry	46,000
Stocks and bonds	Anne	103,000
Millers, Inc., stock	Larry	506,172
Millers, Inc., stock	Anne	173,760
Personal residence	Larry	400,000
Household furnishings	Anne	100,000
Resort home	Anne	150,000
Resort home	Larry	16,000
Store building	Larry	530,000
Note receivable (second store)	Larry	159,000
Profit-sharing plan	Larry	65,800
Cash value (life insurance)	Larry	26,940
Cash value (life insurance)	Anne	4,890
Accumulated dividends (life insurance)	Anne	6,430
Total		$2,302,992

If Larry predeceases Anne, he would like her to be financially independent for the rest of her life. Although there is no friction between Anne and her children, she does not wish to depend on them for assistance and wishes to be able to pay for any household help or luxuries that she requires as she gets older. Larry wishes any assets remaining at Anne's death to be divided equally among his children and the share of any deceased child to be split equally among the deceased child's children.

Both Larry's parents are deceased, but Anne's mother is still living. Although she is in her late seventies, she continues to enjoy good health and a luxurious lifestyle. Anne's mother was the primary beneficiary under Anne's father's will, which left the bulk of his estate to her outright. Anne believes that she and her younger brother are the principal beneficiaries of their mother's will and that their inheritances from her could be at least $600,000 to $800,000 each.

Larry's and Anne's wills have not been updated for 16 years. Each leaves all his or her property to the other spouse, if surviving. If there is no surviving spouse, all property is left to their living children or children of a deceased child equally, per stirpes.

Business Information

Larry is proud of the business he has built and thinks he has accumulated a sufficient net worth to allow him a financially untroubled retirement. However, because so much of his accumulated wealth is tied up in Millers, he has requested advice on the implementation of a plan allowing those assets to be transformed into a more liquid form so that they can provide retirement income for Anne and him. Larry also wants to be sure that his business interest is not burdensome for Anne at his death and that she can be assured of an income from his assets. At the same time he does not wish to have an estate plan or a business transition plan that will damage the continuing viability of Millers.

Larry feels that an orderly business transition of Millers to Steve during Larry's lifetime is equitable, since Steve has spent many years working for the corporation, and he should be able to have ownership or at least control of the company without waiting for Larry to die. Larry considers that the sale of the other corporation's stock to Doug has assured Doug of a secure source of income if he is willing to devote himself diligently to the business. He feels that the transition of Millers stock to Steve will achieve the same objective.

Millers is a regular (C) corporation. There are 250 shares of common stock authorized and issued. Of those shares Larry owns approximately 167.5 shares (67 percent), Steve owns 25 shares (10 percent), and Anne owns approximately 57.5 shares (23 percent). The corporation has never paid dividends. It uses a calendar-year accounting period and employs the specific-identification inventory accounting method. At the end of last year the net worth of the corporation was $755,480, and the book value of each of the 250 shares was $3,022, as shown on the corporate balance sheet that follows.

The corporation employs 34 people, 26 of whom are full-time. Last year salaries were $686,000, of which Larry was paid $65,000 and Steve was paid $42,500. Larry expects his and Steve's salaries to increase at about 6 percent a year. Last year the corporation had sales of approximately $2,200,000 and taxable income of $175,000.

The corporation provides a profit-sharing plan for its employees. The plan requires that if corporate pretax profits reach $200,000 a year, a 10 percent contribution will be made to the plan. If corporate profits do not reach $200,000, there is no contribution to the profit-sharing plan. Therefore the plan has been funded only sporadically.

Larry is unhappy with the performance of the plan, which he feels the employees do not view as a motivator. He comments that perhaps this situation exists because most of his employees, except for three or four rank-and-file employees, are under 40 and consequently too young to be concerned about retirement. In addition, the plan's sporadic funding does not strongly motivate employees. Larry's account balance in the profit-sharing plan is $65,800, and he is fully vested.

Table 6-2 CORPORATE BALANCE SHEET Millers, Inc. December 31, last year	
Assets	
Cash	$ 205,000
Accounts receivable	179,000
Inventory	486,000
Office equipment (net of depreciation)	20,000
Delivery vehicles (net of depreciation)	20,000
Leasehold improvements	42,000
Life insurance cash value	77,480
Total assets	$1,029,480
Liabilities and Net Worth	
Current liabilities	$ 274,000
Common stock ($160 par)	40,000
Retained earnings	715,480
Total liabilities and net worth	$1,029,480

Millers provides its hourly employees with 7 days of sick leave per year and a week of vacation after a year of service. Vacation is increased to 2 weeks after 3 years of employment. Hourly employees are allowed to accumulate sick leave up to 21 days. Salaried staff are provided 2 weeks of vacation after a year of employment and 3 weeks of vacation after employment for 5 years. Sick leave for salaried employees is 10 days per year, and salaried employees may carry over unused sick leave up to a maximum of 60 days. Larry carries an excellent medical insurance plan for his employees that provides $1 million of lifetime coverage and, after a $100 deductible, provides coverage of 80 percent of the first $3,000 of covered benefits. After the

$3,000 of covered benefits is reached, additional expenses are paid in full. The corporation provides employee coverage on a noncontributory basis. However, dependent coverage is available only if the employee pays the additional amount. The corporation does not provide long-term disability income benefits or life insurance benefits for employees. The corporation, however, does carry a $200,000 whole life insurance policy on Larry's life that was acquired 20 years ago. The corporation is the owner and beneficiary of this policy, which has a current cash value of $77,480.

Larry individually, and not the corporation, owns the building that houses Millers. It was built 10 years ago and has been leased to the corporation since that time. The cost to construct the building was approximately $185,000. Larry estimates its present worth at $530,000 and assumes that it will increase in value at about 4 percent per year. At present it provides net rental income of $33,000 per year.

INSTRUCTIONS
Based on this information, prepare a working outline for the Millers. When this has been completed, it can be compared with the one that follows. After comparing the working outlines, go to page 6.11 for further instructions.

WORKING OUTLINE

1. Clients' objectives

    a. Lifetime objectives

        (1) Assure that control of Millers goes to Steve during Larry's lifetime.

        (2) Enjoy a secure retirement and maintain some continuing involvement with Millers.

    b. Dispositions at death

        (1) Assure that Anne is well provided for and that Larry's accumulated assets are not burdensome to her at his death.

        (2) Divide any assets remaining at Anne's death equally among the children.

        (3) Achieve his other objectives without damaging Millers.

2. Business planning

a. Tax planning

    (1) Present position

    (2) Business transition

        (a) Installment sales

- General requirements
- Avoiding the limitations on the deductibility of investment interest

        (b) Using an S election to facilitate the transfer of a business interest

- The tax on built-in gains
- Practical considerations in planning for an S election
- Additional principles applicable to the taxation of installment sales

        (c) Redemptions

- Requirements for favorable federal income tax treatment
- Sec. 318 attribution problems
- Sec. 302(c)(2) election—the waiver approach
- Sec. 303 redemptions

        (d) Recapitalizations

- General requirements
- Restrictions

        (e) Private annuity

    (3) Shareholder-employee compensation planning

        (a) Reasonable compensation for shareholder employees

        (b) Employment contracts

        (c) Consulting contracts

          (4) Employee benefits

             (a) Qualified plans of deferred compensation

- Problems with present plans
- General requirements
- Recommendations

             (b) Nonqualified deferred compensation

- Avoiding immediate inclusion in employee's income
- Deductibility by the corporation
- Avoiding imposition of federal estate tax

   b. Insurance planning

       (1) Medical insurance plans

       (2) Disability income plans

       (3) Life insurance plans

       (4) Property and liability coverage for the business—fundamental requirements

3. Personal planning

   a. Tax planning

       (1) Present position

       (2) Assuring Larry's comfortable retirement and continuing involvement with Millers

       (3) Dispositions at death

          (a) Analysis of present plans

          (b) Possible improvements in estate plan

          (c) Concept of estate equalization

          (d) Recommendations

          (e) Life insurance placement

- General discussion
- Structuring the irrevocable life insurance trust

(f) Deferral of estate taxes under IRC Sec. 6166

    b. Insurance planning

        (1) Personal life insurance coverage

        (2) Personal property and liability coverage

    c. Investment planning

        (1) Client profile

        (2) Investment alternatives

            (a) Certificates of deposit

            (b) Municipal bond funds

            (c) Municipal bonds

            (d) Balanced mutual funds

            (e) Convertible bonds or convertible bond funds

        (3) Recommendations

        (4) Preretirement planning

            (a) Repositioning of assets

            (b) Asset conservation

            (c) Plan distribution options

            (d) Retirement income estimation

            (e) Potentially dependent parent

            (f) Recreation/health

            (g) Personal asset acquisition

            (h) Possible new career

INSTRUCTIONS

Now prepare a financial plan for the Millers. When you have completed your financial plan, you can compare it with the suggested solution that follows.

PERSONAL FINANCIAL PLAN FOR LARRY AND ANNE MILLER [SUGGESTED SOLUTION]: CLIENTS' OBJECTIVES

1. Lifetime objectives

   a. Assure that control of Millers goes to Steve during Larry's lifetime.

   b. Enjoy a secure retirement and maintain some continuing involvement with Millers.

2. Dispositions at death

   a. Assure that Anne is well provided for and that Larry's accumulated assets are not burdensome to her at his death.

   b. Divide any assets remaining at Anne's death equally among the children.

   c. Achieve Larry's other objectives without damaging Millers.

The following pages show the 3-year income statement, balance sheet, cash flow, and summary data of the Millers' present personal situation.

BASE CASE

Assumptions

1. The checking account balance is maintained at $3,000 and is noninterest bearing.
2. The savings account earns 5 percent annually. Interest accumulates in the account.
3. Surplus cash earns 5.25 percent annually
4. The money market funds earn 5.5 percent annually. Interest accumulates in the fund.
5. Larry's salary increases at 6 percent annually.
6. Anne's listed stocks and bonds will increase in value at 5 percent annually. Yields on these securities will average 4 percent annually.
7. Stock in Millers is based on year-end book value and will increase in value at 5 percent annually.
8. The personal residence will increase in value at 4 percent annually.
9. Property taxes on the residence last year were $4,150 and will increase at 3 percent annually.
10. The resort condominium will increase in value at 8 percent annually.
11. Property taxes on the condominium will increase at 6 percent annually.
12. Increase or decrease in the value of household furnishings is ignored.
13. The value of the commercial building will increase at 4 percent annually. Net rental income from this property increases at 6 percent annually.
14. Nondeductible living expenses and charitable contributions increase at 6 percent annually.
15. The profit-sharing plan will earn 6 percent annually.
16. The cash values of the life insurance policies will grow at 8 percent annually.

Larry and Anne Miller Balance Sheet

Table 6-3 Base Case Balance Sheet for Larry and Anne Miller			
BASE CASE	**Current Year**	**Next Year (Projected)**	**Two Years (Projected)**
LIQUID ASSETS			
Running Total	$ 9,943.34	$ 24,675.62	$ 54,818.32
Cash			
Checking	$ 3,000.00	$3,000.00	$3,000.00
Savings — Anne	$ 12,600.00	$ 13,230.00	$ 13,891.50
Investable Cash	$ 69,126.00	$ 142,467.00	$ 220,512.00
MMKT — Larry	$ 48,530.00	$ 54,199.00	$ 54,015.00
	$ 133,256.00	$ 213,196.00	$ 291,418.50
Stocks & Bonds			
Stocks/Bonds — Anne	$ 108,150.00	$ 113,557.50	$ 119,235.38
Miller Stock — Anne	$ 182,448.00	$ 191,570.40	$ 201,148.92
Miller Stock — Larry	$ 531,481.00	$ 558,055.05	$ 585,957.80
	$ 822,079.00	$ 863,182.95	$ 906,342.10
Life Insurance			
Larry #1	$ 20,836.00	$ 22,502.88	$ 24,303.11
Larry #2	$ 8,259.00	$ 8,919.72	$ 9,633.30
Anne	$ 5,281.00	$ 5,703.48	$ 6,159.76
	$ 34,376.00	$ 37,126.08	$ 40,096.17
Liquid Assets	$ 999,654.34	$ 1,137,880.65	$1,292,675.08
NONLIQUID ASSETS			
Benefit Plans			
PS Plan	$ 69,748.00	$ 73,933.00	$ 78,369.00
Receivables			
Notes Rec — Doug	$ 148,718.00	$ 135,934.00	$ 121,812.00
Personal Property			
Home	$ 400,000.00	$ 416,000.00	$ 432,640.00
Condo	$ 162,000.00	$ 174,960.00	$ 188,957.00
Commercial Building	$ 530,000.00	$ 551,200.00	$ 573,248.00
Automobiles	$ 13,600.00	$ 11,560.00	$ 9,826.00
Home Furnishings	$ 100,000.00	$ 100,000.00	$ 100,000.00
	$1,205,600.00	$ 1,253,720.00	$1,304,671.00
Nonliquid Assets	$1,424,066.00	$ 1,463,587.00	$1,504,852.00
Total Assets	$2,423,720.34	$ 2,601,467.65	$2,797,527.08
Net Worth	**$2,423,720.34**	**$ 2,601,467.65**	**$2,797,527.08**

Larry and Anne Miller Tax Flow

Table 6-4 Base Case Tax Statement Larry and Anne Miller			
BASE CASE	**Current Year**	**Next Year (Projected)**	**Two Years (Projected)**
Earned Income			
Salaries—Larry	$ 68,900.00	$ 73,034.00	$ 77,416.04
Interest/Dividends			
Notes Rec—Doug	$ 15,508.00	$ 14,296.00	$ 12,958.00
Stocks/Bonds—Anne	$ 4,326.00	$ 4,542.00	$ 4,769.00
Savings Acct—Anne	$ 600.00	$ 630.00	$ 662.00
MMKT—Larry	$ 2,530.00	$ 2,669.00	$ 2,816.00
Investable Cash	$ 1,768.00	$ 5,412.00	$ 9,284.00
	$ 24,732.00	$ 27,549.00	$ 30,489.00
Investments			
Rent—Commercial Bldg	$ 33,000.00	$ 34,980.00	$ 37,079.00
Rent—Condo	$ 6,000.00	$ 6,000.00	$ 6,000.00
	$ 39,000.00	$ 40,980.00	$ 43,079.00
Net Capital Gain	$ 4,629.00	$ 5,114.00	$ 5,649.00
Adjusted Gross Income	$ 137,261.00	$ 146,677.00	$ 156,633.04
Deductions			
Charitable 50%	$ 3,000.00	$ 3,180.00	$ 3,370.80
State Tax Paid	$ 6,757.00	$ 7,275.00	$ 7,822.00
Property Tax—Home	$ 4,150.00	$ 4,275.00	$ 4,403.00
Property Tax—Condo	$ 1,000.00	$ 1,060.00	$ 1,124.00
Gross Deductions	$ 14,907.00	$ 15,790.00	$ 16,719.80
Standard Deduction	—		
Personal Exemptions	$ 7,000.00	$ 7,000.00	$ 7,000.00
Taxable Income	$ 100,447.00	$ 108,097.00	$ 116,193.44
Fed Income Tax	$ 17,799.25	$ 19,711.75	$ 21,735.86
Fed Tax Bracket	25%	25%	25%

Larry and Anne Miller's Cash Flow Statement

Table 6-5 Base Case Cash Flow Statement of Larry and Anne Miller			
BASE CASE	**Current Year**	**Next Year (Projected)**	**Two Years (Projected)**
BEGINNING OF YEAR			
Idle Cash on Hand	$ 3,000.00	$ 9,943.34	$ 24,675.62
SOURCES OF CASH			
Cash Income			
Salaries—Larry	$ 68,900.00	$ 73,034.00	$ 77,416.04
Interest & Dividends	$ 19,834.00	$ 18,838.00	$ 17,727.00
Rents/Royalties	$ 39,000.00	$ 40,980.00	$ 43,079.00
	$ 127,734.00	$132,852.00	$138,222.04
Debt Recovered			
Notes Rec—Doug	$ 11,572.00	$ 12,784.00	$ 14,122.00
Cash Inflow	$ 142,306.00	$155,579.34	$177,019.66
Total Cash Available	$ 145,306.00	$165,522.68	$201,695.27
USES OF CASH			
Charity Contribution	$ 3,000.00	$ 3,180.00	$ 3,370.80
Living Expenses	$ 30,000.00	$ 31,800.00	$ 33,708.00
	$ 33,000.00	$ 34,980.00	$ 37,078.80
Income Taxes Paid	$ 17,799.25	$ 19,711.75	$ 21,735.86
State Tax Paid	$ 6,757.00	$ 7,275.00	$ 7,822.00
FICA/Soc. Sec. Tax	$ 5,298.41	$ 5,616.31	$ 5,953.29
Real Estate Tax	$ 5,150.00	$ 5,335.00	$ 5,526.00
	$ 35,004.66	$ 37,938.06	$ 41,037.15
Investable Cash	$ 67,358.00	$67,929.00	$68,761.00
Total Outflow	$ 135,362.66	$140,847.06	$146,876.95
END OF YEAR			
Cash Balance	$ 9,943.34	$ 24,675.62	$ 54,818.32

CASE II

Installment Sale of Larry's Entire Interest in Millers to Steve

New Assumption

Steve purchases all of Larry's Millers stock on July 1, 2011, at a projected 2011 book value ($531,480) for no down payment at 9 percent interest for a term of 15 years. Larry remains active in the business for at least 4 years.

Continuing Assumptions

1. The checking account balance is maintained at $3,000 and is noninterest bearing.
2. The savings account earns 5 percent annually. Interest accumulates in the account.
3. Surplus cash earns 5.25 percent annually.
4. The money market funds earn 5.5 percent annually. Interest accumulates in the fund.
5. Larry's salary increases at 6 percent annually.
6. Anne's listed stocks and bonds will increase in value at 5 percent annually. Yields on these securities will average 4 percent annually.
7. Stock in Millers is based on year-end book value and will increase in value at 5 percent annually.
8. The personal residence will increase in value at 4 percent annually.
9. Property taxes on the residence last year were $4,150 and will increase at 3 percent annually.
10. The resort condominium will increase in value at 8 percent annually.
11. Property taxes on the condominium will increase at 6 percent annually.
12. Increase or decrease in the value of household furnishings is ignored.
13. The value of the commercial building will increase at 4 percent annually. Net rental income from this property increases at 6 percent annually.
14. Nondeductible living expenses and charitable contributions increase at 6 percent annually.
15. The profit-sharing plan will earn 6 percent annually.
16. The cash values of the life insurance policies will grow at 8 percent annually.

Larry and Anne Miller: Case II Balance Sheet

Table 6-6 Case II Balance Sheet Larry and Anne Miller			
Case II	Current Year	Next Year (Projected)	Two Years (Projected)
LIQUID ASSETS			
Running Total	$ 9,943.34	$ 27,323.37	$ 65,975.31
Cash			
Checking	$ 3,000.00	$ 3,000.00	$ 3,000.00
Savings—Anne	$ 12,600.00	$ 13,230.00	$ 13,891.50
Investable Cash	$ 69,126.00	$ 142,467.00	$ 220,512.00
MMKT—Larry	$ 48,530.00	$ 51,199.00	$ 54,015.00
	$ 133,256.00	$ 203,896.00	$ 291,418.50
Stocks & Bonds			
Stocks/Bonds—Anne	$ 108,150.00	$ 113,557.50	$ 119,235.38
Miller Stock—Anne	$ 182,448.00	$ 191,570.40	$ 201,148.92
Miller Stock—Larry	$ 531,481.00	$ 558,055.05	$ 585,957.80
	$ 822,079.00	$ 863,182.95	$ 906,342.10
Life Insurance			
Larry #1	$ 20,836.00	$ 22,502.88	$ 24,303.11
Larry #2	$ 8,259.00	$ 8,919.72	$ 9,633.30
Anne	$ 5,281.00	$ 5,703.48	$ 6,159.76
	$ 34,376.00	$ 37,126.08	$ 40,096.17
Liquid Assets	$ 999,654.34	$ 1,137,528.40	$1,303,832.08
NONLIQUID ASSETS			
Benefit Plans			
PS Plan	$ 69,748.00	$ 73,933.00	$ 78,369.00
Receivables			
Notes Rec—Doug	$ 148,718.00	$ 135,934.00	$ 121,812.00
Notes Rec—Steve	—	$ 522,893.00	$ 504,521.00
Personal Property			
Home	$ 400,000.00	$ 416,000.00	$ 432,640.00
Condo	$ 162,000.00	$ 174,960.00	$ 188,957.00
Commercial Building	$ 530,000.00	$ 551,200.00	$ 573,248.00
Automobiles	$ 13,600.00	$ 11,560.00	$ 9,826.00
Home Furnishings	$ 100,000.00	$ 100,000.00	$ 100,000.00
	$1,205,600.00	$ 1,253,720.00	$1,304,671.00
Nonliquid Assets	$1,424,066.00	$ 1,986,480.00	$2,009,373.00
Total Assets	$2,423,720.34	$ 3,124,008.40	$3,313,205.08
Net Worth	**$2,420,720.34**	**$ 3,121,008.40**	**$3,310,205.08**

Larry and Anne Miller: Case II Tax Statement

Table 6-7 Case II Tax Statement Larry and Anne Miller			
CASE II	Current Year	Next Year (Projected)	Two Years (Projected)
Earned Income			
Salaries— Larry	$ 68,900.00	$ 73,034.00	$ 77,416.04
Interest/Dividends			
Notes Rec—Doug	$ 15,508.00	$ 14,296.00	$ 12,958.00
Notes Rec—Steve	—	**$ 23,757.00**	**$ 46,315.00**
Stocks/Bonds—Anne	$ 4,326.00	$ 4,542.00	$ 4,769.00
Savings Acct—Anne	$ 600.00	$ 630.00	$ 662.00
MMKT—Larry	$ 2,530.00	$ 2,669.00	$ 2,816.00
Investable Cash	$ 1,768.00	$ 5,412.00	$ 9,284.00
	$ 24,732.00	$ 51,306.00	$ 76,804.00
Investments			
Rent—Commercial Bldg	$ 33,000.00	$ 34,980.00	$ 37,079.00
Rent—Condo	$ 6,000.00	$ 6,000.00	$ 6,000.00
	$ 39,000.00	$ 40,980.00	$ 43,079.00
Net Capital Gain	$ 4,629.00	$ 5,114.00	$ 5,649.00
Adjusted Gross Income	$ 137,261.00	$ 170,434.00	$ 202,948.04
Deductions			
Charitable 50%	$ 3,000.00	$ 3,180.00	$ 3,370.80
State Tax Paid	$ 6,757.00	$ 7,275.00	$ 7,822.00
Property Tax—Home	$ 4,150.00	$ 4,275.00	$ 4,403.00
Property Tax—Condo	$ 1,000.00	$ 1,060.00	$ 1,124.00
Gross Deductions	$ 14,907.00	$ 15,790.00	$ 16,719.80
Standard Deduction	—		
Personal Exemptions	$ 7,000.00	$ 7,000.00	$ 7,000.00
Taxable Income	$ 100,447.00	$ 131,854.00	$ 162,508.44
Fed Income Tax	$ 17,799.25	$ 25,651.00	$ 34,246.36
Fed Tax Bracket-Ord	25%	25%	28%

Larry and Anne Miller: Case II Cash Flow Statement

Table 6-8 Case II Cash Flow Statement Larry and Anne Miller			
CASE II	Current Year	Next Year (Projected)	Two Years (Projected)
BEGINNING OF YEAR			
Idle Cash on Hand	$ 3,000.00	$ 9,943.34	$ 27,323.37
SOURCES OF CASH			
Cash Income			
Salaries—Larry	$ 68,900.00	$ 73,034.00	$ 77,416.04
Interest & Dividends	$ 19,834.00	$ 18,838.00	$ 17,727.00
Rents/Royalties	$ 39,000.00	$ 40,980.00	$ 43,079.00
	$ 127,734.00	$132,852.00	$138,222.04
Debt Recovered			
Notes Rec– Doug	$ 11,572.00	$ 12,784.00	$ 14,122.00
Notes Rec—Steve	—	$ 8,587.00	$ 18,372.00
Cash Inflow	$ 142,306.00	$164,166.34	$198,039.41
Total Cash Available	$ 145,306.00	$174,109.68	$225,362.77
USES OF CASH			
Charity Contribution	$ 3,000.00	$ 3,180.00	$ 3,370.80
Living Expenses	$ 30,000.00	$ 31,800.00	$ 33,708.00
	$ 33,000.00	$ 34,980.00	$ 37,078.80
Income Taxes Paid	$ 17,799.25	$ 25,651.00	$ 34,246.36
State Tax Paid	$ 6,757.00	$ 7,275.00	$ 7,822.00
FICA/Soc. Sec. Tax	$ 5,298.41	$ 5,616.31	$ 5,953.29
Real Estate Tax	$ 5,150.00	$ 5,335.00	$ 5,526.00
	$ 35,004.66	$ 43,877.31	$ 53,547.66
Investable Cash	$ 67,358.00	$ 67,929.00	$ 68,761.00
Total Outflow	$ 135,362.66	$146,786.31	$159,387.46
END OF YEAR			
Cash Balance	$ 9,943.34	$ 27,323.37	$ 65,975.31

CASE III

Installment Sale of 101 Shares of Millers Stock to Steve

New Assumption

Steve purchases 101 shares of Larry's Millers stock on July 1, 2011, at a projected book value ($320,483) for no down payment at 9 percent interest for a term of 15 years. Larry remains active in the business for at least 4 years.

Continuing Assumptions

1. The checking account balance is maintained at $3,000 and is noninterest bearing.
2. The savings account earns 5 percent annually. Interest accumulates in the account.
3. Surplus cash earns 5.25 percent annually.
4. The money market funds earn 5.5 percent annually. Interest accumulates in the account.
5. Larry's salary increases at 6 percent annually.
6. Anne's listed stocks and bonds will increase in value at 5 percent annually. Yields on these securities will average 4 percent annually.
7. Stock in Millers is based on year-end book value and will increase in value at 5 percent annually.
8. The personal residence will increase in value at 4 percent annually.
9. Property taxes on the residence last year were $4,150 and will increase at 3 percent annually.
10. The resort condominium will increase in value at 8 percent annually.
11. Property taxes on the condominium will increase at 6 percent annually.
12. Increase or decrease in the value of household furnishings is ignored.
13. The value of the commercial building will increase at 4 percent annually. Net rental income from this property increases at 6 percent annually.
14. Nondeductible living expenses and charitable contributions increase at 6 percent annually.
15. The profit-sharing plan will earn 6 percent annually.
16. The cash values of the life insurance policies will grow at 8 percent annually.

Larry and Anne Miller: Case III Balance Sheet

Table 6-9 Case III Balance Sheet Larry and Anne Miller			
CASE III	Current Year	Next Year (Projected)	Two Years (Projected)
LIQUID ASSETS			
Running Total	$ 9,943.34	$ 26,272.37	$ 61,728.67
Cash			
Checking	$ 3,000.00	$ 3,000.00	$ 3,000.00
Savings—Anne	$ 12,600.00	$ 13,230.00	$ 13,891.50
Investable Cash	$ 69,126.00	$ 142,467.00	$ 220,512.00
MMKT—Larry	$ 48,530.00	$ 51,199.00	$ 54,015.00
	$ 133,256.00	$ 209,896.00	$ 291,418.50
Stocks & Bonds			
Stocks/Bonds—Anne	$ 108,150.00	$ 113,557.50	$ 119,235.38
Miller Stock—Anne	$ 182,448.00	$ 191,570.40	$ 201,148.92
Miller Stock—Larry	$ 531,481.00	$ 558,055.05	$ 585,957.80
	$ 822,079.00	$ 863,182.95	$ 906,342.10
Life Insurance			
Larry #1	$ 20,836.00	$ 22,502.88	$ 24,303.11
Larry #2	$ 8,259.00	$ 8,919.72	$ 9,633.30
Anne	$ 5,281.00	$ 5,703.48	$ 6,159.76
	$ 34,376.00	$ 37,126.08	$ 40,096.17
Liquid Assets	$ 999,654.34	$ 1,136,477.40	$1,299,585.44
NONLIQUID ASSETS			
Benefit Plans			
PS Plan	$ 69,748.00	$ 73,933.00	$ 78,369.00
Receivables			
Notes Rec—Doug	$ 148,718.00	$ 135,934.00	$ 121,812.00
Notes Rec—Steve	—	$ 315,305.00	$ 304,226.00
Personal Property			
Home	$ 400,000.00	$ 416,000.00	$ 432,640.00
Condo	$ 162,000.00	$ 174,960.00	$ 188,957.00
Commercial Building	$ 530,000.00	$ 551,200.00	$ 573,248.00
Automobiles	$ 13,600.00	$ 11,560.00	$ 9,826.00
Home Furnishings	$ 100,000.00	$ 100,000.00	$ 100,000.00
	$1,205,600.00	$ 1,253,720.00	$1,304,671.00
Nonliquid Assets	$1,424,066.00	$ 1,778,892.00	$1,809,078.00
Total Assets	$2,423,720.34	$ 2,915,369.40	$3,108,663.44
Net Worth	**$2,423,720.34**	**$ 2,915,369.40**	**$3,108,663.44**

Larry and Anne Miller: Case III Tax Statement

Table 6-10 Case III Tax Statement Larry and Anne Miller			
CASE III	Current Year	Next Year (Projected)	Two Years (Projected)
Earned Income			
Salaries—Larry	$ 68,900.00	$ 73,034.00	$ 77,416.04
Interest/Dividends			
Notes Rec—Doug	$ 15,508.00	$ 14,296.00	$ 12,958.00
Notes Rec—Steve	—	**$ 14,325.00**	**$ 27,928.00**
Stocks/Bonds—Anne	$ 4,326.00	$ 4,542.00	$ 4,769.00
Savings Acct—Anne	$ 600.00	$ 630.00	$ 662.00
MMKT—Larry	$ 2,530.00	$ 2,669.00	$ 2,816.00
Investable Cash	$ 1,768.00	$ 5,412.00	$ 9,284.00
	$ 24,732.00	$ 41,874.00	$ 58,417.00
Investments			
Rent—Commercial Bldg	$ 33,000.00	$ 34,980.00	$ 37,079.00
Rent - Condo	$ 6,000.00	$ 6,000.00	$ 6,000.00
	$ 39,000.00	$ 40,980.00	$ 43,079.00
Net Capital Gain	$ 4,629.00	$ 5,114.00	$ 5,649.00
Adjusted Gross Income	$ 137,261.00	$ 161,002.00	$ 184,561.04
Deductions			
Charitable 50%	$ 3,000.00	$ 3,180.00	$ 3,370.80
State Tax Paid	$ 6,757.00	$ 7,275.00	$ 7,822.00
Property Tax—Home	$ 4,150.00	$ 4,275.00	$ 4,403.00
Property Tax—Condo	$ 1,000.00	$ 1,060.00	$ 1,124.00
Gross Deductions	$ 14,907.00	$ 15,790.00	$ 16,719.80
Standard Deduction	—		
Personal Exemptions	$ 7,000.00	$ 7,000.00	$ 7,000.00
Taxable Income	$ 100,447.00	$ 122,422.00	$ 144,121.44
Fed Income Tax	$ 17,799.25	$ 23,293.00	$ 29,098.00
Fed Tax Bracket-Ord.	25%	25%	28%

Larry and Anne Miller Case III Cash Flow Statement

Table 6-11 Case III Cash Flow Statement Larry and Anne Miller			
CASE III	Current Year	Next Year (Projected)	Two Years (Projected)
BEGINNING OF YEAR			
Idle Cash on Hand	$ 3,000.00	$ 9,943.34	$ 23,914.37
SOURCES OF CASH			
Cash Income			
Salaries—Larry	$ 68,900.00	$ 73,034.00	$ 77,416.04
Interest & Dividends	$ 19,834.00	$ 18,838.00	$ 17,727.00
Rents/Royalties	$ 39,000.00	$ 40,980.00	$ 43,079.00
	$ 127,734.00	$132,852.00	$138,222.04
Debt Recovered			
Notes Rec - Doug	$ 11,572.00	$ 12,784.00	$ 14,122.00
Notes Rec - Steve	$ —	$ 5,178.00	$ 11,079.00
Cash Inflow	$ 142,306.00	$160,757.34	$187,337.41
Total Cash Available	$ 145,306.00	$170,700.68	$211,251.77
USES OF CASH			
Charity Contribution	$ 3,000.00	$ 3,180.00	$ 3,370.80
Living Expenses	$ 30,000.00	$ 31,800.00	$ 33,708.00
	$ 33,000.00	$ 34,980.00	$ 37,078.80
Income Taxes Paid	$ 17,799.25	$ 25,651.00	$ 34,246.36
State Tax Paid	$ 6,757.00	$ 7,275.00	$ 7,822.00
FICA/Soc. Sec. Tax	$ 5,298.41	$ 5,616.31	$ 5,953.29
Real Estate Tax	$ 5,150.00	$ 5,335.00	$ 5,526.00
	$ 35,004.66	$ 43,877.31	$ 53,547.66
Investable Cash	$ 67,358.00	$ 67,929.00	$ 68,761.00
Total Outflow	$ 135,362.66	$146,786.31	$159,387.46
END OF YEAR			
Cash Balance	$ 9,943.34	$ 23,914.37	$ 51,864.31

BUSINESS PLANNING: TAXES

Present Position

Millers is not only the largest and most important single asset that Larry and Anne have accumulated, it has also been the primary source of income to support their lifestyle and to allow them to accumulate other assets. Larry has a very strong desire to preserve the business for their oldest son, Steve, who has worked in the business for many years and who Larry thinks is capable of continuing to manage it profitably. Another corporation has already been sold to their younger son, Doug, and a business associate.

Larry has no present plan to retire completely from Millers but would like to cut back his day-to-day responsibilities there. He would like to transfer his responsibilities to Steve before planning to significantly reduce the time he spends at the store. He thinks he is ready to pass management control of the business to Steve, since he is assured that Steve will succeed in a leadership role.

Larry presently owns 167.5 (67 percent) of the corporation's 250 authorized and issued shares. Anne owns 57.5 shares (23 percent) and Steve owns 25 shares (10 percent). The book value of Larry's shares at year end was $506,172, the book value of Anne's shares was $173,760, and the book value of Steve's shares was $75,548.

Larry wishes to accomplish the transition of control to Steve while assuring that his and Anne's interest in Millers will continue to produce income that will allow them to be secure during their later years. At the same time he does not want to implement techniques that will accomplish these personal objectives while compromising the continuing viability of the business.

Business Transition

Installment Sales

  General Requirements. A simple method of transferring Larry's interest in Millers to Steve is an installment sale. Generally an installment sale occurs when property is disposed of in exchange for payments, at least one of which is to be received after the close of the taxable year in which the disposition occurs (IRC Sec. 453(a)).

The seller receives sale-or-exchange federal income tax treatment to the extent of gain realized on the transaction (selling price less adjusted basis = gain realized). When the installment method of reporting is used, the gain portion is recognized and reported as a percentage of each taxable year's payment. The interest portion of the installment payment is, of course, recognized as ordinary income in the year in which it is received. Use of the installment sale method can therefore spread a large gain over a number of years, with significant income tax deferral and possible overall tax savings.

Note, however, that for installment sales of depreciable property all recapture for depreciation must be treated as ordinary income in the year of the sale, regardless of whether any payment is received in that year (IRC Sec. 453(i), 453(i)(2)). However, stock in Millers is not depreciable property.

Installment sales of stock can also provide an important income stream for retirement years, particularly in cases such as this when many of the client's assets are wrapped up in a single business entity that is essentially nonliquid. The 5-year tax, net worth, and cash-flow results of an installment sale of Larry's entire interest in Millers to Steve at book value with a 9 percent interest rate for a term of 15 years are illustrated on the previous pages.

Another important advantage of installment sales is that they take an appreciating asset out of Larry's estate and replace it with one that has a fixed value. In fact, the value of Larry's interest in the business can decrease if the installment proceeds are consumed prior to Larry's death.

If Larry were to sell Steve his entire interest in Millers for no down payment and monthly payments calculated at 9 percent interest for a term of 15 years, Steve's annual level payments of principal and interest would be $64,687 (in 12 monthly payments). Steve's present salary obviously would not allow him to afford such high payments. In fact, it would probably be difficult to raise Steve's salary in the near future to a level that would allow him to afford these payments and avoid an IRS challenge on the reasonableness of his compensation, particularly since Millers is a C corporation.

It would not, however, be difficult to raise Steve's salary to allow him to acquire some of Larry's stock immediately through an installment sale, especially in view of the additional duties Larry would like to see Steve undertake.

Steve could purchase 101 of Larry's 167.5 shares at a projected 2004 book value of $320,483 at 9 percent interest for a term of 15 years for annual principal and interest payments of $39,758. In the early years, close to $35,000 of that amount would be interest. Since Millers is a C corporation, the interest payments would be an investment interest expense to Steve and therefore subject to the limitations on the deductibility of investment interest, discussed in the next section. If Steve purchased 101 shares, he would own 126 shares (101 + 25) and the controlling interest in the corporation.

The 5-year income statement, balance sheet, and cash-flow results to Larry and Anne of such a sale are shown on the previous pages.

Avoiding the Limitation on the Deductibility of Investment Interest.
In an installment sale the purchaser's deductibility of interest payments can be a crucial issue when the purchaser's salary must be raised to make such a purchase possible. In Steve's case the inability to deduct a major portion of the interest would require a substantially greater salary increase. This would increase the likelihood of the IRS's characterizing the compensation as unreasonable and therefore nondeductible by the corporation.

Generally an individual taxpayer can deduct investment interest only up to the amount of the taxpayer's *net investment income,* which means the excess of *investment income* over investment expenses.

Investment income is income from interest, dividends, rents, and royalties. Under the facts of this case Millers pays no dividends. Thus there will be no investment income to Steve as a result of owning any stock in Millers.

Investment expenses are deductible expenses other than interest that are directly connected with the production of investment income. Steve will not be incurring investment expenses as a consequence of this transaction.

The purchase of an ownership interest in a corporation (that is, stock) has traditionally been characterized as a purchase of an asset held for investment.

The Internal Revenue Service treats interest on a debt incurred to purchase an interest in an *S corporation* or a *partnership* as interest incurred in the conduct of a trade or business and *not* as investment interest, as long as the taxpayer purchasing the interest materially participates in the business.

This means that if a taxpayer uses the installment method to purchase an interest in an S corporation or a partnership, the interest payments will be fully deductible as a business expense and not subject to the investment interest expense limitations described above.

Although Steve is not your client at this time, his ability to deduct his interest payments in connection with the purchase of Larry's stock may be very important to Larry in terms of making the transaction affordable for Steve.

Millers is presently operated as a regular (C) corporation. Therefore in order to have the interest payments on Steve's obligation fully deductible as business interest payments under current IRS rules, Millers would have to make an S election. If the S election was in effect prior to the consummation of an installment sale, it is very likely that Steve could take advantage of the position taken by the IRS in Announcement 87-4 and deduct the full amount of his interest payments as a business expense. However, the other effects of making an S election in this case must be explored.

Using an S Election to Facilitate Transfer of a Business Interest

Note

To avoid repetition, background information on S corporations has been omitted. In an actual plan this information should be presented to the client for completeness. If you are not completely familiar with this material, it should be reviewed before proceeding through this suggested solution.

The Tax on "Built-in" Gains

Millers qualifies to be taxed as an S corporation, since it meets the basic requirements for the election. However, qualification is not the only factor that must be considered.

First, a special income tax liability can result in the case of existing C corporations that make elections under Subchapter S. Briefly stated, this tax liability is designed to prevent taxpayers from using S elections to circumvent the corporate-level tax imposed on corporate liquidations. This tax that can result from an S election is referred to as the *built-in gains tax*.

Millers could be subject to both a corporate-level built-in gains tax and a shareholder-level tax upon the subsequent sale of any inventory that existed prior to the time of an S election that is sold within 10 years of the effective date of such election (IRC Sec. 1374(d)). The corporate-level tax in this case would be assessed at a rate of 35 percent on the amount of the inventory's untaxed gain at the time the S election became effective. The shareholder-level tax on the same gain is assessed at the marginal rate of each shareholder.

The inventory appears to be the only significant "ordinary income" type of asset that would be subject to the built-in gains tax if an S election were made in this case. Millers accounts receivable have already been "booked" for income tax purposes under the accrual method of accounting. Since the receivables have already been recognized for tax purposes, they are not subject to the built-in gains tax.

The built-in gains tax will also apply to the corporation's capital assets. Any capital assets sold by the corporation within 10 years of the S election will be subject to a 35 percent corporate-level tax (in addition to the tax on the shareholders) with respect to the amount of appreciation that was "built in" or existing at the time of the S election. However, since Larry owns the store building individually, any property or improvements the corporation owns can be taxed under these rules. If the corporation waits 10 years after an S election before selling its capital assets, the tax will not be imposed. Also any capital assets sold before an S election became effective will be taxed at the corporation's marginal rate but will not be subject to the double tax that would result if the assets were sold after an S election, provided that the proceeds are not distributed to the shareholders as a dividend.

Sales of existing inventory *after* an S election will result in a built-in gains tax. One practical way to minimize this tax is to reduce inventory as much as possible just before the first day of the calendar year in which the S election becomes effective. If there is less inventory existing at the time an S election becomes effective, the built-in gains tax will be less of a problem.

Clearly these are sophisticated tax matters that the financial planner cannot single-handedly resolve. Larry's accountant and attorney must be consulted to determine the built-in gains tax liability that could result from an S election.

Larry's accountant would also have to examine how distributions by the corporation after an S election is made might be affected by the complex rules regarding previously taxed income of S corporations and the shareholders' "accumulated adjustment account" ("triple A account"). These matters are beyond the scope of this text.

Since Millers has substantial retained earnings, dividend treatment can still be applied to certain corporate distributions even after an S election is made because Millers would still have substantial earnings and profits accumulated during its life as a C corporation. As a result the tax rules regarding redemptions (discussed in a later section) will still apply even after an S election is made to determine whether dividend treatment would be applied to the proceeds of any proposed redemption. As discussed below, the treatment of a stock redemption as a dividend for federal income tax purposes is not a desirable result.

Practical Considerations in Planning for an S Election

Once Millers makes an S election, Larry and Steve will no longer be eligible for tax-favored fringe benefits at the corporate level. Most significantly the shareholders will be taxed on their proportionate shares of the corporation's taxable income, regardless of whether the income is distributed. Therefore care must be taken that Larry and Anne will receive at least enough money from Millers in the form of dividends to cover this additional tax liability.

If Steve purchases a controlling interest in Millers, he will have the authority to decide how much of the corporation's taxable income should be distributed to its shareholders. It is unlikely that Steve will refuse to distribute enough to allow his father to pay the additional taxes. However, the contract for the sale of Larry's stock could include a provision requiring Steve to make such distributions if Larry is concerned about the issue. This should be further explored before any agreements are signed.

An S election could provide Larry and Anne with additional retirement income if a substantial portion of their share of corporate taxable income is distributed to them. In addition, these distributions are derived from stock ownership and are not made in exchange for performance of services. Therefore the issue of reasonableness of compensation is avoided. Such distributions could be made regardless of whether Larry is working for the corporation at the time.

The possible problems associated with an S election have been noted. However, there appears to be no substantial disadvantage to Millers if they make an S election. The principal advantage would be to allow Steve to deduct interest payments on his installment obligation incurred to acquire S corporation stock. This would make the purchase much more feasible and affordable for Steve. Another advantage would be the lower individual tax rates (as compared with corporate rates) imposed on taxable income of the corporation in excess of $75,000. Therefore, subject to the agreement of Larry's attorney and accountant, our recommendation would be for Millers to make an election to be taxed as an S corporation, effective for the 2009 tax year. The election should be made in 2009 but in no event may it be made later than March 15, 2010 in order for it to be effective for taxable year 2009. The election must be made before Larry makes an installment sale of his stock to Steve.

In addition, if Anne's stock in Millers is redeemed immediately by the corporation (as will be discussed later), it will not be necessary for Steve to purchase 101 shares from Larry in order to acquire a controlling interest in the business. After Anne's stock is redeemed, Steve need purchase only 72 shares to own more than 50 percent of the total value of the stock then outstanding. This is preferable to Steve's purchasing additional shares because it will reduce his total installment obligation. Also the gain on Anne's shares will be treated in a tax-favored manner (as will also be discussed later), since dividend treatment to Larry and Anne can be avoided for this particular redemption.

A 15-year installment sale of 72 shares will cost Steve $28,342 per year in installment payments, of which close to $25,000 will be deductible interest in the early years. Steve should be able to service this debt through either a salary increase, a distribution of the S corporation taxable income, or a combination of both.

Additional Principles Applicable to the Taxation of Installment Sales. Installment reporting of the income from an installment sale will be allowed even though the parties to the sale are closely related persons. However, abusive tax-motivated transactions have been observed in this area. These generally involve a person selling to a close relative on an installment basis and having the purchaser (who has received a step-up in basis on the sale) dispose of the asset at little or no gain by selling it again almost immediately for cash while still paying for the original purchase over many years. To combat these abuses the Code provides that a disposition of the property that is the subject of an installment sale between related parties cannot be made by the purchaser without the seller's being treated for tax purposes as if he or she has received the balance of the purchase price (subject to some limitations) regardless of whether the price has actually been paid to the original seller (IRC Sec. 453(e)). Unless the property that is the subject of the installment sale consists of marketable securities, the period during which a disposition of the property will trigger adverse consequences to the related seller expires 2 years after the initial sale.

Since the stock of Millers is not a marketable security, only the 2-year rule against dispositions will apply.

Additional rules regarding the tax treatment of certain installment sales also may apply. The installment tax treatment is not permitted for sales of publicly traded property such as marketable securities. In addition, installment sales of property such as inventory and certain real estate may subject the seller to the alternative minimum tax on the full amount of gain in the year of sale. Currently, the alternative minimum tax will not be applied to the full amount of gain in the case of an installment sale of closely held (nonpublicly traded) stock.

One additional potential problem associated with an installment sale is personal, not tax related. An installment purchase by a younger-generation successor of a family business means that for a very long period of time, his or her lifestyle may be curtailed by the purchase. Since Steve's ability to purchase the stock depends on substantially increasing his total income from Millers, the business must expand somewhat in order to allow him to finance the purchase. This means that during the period when he is raising and educating his family, available cash flow may be limited. As long as Steve and his wife have thoughtfully considered this fact and are committed to the business, the transaction may prove to be a favorable one. It is always advisable, however, to point out these implications to the seller as well as to the purchaser.

Redemptions

Few owners of closely held businesses who spend their working life in a small business realize that it may be very difficult to transform their investment in that corporation into another type of investment that may be more appropriate for their later years without paying a heavy price in taxes. Because of the family attribution rules of IRC Sec. 318, this is especially true when several members of a family own stock in the corporation.

Dividends are not deductible to the corporation when distributed and are taxable to the shareholders as ordinary income. A redemption occurs when a corporation purchases its own stock. In most small wholly owned or family-owned corporations, dividends either are never paid or are paid rarely and in small, often insignificant, amounts. The shareholders of these corporations, who are usually employees of the corporation, depend on salaries rather than dividends for their livelihoods.

In the absence of statutory restraints on corporate redemptions, if a shareholder of a wholly owned corporation wished to take money out of the corporation without subjecting these funds to dividend treatment, the shareholder could simply sell some shares back to the corporation for cash and pay the federal income tax on the gain.

An example of this type of transaction follows:

> Mickey MacDonald owns 100 percent (300 shares) of M. M. Corporation, each share of which is worth $1,000. He causes M. M. Corporation, which has earnings and profits, to redeem 10 shares of his stock for $10,000. Result: Mickey still owns 100 percent of M. M. Corporation although he now owns only 290 shares of stock.

> Mickey would like to treat the redemption as the sale of a capital asset and pay taxes only on the gain. Since the redemption is

essentially the same as if a cash dividend had been paid to Mickey, however, the Code requires the entire $10,000 to be treated as a dividend, resulting in ordinary income tax treatment.

If a redemption is treated as a dividend, the taxpayer will pay income taxes on the entire value of the money or other property distributed. If a redemption is treated as a capital gain, only the amount of the gain (amount distributed – basis = gain) the taxpayer realizes on the transaction is subject to tax. Furthermore, the capital-gains rate is generally 15 percent. This principle can be illustrated as follows:

> If Mickey has a basis of $400 in each of his 300 shares of stock, and if he could effect a redemption of 10 shares that would qualify for treatment as a sale or exchange, he would pay tax on only the amount of his $6,000 gain ($600 per share x 10 shares). If, however, the redemption is treated as a dividend (as it inevitably would be in our example), the entire $10,000 distribution is taxable. Note that if the distribution is treated as a dividend, Mickey's basis in the 10 shares of redeemed stock is preserved by assigning it to his remaining 290 shares.

In addition, an individual's capital losses are fully deductible against capital gains but are deductible against ordinary income only up to $3,000 in a given year. Therefore in circumstances where an individual has capital losses (such as stock sales in a down market), the losses can "shelter" capital gains fully. However, an individual's capital losses cannot "shelter" dividend income, except to the extent of $3,000 per year.

Requirements for Favorable Federal Income Tax Treatment.

Particularly as they get older, the shareholders of closely held businesses may wish to take some or all of their investment out of the corporation so that their lifetime accumulation of wealth will no longer be subject to the frailties and errors of new management—even if the new managers are their own children.

If shareholders are willing to sell their stock either to their children or to an outsider, the problems associated with redemptions can be avoided. A redemption is defined by the Internal Revenue Code as the acquisition by a corporation of its stock from a shareholder in exchange for money or other property (excluding stock in the corporation) (IRC Sec. 317).

The purchase of a substantial interest in a business may be difficult for a younger family member to finance without altering his or her lifestyle even if payments are made over a period of years. Therefore redemptions are usually considered in business transition plans for family businesses.

The type of redemption attempted by Mickey in the preceding example is clearly an attempt to take the earnings and profits out of the corporation without treating them as dividends. As noted above, the Code requires that a corporation's purchase of its own stock will generally be treated as a dividend (to the extent of the earnings and profits of the corporation) (IRC Secs. 302(d), 301(c)). This general rule will apply unless the taxpayer can meet one of the exceptions found in Sec. 302(b) that will guarantee capital-gains treatment.

The exceptions include:

- redemptions not essentially equivalent to a dividend (IRC Sec. 302(b)(1)). This is not a precise test but depends on whether there is a meaningful reduction of the shareholder's interest under all the facts and circumstances of the case. For this purpose the shareholder's constructive ownership under the attribution rules of IRC Sec. 318 (discussed below) will be considered. This is not an exception that the client can rely on.

- substantially disproportionate redemptions. A redemption qualifies for capital-gains treatment provided that *immediately after the redemption* (a) the redeemed shareholder's proportion of ownership of both the outstanding *voting* stock and the *common* stock of the corporation is less than 80 percent of his or her proportionate ownership before the redemption, and (b) the redeemed shareholder owns less than 50 percent of the total voting power of all classes of stock entitled to vote (IRC Sec. 302(b)(2)).

  An example of a redemption that would qualify as substantially disproportionate follows:

  X corporation has 100 shares of one class of voting common stock outstanding. A and B each own 50 of those shares. X redeems 20 of A's 50 shares. The corporation now has 80 shares of voting common stock outstanding, of which A owns 30 and B owns 50.

  A's proportion of ownership before the redemption was 50 percent (50 ÷ 100). Her proportion of ownership after the redemption is 37.5 percent (30 ÷ 80). Since 50 percent x 80 percent is 40 percent, and A now owns 37.5 percent, her proportion of ownership of voting and common stock after the redemption (37.5 percent) is less than 80 percent of her proportion of ownership before the redemption (40 percent). Since A also now owns less than 50 percent of the total voting power in the corporation, both the 80 percent and 50 percent tests are met and the redemption will qualify as substantially disproportionate.

- the redemption is a complete termination of a shareholder's interest (IRC Sec. 302(b)(3))

For corporations whose stockholders are not subject to the family attribution rules of IRC Sec. 318, avoiding dividend treatment by using these exceptions is relatively straightforward. However, when the complexities of constructive ownership are present, these rules can become quite difficult. Redemptions that qualify for capital-gains treatment can become virtually impossible to achieve in family-owned corporations.

Sec. 318 Attribution Problems. For purposes of determining the ownership of a corporation before and after a redemption, the redeemed stockholder is considered to own

- all the stock he or she actually owns
- all the stock the stockholder's spouse, children, grandchildren, or parents own
- stock owned by an estate or partnership of which the stockholder is a partner or beneficiary (in proportion to his or her interest in the partnership or estate)
- stock owned by a trust of which the stockholder is a beneficiary (in proportion to his or her actuarial interest in the trust)
- stock owned by another corporation in which the stockholder also owns directly or indirectly 50 percent or more of the outstanding stock (in proportion to his or her stock ownership in the other corporation)

The family and entity attribution rules are complex, and a full discussion of them would be more extensive than necessary for this financial plan. However, some time devoted to an explanation of the family attribution rules is important to Larry and Anne's situation.

When the family attribution rules of IRC Sec. 318(a)(1) are applied to the Millers' situation, the results show that Larry owns

directly	67 %
constructively (Anne's)	23
constructively (Steve's)	10
Total ownership actually and constructively	100 %

If Steve buys 40 percent of the stock from Larry, the result to Larry is unchanged. He then owns 27 percent of the stock directly, *but* he still owns Anne's 23 percent and Steve's 50 percent constructively under Sec. 318. The result is that Larry's ownership for purposes of the tax treatment of a redemption under Sec. 302 is still 100 percent.

Even if Larry sold all but one share of his stock to Steve, the results are unchanged in that Larry would then own

directly	.4 %
constructively (Anne's)	23.0
constructively (Steve's)	76.6
Total ownership actually and constructively	100.0 %

Because Larry will always be deemed to own the stock owned by his wife and son, he will not be able to effect a lifetime redemption that will enable him both to qualify for capital-gains treatment *and* to still remain active in the business. The significance of remaining active in the business will be addressed in the next section.

   Sec. 302(c)(2) Election—The Waiver Approach. The difficulty associated with a corporate redemption for family-owned businesses is burdensome. Consequently the Code allows a waiver of the family attribution rules of IRC Sec. 318, thereby allowing the redemption of a shareholder such as Larry to qualify as a complete termination of his interest (IRC Sec. 302(c)(2)).

In order to waive the attribution rules, the shareholder must dispose of all of his or her stock. In addition, immediately after the redemption the shareholder must have no continuing interest in the corporation (including an interest as an officer, director, or employee) except that of a creditor and must agree not to acquire an interest in the corporation (except by inheritance) within 10 years from the date of the redemption. Furthermore, the employee must file an agreement with the Internal Revenue Service requiring the taxpayer to notify the IRS if an interest is acquired within the prohibited period.

Even if these conditions are met, the redemption will not qualify for capital-gains treatment if

- any portion of the stock that is being redeemed was acquired within 10 years of the date of the redemption from a person whose ownership of the stock would be attributable to the person whose stock is being redeemed, or
- if any person whose stock would be attributable to the person whose stock is being redeemed has acquired that stock within a 10-year period directly or indirectly from the person whose stock is being redeemed, unless his or her stock is also redeemed

For example, a husband cannot have given a portion of his stock to his wife and have the corporation redeem the remainder of the stock he holds under a Sec. 302(c)(2) election (to receive capital-gains tax treatment) unless the gift took place more than 10 years prior to the redemption and Sec. 302(c)(2) election. Also he could not have been the recipient of a gift of Millers stock from his wife during that 10-year period.

Since Larry wishes to continue his involvement with Millers for the foreseeable future, it is unlikely that this election out (waiver approach) would appeal to him. As his involvement with Millers becomes less important to him, however, this type of a redemption may become viable.

Anne, on the other hand, could take advantage of this provision immediately to have her interest in Millers redeemed. This would be beneficial to Anne because she has a basis of $1,000 per share in Millers, which could be recovered tax free when the redemption proceeds are paid. In contrast, Larry's basis in his stock is $160.

If properly structured, the redemption does not have to drain the corporation of needed cash flow and can provide Anne and Larry with a steady income stream as well as an opportunity to spread the gain over a number of years. For example, Anne's shares could be surrendered and a Sec. 302(c)(2) election could be made in return for the corporation's obligation to pay the redemption price over a period of years at an appropriate interest rate. The interest should be deductible to the corporation. The principal payments, however, are not.

In conclusion, the recommendation would be that Anne's shares be redeemed with an appropriate Sec. 302(c)(2) election and that the corporation be allowed to spread payments by an installment payout. If the income picture of Millers requires a lower payment, the term of the obligation could be lengthened, thereby lowering the annual payment. As already noted, this redemption should be coordinated with the installment sale to Steve to allow him to acquire control of the business as a result of both transactions. Larry, on the other hand, can retain his shares until he is ready to retire completely from Millers.

If he continues to be involved with Millers until his death, Larry may wish to leave his remaining shares to Steve with provisions in his will stating that Steve's portion of Larry's residuary estate should be adjusted to reflect the bequest of the stock.

Sec. 303 Redemptions. An estate liquidity problem occurs when many shareholders of family-owned businesses continue to hold stock in their corporations until their death. IRC Sec. 303 provides a method for assuring that sufficient stock can be redeemed without dividend treatment to pay estate taxes and funeral and administrative expenses if certain requirements are met. Redemption proceeds in excess of the estate's funeral, administrative, and tax expenses cannot be recovered under Sec. 303. The threshold test for utilizing a Sec. 303 redemption is that the value of the stock of the corporation owned by the decedent must exceed 35 percent of his or her adjusted gross estate for federal estate tax purposes.

Capital-gains treatment is particularly important in the case of a redemption from a decedent's estate, regardless of whether the redemption is treated under Sec. 302 or Sec. 303. Since the estate has received a stepped-up basis in the redeemed stock, capital-gains treatment will generally trigger little or no income tax liability for the estate. If dividend treatment applies, the estate loses the benefit of the stepped-up basis, since the proceeds will be fully taxed (assuming the corporation has sufficient earnings and profits).

Currently, Larry's shares are valued at $286,601 and his adjusted gross estate is assumed to be $1,507,946. Therefore the 35 percent test is not satisfactorily met.

In short, if Larry were to die with his present stock holdings, his estate would not qualify for a Sec. 303 redemption. Even if Larry's estate were to qualify today for Sec. 303 treatment, the planned sale of shares in Millers to Steve would reduce the stock ownership amount below the 35 percent threshold level.

Since Larry has indicated a strong desire not to force Steve to wait until Larry's death to take control of Millers, planning at this time for a Sec. 303 redemption would not be appropriate in any event.

Recapitalizations

General Requirements. The Internal Revenue Code provides for tax-free treatment of various corporate reorganizations (IRC Sec. 368). One type of reorganization is an "E" reorganization—a "recapitalization" (IRC Sec. 368(a)(1)(E)). The Code does not define a recapitalization and the regulations offer no definition, but they do contain some examples of transactions that would qualify as recapitalizations. The most frequently quoted general definition is from a 1942 United States Supreme Court decision that described a recapitalization as "reshuffling of a capital structure within the framework of an existing corporation" (*Helvering v. Southwest Consolidated Corp.,* 315 U.S. 194 (1942)).

In the past a common type of "reshuffling" of capital was the exchange by older shareholders of all or a part of their common stock in the corporation for preferred stock. This technique was used for some or all of the following purposes: to transfer control to younger-generation management; to assure the older shareholder of an income stream from dividends on the preferred stock; or to attempt to freeze the value of the older shareholder's interest in the corporation for estate tax purposes.

In the typical recapitalization, all the shareholders were offered an opportunity pursuant to a plan of reorganization to exchange their shares of common stock for preferred stock. Normally the older shareholders elected the exchange, while the younger shareholders chose to retain their shares of common stock.

In a recapitalization if the value of the preferred stock received is equal to the value of the common stock surrendered, the transaction is generally tax free at the time of the transfer. If the value of the preferred is less than the common surrendered, the difference in value may be treated as a taxable gift to the other shareholders. To assure equivalency of value, the preferred shares must pay a reasonable dividend, dividends must be cumulative, and the preferred stock must have liquidation preferences. The question of valuation in recapitalizations has been one of the most troublesome issues in planning to recapitalize a corporation.

   Restrictions on the Use of Recapitalizations and on Other Estate-Freezing Techniques. Prior changes in the federal tax laws dealt a severe blow to recapitalizations and other techniques intended to freeze the estate tax value of an older-generation owner's interest in a family business. These changes have been codified in IRC Secs. 2701-2704, sometimes referred to as the chapter 14 estate-freeze provisions.

IRC Secs. 2701-2704 are gift tax provisions that set forth rules for placing a value on a stock interest or a partnership interest transferred by gift or by sale to a family member. The prohibitions set forth in Sec. 2701 are stringent and limit the ability of taxpayers to use a preferred stock recapitalization to freeze the value of their interest in the corporation.

Specifically Sec. 2701 provides rules for determining (a) whether the transfer of an interest in a *controlled* corporation or partnership to (or for the benefit of, such as through a trust) a *member of the family* of the transferor is a completed gift or (b) whether the transferor has retained some interest. If the transferor has retained any interest, and the rules of Sec. 2701 are not complied with, the transferor will be deemed to make a gift of his or her entire interest in the property.

Sec. 2702 deals with transfers in trust and provides for the same type of prohibition with respect to transfers of interests to a member of the family in a controlled corporation or partnership.

The enactment of the chapter 14 estate-freeze rules has made effective use of a corporate recapitalization to shift future appreciation to family members more difficult.

Private Annuity

A private annuity is a contract for a private individual (not a commercial annuity company) to pay the purchase price for an asset over the actuarial life of the seller. If the seller does not live to his or her actuarial life expectancy, the purchaser's obligation ceases, and there is nothing remaining of the obligation to include in the deceased seller's estate. If the seller lives longer than his or her actuarially determined life expectancy, the purchaser must pay the predetermined payments for the seller's actual life.

To avoid inclusion in the seller's income in the year of the sale, the transaction must not be secured; that is, it must be a naked promise to pay.

Payments to the seller are split into several components for tax purposes. First, a portion of each payment will represent a nontaxable return of the seller's basis. Second, a portion will typically be taxed as the sale or exchange of a capital asset. The seller will pay a capital-gains tax on the portion of each payment that represents gain from the sale of the property. Third, there will be ordinary income tax on any portion in excess of the seller's return of basis and capital-gain portions. For purposes of determining gain to the seller, the sale price for the asset transferred is the present value of the total amount of all annuity payments to be made over the seller's life expectancy.

There are some drawbacks to the private annuity arrangement. For example, the purchaser cannot deduct any part of the payment, including the portion taxed as ordinary income to the seller. In contrast, under an installment sale the interest portion of the payments may be deductible subject to the limitations already discussed.

The private annuity does not meet the Millers' needs because the termination of the payment obligation at Larry's death could severely deplete Larry's estate if he died prematurely, depriving Anne of income and resulting in a windfall to Steve. Steve, on the other hand, could not afford to purchase any significant amount of his father's stock without the benefit of the interest deduction.

Shareholder-Employee Compensation Planning

Reasonable Compensation for Shareholder-Employees

The issue of unreasonable compensation is generally raised only in closely held corporations where there is a strong identity of interest between the role of employee and stockholder or where a member of the employee's family is a stockholder. The Internal Revenue Service's position is that an arm's-length transaction setting the value of personal services cannot exist in most closely held corporations. The closer the identity of interest between the corporation and the employee, the more vulnerable to IRS scrutiny compensation becomes. The most vulnerable situation occurs between an employee and his or her wholly owned corporation. Because of the identity of interests, the issue of unreasonable compensation is also frequently raised in family-owned corporations.

If Steve's salary, for example, was substantially raised in order to provide him with funds to buy Larry's stock, Millers might be denied a deduction for a portion of Steve's salary that the IRS deemed to be unreasonable.

However, if Millers elects Subchapter S status as previously recommended, unreasonable compensation will not be an issue as long as Larry is being paid a comparable salary based on actual services rendered.

Steve and Larry will be taxed directly on their proportionate shares of corporate taxable income if Millers makes an S election. Therefore payments to Steve will not be taxable as a dividend as long as the taxable income distributed is attributable to activity of the corporation.

Employment Contracts

Employment contracts between unrelated employees and employers are often used to reduce misunderstandings about the rights and responsibilities of each party. In the case of a shareholder-employee of a closely held corporation, employment agreements are often utilized not only to clarify the duties of the shareholder-employee but also to describe compensation arrangements in an effort to support the reasonableness of compensation. The first consideration is very important for the Millers in this business transition period.

Another benefit of employment contracts is their ability to minimize shareholder dissension, which may be especially important to Larry and Steve as they work at transferring the management of the store to Steve. They should fully and thoughtfully discuss which duties are the responsibility of each, and their agreements on these issues should be included in their employment agreements.

Employment contracts can run for any period of time, but care should be taken to treat the contract as if it were being entered into between an employee and an unrelated employer, that is, as an arm's-length transaction. For this reason contract periods are usually quite short, although some contain options to renew for an additional specified period. These renewals can even be tailored to occur automatically unless the employer gives appropriate and timely notice to the employee.

For the reasons indicated, employment contracts covering corporate duties and compensation agreements should be implemented for both Larry and Steve.

Consulting Contracts

Consulting contracts are specialized forms of employment contracts. As Larry begins to reduce his daily participation in Millers, consulting contracts should be implemented to demonstrate the decrease in his duties and the new compensation arrangements. Since the primary issues that would need to be dealt with (for example, exact duties as well as amounts and methods of payment) may not be ascertainable for several years, it is only necessary to note that these contracts should be drawn at an appropriate time.

Employee Benefits

Qualified Plans of Deferred Compensation

Since Larry has noted that he is displeased with the performance of the profit-sharing plan of Millers, now would be a good time to see if the qualified plan could be improved and its performance enhanced instead of being terminated.

Problems with Present Plans. The utilization of appropriate corporate qualified plans not only reduces shareholder-employees' present tax burden, it also allows them to accumulate earnings on a tax-deferred basis within the plan.

The tax-deferred accumulation within the plan can allow assets to increase at a much more rapid rate than if taxes were currently payable. Amounts deferred in qualified plans are not taxable until they are distributed to the participant. If there is a proper balance between corporate cost and present benefits to the employees, qualified plans can be good employee motivators.

The current profit-sharing plan of Millers is unnecessarily restrictive with its provision for mandatory contributions when corporate profits reach a certain level.

General Requirements. There are basically two types of qualified plans: defined-contribution plans and defined-benefit plans. Defined-benefit pension plans promise the recipient a specific benefit within statutory limits at retirement age, and the funding necessary to provide that benefit for the actuarial life of the recipient is contributed by the employer. Defined-benefit plans usually work best for funding retirement benefits for older shareholder-employees when there is only a short time left to provide significant retirement benefits. These plans can be very expensive to the funding corporation, and most have the additional disadvantage of being subject to regulation by the Pension Benefit Guaranty Corporation. Since defined-benefit plans are "pension plans" under the Internal Revenue Code, contributions to the plan are mandatory once the plan is in place.

Defined-contribution plans set a contribution level that the employer contributes to the plan. The funds are invested over the employee's working life, and the benefits available at retirement consist of the contributions that have been made to the plan, plus forfeitures that have been added to the account, plus earnings on the account assets. Defined-contribution plans are generally preferable to defined-benefit plans for younger employees because the potential benefits are greater. The defined-contribution plans that small corporations most often utilize fall into two categories: profit-sharing plans and money-purchase pension plans.

Note

To avoid repetition of background material on qualified plans, that material has been omitted from this chapter. If you are not familiar with this material, it should be reviewed prior to proceeding through this section of the suggested solution.

Recommendations. There is not enough information in the facts of this case to determine whether the Millers' plans would be top-heavy. Many, if not most, small plans will be subject to the top-heavy rules. However, the fact that Millers employs 34 people indicates that the plan is probably not top-heavy. The qualified retirement plan presently in place has not been perceived as performing well, and the recommendation would be to amend the plan to allow for purely discretionary contributions, which could be made regardless of whether pretax profits reach $200,000 per year. In addition, the plan must immediately comply with the eligibility and vesting requirements of the Internal Revenue Code.

An appropriate vesting schedule might be 2-to-6-year vesting, which is an acceptable vesting schedule under the current tax laws. The schedule is as follows:

Years of Service	Vested Percentage
2	20%
3	40%
4	60%

Years of Service	Vested Percentage
5	80%
6 or more	100%

The plan will also have to meet the minimum coverage requirements. A plan cannot discriminate in coverage or in the amount of contributions made. Several safe-harbor design strategies could be recommended. Also an alternative vesting schedule would have to be included in case the plan becomes top-heavy.

An integrated money-purchase pension plan could also be instituted. Plan integration with Social Security would allow a higher rate of contributions to be applied to compensation earned over specified levels. In effect it is a permitted form of discrimination that would skew plan contributions in favor of Larry Miller.

Since Larry has expressed satisfaction with his overall net worth, assuming it can provide liquidity for his retirement, this package of qualified plans is aimed at the younger employees (primarily Steve) and will benefit them most. The plans would not, however, exclude Larry, since qualified plans cannot exclude employees from participation based on age.

Nonqualified Deferred Compensation

Another important benefit that can be available to shareholder-employees of a closely held corporation on a discriminatory basis is a nonqualified deferred-compensation arrangement. These arrangements do not have to meet the funding, employee coverage, and other requirements necessary to satisfy the qualified plan definition under IRC Sec. 401(a), as ERISA exempts from almost all its requirements an unfunded arrangement maintained "primarily for the purpose of providing deferred compensation for a select group of management or highly compensated employees." (There are a few minor requirements, however, even for nonqualified deferred-compensation plans.)

While nonqualified plans of deferred compensation may involve compensation in the form of money or other property, many are salary continuation plans of various types.

Nonqualified salary continuation plans, for example, may provide significant disability or retirement income for shareholder-employees or death benefits for the spouse or beneficiaries of shareholder-employees. They may be particularly appropriate in the case of a corporation that wishes to provide such benefits to shareholder-employees but finds a qualified plan too costly because of ERISA requirements. Alternatively these plans may be used to provide benefits to shareholder-employees in addition to those allowable under qualified plans.

There are generally three fundamental hurdles in structuring a nonqualified deferred-compensation plan. The first is structuring the arrangement so that compensation is in fact deferred, thereby escaping immediate inclusion in the shareholder-employee's income. The second is the question of whether the deferred-compensation arrangement will be deductible to the employer corporation. The third is the question of whether an attempt should be made to structure the deferred-compensation plan to escape federal estate taxation at the employee's death.

> ***Avoiding Immediate Inclusion in the Employee's Income.*** Initially the deferred amount must qualify as bona fide deferred compensation to escape immediate inclusion in the employee's income. The IRS can argue for inclusion in current income under either a constructive receipt or an economic benefit theory.

The concept of constructive receipt is explained by the Treasury Regulations as follows:

> Income although not actually reduced to a taxpayer's possession is constructively received by him in the taxable year in which it is credited to his account, set apart for him or otherwise made available so that he may draw upon it at any time, or so that he could have drawn upon it during the taxable year if notice of intention to withdraw had been given. However, income is not constructively received if the taxpayer's control of its receipt is subject to substantial limitations or restrictions. (Reg. 1.451-2(a)).

The economic benefit theory provides that if compensation is readily convertible into cash, it is not bona fide deferred compensation. The economic benefit theory has not generally been extended to tax the value of an employer's unsecured contractual obligation to pay deferred compensation. However, if the contractual obligation is (1) unconditional, (2) that of a solvent employer, (3) freely assignable or transferable or immediately convertible into cash, and (4) of a type frequently transferred to banks or investors at a discount not greater than the prevailing premium for the use of money, the IRS position for immediate inclusion in income has been upheld by the courts (*Cowden v. Comm'r, Watson, Jones Co., Steen, Evans,* Rev. Rul. 68-606). It appears that the addition of a clause in the deferred-compensation agreement that prohibits the assignment, transfer, or pledging of the agreement would be sufficient protection against the inclusion of deferred compensation in present income under the economic benefit theory. It would be prudent to include such a provision.

The best guidance for avoiding immediate taxation under nonqualified deferred-compensation plans is contained in Rev. Rul. 60-31, 1960-1 C.B. 174. This revenue ruling sets forth the IRS position that when an employee receives an unfunded promise to pay an amount in the future, deferral of the promised amount will generally be allowed provided the amount of compensation to be delivered at a future date is not set apart in any type of special fund that would be protected from the employer's creditors.

Also deferred-compensation contracts or agreements entered into prior to performance of services appear to have the best chance to withstand IRS attack (Rev. Rul. 60-31, 1960-1 C.B. 174).

Prior to the issuance of Rev. Rul. 60-31 practitioners and commentators generally believed that the one safe way to keep an amount under a deferred-compensation contract from being currently taxable was to make the payment "subject to forfeiture." Forfeiture provisions often condition payment under a deferred-compensation arrangement on the employee's agreement to (1) work for the employer for a specified number of years or until retirement; (2) render advisory or consulting services after retirement at the request of the employee; (3) refrain from disclosing customer lists, trade secrets, or other information valuable to the employer's business; or (4) refrain from engaging in a competitive business as an owner, stockholder, partner, employee, or otherwise.

Although these forfeiture provisions may no longer be necessary to avoid current income taxation after Rev. Rul. 60-31, they often offer desirable protection for the employer for other business reasons and are therefore still found in many deferred-compensation arrangements. The maintenance of forfeiture provisions may again have taken on increased importance to prevent current withholding of income tax, FICA, and other employment taxes due to recent legislation that authorizes such withholding upon the lapse of the substantial risk of forfeiture to the employee.

Well-known private rulings issued by the IRS indicate that the employer may set aside funds in a so-called *rabbi trust* (PLR 8113107) without creating problems under the constructive receipt or economic benefit doctrines. Rabbi trusts can provide additional assurance to the participants that funds will be available to pay benefits actually promised by the plan.

Rabbi trusts are trusts established by the employer in which contributions are periodically made to finance the promised benefits. The trust can be irrevocable in favor of the plan participants except that trust assets must be subject to claims of the employer's creditors. The employee-beneficiary must be prohibited from transferring or assigning any part of his or her interest in the trust assets. If these conditions are met, the funds will not be includible in the employee's income until the employee actually receives them; that is, the plan will be treated as an unfunded plan for tax purposes. The trust itself will be taxed as a grantor trust, which means that the employer will be taxed on any income the trust generates.

The deductibility of payments by the employer falls within the general rules for nonqualified arrangements discussed below.

Deductibility by the Corporation. To be deductible all compensation paid to an employee, including deferred compensation, must be reasonable and in fact paid purely for services (Treas. Reg. Sec. 1.162-7; Treas. Reg. Sec. 1.162-9). In determining reasonableness of compensation, the entire amount of compensation, present and deferred, is examined. Although the courts have enumerated factors that are important in making a determination on the issue of reasonableness, no single factor appears decisive since each situation must be considered as a whole (*Mayson Mfg. Co. v. Comm'r*).

If a deferred-compensation agreement is reasonable and is intended to provide only retirement or disability benefits to the employee, generally the corporation is entitled to a deduction for a deferred-compensation payment in the year in which the payment is made (Treas. Reg. Sec. 1.404(a)-12).

If the employer is legally obligated to pay an employee's estate or specified beneficiaries under a death-benefit-only plan, the benefits paid to the surviving spouse or beneficiary will generally be deductible by the corporation in the year paid (Treas. Reg. Sec. 1.404(a)-12).

The deductibility of a death benefit payment to a surviving spouse or beneficiary may be called into question when the survivor is a shareholder in a closely held corporation. If, in fact, the employee has been adequately compensated during his or her lifetime and the corporation will be controlled by the surviving spouse or other members of the deceased's family, extreme care should be taken to enter into an agreement with the corporation at the earliest possible date. The contract must emphasize that certain payments that will be made to a surviving spouse or other beneficiary are deferred compensation to the employee.

Avoiding the Imposition of Federal Estate Tax. In order to escape the inclusion of the benefits of a salary continuation plan in the deceased employee's estate, it must be a death-benefit-only plan. If exclusion is not a primary concern, the plan can also provide for benefits to be paid to the employee upon retirement or disability. Such a nonqualified retirement or disability agreement can provide substantial amounts of income during retirement or prolonged disability in addition to providing income to a surviving spouse after the employee's death. The tax price paid for this increased security is that the remaining value of the survivor's interest is included in the estate of the deceased employee and is subject to estate tax (IRC Sec. 2039(a)).

Even if the plan is a death-benefit-only plan, the proceeds are not automatically excluded from estate taxation. This area involves some complexity. IRC Sec. 2039(a) requires that the value of any annuity or other payment (other than from a qualified plan) receivable by a decedent as the result of a contract or agreement be included in calculating the decedent's gross estate if the decedent had the right to receive such annuity or other payment in any of the following situations:

- for life
- for a period not ascertainable without reference to the decedent's death
- for a period that does not, in fact, end before the decedent's death

An annuity or other payment is not restricted to commercial annuity payments but includes any annuity or other payment that, according to the regulations, may be equal or unequal, conditional or unconditional, periodic or sporadic, and that may be one or more payments extending over any period of time (Treas. Reg. Sec. 20.2039-1(b)(1)).

In order for the proceeds of a death-benefit-only deferred-compensation plan to be included under Sec. 2039(a), the annuity or other payment must have been "payable to the decedent"; that is, the decedent must have been receiving payments at death, or the decedent must have possessed the right to receive such payment or annuity. In other words, inclusion in the employee's estate results if the employee possessed an enforceable right to receive payments at some time in the future, regardless of whether he or she was receiving payments at the time of death (Treas. Reg. Sec. 20.2039-1 (b)(1); *Estate of Bahen*).

The inclusion of plan proceeds in an employee's estate may not be such a poor result, considering that it will generate an income stream during retirement. Furthermore, if the intended beneficiary is the employee's spouse, the proceeds may qualify for the marital deduction.

Note that even if a death-benefit-only plan is selected, other nonqualified plans (such as disability plans) will all be viewed together when determining whether the tests for includibility under Sec. 2039 are met (Reg. Sec. 20.2039-2). Benefits receivable under qualified plans of deferred compensation will not be included in determining whether the employee had the right to an annuity or other payment that meets the other criteria of Sec. 2039(a) and that would require inclusion of a death-benefit-only plan in the employee's gross estate (Rev. Rul. 76-380, 1976-2 C.B. 270).

Since Larry is concerned about providing Anne with a good income stream for her life, a death-benefit-only plan could be implemented to continue some portion of his salary to her for 5 to 7 years. Funding for this purpose could come from the insurance the corporation has on his life.

In this area care should be taken to enlist a competent attorney to draft documents to implement these plans.

BUSINESS PLANNING: INSURANCE

Medical Insurance Plans

Since the present medical insurance plan provides Millers employees with excellent benefits, no improvements appear necessary.

Disability Income Plans

As already noted, no disability income plan exists for Millers employees. It is questionable whether many of the rank-and-file employees would benefit materially from a long-term disability plan because of their modest average salaries. Most of the employees would probably have their disability benefits either eliminated or substantially reduced because of coordination with Social Security.

Disability income protection for Larry and Steve is a different matter entirely. The installment sale to Steve would provide income to Larry regardless of disability. In addition, a nonqualified deferred-compensation plan could continue Larry's salary if he became disabled before leaving Millers. As discussed in the section on nonqualified deferred compensation, a disability plan of this type would almost certainly cause inclusion of the death-benefit-only plan in Larry's estate. However, Steve should obtain the maximum amount of long-term disability income coverage that insurers are willing to underwrite. Since the S election will prevent tax-favored coverage through the corporation, Steve should obtain personal coverage. Any benefits paid are not subject to income tax. If Steve becomes disabled, he will need additional financial protection to complete the payments for the purchase of Larry's stock.

Life Insurance Plans

The group insurance coverages of Millers are characterized by an extreme dichotomy—a very comprehensive medical expense plan and an obvious lack of anything else. In reviewing an employee benefit plan it is necessary to understand the objectives of a firm in providing employee benefits. Is it primarily to meet the needs of the employees or to meet the needs of the owners? The latter tends to be particularly true for many small firms such as Millers.

If the employees' needs are of concern, the lack of a group life insurance plan is conspicuous. Most firms of this size with a relatively stable employment would provide some coverage, even if only a modest flat amount per employee, such as $5,000 or $10,000. In fact, with salespeople who are often paid on a commission basis, a flat amount of coverage may be appropriate. Salespeople could be provided with a level amount of insurance that is roughly equivalent to that provided to salaried personnel.

Millers should consider a group life insurance policy for its employees with coverage based on a multiple of salary. The multiple would depend on the corporation's ability and willingness to pay premiums. It is common for these plans to provide between one and two times salary for salaried employees.

It is important to remember that Larry and Steve would have to include the value of this coverage in their gross incomes after an S election is made because of their stock ownership.

Larry has over $1 million in separately owned assets, but only about $100,000 of this is in liquid assets. This liquidity and his present insurance coverage are currently adequate to cover the estate taxes and administrative costs at Larry's death. As long as Larry remains active in the corporation, group life insurance for him would provide additional contingency protection. Group coverage may be less expensive than individual coverage even though Larry cannot participate in a group plan on a tax-advantaged basis. The coverage could be assigned to an irrevocable life insurance trust to avoid inclusion of the proceeds in his estate. Group life coverage on Steve could help pay off the installment contract in case Steve predeceases Larry.

Although Steve is not currently a planning client, some planning for Steve is important to Larry and Anne because of the possibility that Steve could die or become disabled before the installment sale is fully paid for. If this happens, the security of Larry and Anne's retirement could be in peril because of Steve's inability to meet his obligations under the installment sale contract.

In addition, the corporation should consider a key person life insurance policy to cover Steve. Millers would be both owner and beneficiary of the policy. If Steve should die, especially after Larry has substantially withdrawn from Millers, the corporation will almost certainly have to hire someone else to replace Steve in order to keep the corporation viable. The corporation may also need to redeem Steve's shares in the corporation if he predeceases Larry. Planning for this redemption should be carefully considered and coordinated between Millers and Steve (and his family's personal objectives) to assure that Steve's estate will be able to qualify for exemption from the family attribution rules and to achieve capital-gains treatment.

The $200,000 policy owned by Millers insuring Larry can be left in place to provide funding for a salary continuation death-benefit-only plan or to fund the survivorship benefit portion to Anne of any salary continuation plan for Larry by the corporation. If necessary, Millers can always fall back on the cash value of the life insurance to help make the installment sale payments to Anne for the redemption of her stock.

Property and Liability Coverage for the Business—Fundamental Requirements

In analyzing the property and liability needs of a business, it is important to realize that the needs of businesses are much less uniform than those of individuals, and more flexibility is needed in designing their insurance coverages than in designing those of an average homeowner.

In general loss exposures of a business can be divided into four categories:

- damage to or destruction of property
- loss of possession of property
- loss of income or the imposition of extraordinary expenses
- liability for payment of damages to others

The first category is self-explanatory and includes loss or damage by fire, wind, flood, and many other perils. The second category includes loss of possessions resulting from criminal activities of others, including employee dishonesty. The third category includes such items as lost profits and additional expenses following the damage or destruction of business property. The last category includes obligations to reimburse others for legal injuries for which a business is liable.

Historically many separate policies had to be purchased to meet all a business's needs. However, in recent years package policies have been made available to most businesses so that these needs can be met with a minimum number of insurance contracts. It has also become common in situations like the one in this case (when the owner of a business also owns the real estate rented by the business) to insure the building and the business under a single package policy, with the owner of the building and the owner of the business both being named as insureds as their interests may appear.

Most of the needs of Millers (and Larry's needs for property and liability insurance on the building rented by Millers) can be met under a business owner's policy for small and medium-sized businesses. The business owner's policy is standardized and is designed for small businesses that have little need for flexibility in insurance coverages. Based on the information in the case, Millers has no unusual insurance exposures with regard to property and liability insurance and would be well suited for this contract.

The business owner's policy can now include coverage for automobiles. However, a separate workers' compensation policy will be necessary since this coverage is not included. In addition, the Millers may decide that a commercial excess-liability policy is needed to supplement the liability coverages available under the business owner's policy.

The typical business owner's policy (some variations exist among insurers) provides the following basic coverages, with the insured selecting the amount of insurance for each coverage:

- buildings. All buildings on the premises are covered on a replacement-cost basis. No coinsurance applies, but the amount of insurance must usually be equal to the full replacement cost of the property. The amount of insurance increases quarterly with inflation. Buildings can be insured on either a named-peril or an open-peril basis, with the latter providing broader protection at a slightly increased cost.

- business personal property. This is also on a replacement-cost basis without coinsurance. In addition to inventory and office equipment, it also covers tenants' improvements. There is limited coverage ($1,000) for goods away from the insured premises, such as those being delivered on the company's trucks. Additional coverage can be added if this exposure is significantly greater. Coverage also exists for the property of others in the care, custody, or control of the insured if the insured is legally liable. This coverage, for example, would cover the liability of Millers for damage to furniture that was being repaired or reupholstered for customers. One concern of a business such as Millers is to see that proper insurance is maintained on inventory that fluctuates in value. As long as the amount of insurance carried is equal to at least 100 percent of the average inventory during the 12 months prior to the loss, the amount of insurance can be increased automatically by up to 25 percent to cover peak season values.

- loss of income. Coverage for lost profits, continuing expenses, and extra expenses is provided for up to 12 months if a business suffers a loss resulting from an insured peril.

- optional property coverages. Numerous endorsements are available that provide coverage for many types of property and liability situations not adequately covered under other sections of the policy. These include employee dishonesty, plate glass, outdoor signs, earthquake, and boiler and machinery coverage.

- business liability. Coverage of up to $1 million is available for liability arising from the premises and operations. Personal injury coverage (for example, libel, slander, false arrest) is also provided.

PERSONAL PLANNING: TAXES

Present Position

Larry and Anne appear to have achieved a good deal of success in their lives both financially and personally. They have created a successful business that has provided the means for them to enjoy a comfortable lifestyle both in the past and, through proper planning, in future years. Their children are all grown and seem to have found careers in which they are content.

The primary objectives to be dealt with in Larry and Anne's personal plan are that they are able to be secure during their retirement and that Anne is well provided for as long as she lives should Larry predecease her.

Assuring Larry's Comfortable Retirement and Continuing Involvement with Millers

Most of the techniques for assuring that Larry and Anne will be guaranteed a comfortable retirement income have been discussed at length in the business plan. These techniques include (1) the installment sale of 72 shares of Millers stock to Steve for an installment obligation with a term of 15 years, (2) the redemption of Anne's Millers stock for an installment obligation with a term of 10 years, and (3) the possible later redemption of Larry's remaining Millers stock if future circumstances warrant.

Steve's installment obligation will add approximately $28,340 per year to Larry and Anne's cash flow for a 15-year period. If the corporation redeems Anne's stock with a 10-year note at 9 percent, another $28,400 will be added to the Millers' cash flow for 10 years. However, if a 10-year note places too heavy a cash drain on Millers, a longer-term obligation would still provide the Millers with substantial cash payments well into their retirement years. In addition, there will also be retirement income available from the qualified plan. Since Larry is very concerned about providing income to Anne should he predecease her, he might consider electing a term certain or a joint and survivor annuity as the method of payment for benefits from the defined-contribution plan.

Dispositions at Death

Analysis of Present Plans

The Millers' present estate plan, in which each leaves everything to a surviving spouse and then to living children or children of a deceased child, per stirpes, may have been perfectly adequate 16 years ago when it was implemented. Since the Millers have acquired a substantial amount of additional assets, however, their present plan is unnecessarily expensive in terms of estate tax liabilities. This fact remains true despite the current availability of the unlimited marital deduction, because their current wills could result in all the assets of both Larry and Anne being taxed in her estate at marginal rates of up to 48 percent (in 2004 under the changes set forth in EGTRRA 2001). Larry's unified credit is wasted. In cases like this when the surviving spouse has substantial assets (and especially considering the fact that an outright inheritance from her mother could materially increase her taxable estate), an estate plan that uses only the unlimited marital deduction is not indicated.

Although Larry has expressed his desire that any assets Anne does not consume during her lifetime be divided equally among their three children, the present estate plan contains no provision for assuring this result.

In addition, the present placement of Larry and Anne's personal insurance results in the inclusion of the proceeds in their estates for estate tax purposes.

Possible Improvements in Estate Plan

Because Anne already owns significant assets, it is not advisable to add to her taxable estate unnecessarily. This can be avoided by structuring an estate plan to make the bulk of Larry's assets available to Anne but to shield them from federal estate taxation at the time of her subsequent death. The fact that she is the potential beneficiary of a significant inheritance from her mother somewhat complicates the issue of the exact amount. It does not, however, alter the fact that at least an amount sufficient to allow Larry to utilize his unified credit should be left in a trust that will not be taxed again at Anne's death.

The issue of whether to utilize a marital trust or to leave the marital deduction property to Anne outright is one that should be decided between Larry and Anne.

The marital portion of the bequest can be left in a trust and can still qualify for the marital deduction provided that the trust is required to pay all the income from the trust to the spouse in annual or more frequent payments. The spouse may be given a general power of appointment (the power to appoint the property to himself or herself, his or her estate, his or her creditors, creditors of his or her estate, and any other appointee) exercisable either during his or her life or by specific reference to the power in his or her will, or both. In other words, the spouse can either be allowed to appoint property as he or she sees fit to self or others during lifetime, or the spouse can be effectively restricted from withdrawing the principal of the marital trust until the time of death by the use of a testamentary power alone. Alternatively a trust that pays all the income to the spouse annually or more frequently but provides for no power of appointment for the spouse qualifies for the marital deduction if the executor of the estate elects to treat the trust as qualified terminable interest property (a QTIP trust). Typically a QTIP trust will contain provisions governing the disposition of the property after the death of the surviving spouse. Many spouses, however, object to having all or most of their inheritance tied up in trusts, as they feel they must deal continuously with bank trust officers who may be less than sympathetic to their wishes.

The use of a marital trust does not seem indicated in this case, especially when considered in light of Anne's investment experience. However, if a trust is used, there are some assets, such as the principal residence, that should not be included in the marital trust. The management of a residence by a trustee may present practical administrative problems. For these reasons it may be advisable to convey the house as a separate item in the will, and such a bequest should be an outright bequest of all the decedent's interest to the spouse.

Concept of Estate Equalization

Some planners recommend that in addition to the utilization of the unified credit, an estate plan for clients such as the Millers should provide for the payment of some federal estate tax when the first spouse dies, instead of a complete deferral of estate tax liability to the surviving spouse's estate. This is accomplished by intentionally failing to fully use the federal estate tax marital deduction with respect to the taxable estate in excess of the applicable credit exemption equivalent in order to achieve estate equalization. The potential benefit of estate equalization is a lower estate tax bracket applied to the portion of the estate that would otherwise be taxed in a higher estate tax bracket if the property passed to the surviving spouse under the marital deduction and thus increased the surviving spouse's estate. "Splitting" or "equalizing" the spouses' taxable estates can cause lower estate tax brackets to be utilized in each estate instead of only in the surviving spouse's estate.

This technique may be desirable for older clients and may result in a tax savings if both spouses die within a relatively short time of one another.

One problem with the equalization approach is the applicability of the time-value-of-money concept. The surviving spouse and the other family members lose the use of the money paid out for the "prepaid" estate tax. If the surviving spouse lives for many years, the future value of the tax paid may be greater than the higher tax that would be payable later if the equalization approach had not been used.

Another drawback of equalization is that the surviving spouse can employ other and sometimes better planning devices, such as gifts, to reduce his or her taxable estate after the first spouse's death, which in turn will reduce the ultimate tax liability.

A third drawback is that clients generally prefer to defer taxes when possible. When both spouses are in good health, it may not make sense to them to "prepay" federal estate taxes.

It should also be borne in mind that there is always the danger that the surviving spouse might dispose of these inherited assets in a manner not intended by the deceased spouse.

For these reasons it is recommended that the equalization approach not be used for the Millers. The assets in excess of the applicable credit amount of the first spouse to die should pass to the surviving spouse under the marital deduction.

Recommendations

Our recommendations for Larry's estate plan would be an outright bequest of the cars and the residence to Anne, an outright bequest of a marital portion equal to the excess of Larry's taxable estate over the applicable credit exemption equivalent, and an applicable credit shelter residuary trust of which Anne is the primary beneficiary for her life. Anne could be the sole beneficiary of the residuary trust; however, it might be more prudent to allow the trustee to invade the trust for the benefit of Larry and Anne's children and grandchildren for specified purposes, such as education or catastrophic medical expenses. In some states, however, such as Pennsylvania, this provision may cause increased exposure to state inheritance tax. Since Anne has assets of her own and stands to inherit substantial assets from her mother, her estate plan should take the same approach (except for the specific bequests).

Whichever form the trust takes, the trustee should be empowered to pay income and to invade the corpus of the trust as necessary for Anne's benefit. If an independent trustee is used, the trustee can be instructed to pay income and invade the corpus for her comfort and happiness.

At Anne's death the trust will terminate, and the principal remaining in the trust will be divided equally among their three children, if living. If a child has died but leaves living children, the will should be designed so that the child's portion goes to his or her living children, per stirpes. If the child leaves no living children, the assets will be shared among Larry and Anne's remaining children.

Life Insurance Placement

General Discussion. At present Larry has $93,500 in personal life insurance death benefits. The most significant problem with this coverage is that Larry is the owner of each of the policies, so the proceeds will be includible in his estate for estate tax purposes at his death (IRC Sec. 2042(2)) and ultimately will increase Anne's estate if Larry dies first.

The positioning of the insurance policies is very important and may become more so if Larry's estate grows, since inclusion of life insurance proceeds in his taxable estate will result in unnecessary additional estate tax liabilities. Also in order to achieve maximum economy with life insurance proceeds, each dollar should be available to meet several financial needs or contingencies should the occasion arise. These objectives can be achieved by the utilization of an irrevocable life insurance trust to own and be the beneficiary of the life insurance coverage. The terms of the trust instrument can control the distribution of the proceeds. This is a much more flexible arrangement than the use of individual beneficiary designations.

Structuring the Irrevocable Life Insurance Trust. In the usual case the terms of the irrevocable life insurance trust are tailored much like those in the residuary (nonmarital) trust under the client's will. Although this type of design is not required, we would recommend it in this case, since this would make the entire amount of the insurance proceeds available to Anne until her death.

An additional provision that is often advantageous in life insurance trusts is a provision that allows but does not require the trustee to loan money to the estate of the deceased or the deceased's spouse or to purchase assets from the estate of the deceased or the deceased's spouse. This can provide the estate with needed liquidity. However, the trust instrument cannot require loans or purchases. The Internal Revenue Service has construed loan or purchase requirements as making the proceeds available to the executor for the use of the estate and has included them in the estate tax valuation of the decedent's gross estate, defeating the purpose of the insurance trust. That purpose is to protect the insurance proceeds from estate taxation (Reg. Sec. 20.2042-1(b)(1)). When the recommended design is implemented, the insurance proceeds are protected from estate taxation in both spouses' estates. In addition, as a general rule, the proceeds of life insurance in a life insurance trust are not subject to the claims of either the insured's or the beneficiaries' creditors.

One estate tax problem remains—the fact that gifts of life insurance policies within 3 years of death will result in taxation of the proceeds of the policy in the insured decedent's estate (IRC Sec. 2035(d)(2)).

If restrictions are placed on the beneficiaries' rights to exercise immediate ownership rights on the policies or the funds to pay premiums on the policies, the gift is a gift of a future interest and the annual gift tax exclusion does not apply. The result is that an immediate gift tax liability arises. This problem can be avoided by giving the beneficiaries a withdrawal right called a *Crummey provision* (derived from the tax court case *Crummey v. Comm'r*), which gives the trust beneficiaries the right to demand the annual gifts to the trust. This withdrawal right usually lasts for only a short period of time and then lapses. The period of time must be reasonable—usually 30 to 60 days are sufficient—and notice of the withdrawal right must be given to the beneficiary. The fact that the beneficiary is a minor without an appointed guardian will not invalidate the Crummey provision. To avoid adverse federal gift tax consequences in the event of a lapse of the withdrawal right, the annual amount subject to withdrawal should not exceed $5,000.

From a legal and statutory point of view the Crummey doctrine must be viewed in light of the Code provisions dealing with the lapse of a general power of appointment. Secs. 2514(e) and 2041(b)(2) provide that the lapse of a general power of appointment (created after October 21, 1942) is a release of such power. The release of a general power of appointment is "deemed to be a transfer of property by the individual possessing such power." This concept of a release or transfer of a power, although technical and complex, is very important because it is limited to the greater of $5,000 or 5 percent of the value of the assets held by a trust. It is this "5-and-5 power" that applies to Crummey trusts. The annual contribution to the trust must never exceed the greater of $5,000 or 5 percent of the value of the assets held by a trust if the grantor wishes to avoid a lapse of a general power of appointment.

Prior to the enactment of the Economic Recovery Tax Act of 1981 (ERTA), the 5-and-5 power was not an issue for Crummey-type trusts because the gift tax annual exclusion was $3,000 per donee. Since the gift tax annual exclusion was less than the $5,000 standard amount, a problem was never created. However, ERTA increased the annual exclusion from $3,000 per donee to $13,000 per donee. Although the annual exclusion is now $13,000 per year per donee, the maximum nonlapsing withdrawal amount that may be taken as part of the Crummey power is the greater of $5,000, or 5 percent of the trust corpus.

If Larry's present life insurance coverage is transferred to the trust, there will be a taxable gift in the amount of the interpolated terminal reserve of the polices. Proper structuring of the Crummey provision ensures that this amount should not exceed the annual gift tax exclusion.

There are also income tax consequences to a grantor of a trust that is empowered to use the trust income to pay premiums on policies of insurance on the life of the grantor or the grantor's spouse. In this case since no assets other than an existing life insurance policy would be transferred to the trust, as in the case of most irrevocable insurance trusts, there is little or no trust income to be taxable to the grantor.

Under the revised plan the removal of the insurance proceeds from both Larry's and Anne's estates should ultimately produce an additional federal estate tax savings of approximately $39,000.

Deferral of Estate Taxes under IRC Sec. 6166

Sec. 6166 provides that if more than 35 percent of a decedent's adjusted gross estate consists of an interest in a closely held business, the executor may elect to pay the federal estate tax attributable to such stock over a period of up to 14 years and 9 months. You will recall that Larry's estate would not qualify for a Sec. 303 redemption after the recommended installment sale to Steve because it failed to meet the 35 percent test. For the same reason—failure to meet the 35 percent test—deferral of estate taxes under

Sec. 6166 will not be available. Note that the availability of Sec. 6166 is not limited to corporations but applies to all closely held business interests as defined in IRC Sec. 6166(b). Sec. 303, on the other hand, applies specifically to redemptions of corporate stock.

PERSONAL PLANNING: INSURANCE

Personal Life Insurance Coverage

Although Larry presently has life insurance and other liquid assets that are sufficient to pay his estate taxes and administrative expenses, he should at least participate in the corporation's group insurance plan as long as he remains an employee to give him an extra margin of protection. As his investment is withdrawn from Millers and becomes more liquid, his present coverage may be sufficient.

Personal Property and Liability Coverage

From the information given in the case, two questions can be raised about the Millers' personal property and liability needs. First, the amount of insurance on the Millers' residence is inadequate to satisfy the replacement-cost provision of their homeowners policy. Under homeowners form 3, property losses are settled on a full-replacement-cost basis only if the amount of insurance carried at the time of loss is equal to 80 percent or more of the full replacement cost of the dwelling. However, loss settlements are limited to the amount of insurance carried, and an insured suffering a total loss will be fully indemnified only if insurance equal to 100 percent of the full replacement cost is carried. If the amount of insurance is less than 80 percent of the full replacement cost, the insurer's liability will be limited to the greater of (1) an amount calculated as if the policy contained an 80 percent coinsurance clause, based on the full replacement cost, or (2) the actual cash value of the damaged property. Thus the Millers will not have any losses paid in full unless they carry an amount of insurance equal to at least $360,000 or 80 percent of the dwelling's $450,000 replacement cost. (Since the actual replacement value seems to be only an estimate, an appraisal is probably in order.)

Second, no mention is made of any insurance on the condominium in another state. It can be adequately insured under a homeowners form 6, which is specifically designed to meet the needs of condominium owners. In addition to providing liability protection, it insures the real property that comprises the individual condominium unit. It is, however, up to the condominium association to insure the shell of the building. The basic form applies only to owner-occupied units, and an endorsement will be necessary since the unit is occasionally rented to others. The charge for this endorsement reflects the increased exposure resulting from tenant-occupied property. In addition, an endorsement is also needed if the real property within the unit (for example, fixtures, improvements, and alterations) is valued at more than $1,000. Finally, the basic contract provides named-peril coverage but can be endorsed to all-risks coverage as exists for real property in homeowners form 3.

PERSONAL PLANNING: INVESTMENT

Client Profile

Larry's current assets reflect his risk avoidance attitude and result in an investment program seeking stability of value and modest earnings. Their modest home and avoidance of debt also suggest that the Millers are quite conservative in their total outlook. Any recommendations for investments must recognize these views.

The projections over the next several years indicate that the Millers will have a substantial amount of cash available annually for investment purposes if the recommended solutions (the sale of 72 shares to Steve and the redemption of Anne's shares) are implemented. Larry's income from continued employment is almost sufficient to meet their cash needs. Unless the Millers drastically alter their lifestyle, most of their additional income is available for reinvestment. Any recommendations for specific investment assets should also recognize that convenience of reinvestment of income is a desirable characteristic.

Anne inherited some blue-chip stocks and bonds from her father. She has been managing the portfolio with the advice of her stockbroker, with whom she has been associated for many years. She enjoys trading the portfolio and has been successful. Since Anne enjoys successfully managing her securities, no repositioning of her portfolio is appropriate. Larry, on the other hand, keeps his cash in money market mutual funds. The following investment recommendations are directed at the cash the Millers will be receiving in the future. These recommendations should be reviewed by Anne as well as Larry.

The bulk of the Millers' investable cash will come from the sale of Millers stock owned by Larry. A portion, however, will come from the redemption of Anne's stock.

Except for Anne's inheritance the Millers should consider dividing ownership of investment assets equally between them. This is preferable to joint ownership because it will assure that both Larry and Anne will be able to make full use of the applicable credit for estate tax purposes. Jointly held assets, on the other hand, would pass under the marital deduction regardless of any estate planning documents.

Investment Alternatives

Certificates of Deposit

These are term deposits with either banks or savings and loan associations that are available with varying maturity dates and interest yields. Currently certificates of deposit (CDs) are yielding approximately 5.25 percent interest for 5-year maturities. Provided no more than $100,000 is in any one account at any one bank (or savings and loan), the account is insured by the FDIC—a desirable feature for this client's risk profile. Five-year maturities should reduce the likelihood of forced-sale problems since the Millers' annual cash flow is projected to be quite sizable. Another characteristic of CDs is that interest income can be either left to accumulate at the stipulated rate or withdrawn on a regular basis. Since the Millers will have a need for income reinvestment each year, the reinvestment feature is desirable. Furthermore, the Millers can later decide to take the current earnings on a regular basis if the return on newly issued CDs becomes higher than those already in their portfolio.

One disadvantage of CDs is that there is no growth in value other than through interest accumulations since CDs are a bank deposit. This lack of growth means CDs are subject to inflation risk. There is also a form of the interest-rate risk. Higher earnings can be realized by having investable cash in a more liquid form if interest rates rise. If interest rates do rise after any CDs are purchased, the CDs can be turned in for early redemption, the early redemption penalty paid, and the proceeds reinvested in the then-higher rate being paid on newly issued CDs. Each rollover of this type should be analyzed to determine if the higher interest rate being earned justifies paying the redemption penalty. Some banks are now issuing CDs that do not have an early redemption penalty. However, those CDs carry a lower interest rate than those with the penalty.

The Millers should plan a schedule of purchasing some CDs each year as a means of reducing a portion of the potential interest-rate risk during the period of acquisition. Also they should not have all their CDs mature in the same year. This spreading of maturity dates avoids the possibility of having to reinvest large portions of their portfolio at a particularly low point in the interest-rate cycle.

Municipal Bond Funds

This form of fund acquires a portfolio of tax-exempt bonds. The fund can pass the federal tax exemption on municipal bond income to its shareholders. Most municipal bonds issued on or before August 7, 1986, and bonds issued after that date that are deemed to be public-purpose bonds produce income that is fully exempt from federal income taxation. Bond funds that have a portfolio consisting totally of bonds issued by the states or their subdivisions in which the shareholder resides are typically free of that state's income tax. Although a state income tax exemption is a nice feature, the overriding consideration should be the quality of the bond portfolio held by the fund. For risk averters the bond fund portfolio should be high-investment grade with only a small or minor portion of the holdings having bond ratings less than AA. These funds are currently yielding approximately 5.5 percent on a tax-exempt basis, a yield that converts to an equivalent before-tax yield for clients in the 28 percent bracket of 7.64 percent (5.5%/1 − .28). Money market tax-exempt funds are currently yielding 4 percent after tax, which is equivalent to a 5.7 percent before-tax yield.

Since these bond funds are invested solely in debt instruments, the interest-rate risk is a cause for concern. Should interest rates rise, the fund's per-share value will fall although the interest income stream might not be affected. In addition, as with all fixed-income securities, the purchasing-power risk is an inherent characteristic and will affect the buying power of the income stream.

Municipal Bonds

Direct ownership of municipal bonds can be a desirable investment for risk-averse clients provided sufficient diversification can be achieved. Newly issued investment grade municipal bonds have a tax-exempt yield of approximately 5.5 percent (7.64 percent before tax if the owner is in the 28 percent tax bracket) for 25- to 30-year maturity dates. The disadvantages are a lack of sufficient diversification if the portfolio consists of only one or two issues and also the same disadvantages that municipal bond funds have.

Balanced Mutual Funds

These funds distribute their portfolio among the various classes of securities: bonds, common stocks, and preferred stocks. The proportion of their assets in any one security can be either at the fund manager's discretion or specified in the prospectus. These funds are generally the most conservative of any mutual fund that invests in common stock. Their investment objectives in order of priority are to preserve capital, to generate income, and to obtain capital gains if possible. During declining markets the holding of different types of securities provides protection for the investor since typically not all markets—bond, preferred stock, and common stock—fall simultaneously.

In addition to the conservative nature of balanced funds, they, like all other funds, provide diversification and professional management, and they offer automatic reinvestment of dividends, all features desirable to the Millers. These funds provide minimal growth opportunities since only a portion of their assets is invested in common stocks. But this limited potential growth can nevertheless serve as a means of offsetting some effects of inflation.

Any investor using balanced funds, or any fund for that matter, must choose between load versus no-load funds and must also time acquisitions after the date of record to avoid having a portion of the investment immediately returned as a taxable dividend or capital gain.

Convertible Bonds or Convertible Bond Funds

The unique feature of convertible bonds is the option the bondholder has to convert the bond, when desired, to common stock of the issuing corporation. Should the common stock of the issuer rise substantially in price, the holder can convert and obtain the benefit of the increased market price of the stock. The conventional wisdom is that over long periods of time, common stocks in general tend to outperform inflation. If this holds true, this form of bond provides potential inflation protection while still spinning off interest income that is greater than the dividend flow on the underlying common stocks during the years immediately following the bond's issue. However, the bond never has to be converted. At maturity the face amount is returned to the bondholders.

Like all bonds, convertibles are subject to the interest-rate risk, and unless the underlying common stock rises faster than the price level so that conversion is desirable, they are also subject to the purchasing-power risk.

Risk-averse investors could well consider purchasing convertibles, either directly or through a convertible bond fund (with the usual fund advantages and disadvantages), provided the portfolio of these bonds (individually owned or through the bond fund) is of investment-grade quality. The yield will perhaps be one-eighth of a percent less than could be earned on nonconvertible debt of the same risk. It is the potential increase in the value of the underlying common stock to offset inflation that makes this form of debt attractive, particularly to investors like the Millers. They are nearing retirement, do not wish to take undue investment risks, but will probably experience inflation during the remainder of their lives.

Preretirement Planning

At this point in their lives Anne and Larry should consider preretirement planning. They have devoted a major portion of their financial activities to the establishment and prosperity of their furniture business and are now nearing the conclusion of their peak wealth-accumulation years. Their efforts should focus on preparing the way for their actual retirement in a manner that will provide financial security during those years. Important factors for Larry and Anne to consider at this time include

- repositioning of assets
- asset conservation
- plan-distribution options
- retirement income estimation
- potentially dependent parent
- recreation/health
- acquisition of personal assets (autos, home appliances, and so on)
- possible new career

Many of these factors have received some attention in the solution as presented up to this point. Each of these factors will now be examined for the Millers.

Repositioning of Assets

The recommendation is for Larry to sell a portion of his stock in Millers through an installment sale to their son, Steve. This sale will convert a portion of his ownership in Millers to an annual cash flow that will provide income for both himself and Anne during retirement. Larry will still have 95.5 shares in Millers that are not available for repositioning due to their general nonmarketability. At some time in the future consideration could be given to a disposition of Larry's remaining shares in Millers, possibly by means of a redemption.

Anne will have her Millers stock redeemed by the corporation, thus producing a stream of income that will increase their cash flow.

An examination of the Millers' balance sheet discloses that they own few other assets that can be repositioned. Although the potential for repositioning Anne's portfolio of stock and bonds does exist, Anne enjoys managing these assets and has been successful in doing so. Any repositioning of these securities by the planner appears to be undesirable. However, this is a matter that should be explored with the client.

Another asset that might be repositioned is the store building. Again, in situations such as this the sale of the building to a third party could jeopardize much of this family's well-being. Steve would be at the mercy of an unsympathetic owner of the building and could have little option but to renew leases at the owner's terms. Although the asset is worth close to one-third of a million dollars, Larry would probably prefer to retain the ownership to protect both his installment sale, Anne's installment redemption, and Steve's livelihood from the furniture store. Larry should discuss with Steve the need for some long-term inflation protection from the rents that Steve will be paying. Perhaps the lease agreement should incorporate a form of escalator clause adjusting the rent either for some broad-based inflation measure or linked to increases in rents being paid in the town. Larry might consider doing this while he retains working control of Millers as part of his preretirement planning.

The beach condo Anne owns provides her with the satisfaction of being able to use it as she and the family desire. With approaching retirement promising to bring Anne and Larry more leisure time, it does not seem prudent to convert the condo into either a more full-time, rental real estate property or to sell it and use the proceeds to acquire additional income-producing securities. Under the current situation since the property is free of any debt, the modest rental income earned more than covers the annual cash drain for taxes and insurance. Continued ownership should enhance their retirement leisure time. Fortunately the Millers' financial position is such that the opportunity cost (forgone interest earnings) of the money invested in the condo does not affect their ability to meet their financial goals. Of course, the potential does exist for a subsequent sale should the need arise.

The remaining assets do not appear suited for repositioning. Perhaps the return being earned on Anne's accumulated life insurance dividends could be examined to determine whether a higher return could be obtained on the funds if placed elsewhere. The remaining assets, such as the checking and savings accounts, money market fund, automobiles, and life insurance cash values, need not be considered for repositioning at this time.

Asset Conservation

Asset conservation has two elements. The first is to create a relatively risk-free portfolio. The second is to keep the bulk of the assets available for the clients' use should the need arise.

As is the case with many owners of small businesses, most of the Millers' wealth accumulation is in their family business, so these ventures typically involve high risk. Through the mechanisms of the installment sale to Steve and the installment payout of Anne's stock redemption, the Millers will begin to move some of their wealth out of the family business. However, their retirement income flow will depend on the ability of the furniture store to produce income to meet these obligations. Also Larry will continue to own some shares in Millers.

Only two of their existing assets—the store building and Anne's stock and bond portfolio—exhibit high-risk characteristics. The store building probably has alternative uses and in that sense is less risky than a special-purpose building would be. The composition of Anne's portfolio is not specifically stated, and perhaps a somewhat less risky mix of stocks and bonds could provide additional asset conservation.

The recommendations presented earlier for the Millers to employ for their investable cash flow during the next several years are relatively conservative in nature and are consistent with an asset-conservation objective.

Maintaining their accumulated assets for their use is the method recommended for the Millers (that is, the installment sale) in transferring ownership in Millers. In addition, their recommended estate plans provide the maximum protection to the surviving spouse. Thus their assets are being managed in a manner that will provide them with the desired economic benefits.

Plan Distribution Options

Larry presently has almost $70,000 in the profit-sharing plan of Millers. He plans to continue his employment for several years before withdrawing from any active involvement in the business. Even if no further contributions are made for his benefit, and assuming the plan earns about 8 percent annually over the next several years, Larry should have at least $90,000 of plan assets available for income-producing purposes. Since retirement is not imminent, there is no immediate need for Larry and Anne to choose between a lump-sum distribution and installment distribution or a joint and survivor annuity. Given their expected cash flows during the next few years, the Millers should continue deferring the removal of plan assets as long as is feasible without incurring penalties in order to obtain the maximum benefit of tax deferral.

Retirement Income Estimation

The table below projects the amount of cash inflow Larry and Anne will have during the first 5 years of their retirement under the assumption that Larry retires from Millers in 2014.

During the first 5 years of retirement the Millers' cash outflows will rise less than the increase in their cash inflows from sources presently available to them.

Table 6-12 Retirement Cash Inflow/Cash Expense Estimation					
	2013	2014	2015	2016	2017
Cash Inflow					
Installment sale (Doug)	$ 27,080	$ 27,080	$ 27,080	$ 27,080	$ 27,080
Installment sale (Steve)	27,800	27,800	27,800	27,800	27,800
302 redemption	27,734	27,734	27,734	27,734	27,734
Social Security	17,484	18,009	18,549	19,105	19,678
Pension plan	10,500	10,500	10,500	10,500	10,500
Building rental	44,000	46,640	49,438		55,549
Anne's portfolio	5,466	5,739	6,026	6,328	6,644
Investment portfolio (reinvested cash flow [12/31/04])	27,388	27,388	27,388	27,388	27,388
Interest on retirement savings	0	3,687	73,393	11,112	14,842
Total cash inflow	$187,452	$194,577	$201,908	$209,452	$217,216
Cash Outflow					
Expenses	47,000	49,820	52,809	55,978	59,336
Federal and state income taxes	69,000	72,000	75,000	78,000	81,000
Vacation/travel	10,000	11,000	12,100	13,310	14,641
Total cash outflow	$126,000	$132,820	$139,909	$147,288	$154,977
Net cash inflow (annual cash savings)	$ 61,452	$ 61,757	$ 61,999	$ 62,164	$ 62,238
Accumulated net savings during retirement	$ 61,452	$123,209	$185,208	$247,372	$309,610

The effect of this is shown on the net cash inflow line. Based on this data the Millers will be able to save a rather sizable sum each year, which, if invested in bonds yielding a 6 percent return, will result in a year-to-year increase in their income. The Millers should be financially secure during their years of retirement.

One important point to consider is that the annual cash inflow from the proposed redemption of Anne's stock in Millers will cease with the payment in 2019 (if a 10-year installment term is in fact implemented). The payments from Doug for the purchase of the second store will end in 2019. The combined effect of these two events is to reduce their annual saving by the after-tax cash inflow from these two installment transactions.

Potentially Dependent Parent

Anne's mother, the sole surviving parent of Anne and Larry, appears to be financially independent and in good health at this time. Unless serious medical problems or long-term nursing care deplete her assets, it is unlikely that the Millers will be called upon to provide financial support. Therefore they need not include any expenditure planning for the benefit of Anne's mother in their retirement plans. However, they might have to consider the possibility of providing some personal time to care for her should she experience a deterioration in health.

Recreation/Health

At this time both the Millers expect to travel and to use their condo to a greater degree when Larry either spends less time with Millers or fully retires. Fortunately the Millers enjoy good health, so these factors do not create any unique planning considerations at this time.

Personal Asset Acquisition

Since Larry is in the furniture business, it can be assumed that furniture for the home is not needed now or at retirement. The Millers might wish to consider the purchase of a new car when Larry retires completely if their travel plans include lengthy car trips. Other than the car, it does not appear they have any unfulfilled wishes in this category.

Possible New Career

Larry has not indicated any interest in possibly embarking on a different career upon retirement. His expressed desire to travel and to spend more time with Anne and their grandchildren is the extent of his expected use of his retirement time.

Chapter Review

Review Questions

These questions are intended to help students answer questions about case studies, goals and assumptions. Answers to these questions can be found in the study supplement.

1. What are distinct challenges for financial service professionals when working with family run small businesses? [1]

2. Describe the mechanics of an installment sale and a private annuity. What are the advantages and disadvantages of transferring property using both techniques? [2]

3. Jill owns an engineering firm and actively works as the firm CEO. Jill decides to decrease her salary to $1.00 for 2011 and pay herself with dividend income in order to avoid paying FICA taxes. Why is Jill's decision worrisome? [2]

4. What types of property and liability coverage should be considered when working with a family owned small business? [2]

5. What preretirement factors should small business owners consider as they approach their retirement years? [1]

Learning Objectives

An understanding of the material in this chapter should enable the student to

1. Review planning for the officer of a large organization.
2. Discuss unique challenges of planning for higher income individuals.

Officers of large organizations are rapidly becoming clients of professional financial planners. These clients often have a comprehensive set of benefits from their employment, but they also have many of the same priorities and concerns that can benefit from a financial planner's expertise. With increasing awareness of the availability of comprehensive, well-trained financial planners, some large organizations offer personal financial counseling as an executive benefit. In other cases the relationship with the financial adviser is developed as an outgrowth of some single-purpose planning provided by an insurance agent, a securities broker, a CPA, or a lawyer.

In contrast to the young couple with only the potential to accumulate substantial assets, these clients, typically between 45 and 60 years of age, have reached or are nearing the peak of their careers. Hence a portfolio of investment assets is commonly present. In addition, the prospect of further significant accumulation exists, since children's education expenses are actually or almost completely paid. These clients can focus on the adequacy of their retirement planning. Although included in the upper ranks of their employer's management team, these clients lack the requisite clout to install benefit programs suited to their specific situation, and any desirable changes in employment-related benefits may be beyond their power or influence. Thus individual plans, although lacking some of the tax advantages found in corporate plans, provide the means to meet the clients' financial objectives.

Today medical advances and increased longevity enhance the likelihood that clients in this age bracket should consider their potential need for long-term care outside their home for themselves and their spouse. Also some of these clients may need to provide financial assistance to care for a parent or to provide resources for the care of a disabled child over a long period. Once again, personal planning and funding techniques may provide the only adequate basis for a satisfactory course of action that will meet the objective.

CASE NARRATIVE

Personal Information

Edgar (Ed) and Amy Martinson are 54 and 45 respectively and reside in a suburb of Atlanta, Jefferson. They have been married 24 years and have two children. Beatrice (Bea) is 22, single, and has been employed in the international division of a large bank since graduating from college 2 years ago. Their son, Scott, is 16 and attends high school.

Shortly after Amy and Ed were married they had simple, reciprocal wills drafted in which each left all of his or her respective estate properties to the surviving spouse. No revisions have been made to these wills.

Ed joined Inc, Inc., 20 years ago as an assistant to the plant superintendent. He has progressed to his current position of vice president of manufacturing, which became effective on December 1 of last year. Details of Ed's employment and benefits are described in the section titled "Employment Information."

Amy began a career in retailing as a buyer for a large department store but interrupted her career at their daughter's birth. When Scott entered kindergarten, she returned to her former employer. When their son was injured 7 years ago, Amy resigned to care for him and presently has no plans to continue her career.

Ed, Amy, and Bea all enjoy excellent health, but Scott has serious health problems. Seven years ago he fell from a tree, severely injuring his leg and hip. After a long hospital stay and months of rehabilitation therapy he appeared to be fully recovered. However, about 3 years ago Scott began to experience pain and stiffness in the hip joint and eventually was unable to move about. Although he had a hip replacement at that time, it only slightly alleviated the pain and did little to improve his mobility. Ed's health insurance under Inc's plan has covered most of the medical expenses resulting from the accident, but the Martinsons are uncertain about Scott's future medical costs. In addition to paying the deductible and other out-of-pocket medical expenses, Amy took several specialized courses at their expense at the local hospital so she could give Scott some care that would otherwise have required hospitalization or semiskilled nursing experience.

As a result of this serious health problem Scott has become rather frail physically. Although he continues to attend school, he lacks a positive attitude toward education. Since his grades reflect this attitude, the Martinsons doubt that he will continue any education beyond high school. They worry that this lack of education beyond the high school level, combined with his physical condition, will make it impossible for him to support himself adequately.

By the time Bea started college, the Martinsons had accumulated about $25,000 for her educational expenses. These funds, plus some of their annual income, were sufficient to cover Bea's college expenses. Ed's mother, who was very fond of Bea, died when Bea was 4. Her will established a testamentary trust for Bea's benefit with Grass Roots Bank as the trustee. The terms of the trust permit each year's trust income to be paid out annually if Bea notifies the trustee, but Bea has not yet exercised her option to withdraw any trust income. The corpus and accumulated income, if any, can be invaded to fund an elaborate wedding or a down payment on a home. When Bea is 35, any funds remaining must be distributed to her. Trust assets have a current market value of $70,000.

Since Bea's prospective financial concerns appear to be largely taken care of, the Martinsons want to focus their attention on providing for Scott. Currently they have about $26,000 set aside for him. These funds are invested in conservative common stocks, and although Ed and Amy are the owners, the stocks are held in street name in a separate account maintained with a large brokerage firm. The stocks are increasing in value at a rate of 6 percent a year and are paying a dividend of 3 percent a year. All dividend income is automatically invested in the issuers' dividend reinvestment plans. Until Ed retires and perhaps for a few years thereafter, the Martinsons anticipate that they can provide for Scott's needs from their current income. However, by the time Ed retires they would like to have some provision in place for a lifelong stream of income to supplement Scott's impaired earning capacity and to cover his continuing medical expenses. At today's prices the Martinsons' target is to provide Scott with an annual supplemental income of $3,000, adjusted for inflation. Ed planned to retire by age 62 but is now unsure whether this will be feasible in light of their objective to provide long-term support for Scott.

A further concern of Ed's is Amy's life expectancy. Not only is she a bit younger than he, but her family history indicates it is likely that she will have a longer-than-normal life expectancy. Although he doesn't need to make any decisions now about distributions from the corporate defined-benefit, noncontributory pension plan and the contributory 401(k) plan, Ed and Amy believe these decisions must be considered in conjunction with some retirement planning necessary to supplement the retirement benefits available from both Inc and Social Security.

Both of Amy's parents are in their 70s, and three of her four grandparents are still hale and hearty folk. Although some of Amy's elderly relatives may need support, Amy and Ed are not concerned about accumulating any funds for this contingency because fortunately Amy's father was very successful financially and is able to afford the support necessary at this time. He has been open with Amy about his finances and, barring unforeseen financial reverses, expects to provide economic assistance for Amy's grandparents as well as provide for his and his spouse's support. Amy has a brother, Bob, aged 48, who is a physician in a different state.

Ed's family does not include such long-lived ancestors. Both his parents died in their early 70s. Except for an unmarried brother, Jack, who is 10 years younger than he, Ed has no living relatives other than his spouse and children.

Seven years ago, expecting that Ed would rise to the executive ranks of Inc, the Martinsons sold their home for $200,000 and purchased a newly built $350,000 home in an exclusive suburb. Their adjusted basis in the old home was $58,000. The Martinsons made a down payment of $225,000 and financed the remainder of the acquisition cost with a 25-year mortgage at a fixed interest rate of 8.5 percent. The estimated fair market value of their home is $575,000.

When Ed and Amy were married 24 year ago, Ed purchased a $50,000 whole life policy with an annual premium of $1,120. He is the owner and Amy is the primary beneficiary. He has since named Bea and Scott as the contingent beneficiaries, per stirpes. This policy has a current cash value of $18,100. Amy converted her group term life insurance into a $5,000 whole life policy 21 years ago, naming Ed as the primary beneficiary. The children are the contingent beneficiaries, per stirpes. The policy has a $120 annual premium and a cash value of $1,800. Ed has two $25,000 policies with combined premiums of $1,215 and a total cash value of $16,325. Each of these policies was purchased when a child was born. Each child is the named primary beneficiary on a policy, and Amy is the contingent beneficiary for both policies.

Over the years the Martinsons have invested their excess income in several different instruments. First, during the years when the IRA window permitting fully tax-deductible contributions of up to $2,000 annually without an income limitation was open for participants in qualified pension plans, Ed funded an IRA and a spousal IRA at the local savings and loan when their finances permitted. CDs were used as the investment instrument. The blended current return based on differing maturity dates of the CDs is 8.1 percent. When the contributions ceased being tax deductible, Ed discontinued adding money to the IRA. Overall he put $9,800 into his IRA, which now has an accumulated value of $22,800. The spousal IRA for Amy, with $1,250 invested, has an accumulated value of $2,400. Its current return is about the same as Ed's.

They maintain a regular joint checking account that currently has a $12,000 balance. They also have a money market deposit account at the same bank. The account typically has a target average balance of about $25,000 and currently earns 4.75 percent. Their monthly mortgage payment and other large bills are paid by drafts drawn on this account. If the deposit account becomes too large, the excess is divided between investments in a balanced mutual fund and a growth mutual fund. In both funds all dividends and capital gains have been reinvested. Their basis is $45,000 in the balanced fund, which now has a current value of $184,000. The investment in the growth fund is worth $220,000 and has a basis of $57,000. The estimated annual return on these funds has averaged 9.5 percent and 13 percent respectively over the last 5 years.

The taxable portion of the total return from the balanced fund averages 4.3 percent and from the growth fund it is 1.5 percent. The remainder of each fund's return is unrealized capital gains on the portfolio and increases in the net asset value of their shares.

Amy has furnished their new home with $30,000 worth of additional purchases, which were partially financed over 2 years. Furnishings and other personal property they own increase the value of the contents to about $75,000.

Ed's auto was purchased in December of last year and is being financed with 42 monthly payments of $440. Currently the vehicle is worth about $20,000. Amy's station wagon is fully paid for and has a value of $12,000.

Until the additional problems with Scott began to drain some of their potential savings, Ed and Amy anticipated having Scott's education fully funded before he entered college. They then expected to establish a side fund for their retirement. Their target was and still is to have an additional $5,000 of annual income beginning at the expected retirement date. This additional income, they thought, would enable Ed to retire at age 62, the earliest date permitted under Inc's pension plan. They felt the side fund was needed because of the difference in their ages and Amy's potential long life.

Employment Information

Ed's job requires him to spend about 30 percent of his time on visits to Inc's facilities in North America and Europe. Inc plans to commence building at least one manufacturing operation in an Asian country during the next 2 years. Whenever Ed is traveling on company business, he is covered by accidental death insurance that is double his annual base salary. This is in addition to other employment-related life insurance described below.

In his new position Ed's salary is $100,000 per year, and he is now eligible for Inc's executive bonus plan that over the past several years has distributed an annual bonus equal to 10 percent of each participating executive's salary. The total bonus distributed by the plan is directly related to corporate profits. The percentage of corporate profits distributed by the bonus plan has remained constant over the past several years. Each plan participant's potential share of next year's profits is determined by Inc's board at its December meeting. Inc uses the calendar year for financial statement and income tax purposes.

Coverage for 100 percent of lost salary for short-term disability (maximum of 6 months) is provided under a nonfunded sick-pay plan. Salary lost due to a disability's preventing a return to employment status after a period of 6 months is replaced at 75 percent, including Social Security disability benefits, for the duration of the disability or until normal retirement age, whichever comes first. For Ed this would amount to almost $6,250 a month. Inc will continue to credit years of employment for pension plan coverage and make both the employer and the employee contributions to the 401(k) plan. In addition, coverage will be continued under the company's insured medical plan at no cost to the disabled employee. If Ed should become disabled, the Martinsons stated that they want to have the equivalent of Ed's current salary of almost $8,750 a month. Therefore they have a shortfall of $2,000 a month.

Inc's qualified noncontributory defined-benefit pension plan will provide a maximum retirement income of 1.5 percent of the average of an employee's highest 5 years of income times the number of years of service, with the maximum number of years of service for the purpose of the plan being 25 years. The pension benefit is not offset by retirement income provided under

Social Security. The value of the future pension benefit, reduced to present value, is approximately $190,000.

Six years ago Inc instituted a voluntary-participation, salary reduction type 401(k) plan for its employees. About 85 percent of Inc's employees participate in the plan. For employee contributions up to 5 percent of salary, Inc will contribute 50 percent of the employee's contribution during the first 5 years of service and 75 percent until 10 years of service are achieved. At that point Inc will match the employee's contribution. The plan permits lump-sum withdrawals upon retirement or severance from the employer. The 401(k) plan is self-directed; plan participants may choose the investment instruments and may shift invested funds within a limited set of alternatives. Investment options include Inc's common stock, which is traded on a national exchange; a no-load family of mutual funds that includes a money market, a U.S. government bond, a corporate bond, a balanced, a growth, and an international fund as its "family"; and Series EE U.S. government savings bonds. Ed has participated in the plan since its inception and divides both his and Inc's contributions equally between the U.S. government bond fund and Inc's stock. At the end of last year Ed's account in the bond fund was $50,000, and Inc's stock had a market value of $74,000. He anticipates contributing 5 percent of salary each year until retirement.

As a result of Ed's promotion last December he became a participant in Inc's nonqualified deferred-compensation plan. Assuming that Ed remains with Inc until normal retirement age (65), the plan will provide a benefit of $1,500 per month for a period of 10 years provided Ed does not engage in activities deemed to be in direct competition with Inc. Should Ed die before the end of the 10-year period, the plan will continue the payments to Amy for the unpaid period of time. If Amy fails to live until the end of the 10-year period, the remaining payments will be made to her estate. Although Inc is placing funds into a separate account earmarked to fund the deferred-compensation obligation, these funds are part of Inc's assets and are available to its creditors.

Inc provides noncontributory group term life insurance in the amount of 1.5 times annual base salary for all employees. Ed has named Amy as the primary beneficiary of the policy and Bea and Scott, per stirpes, as the contingent beneficiaries. Upon retirement the insurance protection decreases to $10,000 and then declines over the next 5 years to a face amount of $5,000.

Inc's comprehensive medical insurance plan provides $500,000 of lifetime coverage for each family member. Each year after a $250 per-person deductible, the insurance provides coverage for 80 percent of the first $5,000 of each year's covered benefits for the family. After the $5,000 of covered benefits is incurred in any one year, additional medical expenses are paid in full. The plan is noncontributory for employee coverage, but dependent coverage is available only if the employee contributes $20 monthly to the cost of coverage. Scott is covered under the plan until graduation from high school, and coverage would be continued if he were a full-time, post-high-school student until age 23. When Scott's qualification as a student for participation in the health plan ends, the COBRA rules permit coverage to extend for 36 months as long as the premium is properly paid.

When an employee retires at normal retirement age (65), Inc pays the full cost of medical insurance to supplement Medicare for both the employee and the employee's spouse. If the joint and survivor option is selected under Inc's pension plan, Inc will continue to pay the supplemental premium for the surviving spouse. If the retired or deceased employee's spouse is not eligible for Medicare, then Inc provides a group supplemental plan that will pay 80 percent of the surviving spouse's medical expenses in excess of a spouse's basic Blue Cross/Blue Shield plan until such time as the spouse is eligible for Medicare. Before Medicare coverage is available, the spouse pays the premium for the basic insurance, and Inc pays for the supplemental insurance. When Medicare coverage becomes available, the spouse is provided the Medicare supplemental insurance as described above.

Because of the Financial Accounting Standards Board requirement that the present value of retirees' medical expenses must be reported in a company's annual financial report and because of the rapid inflation of medical costs, Inc is currently studying the possibility of (1) discontinuing its payments for the supplemental medical insurance, (2) having the retired employee pay for the coverage under a group plan, or (3) having the employee make contributions during his or her employment years toward the retirement medical insurance. If either of the first two options were implemented, Inc would make some improvements in its pension plan to partially compensate for the loss of the full payment of the supplemental medical insurance. Whatever changes are made will affect only future retirees, such as Ed.

The Martinsons' property tax assessment is $70,000 for the land and $310,000 for home improvements, although they anticipate that the property would sell for no more than $375,000. They carry an HO-3 homeowners policy that insures the dwelling for $300,000, which is the amount they anticipate it would cost to replace the structure. The contents are insured for one-half the limit on the dwelling. The policy provides $500,000 of liability coverage and what they believe is adequate additional living expense coverage should a loss occur that precludes living in their home. Although the homeowners policy would provide some coverage, the Martinsons have opted to insure Amy's jewelry and furs for scheduled values on a separate policy.

The automobiles are covered under one policy that has a liability limit of $500,000 and medical expense coverage of $10,000. In addition, the policy includes uninsured motorists, towing, collision, and other-than-collision coverages (comprehensive). The latter coverages have $500 deductibles.

To further protect themselves, the Martinsons carry a $1 million umbrella policy that requires liability insurance for both the home and the automobile in the amount of $500,000.

INSTRUCTIONS
Based on this information, prepare a working outline for the Martinsons' financial plan. When this has been completed, it can be compared with the suggested solution that follows. After comparing the two working outlines, see further instructions that follow.

WORKING OUTLINE

1. Client's objectives

    a. For lifetime planning

        (1) Accumulate sufficient wealth to assure that current lifestyle continues following retirement.

        (2) Address the retirement planning issues stemming from Amy's family history of longevity and Amy's likelihood of surviving Ed by many years.

        (3) Accumulate a fund that will assure an adequate stream of income to Scott for purposes of maintenance and medical costs

        (4) Provide current medical insurance coverage for Scott both while he is covered by Inc's plan and after he is no longer covered by the plan.

(5) Assess current insurance coverage and restructure such coverages optimally.

b. For disposition at death

(1) Provide for Amy since she is likely to outlive Ed.

(2) Construct the estate plan so that Scott's disability is adequately addressed should Ed and/or Amy predecease him.

(3) Plan eventual inheritances in some equitable manner to allow Bea to receive an equal benefit and an equal amount of estate property.

(4) Ensure that the entire family will have sufficient assets to maintain their lifestyle if Ed should die prematurely.

(5) Provide for estate liquidity at death.

(6) Avoid unnecessary taxes at the death of either Ed or Amy.

2. Personal planning

a. Tax planning

(1) Present situation

(2) Treatment of distributions from nonqualified deferred-compensation plan

(3) Creation of fund for Scott

(a) Outright gifts

(b) 2503(b) trust

(c) 2503(c) trust

(d) UGMA gifts

(4) Dispositions at death

(a) Revision of estate plan

(b) Analysis of present situation

(c) Imposition of the excise tax

(d) Modification of present plan to consider concept of "equity of inheritance"

(e) Considerations stemming from Amy's family's history of longevity

(f) Use of irrevocable life insurance trust

b. Accumulation planning

c. Insurance planning

(1) Long-term care protection for Scott

(2) Long-term care protection for Amy

(3) Current life insurance coverage and recommendations

(4) Insurance to fund income supplements for retirement and for Scott

(5) Equalization of benefit for Bea

(6) Additional income for Amy should Ed die first

(7) Review of accidental death and dismemberment coverage

(8) Review of disability insurance

(9) Review of medical coverages for Ed and Amy

(10) Evaluation of existing personal property and liability coverage

(11) Summary of insurance needs

d. Investment planning

(1) Refinancing the home

(2) Evaluation of portfolio with regard to objectives

(3) Recommended portfolio

(4) Additional considerations

(a) Maximizing use of Inc's 401(k) plan

(b) Family of funds

(c) Ownership considerations

INSTRUCTIONS

Now prepare a financial plan for the Martinsons. When you have prepared your solution, you can compare it with the suggested solution that follows.

PERSONAL FINANCIAL PLAN FOR EDGAR AND AMY MARTINSON [SUGGESTED SOLUTION]: CLIENTS' OBJECTIVES

1. For lifetime planning

    a. Accumulate sufficient wealth to assure that current lifestyle continues following retirement.

    b. Address the retirement planning issues stemming from Amy's family history of longevity and Amy's likelihood of surviving Ed by many years.

    c. Accumulate a fund that will assure an adequate stream of income to Scott for purposes of maintenance and medical costs.

    d. Provide current medical insurance coverage for Scott both while he is covered by Inc's plan and after he is no longer covered by the plan.

    e. Assess current insurance coverage and restructure such coverages optimally.

2. For disposition at death

    a. Provide for Amy since she is likely to outlive Ed.

    b. Construct the estate plan so that Scott's disability is adequately addressed should Ed and/or Amy predecease him.

    c. Plan eventual inheritances in some equitable manner to allow Bea to receive an equal benefit and an equal amount of estate property.

    d. Ensure that the entire family will have sufficient assets to maintain their lifestyle if Ed should die prematurely.

    e. Provide for estate liquidity at death.

    f. Avoid unnecessary taxes at the death of either Ed or Amy.

BASE CASE

Assumptions

1. The checking account balance is maintained at $12,000; the account is noninterest bearing.
2. Ed's salary is increased at 5 percent annually.
3. The money market deposit account earns 4.75 percent annually.
4. Investable cash is invested and earns 5 percent annually.
5. Expenditures for food, clothing and cleaning, utilities, phone, vacations, and charitable contributions will increase annually at 3 percent.
6. Expenditures for transportation will increase 4 percent annually.
7. Expenditures for entertainment will increase 5 percent annually.
8. Expenditures for medical insurance and other medical expenses will increase at 6 percent annually.
9. Decreases in the value of furniture have been ignored.
10. Automobiles decrease in value at a rate of 15 percent annually.
11. The value of the home will increase at one percent annually.
12. The common stock portfolio will increase at 9 percent annually.
13. Dividends from the common stock portfolio are currently $3,120, will increase 4 percent annually, and are reinvested in the portfolio.
14. IRAs will earn 8.1 percent annually over the next 4 years.

Base Case: Inventory of Assets—Ed and Amy Martinson

Table 7-1 Base Case: Inventory of Assets—Ed and Amy Martinson								
Assets	Cost or Basis	Fair Market Value	Current Return		Form of Owner-ship[1]	Avail-able for Liquid-ity	Collat-eral-ized	Location
			%	$				
Checking account	$12,000	10,000	—	—	JT	Yes	No	Bank
Money market deposit account	25,000	25,000	4.75	1,188	JT	Yes	No	Bank
Residence	183,000	575,000	—	—	JT	No	Yes	—
Life ins. cash value	18,100	18,100	—	—	S(H)	Yes	No	Safe-deposit box
Life ins. cash value	1,800	1,800	—	—	S(W)	Yes	No	Safe-deposit box
Life ins. cash value	16,325	16,325	—	—	S(H)	Yes	No	Safe-deposit box
IRA	9,800	22,800	8.1	1,720	S(H)	No	No	Safe-deposit box
IRA	1,250	2,400	8.1	180	S(W)	No	No	Safe-deposit box
Balanced fund	45,000	184,000	4.3	3,612	S(H)	Yes	No	Mutual fund
Growth fund	57,000	220,000	1.5	1,800	S(H)	Yes	No	Mutual fund
401(k) bond fund	—	50,000	6.5	3,250	S(H)	No	No	Mutual fund
401(k) stock	—	74,000	2	1,480	S(H)	No	No	Mutual fund
Group term life	—	142,500[2]	—	—	S(H)	Yes	No	Employer
Nonqualified deferred compensation	—	52,000[2]	—	—	S(H)	No	No	Employer
Vested pension benefit	—	190,000[2]	—	—	S(H)	Yes	No	Employer
Common stock	60,000	104,000	3	3,120	S(H)	Yes	No	Safe-deposit box
Household furnishings	75,000	75,000	—	—	JT	No	No	—
Auto	28,000	20,000	—	—	S(H)	Yes	Yes	—
Auto	20,000	2,000	—	—	S(W)	No	No	—

[1] JT = joint tenants with right of survivorship; S = single ownership; H = husband; W = wife

[2] Value of plan benefits

BASE CASE: INCOME TAX STATEMENT OF ED AND AMY MARTINSON

Table 7-2 Base Case: Income Tax Statement of Ed and Amy Martinson			
BASE CASE	**Current Year**	**Next Year (Projected)**	**Two Years (Projected)**
Earned Income			
Compensation	$100,000.00	$105,000.00	$110,250.00
Company Bonus	$10,000.00	$10,500.00	$11,025.00
401(k) Contribution—Ed	$ (4,750.00)	$ (4,987.50)	$ (5,236.88)
	$ 105,250.00	$ 110,512.50	$ 116,038.13
Interest/Dividends			
Money Market Fund	$ 1,188.00	$ 14,296.00	$ 12,958.00
Stock Portfolio	$ 850.00	$ 4,542.00	$ 4,769.00
Investable Cash	$ 1,181.20	$ 2,262.45	$ 3,543.45
Growth Mutual Funds	$ 6,133.00	$ 2,669.00	$ 2,816.00
Balanced Mutual Funds	$ 7,765.00	$ 5,412.00	$ 9,284.00
	$ 17,117.20	$ 29,181.45	$ 33,370.45
Adjusted Gross Income	$ 122,367.20	$ 139,693.95	$ 149,408.58
Deductions			
Charitable 50%	$ 2,000.00	$ 2,120.00	$ 2,247.20
State Tax Paid	$ 5,164.00	$ 7,275.00	$ 7,822.00
Property Tax—Home	$ 3,000.00	$ 4,275.00	$ 4,403.00
Points Amort	—	—	—
Mortgage Interest	**$ 12,893.00**	**$ 12,713.00**	**$ 12,511.00**
	$ 23,057.00	$ 26,383.00	$ 26,983.20
Gross Deductions	$ 23,057.00	$ 26,383.00	$ 26,983.20
Standard Deduction	—		
Personal Exemptions	$ 10,500.00	$ 10,500.00	$ 7,000.00
Taxable Income	$ 88,810.20	$ 102,810.95	$ 115,425.38
Fed Income Tax	$ 14,890.05	$ 18,390.24	$ 21,543.84
Fed Tax Bracket-Ord	25%	25%	25%

BASE CASE: BALANCE SHEET OF ED AND AMY MARTINSON

Table 7-3 Base Case: Balance Sheet of Ed and Amy Martinson			
BASE CASE	**Current Year**	**Next Year (Projected)**	**Two Years (Projected)**
LIQUID ASSETS			
Running Total	$ 12,000.00	$ 31,240.95	$ 65,057.71
Cash			
Investable Cash	**$ 23,624.00**	**$ 45,249.00**	**$ 70,869.00**
IRA — Ed	$ 24,323.00	$ 26,293.16	$ 28,422.91
IRA — Amy	$ 25,944.00	$ 28,045.46	$ 30,317.15
MMKT — Larry	$ 25,000.00	$ 25,000.00	$ 25,000.00
	$ 98,891.00	$ 124,587.63	$ 154,609.06
Stocks & Bonds			
Stocks/Bonds — Anne	$ 109,000.00	$ 118,810.00	$ 129,503.00
Growth Mutual Funds	$ 252,138.00	$ 288,970.00	$ 331,183.00
Balanced Mutual Funds	$ 202,312.00	$ 222,446.00	$ 244,584.00
	$ 563,450.00	$ 630,226.00	$ 705,270.00
Life Insurance			
Life insurance CV — Ed	$ 34,425.00	$ 34,425.00	$ 34,425.00
Life insurance CV — Amy	$ 1,800.00	$ 1,800.00	$ 1,800.00
	$ 36,225.00	$ 36,225.00	$ 36,225.00
Liquid Assets	$ 710,566.00	$ 822,279.58	$ 961,161.77
NONLIQUID ASSETS			
Retirement Plans			
401(k)	$ 134,540.00	$ 145,976.00	$ 158,384.00
Ed's Contribution	$ 4,750.00	$ 9,738.00	$ 14,975.00
Ed's Match	$ 4,750.00	$ 9,738.00	$ 14,975.00
Vested Pension	$ 149,625.00	$ 157,106.00	$ 164,961.00
	$ 293,665.00	$ 322,558.00	$ 353,295.00
Personal Property			
Home	$ 580,750.00	$ 586,558.00	$ 592,423.00
Ed's Car	$ 17,000.00	$ 14,450.00	$ 12,283.00
Amy's Car	$ 10,200.00	$ 8,670.00	$ 7,370.00
Home Furnishings	$ 75,000.00	$ 75,000.00	$ 75,000.00
	$ 682,950.00	$ 684,678.00	$ 687,076.00
Nonliquid Assets	$ 976,615.00	$ 1,007,236.00	$ 1,040,371.00
Total Assets	$ 1,687,181.00	$ 1,829,515.58	$ 2,001,532.77
Liabilities			
Mortgage Loan	**$ 117,973.00**	**$ 116,237.00**	**$ 114,370.00**
Car Loan	$ 11,429.00	$ 6,998.00	$ 2,151.00
	$ 129,402.00	$ 123,235.00	$ 116,521.00
Net Worth	**$ 1,557,779.00**	**$ 1,706,280.58**	**$ 1,885,011.77**

BASE CASE: CASH FLOW STATEMENT FOR EDGAR AND AMY MARTINSON

Table 7-4 Base Case: Cash Flow Statement for Edgar and Amy Martinson			
BASE CASE	Current Year	Next Year (Projected)	Two Years (Projected)
BEGINNING OF YEAR			
Idle Cash on Hand	$ 12,000.00	$ 31,240.95	$ 65,057.71
SOURCES OF CASH			
Cash Income			
Compensation	$ 100,000.00	$ 105,000.00	$ 110,250.00
Bonus	$ 10,000.00	$ 10,500.00	$ 11,025.00
Interest & Dividends	$2,038.00	$ 2,072.00	$2,107.00
	$ 112,038.00	$ 117,572.00	$ 123,382.00
Cash Inflow	$ 112,038.00	$ 117,572.00	$123,382.00
Total Cash Available	**$ 124,038.00**	**$ 148,812.95**	**$ 188,439.71**
USES OF CASH			
401(k) Contribution	$ 4,750.00	$ 4,988.00	$ 5,237.00
Mortgage Payment	**$ 14,485.00**	**$14,485.00**	**$14,485.00**
Med Ins	$ 240.00	$ 254.00	$ 270.00
Med Expense	$ 2,800.00	$ 2,968.00	$ 3,146.00
Charitable Contribution	$ 2,000.00	$ 2,060.00	$ 2,122.00
Car Loan	$ 5,280.00	$ 5,280.00	$ 5,280.00
Food	$ 8,000.00	$ 8,240.00	$ 8,487.00
Clothing	$ 3,000.00	$ 3,090.00	$ 3,183.00
Entertainment	$ 2,000.00	$ 2,100.00	$ 2,205.00
Vacations	$ 3,000.00	$ 3,090.00	$ 3,183.00
Transportation	$ 1,000.00	$ 1,040.00	$ 1,082.00
Home Insurance Premium	$ 500.00	$ 510.00	$ 520.00
Prop/Liab Ins	$ 100.00	$ 102.00	$ 104.00
Auto Insurance	$ 1,000.00	$ 1,040.00	$ 1,082.00
Ed Life Premium	$ 2,335.00	$ 2,335.00	$ 2,335.00
Amy Life Premium	$ 125.00	$ 125.00	$ 125.00
Additional Insurance	—	—	—
Home Improvements	$ 1,000.00	$1,030.00	$ 1,061.00
Refinance Costs	—	—	—
Points Paid	—	—	—
Utility/Phone	$ 2,000.00	$ 2,060.00	$ 2,122.00
Personal Care Items	$ 1,300.00	$ 1,339.00	$ 1,379.00
	$ 54,915.00	$ 56,136.00	$ 57,408.00
Income Taxes Paid	$ 14,890.05	$ 18,390.24	$ 21,543.84
State Tax Paid	$ 5,164.00	$ 7,275.00	$ 7,822.00
FICA/Soc Sec Tax	$ 7,963.00	$ 8,416.95	$ 8,627.00
Real Estate Tax	$ 3,000.00	$ 4,275.00	$ 4,403.00
	$ 31,017.05	$38,357.19	$ 42,395.84
Investable Cash	**$ 18,865.00**	**$ 20,503.00**	**$ 24,978.00**
Total Outflow	$ 104,797.05	$ 114,996.19	$ 124,781.84
END OF YEAR			
Cash Balance	$ 31,240.95	$ 65,057.71	$ 128,715.58

PERSONAL PLANNING: TAXES

Present Situation

There are 10 issues stemming from the Martinsons' current tax planning situation that need to be addressed. Each of the following involves financial and/or tax considerations that will affect the Martinsons' ability to achieve their objectives:

- the corporate defined-benefit noncontributory pension plan
- the contributory 401(k) plan
- the tax implications of the residential real estate purchase
- the $50,000 whole life insurance policy
- the individual retirement account (IRA)
- taxability of money market account income
- the reinvestment of income and capital gains in the mutual funds
- the current salary of $100,000
- the nonqualified deferred-compensation plan
- the group term life insurance

The Corporate Defined-Benefit Noncontributory Pension Plan

Ed's employer, Inc, established a qualified noncontributory defined-benefit pension plan that provides a maximum retirement income benefit of 1.5 percent of the average of an employee's highest 5 years of income times the number of years of service, with a maximum of 25 years of service. The plan benefit is not offset by retirement income provided under Social Security.

The Contributory 401(k) Plan

Inc also established a voluntary participation salary-reduction-type 401(k) plan for its employees 6 years ago. At this time almost 85 percent of Inc's employees participate in the plan. For employee contributions up to 5 percent of salary, Inc will contribute 2.5 percent of salary during the first 5 years of service and 3.75 percent until 10 years of service are achieved. After that time Inc will match the employee's 5 percent contribution. The plan further stipulates that employee contributions in excess of 5 percent are permitted but that no increased contribution on the part of Inc shall be made. The 401(k) plan does permit lump-sum withdrawals upon retirement or severance from the employer. The 401(k) plan is self-directed so that plan participants may choose the investment instruments and may shift invested funds within a limited set of alternatives.

Tax Implications of the Residential Real Estate Purchase

When the Martinsons sold their house for $200,000 in 1997 (under pre-1998 tax law), they paid $350,000 for their newly built house, which today has a fair market value of $575,000. The Martinsons' basis in the first house was $58,000. Since a new principal residence was purchased within a 2-year period following the sale of the prior principal residence, the Martinsons' gain on the sale was not recognized for purposes of federal income taxation. However, the original basis in the prior principal residence was carried over. Therefore if the Martinsons were to sell their new home today for $575,000, the cost basis to be used for purposes of determining the capital gain after the Sec. 121 exclusion would be $58,000 plus any additional after-tax funds added to the purchase price.

The $50,000 Whole Life Insurance Policy

When Ed and Amy were married, Ed purchased a $50,000 whole life policy. He is the owner of the policy, and Amy is the primary beneficiary.

Under federal estate tax law if an insured has any "incidents of ownership" in a life insurance policy at the date of death, the face amount of the policy will have to be included in the insured's gross estate for federal estate tax purposes. Since Ed is the policyowner, if he dies today the face amount of the life insurance policy, $50,000, will be included in his gross estate.

The Individual Retirement Account (IRA)

The Martinsons have continuously invested their excess income in several different instruments. During the years that the individual retirement account (IRA) provisions under IRC Sec. 408 permitted fully tax-deductible contributions of up to $5,000 annually for everyone, including those who were also participating in other qualified plans without limitation, Ed funded a personal IRA at the local savings and loan. Although Ed can no longer make deductible contributions to an IRA, the funds that were previously contributed to the plan will continue to generate interest income on a tax-deferred basis until distributions are taken from the plan. (Because Ed is a participant in a corporate pension plan and because his adjusted gross income exceeds the allowable amount, he is prevented under current tax law from making deductible contributions to an individual retirement account.) Ed could consider the possibility of making a contribution to a Roth IRA, since the Martinsons' adjusted gross income is less than $150,000. Contributions to a Roth IRA will not be tax deductible, but future withdrawals will be tax free if the Martinsons comply with the new Roth IRA requirement.

Taxability of Money Market Account Income

The Martinsons jointly own a money market deposit account at the local savings and loan. The account typically has an average balance of about $25,000. Since these funds are not invested in tax-exempt vehicles, the interest income generated by the money market deposit account is currently taxable as ordinary income.

The Reinvestment of Income and Capital Gains in the Mutual Funds

The Martinsons monitor the money market account and if the balance grows too large, the excess is divided between investments in a balanced mutual fund and a growth mutual fund. In both these funds, all dividends and capital gains are being reinvested. The capital gains and dividend reinvestments in the mutual funds will have to be recognized currently as part of the Martinsons' gross income.

The Current Salary of $100,000

Currently Ed's salary is $100,000 per year. This amount is taxable as ordinary income and will translate into a sizable federal income tax liability each year. Unfortunately, there is little that can be done when a taxpayer/client is an employee of a large corporation and does not have the power or influence to determine the internal salary/benefit structure.

The Nonqualified Deferred-Compensation Plan

When Ed was promoted last year, he became a participant in Inc's nonqualified deferred-compensation plan. During the years that Ed will work at Inc, the firm will earmark funds in a separate account to fulfill the deferred-compensation obligation. It should be remembered, however, that these funds are part of Inc's assets and are available to its creditors and not to Ed. At this time, Ed does not have to recognize any current income on these assets.

The Group Term Life Insurance Plan

Inc provides noncontributory group term life insurance in the amount of 1.5 times annual base salary for all employees. IRC Sec. 79 permits the cost of the first $50,000 worth of coverage on an insured-employee to be free of federal income tax. Furthermore, the cost of the additional coverage will be taxable to the insured-employee on a tax-favored basis because of the IRS-approved rate-of-insurance tables.

Treatment of Distributions from the Nonqualified Deferred-Compensation Plan

Nonqualified deferred compensation is an extremely popular employee benefit for executives such as Ed Martinson. The highlights of nonqualified deferred-compensation plans are

- Nonqualified deferred compensation is an employee benefit that allows an employee to defer income taxation of compensation that is earned currently and would therefore be subject to current taxation.
- A properly structured plan will pay the former employee income over a period of years following retirement. The fact that it is *nonqualified* will permit the employer to escape the strict nondiscrimination, reporting, and disclosure requirements that ERISA imposes on qualified plans.
- The employee who participates in the plan enters into an agreement with his or her employer providing that specific payments are to be made to the employee or beneficiaries named by the employee in the event of death, disability, or retirement. Because certain standards must exist in the employer-employee relationship before federal income tax may be effectively deferred, the agreement must contain a clause establishing a contingency that can cause the employee to forfeit rights to future payments.

There are several federal income tax consequences of nonqualified deferred compensation that must be considered. It is helpful to separately analyze the federal tax implications affecting the employer and those affecting the employee.

The Employer

- Usually the employer funds the nonqualified deferred-compensation plan with life insurance acquired on the life of the employee. The employer pays the premiums, but premiums are not deductible for federal income tax purposes.

- To fund the retirement obligation, the employer frequently uses one of the settlement options available under the terms of the life insurance policy. A part of each installment payment the employer receives will be taxable income under the annuity rules. Sometimes, however, the employer will choose to surrender the policy and receive a lump-sum payment. In this case the amount that exceeds the employer's cost will be taxed as ordinary income.

- Any death proceeds the employer receives at the employee's death are free of federal income tax.

- The employer will generate a federal income tax deduction when the benefits are paid either to the employee or to the employee's family after the employee's death.

The Employee

- While employed, the plan participant is not required to include in gross income the portion of compensation that is deferred under the deferred-compensation plan.

- Any benefit the employee or the employee's named beneficiaries receive will be taxed as ordinary income when received.

There are also federal estate tax implications stemming from participation in a nonqualified deferred-compensation plan. The present value of the future benefits of a nonqualified deferred-compensation benefit payable to an employee or an employee's named beneficiary will be includible in the employee's gross estate for federal estate tax purposes. Estate inclusion is required because the employee had a present right to receive a future income stream under the deferred-compensation plan.

Creation of a Fund for Scott

Because of Scott's medical situation, the Martinsons should begin to fund a separate account for Scott's benefit. Several approaches may be considered including

- outright gifts
- 529 Accounts
- 2503(b) trusts
- 2503(c) trusts
- UGMA gifts

Each of these vehicles will be explored separately.

Outright Gifts and 529 Plans for Scott — Limited Viability

IRC Sec. 2503(b) allows a donor to exclude the first $13,000 of value from gift tax if a gift of a present interest is made. If the donor of the gifted property is married, the spouse can split the gift, doubling the amount of the allowable annual exclusion to $26,000. This annual exclusion applies to each donee of the gifted property and applies per calendar year. Since Scott will need funds for the balance of his life, it would be a prudent planning step for Ed and Amy to begin a continuous and concerted gifting effort. However, making outright gifts to Scott would not be wise under these facts since no control could be imposed on Scott's spending.

Sec. 529 College Savings Accounts may also be a way to save money toward's Scott's future. The accounts would grow tax deferred, and if distributions were used for eventual higher education expenses, they would be free of income taxation. Considering Scott's medical condition, they may limit the amount used to fund a 529 plan.

The Sec. 2503(b) Trust

Given Amy and Ed's objective to provide Scott with a lifetime supplemental income, they should consider lifetime or testamentary transfers of assets into a trust so that Scott will have the supplemental income available to him. It is advisable for Ed and Amy to begin to transfer assets now to a trust for Scott's benefit in order to avoid gift or estate taxation on the posttransfer appreciation.

Ed and Amy could make inter vivos asset transfers to a trust. IRC Sec. 2503(b) provides that $13,000 ($26,000 for a married couple) worth of property may be transferred free of federal gift taxation as long as the gift is a completed gift and as long as it is a "gift of a present interest." Because this annual exclusion is such a valuable technique, it is prudent to make use of it on a regular basis.

The Sec. 2503(b) trust permits the donor to apply the annual exclusion to property transferred into the trust. The trust *requires* income to be distributed at least annually to (or for the use of) the minor beneficiary. The trust agreement identifies the income beneficiary. The minor beneficiary receives the trust's principal whenever the trust agreement specifies. A distribution of principal does not have to be made by age 21; corpus may be held for as long as the beneficiary lives—or for any shorter period of time. As a practical matter the principal can actually bypass the income beneficiary and go directly to other individuals whom the grantor—or even the named beneficiary—has specified. The trust instrument itself can also control the pattern of asset distribution in the event that the minor dies prior to receiving the corpus of the trust. It is not necessary that trust assets be paid to the minor's estate or appointees.

Many feel that the mandatory payment of income to (or in behalf of) the beneficiary will become burdensome—especially while the beneficiary is still a minor. Income distributions could be deposited in a custodial account and used for the minor's benefit or left to accumulate in a custodial account until the minor attains majority. Ed and Amy should create a 2503(b) trust at this time for Scott's benefit. The primary advantage of using the Sec. 2503(b) trust is that principal need not be distributed when the minor reaches age 21. Since Scott is 16, the adverse consequences of the kiddie tax are not a consideration.

The Sec. 2503(c) Trust

Unlike a Sec. 2503(b) trust, a Sec. 2503(c) trust requires that income and principal be distributed when the beneficiary attains age 21 but does not require the trustee to distribute income on an annual basis.

Gifts to a Sec. 2503(c) trust qualify for the gift tax annual exclusion if the following requirements are met:

- income and principal must be expended by or on behalf of the beneficiary
- to the extent that it is not so expended, income and principal must pass to the beneficiary at age 21 or
- if the beneficiary dies prior to that time, income and principal will go to the beneficiary's estate or to appointees under a general power of appointment

One of the primary advantages of the Sec. 2503(c) trust is the significant degree of flexibility that can be built into the arrangement. Income that has been accumulated, in addition to any principal in the trust, can be paid to the donee when he or she attains age 21. Given the facts presented here, however, Ed and Amy will probably want the trust to continue to age 25, 30, or even longer. It is possible to provide continued management of the trust assets and at the same time avoid forfeiting the annual exclusion by giving the donee, at age 21, a right for a limited period to require immediate distribution by giving written notice to the trustee. If the beneficiary fails to give written notice, the trust can continue automatically for whatever period the donor specified when he or she created the arrangement. This is a technique that Ed and Amy will want to consider.

To summarize, Ed and Amy anticipate that because of their son's unfortunate medical situation, he will need financial assistance throughout his life. Rather than having assets pass through Ed and/or Amy's estate and having federal estate tax imposed at what will be a higher tax liability (particularly if the assets appreciate in value), the assets can be gifted into either a Sec. 2503(b) or 2503(c) trust. The annual exclusion will be available in both types of trusts. To the extent that the value of the property transferred into the trust exceeds the annual exclusion amount, a gift tax will be payable, but the applicable credit will eliminate the need to actually pay any gift tax. As a practical matter it is more prudent to pay federal transfer tax on assets valued at today's lower values than to have appreciating assets pass through an estate, triggering a higher federal transfer tax.

Uniform Gifts to Minors Act

The Uniform Gifts to Minors Act (and Uniform Transfers to Minors Act) provide an alternative to the Sec. 2503(c) trust. The UGMA (and UTMA) is frequently used for smaller gifts because of its simplicity and because it offers the benefits of management, income and estate shifting, and the investment characteristics of a trust with few or none of the start-up costs associated with the use of trusts.

The Uniform Gifts to Minors Act and Uniform Transfers to Minors Act have been adopted in every state. The acts allow lifetime gifts of securities, money, a life insurance or annuity policy, or other property (which differs on a state-by-state basis) to an individual who is a minor on the date of the gift.

Because Scott is 16 and already in high school, he will attain majority in a few short years and have ready access to the accumulated funds. Therefore the use of the UGMA approach is not recommended in this case.

Dispositions at Death

So far our analysis has focused primarily on lifetime planning concerns. These issues should be addressed as soon as possible. Another integral component of the comprehensive financial planning process is estate planning.

Revision of Estate Plan

The Martinsons have wills they have not updated since they were married, and these wills no longer address their estate planning needs. At this time revision is needed to reflect their changed personal and financial situation. Because of the unlimited federal estate tax marital deduction, many tax advisers encourage the full use of the unlimited marital deduction of the estate by the first spouse to die. This approach will assure a deferral (but not a total forgiveness) of federal estate taxation at the first death. Of course, the tax will be imposed at the death of the second spouse. When the first spouse dies, the applicable credit should be used in combination with the federal estate tax marital deduction in estates where the combined assets of the husband and wife are greater than the amount of a single applicable credit exemption equivalent.

The most important objective within the estate planning framework is not only to plan the estate of the first spouse to die but also to anticipate the planning needs at the surviving spouse's subsequent death. In any situation in which the unlimited federal estate tax marital deduction is utilized (as it is here because of the Martinsons' use of their respective "simple wills" that leave all estate assets to the surviving spouse), the applicable credit of the first spouse to die is wasted. The result is that the entire value of marital deduction assets will end up being taxed in the estate of the surviving spouse.

The Martinsons' revised wills should direct the integration of the applicable credit exemption equivalent with the marital deduction amount. Use of a credit shelter trust prevents over qualification of the marital deduction as illustrated under the current scenario. This revision ensures that the applicable credit will not be "wasted."

An alternative approach would be an estate plan in which assets equal in value to the applicable credit equivalent can be directed by an appropriate will to a trust that provides the surviving spouse with access to the funds without requiring inclusion of the trust's assets in the surviving spouse's gross estate. The surviving spouse's access may be totally unrestricted, or it may be restricted if that is the Martinsons' wish.

Assuming Ed predeceases Amy, a portion of his estate assets should be placed into a testamentary trust for the benefit of Scott. Of course, a sufficient amount of assets would need to pass for the benefit of Amy in order to qualify for the estate tax marital deduction.

Analysis of Present Situation

All property a decedent owns at the date of death is included in the gross estate. The larger the taxable estate, the larger the estate tax liability. Therefore the starting point is determining the size of the gross estate. Once this has been accomplished, we can then make recommendations to reduce the amount of the projected federal estate tax liability.

The current ownership of the life insurance policies poses a problem because Ed possesses incidents of ownership over the policies. Under IRC Sec. 2042(2) the face amount of these policies will be required to be included in Ed's gross estate for federal estate tax purposes.

Concept of "Equity of Inheritance"

Ed and Amy are caring and fair parents who love both their children. They do not show favoritism to either one of them. However, Scott's accident and subsequent medical problems have made it difficult to reconcile their philosophy of equity with the fact that Scott will need more financial aid than Bea.

One vexing issue that Ed and Amy have discussed is the favorable treatment that Bea has already received. First, they paid her college education expenses, and her degree has enabled her to begin a promising career with the potential for a high income. In addition, Bea was the sole recipient of Ed's mother's largesse (Scott was not born at the time of her demise) and now has a nice nest egg of her own. Because of these two considerations, Ed and Amy believe that their objective to fund a program designed to provide a lifetime income for Scott tends to equalize the financial benefits bestowed on both children. This view of equity may also involve unequal distributions from their estates.

Should the funding for Scott result in any inequitable treatment for Bea, Ed and Amy could acquire some life insurance on their lives at a later date, naming Bea as the beneficiary.

Considerations Stemming from Amy's Family History of Longevity

Because of their age difference the chances are quite good that Amy will outlive Ed by many years. An integral part of the planning process involves resolving the problems stemming from this fact. It is clear that supplemental coverage will be necessary to add to the retirement benefits available from Inc and from Social Security.

The Use of the Irrevocable Life Insurance Trust

The face amount of certain life insurance policies will be included in Ed's gross estate for federal estate tax purposes on the date of his death. Specifically the $50,000 whole life policy will be included in Ed's gross estate because he will own the policy on his life at the time of his death and because IRC Sec. 2042(2) requires inclusion of the policy proceeds of any life insurance policy owned by the decedent-insured at the date of death. For the same reason the two $25,000 policies will also be included in his estate. Removal of the life insurance from Ed's gross estate is an easy yet effective step in the right direction.

IRC Sec. 2042 addresses the issue of includibility of life insurance proceeds in the insured's gross estate. IRC Sec. 2042(1) provides that the face amount of the policy will be included in the insured's gross estate if the estate is named as the beneficiary of the life insurance policy. Nothing in the facts indicates that this is the case here. IRC Sec. 2042(2) provides that to the extent that the decedent-insured possesses any incidents of ownership in the policy, the proceeds will likewise be included in the insured's gross estate. Incidents of ownership not only include situations in which the insured is named as the owner but also include the right on the part of the insured to borrow against the policy, change the beneficiary, pledge the policy against a loan, and so on. If Ed has any incident of ownership in a policy, he must relinquish ownership of the policy to remove the policy proceeds from his gross estate.

Ed could transfer the three whole life insurance policies that he currently owns to Amy, which would clearly remove all policy proceeds from Ed's gross estate (provided he lives for 3 more years) since he would no longer possess any incidents of ownership over the policy. However, cross-ownership of life insurance policies between spouses is not the best approach since the transferee-spouse could predecease the transferor. Furthermore, since divorce is so prevalent in this country, cross-spousal ownership is often unwise.

The preferable approach would be to use an irrevocable life insurance trust (ILIT). Ed could create an ILIT and transfer the three life insurance policies that he currently owns to the trust. Amy and the two children would be named as beneficiaries of the trust. Upon Amy's death, her share of the trust assets would be distributed to the children in equal shares, per stirpes. Because of Scott's medical situation his portion of the policy proceeds should remain in trust for the balance of his life with the named trustee directed to apply income (and principal if necessary) for Scott's benefit. Upon Scott's death, the trust is to terminate, with the trust assets to be distributed to Scott's heirs, if any; if none; to Bea if living; if Bea has predeceased Scott, to her heirs, if any; if none, to a named charity, Ed's college. Bea's portion could be distributed to her outright. The beneficiary of the whole life policies would be the ILIT.

IRC Sec. 2035 provides that if a decedent-insured transfers a life insurance policy and fails to live 3 years following this transfer, the policy proceeds still must be included as part of the insured's gross estate. Therefore Ed should be advised that if he fails to live 3 years following the creation of the irrevocable life insurance trust and the transfer of the policy into the trust, the policy proceeds will still be included in Ed's gross estate for federal estate tax purposes.

PERSONAL PLANNING: WEALTH ACCUMULATION

Amy and Ed desire to accumulate additional funds to ensure an adequate income during their retirement. Until Scott's accident and subsequent medical expenses they anticipated that between Scott's graduation from high school and Ed's retirement they would be able to concentrate their assets on this objective: the accumulation of sufficient funds to provide an additional $5,000 annual income (in current dollars) during their retirement. Considering Scott's failure to recover fully from the accident, they feel they have an obligation to provide a source of income for him for life, apart from sources they might develop for themselves. Their goal is $3,000 per year in current dollars. They estimate that prices will rise an average of 4 percent per year over the entire planning period; therefore the 4 percent inflation rate will apply before and after retirement.

Ed is now 54, and both Amy and he wonder how meeting these two accumulation goals will affect their cash flow. In addition, they are concerned about the impact of these accumulation goals on the possibility of Ed's retiring at age 62 in 8 years. Their target annual income for the income supplements, allowing for 4 percent inflation, is $6,842 for their supplement at age 62 and $7,696 at age 65. For Scott's funding, the target annual income is $4,105 if Ed retires at age 62 and $4,618 at age 65. They have indicated that the retirement supplement should provide an annual income stream for 40 years and that the funds available for Scott should provide him an income stream for 50 years. In both cases they prefer to begin with an age 62 retirement, but Ed does not want to reduce the payout time if his retirement is delayed.

The following table shows the estimated accumulation and annual funding needed for retirement at age 62 and age 65. A 4 percent rate of inflation is assumed for both the preretirement and postretirement periods. Also a 6 percent after-tax rate of return is used for both periods. The funds will be liquidated over the 40-year period as stated above.

Table 7-5 Funding for Retirement Income Supplement				
			Annual Funding	
Ed's Age	Target Annual Income	Lump Sum at Target Age	Level	Rising at 5 Percent Each Year
62	$6,842	$193,378	$16,381	$14,016
65	7,696	217,514	13,705	11,437

The following table shows the estimated accumulation and annual funding needed to achieve their goal of having funds set aside for Scott's benefit. Again the assumptions are made that Ed retires at age 62 and at age 65. The after-tax earnings assumption is 6 percent, the inflation assumption is 3.5 percent, and the payout period for liquidating the accumulation is 50 years.

Table 7-6 Funding for Scott's Income Supplement				
			Annual Funding	
Ed's Age	Target Annual Income	Lump Sum at Target Age	Level	Rising at 5 Percent Each Year
62	$4,105	$133,632	$13,337	$10,831
65	4,618	150,332	9,472	7,547

The Martinsons have $22,000 set aside for Scott's education and doubt that these funds will be used for that purpose. If these funds were integrated into their funding plans, the $22,000 would grow to $35,064 during the next 8 years and to $41,762 during the next 11 years. Using these accumulated educational funds as part of the accumulated funds for Scott's benefit will reduce their annual contributions to those shown in the following table.

Table 7-7 Annual Funding for Scott's Income Supplement Using the Accumulated Educational Funds				
		Lump Sum at Target Age (in Addition to $22,000 Already Accumulated)	Annual Funding	
Ed's Age	Target Annual Income		Level	Rising at 5 Percent Each Year
62	$4,105	$98,568	$9,395	$7,989
65	4,618	108,569	6,841	5,449

The following table consolidates the information developed for the annual funding (both level and at a 5 percent rising amount) with the amount of their cash flow as shown in the base case.

If the Martinsons were to fund these objectives with either a level contribution or an annual contribution that increases by 5 percent each year over an 8-year period, their annual cash flow would be sufficient to meet the amount needed.

Table 7-8 Comparison of Annual Cash Flow and Needed Annual Funding					
Year	Investable Cash Flow (Base Case)	Annual Funding Increasing		Level Funding	
		8-Year	11-Year	8-Year	11-Year
2011	$28,384	$22,005	$16,886	$25,776	$20,546
2012	$30,125	23,105	17,709	25,776	20,546
2013	$34,619	$24,161	18,594	25,776	20,546

The Martinsons also have the following objectives that require use of their cash flow:

- long-term care protection for Scott
- long-term care protection for Amy
- life insurance protection against reduction in income should Ed die first and the pension benefit be reduced
- life insurance protection against estate shrinkage due to loss of the marital deduction

Until the annual costs of these other dimensions of their financial planning are determined, the final recommendation for these two accumulation objectives will be postponed.

PERSONAL PLANNING: INSURANCE

Long-Term Care Protection for Scott

Scott's medical condition is probably the most critical component of the Martinsons' overall financial plan. Since it is likely that Scott will require some form of long-term care protection, the Martinsons must take steps to be sure that this virtually certain development is appropriately addressed as part of the financial planning process.

Scott could be considered uninsurable because of the preexisting medical condition. Therefore the Martinsons must be prepared to provide funding for long-term care for Scott's benefit without the assistance of long-term care coverage.

Long-Term Care Protection for Amy

With Amy's family history of longevity, the Martinsons should acquire long-term care protection for her. The situation is different from Scott's, and the Martinsons will have no problem acquiring this coverage on Amy, as she is in excellent health.

Because a growing number of people over the age of 65 face a significant risk of requiring nursing home services sometime during their remaining years, the insurance industry has made long-term care policies available. The Martinsons should seriously consider acquiring one on Amy as soon as possible.

Long-term care policies contain many differing provisions, and they also differ from one insurance company to another. There are many insurance companies offering long-term care coverage, and the specific range of coverage goes from very limited protection to total and complete protection. The Martinsons need to address the following issues before the appropriate policy can be selected:

- preexisting conditions
- elimination periods
- exclusions

- premium structure
- underwriting
- benefit provisions
- renewability
- inflation protection
- long-term care added to an existing life insurance policy

Preexisting Conditions

Long-term care insurance policies often contain preexisting-condition provisions. For an established time after the policy has been issued benefit payments are excluded for causes stemming from conditions that existed—and for which the insured has previously received medical advice and treatment—within a specified period of time before the policy was issued. Of course, the rationale behind a preexisting condition clause in a long-term care policy is to prevent adverse selection against the insurance company issuing the policy.

The National Association of Insurance Commissioners (NAIC) model contract provides that the preexisting-condition provisions should not exclude benefits for more than 6 months after policy issue and that specific exclusions should not be predicated on conditions that initially showed up more than 6 months prior to the date the policy was issued. Although most of the long-term care policies available today have incorporated and accepted the NAIC model concerning the 6-month standard, some states still permit long-term care policies to adopt a longer preexisting-condition provision. Some insurance companies will require a preexisting-condition provision of longer than 6 months for long-term care policies being issued to persons under the age of 65.

Since Amy is in good health, the preexisting-condition issue will not be a problem for the Martinsons.

Elimination Period

All long-term care policies contain a provision for an elimination or waiting period. The elimination period may be thought of as a form of deductible that establishes the specific time at which the benefits will begin. In essence the elimination or waiting period is the amount of time that will elapse following the point when an insured can satisfy benefit eligibility but when no benefit will be paid. For example, if a long-term care policy contains a 120-day elimination period, the insured would have to be in the caregiving facility for 120 days before the policy benefits would be payable. There would be 120 days of long-term care with no benefits paid, but on the 121st day the benefits would begin and payment would occur 30 days later.

The length of the elimination period affects the premium. The longer the elimination period under the terms of the policy, the lower the premium.

The actual length of elimination periods in long-term care policies can vary dramatically. It is possible for the Martinsons to acquire a long-term care policy with no elimination period (which would be very expensive), with an elimination period of 2 years (with a much lower premium), or with some time period in between. Since this decision involving the elimination period will directly affect costs, it will have to be considered very carefully in light of the their total financial resources available to meet the costs incurred during the elimination period.

Exclusions

All insurance policies that provide any form of health care coverage contain provisions dealing with exclusions. Although the actual exclusions in long-term care insurance policies are usually not very extensive, it is possible that a single exclusion might eliminate benefit payments for a cause for which other carriers could conceivably provide full coverage. Consequently the Martinsons must "shop" very carefully when choosing the appropriate coverage for Amy's long-term care.

Premiums

How the Martinsons pay for the long-term care coverage is of paramount importance. Although the immediate acquisition of this insurance is vital, the premiums can be relatively expensive, so care will have to be devoted to selecting the most cost-effective package. Most long-term care policies have level premiums for the balance of the insured's life, although some insurance carriers structure costs of long-term care products as increasing premiums. In this type of situation premiums will increase on an annual basis or at 2-, 3-, or 5-year intervals with level steps between adjustment points.

Regardless of whether the long-term care premium is level or increasing, the amount of the premium will be determined by the age of the insured at the time the policy is issued. Historically premium increases are significant only after age 40, and they become very steep after age 65. Waiting until age

70 to purchase this coverage could mean a tenfold increase in premium compared to a purchase at age 45.

One last point on the subject of premiums is that insurance carriers will not guarantee premium levels because the concept of long-term care coverage is a new one, and to date there are very few statistics on experience available to carriers. Long-term care policies are presently "guaranteed renewable," which means that the carrier can increase premium rates for all policyowners (for an entire class of policies) but only on the basis of claims experience rather than on the basis of changes in an insured's age or health. This arrangement is due to the fact that, since long-term care policies are so new, there is limited experience data, so all insurance companies could have computed premium levels at too low a figure. If so, in the future the industry might be forced to increase premium levels for existing policies as well as for newly issued products.

Some representative premiums are as follows:

Table 7-9 Female Aged 45		
	Yearly Premium	
$110/Day Benefit	No Inflation Protection	Inflation Protection
3-year benefit period, 20-day waiting period	$247	$413
6-year benefit period, 20-day waiting period	294	491
Lifetime benefit period, 20-day waiting period	N/A	594

Underwriting Principles

The underwriting process has always been a complex aspect of any insurance company's internal operation. Because long-term care policies deal with the health of the insured and because these types of policies are sometimes issued through the older ages, a series of specialized underwriting principles is often necessary. Most carriers that currently market long-term care products have adopted a single classification approach for purposes of underwriting, which means that the insurance carrier will either accept or reject the application for the insurance coverage. However, a few of the carriers that are more involved in the marketing of long-term care products have begun rating policies. As long-term care products continue to grow in popularity and use, it is likely that additional underwriting classifications will be developed.

Benefits

When the Martinsons choose the right long-term care policy for Amy, they will need to be concerned primarily with benefits. Issues to be concerned about are the maximum duration of the benefits provided, the types and levels of care for which benefits will be provided, prerequisites for benefit eligibility, and the actual level of benefits payable.

With respect to duration the Martinsons will consider the fact that some long-term care policies provide unlimited benefit periods that would allow the insured to enjoy coverage for any length of stay required in a nursing home. The Martinsons will also learn, however, that some long-term care policies specify a maximum benefit duration such as 3 years or 5 years. Some policies will provide coverage for as short a period as one year. The Martinsons will need to select the appropriate coverage realizing, of course, that the longer the benefit period is, the more comprehensive the policy's level of protection will be.

With respect to the benefit payable, most long-term care policies will set forth the benefit as a specified dollar amount per day of benefit eligibility. The Martinsons must be especially cautious to select an adequate benefit level to provide the necessary protection for Amy.

Inflation Protection

Almost all long-term care policies contain some form of inflation protection or offer an inflation rider. This protection will come in the form of either an automatic increase in the benefit each year on a formula basis linked to a measure of inflation or a guarantee that the insured will have the opportunity to purchase additional increments of coverage at certain specified, preestablished intervals. Which approach is used is not too critical. The important thing is that the Martinsons must be sure to have some form of inflation protection.

Renewability

From the perspective of renewability there are two different types of long-term care policies currently available in the marketplace. Some insurance carriers market a long-term care product that is *conditionally renewable*. This type of policy sets forth specified, preestablished conditions that authorize the carrier either to refuse to renew the policy or to cancel the in-force protection. The Martinsons should be sure to avoid this type of policy. The other, referred to as *guaranteed renewable,* provides that the insured will be able to maintain the coverage in force as long as the premiums are paid when they come due. The insurance carrier that has issued the long-term care policy will be unable to refuse to renew the insurance protection or otherwise terminate the coverage for any reason whatsoever other than for nonpayment of premiums. Although this is the type of coverage that the Martinsons should select, it is somewhat more costly.

Benefit Period

Studies have shown that the average stay in a full-service care facility is less than 3 years. Many carriers are currently offering policies that provide coverage at the customer's preference, for any number of years from one to 6 inclusive or for life. Since the average stay in a full-service care facility is less than 3 years, it is tempting for clients to select a 3-year benefit period. In Amy's case purchasing a policy with a $110-per-day benefit, a 3-year benefit, a 20-day elimination period, and inflation protection represents an approximate annual savings of $181 per year when compared to a similar policy with a lifetime benefit—$594 versus $413. However, the major purpose of insurance is to protect against the worst-case financial scenario, not the average case. Thus Amy should select lifetime coverage, especially because of her family history of higher-than-average longevity.

Medicaid Spend-Down Strategy

Some planners have advised clients to select a short benefit period as part of a so-called "spend-down" strategy to maximize benefits available from Medicaid. This Medicaid benefit would be automatically processed if the care facility were Medicare approved. (Medicaid cannot reimburse a facility for services provided unless it is Medicare approved.) This strategy poses ethical hazards for financial advisers. They may wish to maximize public benefits available to a client, but this strategy could be considered taking advantage of an economically strapped public system.

One of Medicaid's programs provides financial assistance for individuals who need long-term care and whose income and nonexempt assets fall below state-specified levels. For individuals whose income or assets are above these levels, this spend-down strategy circumvents the restrictions so that the government, rather than the clients, will foot the bill for long-term care.

The spend-down approach usually involves the client's gifting enough assets to his or her adult children to reduce the individual's nonexempt assets below the state's threshold level. Assets exempt under federal guidelines include a primary residence if the spouse or a minor or disabled child still lives there, household effects, an automobile, and a prepaid burial contract. Each state has its own rules regarding other exemptions such as life insurance and securities.

Since Social Security payments and pension income are included in the maximum income threshold and cannot be gifted, it is critical to verify whether these income flows will preclude the client from qualifying for Medicaid.

Gifts must be irrevocable with no strings attached, and the client must refrain from filing for Medicaid coverage until at least 60 months after gifting the assets. If the client files before 60 months pass, Medicaid will deny benefits under its look-back provision according to the following formula:

Number of months ineligible for Medicaid benefits =

Total value of all assets transferred during look-back period ÷ Average monthly cost of private nursing home

---

EXAMPLE
An incapacitated client applies for admission to a high-quality, Medicare-approved care facility. He retains assets until admitted in case the facility questions the ability to pay the monthly bill. The client then gifts assets to his adult children. The client retains an amount of nonexempt assets sufficient to make 60 months of care facility payments plus just enough additional nonexempt assets to stay below the Medicaid asset threshold. Sixty months after gifting the money, the client applies for Medicaid to pay for his care in the facility. Since the care facility is Medicare-approved, it must accept Medicaid's compensation as payment in full and cannot evict the client even though the payment may be below market rates.

If the spend-down strategy is designed in advance of the client's incapacity, he can purchase long-term care insurance with a benefit period equal to or slightly greater than the Medicaid look-back period. Thus, instead of paying out-of-pocket for 60 months while in the facility, the client receives insurance benefits.

A more efficient approach for the Martinsons to insulate themselves from potential financial disaster resulting from long-term care is to purchase a long-term care insurance policy with a lifetime benefit period. The additional expense relative to a 5-year benefit is relatively small, and owning such a policy eliminates the need for a strategy that may prove counterproductive.

Long-Term Care Added to Existing Life Insurance Coverage

So far we have looked at long-term care policies that are issued for a specific, one-dimensional purpose. There are some insurance carriers that have combined life insurance coverage with long-term care protection. This is accomplished administratively by adding a rider to the existing life insurance policy.

This rider accelerates the payment of a previously established portion of the death benefit to the insured when the insured becomes critically ill, requires custodial care, and is not expected to recover. In this situation a percentage of the face amount will be paid each year for a specified number of years.

Until the passage of the Health Insurance Portability and Accountability Act of 1996, life insurance proceeds when distributed in this manner to the insured have been treated as ordinary income for federal income tax purposes. This act provides that accelerated death benefits received by an individual from the insurer may be excluded from gross income if certain requirements are met. The act distinguishes two categories of individuals who can meet these requirements in whole or in part:

- The first is a terminally ill individual. This individual has obtained certification from a physician that death is reasonably expected to occur within 24 months of the date of certification. For this individual, the accelerated death benefits would be excluded from his or her gross income.

- The second is a chronically ill individual. This individual has been certified within the preceding 12-month period by a licensed health care practitioner as being unable to perform at least two activities of daily living for at least 90 days, certified as having a similar level of disability or requiring substantial supervision because of severe cognitive impairment. This individual can exclude accelerated death benefits from income if the benefit payment is for the actual costs of incurred qualified long-term care not compensated by insurance or otherwise. This rule applies for lump-sum accelerated death benefits that are received by the individual. However, if the accelerated death benefits are determined by a per diem, rather than a lump-sum, method, then the entire amount received from the insurer would be excludible from gross income regardless of the actual costs incurred by the individual.

In the Martinsons' situation, adding the rider that obtains accelerated death benefits to an existing life insurance policy is not appropriate for two reasons. First, when a separate long-term care policy is used, the annual premium qualifies as a potential medical deduction subject to the 7.5 percent-of-adjusted-gross-income rule. Second, at this time there is not sufficient life insurance coverage on Amy's life to make this a feasible rider to an existing policy.

Current Life Insurance Coverage: Comparison of Present Status with Estimated Needs and Recommendations for Coverage and Form of Ownership

The case narrative explains Ed and Amy's current life insurance situation. Ed is the insured on a $50,000 whole life insurance policy with an annual premium of $1,120. He is the owner of the policy, and he named Amy as the primary beneficiary. He subsequently named his two children, Bea and Scott, as the contingent beneficiaries, per stirpes.

Amy converted her group term life insurance to a $5,000 whole life policy with a $5,000 face value and named Ed as the primary beneficiary. For this policy it is recommended that the children be named as primary beneficiaries and that a charity be named as successor beneficiary. The two children have been named as contingent beneficiaries, per stirpes. Ed is also the owner and the insured on two $25,000 policies that have a combined premium of $1,215 and a total cash value of $16,325. Each of these $25,000 policies was acquired when a Martinson child was born. Each child is the named primary beneficiary on one policy, and Amy is the contingent beneficiary for both policies.

The financial services professional must determine whether the current coverage is adequate. Our starting point will be to compute the approximate "cost of dying." Expenditures such as costs of administration, paying off debts, federal estate tax, and state inheritance tax (if any) need to be considered. Next the amount of available liquid assets will be ascertained. Finally a decision about the adequacy of the current life insurance coverage can then be reached.

From the data presented in the case, Ed and Amy's gross estates are $1,627,800 and $362,900 respectively, determined as follows:

	Ed's Gross Estate	Amy's Gross Estate
Checking account	$ 6,000	$ 6,000
Money market deposit account	12,500	12,500
Residence	287,500	287,500
Life insurance—whole life	50,000	
Life insurance	25,000	
Life insurance	25,000	
Life insurance		5,000
IRA	22,200	
IRA		2,400
Balanced fund	184,000	
Growth fund	330,000	
401(k) bond fund	50,000	
401(k) stock fund	74,000	
Group term life insurance	157,500	
Nonqualified deferred compensation	52,000	
Vested pension benefit	190,000	
Common stock	104,000	
Household furnishings	37,500	37,500
Auto	20,000	
Auto		12,000
Miscellaneous	600	
Gross estate	$1,627,800	$362,900

The case narrative states that Ed and Amy have simple, reciprocal wills. This type of will leaves all of the deceased's respective estate properties to the surviving spouse.

Based on the data above, Ed's gross estate is $1,627,800, and his total costs at the date of death will be as follows:

Table 7-10 At Ed's death:

Ed's Estate Computations	Ed's Estate	Shrinkage
Gross estate	$1,627,800	
Less costs of administration (8 percent)	130,224	$130,224
Less mortgage	120,097	
Adjusted gross estate	1,377,479	
Less federal estate tax marital deduction	1,377,479	
Taxable estate	-0-	
Federal estate tax	-0-	
Less unified credit	N/A	
Federal estate tax owed	-0-	-0-
State inheritance tax	-0-	-0-
Total estate shrinkage at Ed's death		$130,224

Table 7-11 At Amy's subsequent death:

Amy's Estate Computations	Amy's Estate	Shrinkage
Gross estate*	$1,740,379	
Less costs of administration (8 percent)	139,230	$139,230
Adjusted gross estate	1,601,149	
Less federal estate tax marital deduction		-0-
Taxable estate	1,601,149	
Federal estate tax	601,317	
Less unified credit	601,317	
Federal estate tax owed	0	0
State inheritance tax	-0-	-0-
Total estate shrinkage at Amy's death		$139,230
Total shrinkage at both deaths		$278,460
*Assumes no increase in value of assets in her name		

In a simple will arrangement, all estate property passes to the surviving spouse. Therefore, all of Ed's property passes to Amy. This means that although the full federal estate tax marital deduction is available for use by Ed's estate at his (the first) death, too much estate property could be passed to Amy and would be taxed without the benefit of a marital deduction at her subsequent death. While there is no estate tax at this time, a marital deduction that integrates the benefits of the applicable credit with the marital deduction concept would be more prudent.

There are sufficient liquid assets available at the time of Ed's death (including the present value of the future benefit of the vested pension). Therefore from an estate liquidity perspective there is no need for additional life insurance.

However, there are several reasons why additional life insurance coverage on Ed's life may be necessary:

- to fund Scott's income supplement
- to fund retirement income supplements for Amy
- to provide funds to pay estate obligations at Ed's and Amy's deaths
- to supplement loss of income when Ed dies
- to equalize Bea's inheritance, if needed

Insurance to Fund Income Supplements for Ed and Amy's Retirement and for Scott

To achieve Ed's desire to retire at age 62, the Martinsons will need to accumulate approximately $200,000. An additional $100,000 for Scott's benefit must also be accumulated. This combined amount of $300,000 will be in jeopardy if Ed dies before funding is completed. If an after-tax rate of return of 6 percent can be earned, then the present value of the $300,000 is about $190,000. This is the amount of life insurance needed on Ed's life. Since this insurance need is temporary, term insurance would be appropriate. Level term would have the Martinsons paying an annual premium for more insurance than they need for this purpose. The additional premium needed to pay for the level term is a relatively small cost that the Martinsons should be able to afford. This insurance will cost approximately $800 per year. Note that the group term insurance on Ed's life is not taken into consideration here since Ed would like to use the group term insurance as an additional cushion to ensure he can meet his goals.

Because of the cost saving in having only one policy in the amount of $190,000 rather than two separate policies, a single policy should be purchased. The Martinsons' interests will be best served if Ed does not have any incidents of ownership in this policy because at his death the face amount of the policy will be included in his estate. An irrevocable life insurance trust containing a Crummey provision can be established that will apply for and own the policy. Ed will contribute sufficient money each year to pay the premium, and at his death the trust will use the proceeds to complete the funding for Scott and Amy.

Equalization of Benefit for Bea

Scott's unfortunate medical condition means that more of Ed and Amy's estate assets will probably pass to him so that after his parents' deaths he will be assured of being adequately cared for. Bea may have mixed feelings about this situation. Surely she understands that she is more fortunate than her brother and does not actually fault her parents for leaving more assets to Scott than to her. After all, Bea is healthy, self-sufficient, and better able to take care of herself. Despite Bea's understanding attitude about the situation, at some times she might feel that an inequity has transpired.

Ed and Amy are good parents as well as perceptive individuals. They know that a form of inequity would take place if Scott received more of the estate assets. To prevent any perceived inequity of treatment, the use of life insurance is recommended. Ed should acquire a life insurance policy on his own life with a face amount equal to the excess value of assets that will ultimately pass to Scott. In order to avoid inclusion of the policy proceeds in Ed's gross estate for federal estate tax purposes, Bea could be named as owner of the policy. More significantly, however, Bea should also be named as the primary beneficiary of the policy. At Ed's death Bea will receive policy proceeds in an amount that will eliminate what would otherwise be an inequity between her and her brother regarding the receipt of valuable estate assets.

Since the Martinsons want to treat both children in an equitable manner, they feel that some specific assets should become available to Bea to balance the funds being accumulated for Scott's benefit. The total accumulation for Scott will be about $122,000. Since the Martinsons spent about $60,000 for Bea's education, an additional $60,000 would be a reasonable amount to give Bea to achieve their desire for equalization.

A $60,000 whole life insurance policy on Ed's life should be acquired for this purpose. An interest-sensitive insurance product would place too much risk on the Martinsons, given their age. As with the previous insurance recommendation, the same life insurance trust would be the appropriate vehicle. The premium would then be a gift of a present interest for federal gift tax purposes, and the proceeds, *if* the trust applied for and owned the policy, would not be included in Ed's estate.

This insurance need, as well as the insurance need described in the next section, should be purchased as one policy. The trustee can be directed to distribute $60,000 of the total proceeds to Bea.

Additional Income for Amy Should Ed Die First

Should Ed predecease Amy, there will be a reduction in the amount of the Social Security benefits payable to her. Indeed, there may be a period of years when her age prevents her from receiving a surviving spouse's benefit, and this gap must be provided for. In addition, if Ed and Amy choose a joint and 50 percent survivor pension, there will be a sizable setback due to the age difference. This is part of the reason why the Martinsons want to set up the fund that will provide them with the additional $5,000 income each year. Also if Ed dies first, Amy will have a reduction in the benefit from Inc's pension plan, so some additional provision for the Social Security and pension reductions should be part of their overall financial plan.

If Amy was old enough to receive Social Security benefits as Ed's surviving spouse, there would be a reduction (loss of spousal benefit) in these benefits of approximately $400 per month ($4,800 per year). Ed's pension, based on $105,000 as his estimated 5-year average salary under the plan, would be $37,500 before applying the plan's setback for both early retirement at age 62 and the age differential. The combined effect of these setbacks reduces the pension by $12,000 to $25,500 yearly. At Ed's death this amount would be further reduced by 50 percent. It is this subsequent reduction for which the Martinsons must make some provision.

Although the Social Security benefit will decline, it is not necessary for the Martinsons to replace this income for Amy except for the few years during which she might not qualify for the benefit if she is under age 60. A fund of about $50,000 should be adequate. For the pension reduction the replacement need is $12,500 annually. If this annual total reduction of $17,300 for the Social Security gap and pension-reduced benefits is capitalized at 7.2 percent, then $240,000 of income-producing assets will be needed to provide the income replacement for Amy. Since the Martinsons' excess cash flow will be used to fund the supplemental income streams for their retirement and for Scott's need, they will also need insurance to fund Amy's need for income replacement.

However, there is an existing $50,000 of insurance on Ed's life, which can be used to reduce the amount of insurance protection needed for meeting Amy's need. (The two $25,000 policies on Ed's life were purchased to benefit the children and should therefore not be used to fund additional income replacement coverage for Amy.) Therefore an additional $190,000 ($240,000 – $50,000) of insurance is needed to achieve the necessary target. Ed should be the insured, and the life insurance trust should apply for and own the policy. The annual cost for one participating whole life policy in the amount of $250,000 ($190,000 + $60,000) is $8,800.

Review of Accidental Death and Dismemberment Coverage

Ed has an accidental death and dismemberment policy as an employee benefit from Inc. The policy carries a death benefit of double Ed's annual base salary. This coverage is in addition to other employment-related life insurance. Because Ed travels frequently on business, such a benefit is a good one and is adequate. There seems to be no need for Ed to have any additional accidental death coverage on an individual basis. To the extent that Ed does decide to acquire more coverage, whole life or universal life would be more appropriate than additional accidental death coverage.

Review of Disability Insurance

The case narrative indicates that Ed receives short-term disability benefits as part of his benefits package from Inc. Specifically coverage for 100 percent of lost salary for short-term disability (maximum of 6 months) is provided under a nonfunded wage contribution plan. Salary lost due to a disability that is serious enough to prevent a return to work after a 6-month period is replaced at 75 percent (including Social Security disability benefits) for the duration of the disability or until normal retirement age, whichever comes first. In the event of disability Inc will continue to credit years of service for purposes of coverage in the qualified pension plan and will make both the employer and the employee contributions to the 401(k) plan. Also the facts indicate that coverage will be continued under Inc's medical insurance plan at no charge to the disabled employee.

The issue is whether the employer-sponsored disability benefit is ample or whether Ed should purchase additional coverage on an individual basis. As stated earlier, Ed estimates a need of an additional $2,000 per month if he becomes disabled. It is therefore clear that the current employer-provided disability package is inadequate. One recommendation is for Ed to purchase individual disability insurance coverage that pays $2,000 a month until age

65 and has an annual cost of $1,220. Having the insurance until age 65 protects Ed should he not retire at age 62 as planned.

Review of Medical Coverage for Both Ed and Amy

Under the current arrangement Ed is covered by Inc's comprehensive medical insurance plan. Such coverage provides $500,000 of lifetime coverage for each family member. Each year after a $250 per-person deductible the insurance provides coverage for 80 percent of the first $5,000 of covered benefits for the family. After $5,000 of covered benefits is reached, additional covered medical expenses are paid in full under the terms of the policy.

The plan is noncontributory for employee coverage. Dependent coverage is available only if the employee will contribute to the cost of the coverage, for which the employee will pay $20 monthly. When an employee retires at normal retirement age (65), Inc pays the full cost of the Medicare supplemental insurance for both the employee and the employee's spouse. Inc is currently studying the possibility of (1) discontinuing its payments for the supplemental Medicare insurance, (2) having the retired employee pay the coverage under a group plan, or (3) having the employee make contributions during his or her employment years toward the retirement medical insurance. Ed would be affected as a future retiree and may need to review expected postretirement medical coverage should Inc change its existing plan.

Summary of Insurance Needs

The following table summarizes the Martinsons' insurance needs, for which the yearly costs total $11,414.

Table 7-12 Recommended Insurance for the Martinsons		
Purpose	Policy Type	Cost Per Year
Disability income protection for Ed	Disability income	1,220
Income supplements for Scott and the Martinsons	Yearly renewable term	800
Income supplement for Amy when Ed dies	Whole life	8,800
Long-term care for Amy	Long-term care	594

Recommendations for the Martinsons

Comparison of their cash inflow and cash outflow over the 4-year period shows that the Martinsons currently have sufficient cash to provide the supplemental income funding and acquire their needed insurance. For 2008–2010, they could consider reducing their idle cash at the start of the year with the intention of replacing the funds using their excess cash inflow for 2010 and future years.

| | | Cash Outflow | | |
Year	Investable Cash Inflow (Base Case)	8-Year Increasing Annual Funding	Projected Insurance Costs	Cash Inflow Minus Cash Outflow
2011	$28,384	$22,005	$11,414	($5,035)
2012	30,125	23,105	11,414	(4,394)
2013	34,619	24,161	11,414	(956)

Table 7-13 Martinsons' Projected Cash Inflows and Outflows to Meet Objectives

In family situations where financial success depends on the earnings of one family member—in this case Ed—adequate life and disability income insurance to provide the future income stream of the surviving family members normally takes precedence over competing uses for scarce dollars. For the Martinsons, then, the recommendation is that they acquire the following insurance in the amounts previously stated in the insurance section:

- whole life insurance on Ed for the purpose of protecting Amy in case he should die before her
- level term life insurance on Ed to assure completion of the accumulation funding for their retirement years and for Scott
- disability income insurance to provide income equal to what would have been earned until age 65

The long-term care insurance covering Amy could be deferred for several years without significantly increasing the current annual premium. Other insurances are assumed to be purchased today.

One point to note with this recommended insurance package is that Ed is slightly overprotected with the level term insurance used to fund the income supplements. Should Ed die, these excess insurance proceeds can be channeled to provide additions to the income stream being provided for Amy.

These recommendations specify that the remainder of their cash flows be channeled into investment assets as outlined in the investment section. In addition, if Ed's income from Inc increases more than anticipated over the 4-year planning horizon, then every effort should be made to add this income to the after-tax fund. Their net cash flow will become positive in 2013.

Although Ed expressed a desire to retire early, he did not make a firm commitment to retiring at age 62. Subsequent evaluations of the progress toward goal achievement might reveal that age 62 is feasible or perhaps that retirement at age 63 would best serve their aggregate goal achievement if sufficient funds have not been accumulated.

PERSONAL PLANNING: INVESTMENT

Refinancing the Home

Because of the decline in mortgage rates, the Martinsons should consider refinancing their home to lower the current monthly payment of $1,207.11, of which $1,080 is interest. When questioned, they reveal that they prefer a fixed-rate mortgage since they want to avoid the risk associated with mortgages that have an adjustable rate. They are willing to finance the existing $120,097 balance of their loan. However, they do not want to remove any of their equity in their home by refinancing more than the unpaid balance.

Because of a trend in standardization in the secondary mortgage market, most lenders offer fixed-rate mortgages with only 15- and 30-year maturities. A review of local rates has revealed that a 15-year mortgage at a rate of 7.25 percent with three points is available for a monthly principal-plus-interest payment of $1,096.32.

If the Martinsons choose a 30-year mortgage, the rate rises to 7.5 percent with three points, but the payment drops to $839.74, of which $750.61 is interest. Of course, this means that they have to make payments for 9 years longer than the current mortgage requires.

An alternative approach involves obtaining a 30-year mortgage and then making payments using a 21-year amortization schedule to match the current loan. This appeals to many clients since they often prefer not to extend the payment period beyond their original obligation. This calculation results in a planned payment of $947.76, but the required payment remains at $839.74.

The Martinsons' home mortgage interest is tax deductible. The interest payment in the 49th (current) month of the existing loan is $1,080.88. The after-tax mortgage payment for the 25 percent tax bracket is $936.89, calculated as follows: $1,207.11 – ($1,080.88 × 0.25). (Note that if mortgage interest is deductible at the state and/or local level, those marginal rates should be added to the federal marginal rate for this calculation.) Of course, interest on the mortgage declines every month, so the after-tax cost rises every month. At the time of the last mortgage payment, the after-tax cost will be within $5 of the mortgage payment. For the 30/21 year approach, the initial monthly after-tax cash outflow is $760.11, calculated as follows: $947.76 – ($750.61 × 0.25).

Both the 15-year mortgage and the 30-year mortgage require an immediate payment of three discount points to the lender ($3,602.92). Under current regulations, this is deductible but must be amortized over the life of the loan. (The original loan had no discount points.) Each of the proposed loans will also require other fees, including legal expenses, appraisal fees, and title insurance, totaling $2,850, which are not deductible.

The Martinsons should evaluate the proposed refinancing carefully. First, they must decide if the changes in cash flows caused by the new loan are affordable since discount points plus other fees total $6,452.92. Fortunately, the Martinsons have the ability and willingness to commit the funds. Second, they should analyze the proposals in greater detail, including the use of discounted cash-flow techniques.

The Martinsons can calculate break even months by dividing any discount points and fees over monthly tax savings. $6,452.92/$179.28 yields 36 months.

Based on the foregoing, it will be 36 months before the monthly savings of the new loan total the costs associated with obtaining that loan. (It should be noted that the break-even would have been shorter if payments were made on a 30-year amortization, but the Martinsons' monthly payments would continue for 9 additional years.) If the Martinsons plan to move within that period, refinancing would not make sense.

Another approach to analyzing the proposed refinancing is to use the concept of time value of money. Two methods that consider the time value of money are the net present value approach and the after-tax internal rate of return approach. Each is theoretically sound, but the after-tax internal rate of return approach is more understandable. Both methods reach the same conclusion but the after-tax internal rate of return is easier to explain and will be used to analyze the refinancing.

Calculating the internal rate of return is a job for specialized computer software or a custom spreadsheet package. Again, there are outflows and inflows, although we handle them differently. For the existing loan the inflow is simply the current balance of the loan, and the outflows are the monthly after-tax mortgage payments. (Recall that the after-tax mortgage payment rises over the life of the loan due to the reduction in interest.) The annual rate that discounts the future outflows back to the present to equal the inflows is the after-tax internal rate of return.

For the new loan the process is more complicated. The inflow consists of the current balance of the loan reduced by any points and fees that are required. Outflows for the new loan are the after-tax monthly payments on the loan reduced by the monthly tax savings from the allocation of discount points on the new loan. However, since the Martinsons would be paying a 30-year mortgage over 21 years, they would have received only 70 percent (21/30) of the tax savings due to them from the allocation of discount points. Thus we reduce the last monthly cash outflow by an amount equal to the discount points times 30 percent times a projected tax rate of 25 percent (assumed to equal their current rate).

Our calculations reveal that the after-tax rate on the old loan is 8.06 percent, while the after-tax rate on the new loan is 6.14 percent. This implies that the new loan, even when we consider points and fees, is the better option.

Since the Martinsons have no intention of moving from their house, refinancing makes sense. They can obtain the funds necessary for refinancing, and the break-even point is only 36 months. A 30-year mortgage gives the flexibility of a much lower monthly house payment, and using a 21-year amortization period makes the time frames of both loans identical. Most important, the after-tax financing rate over the intended holding period is better for the new mortgage than for the old mortgage.

The new mortgage will be in place so that the first payment will be in January of next year.

Evaluation of Portfolio with Regard to Objectives

The investment instruments that a client will use depend on the following variables:

- the client's risk profile
- the relative importance of the objective
- the possibility of postponing the date when the funds are needed
- the purpose for which the income from the accumulated assets or the assets themselves will be used

In light of the Martinsons' current situation, the first of these variables would suggest that relatively conservative investment instruments should be their choice. Their existing portfolio of common stocks and mutual funds is not overly aggressive and implies that the Martinsons are not high-risk takers. Some of their investment is in Inc common, which could be doubly risky if Inc's fortunes decline, since both Ed's position and the value of the stock could be affected. Also their ages, especially Ed's, would indicate that their portfolio should not be incurring higher and higher risk each year as Ed approaches his retirement date. The portfolio should slowly be restructured to move away from investments stressing capital appreciation, thus reducing its overall risk and increasing its income stream.

The Martinsons consider their two accumulation objectives, their retirement supplement and the income supplement for Scott, extremely important. Therefore placing any of these future savings funds into high-risk instruments could jeopardize their situation. (The extra retirement supplement, outside of the qualified and nonqualified pension plans, also helps to accomplish Ed's vital objective of providing for Amy.) When the funds accumulated are for achieving highly rated objective(s), appropriate investments typically include only those having a relatively low risk of loss.

Although Ed has expressed a desire to retire at age 62 if the needed funds can be accumulated within the next 8 years, the retirement date can be postponed until he reaches 65 and perhaps beyond if he is not considered an executive or employee in a high policymaking position as specified in the federal Age Discrimination in Employment Act. The fact that the date by which the funds will be needed can be deferred would make the use of investments with a somewhat higher risk/return profile appropriate.

The objective that these accumulations will seek to meet is an income stream over a long period. Once the long-term income stream begins, inflation starts to erode the dollar's buying power. Although the accumulation amounts and target sums specified the tables are adjusted for 4 percent inflation during the accumulation and payout periods, inflation can exceed that rate, making the buying power of the income stream diminish for both the Martinsons and their son. One way to offset this effect would be to place part of the funds in investments that would tend to provide after-tax returns in excess of the anticipated 4 percent inflation rate. The remainder of the funds would use relatively low-risk investment instruments.

A second aspect of this long-term income flow is the erratic behavior of investment returns. Some financial experts suggest that the direction of interest rates over the next several years will be downward. If this should transpire and if the Martinsons are planning to use only conservative, fixed-income instruments, the likelihood of achieving the estimated 6 percent after-tax return might not be realized. However, periods of declining interest rates during the past 20 years have been associated with a generally buoyant and rising stock market.

Recommended Portfolio

Since both accumulation objectives are similar except for the income recipients, the same portfolio design can be appropriate for both. Based on the previous discussion of these objectives, the funds set aside for each portfolio could be allocated as follows:

U.S. government 5-year notes	25 percent
No-load corporate bond fund	25 percent
No-load balanced fund	30 percent
Individual common stock investments (such as Inc or conservative, defensive stocks)	20 percent

The government notes should not have more than a 5-year duration at this time due to the uncertainty of the direction of long-term interest rates. Currently they are lower than during the past few years, and they continue to move downward. If this direction should change, the Martinsons could end up in the unfortunate position of owning low-yield investments for their long-term purpose if they purchased 25- or 30-year bonds at this time. The government bonds do provide safety and a base of stability for their portfolio.

For the various mutual funds that comprise a sizable portion of the proposed portfolio, no-load funds are recommended, assuming that the returns are comparable. The amount of funding shown is the gross amount that must be invested at the assumed, blended, after-tax return of 6 percent. If load funds are used, the net amount the Martinsons will have working for them will be less. Thus a higher return would be needed from the load fund, for an equivalent risk, to achieve their targets.

Like the government notes, the bond fund provides stability but with a slightly higher rate of return. The balanced fund, with its slightly increased risk, provides some degree of potential growth due to this type of fund's being partially invested in common stock. Usually a balanced fund has safety of principal and current income as its primary investment objectives, which blends with the Martinsons' situation.

The last two categories, a growth stock fund and direct ownership of common stocks, provide the somewhat higher-risk section of the portfolio and over the long term should also offer somewhat higher returns that can compensate for unexpected variations in interest rates or inflation.

Additional Considerations

Maximizing the Use of Inc's 401(k) Plan

Ed participates in Inc's 401(k) plan by contributing 5 percent of salary, a contribution of approximately $5,000 this year. Although the Internal Revenue Code permits a maximum annual employee contribution of $16,500 (in 2011), subject to a possible lower limit because of rules in other sections of the Code, Ed has been unable to verify that Inc permits contributions in excess of 5 percent of salary. If the plan permits additional contributions, Ed should further reduce his salary by making larger, tax-deferred contributions that Inc does not match through the plan. Sufficient cash flow in excess of his additional insurance premiums permits him to take advantage of this feature, if permissible, in the 401(k) plan and still have after-tax cash flow available to make individual investments outside the qualified plan.

Several of the investment choices in Inc's plan are consistent with the recommendations made earlier regarding the composition of the Martinsons' portfolio for this accumulation objective. Allocating a portion of their 401(k) contribution to the corporate bond or balanced mutual fund and then investing the remaining cash flow in other investment instruments as recommended previously will meet their objective.

Taking advantage of the favorable tax treatment currently afforded 401(k) plans will reduce the underfunding of the supplemental income streams that they plan to fund.

Family of Funds

Many sponsors of mutual funds offer a variety of funds referred to as a *family of funds.* The reasons for doing this are twofold. First, investors who might want to allocate their portfolio in funds with different objectives and risk/return characteristics can do so without seeking a competing firm's product. Second, many investors prefer to switch their holdings, essentially those practicing market timing, as economic conditions have changed or are expected to change.

Most authorities recommend that investors using common stocks or stock-invested mutual funds within a portfolio have a minimum planning horizon of 3 to 5 years for these securities. They also advise not allowing short-run market fluctuations to influence investment choices or decisions to buy or sell. But should fundamental conditions in the economic or securities spheres change, then portfolio restructuring can be desirable. For the convenience of making changes within their portfolio and not for the purpose of short-term trading, the Martinsons could consider selecting such a family of funds.

Ownership Considerations

Retirement Income Supplement. The age disparity between Ed and Amy plus Amy's family history suggests she will outlive him. In addition, she currently owns few assets. For these two reasons the best recommendation for the Martinsons to follow would be to title the assets being acquired in Amy's name. The advantages of this course of action would be as follows:

- No gift tax would be incurred because of the unlimited deduction for gifts between spouses.
- Should Amy predecease Ed, she would have assets that could be shielded from estate taxation by using the $3.5 million applicable credit amount (for 2009). To continue Ed's retirement income supplement for which these funds were accumulated, she could set up a testamentary trust that would give Ed the trust income for life and at his death have the corpus pass equally to the children, per stirpes.

One disadvantage of this ownership structure is that should Ed predecease Amy, his assets that pass to her could create estate tax liabilities and shrinkage before the net estate passes to the children. It is recommended that Ed's estate be structured so that most of his income-producing assets are placed in a bypass trust for Amy's benefit. Thus the total estate assets passing to Amy would not create major estate tax liabilities at her subsequent death.

   Scott's Income Supplement. Using a trust for this objective would give the Martinsons the assurance that the funds they set aside would be used solely for Scott's benefit and that prudent supervision of trust assets and their disposition would take place over a long period.

The funding for this objective will continue past the time that Scott reaches age 21. Since the 2503(b) trust requires the annual distribution of trust income, funds could not be accumulated over the next few years that would provide a portion of the necessary long-term income flow to Scott. Therefore a 2503(c) trust would meet the Martinsons' needs because it would have two desirable features. First, the trust can accumulate income. Second, gifts made to the trust qualify for the annual gift tax exclusion. A disadvantage is that the trust corpus must be distributed when Scott attains age 21. At that time, 5 years from now, the Martinsons will not have completed the funding for this purpose. In addition, the corpus, when Scott receives it, could be dissipated rather quickly.

To use the 2503(c) trust in this situation, the instrument should contain a Crummey provision that will allow Scott to withdraw trust income for a period of 20 consecutive days each year. With this clause in the document the life of the trust will extend beyond the time that Scott reaches age 21. In addition, whether the Martinsons fund the trust over the next 8 or 11 years (or some intermediate time), their annual contributions will continue to qualify for the annual gift tax exclusion because Scott has this withdrawal power.

Of course, if he makes any withdrawals, the total amount needed at the end of the funding period will not be available for his long-term income supplement. Ed and Amy hope they will be able to convince him of the need for restraint during the funding period. They will also need to stress the importance of his withdrawing only the amount of the annual income after the funding is completed each year so the desired income stream will not be jeopardized.

Since the possibility exists that Scott might not live as long as the 50 years for which the trust income stream is designed to provide the supplemental income, one or more corpus beneficiaries should be named. Since Ed has indicated that providing for Amy is his primary objective, Amy should be the corpus beneficiary if she survives Scott. Should Amy predecease Scott, Bea and her issue, per stirpes, would become the corpus beneficiaries. If Bea also predeceases Scott and leaves no issue, the corpus could be given to a qualified charity, such as Ed's college.

Finally, although Ed can retire anytime between age 62 and age 65 or perhaps later, he may not prefer this course of action. Indeed, instead of staying with Inc until the normal retirement age, 65, he has expressed a preference to leave at 62. Depending on the Martinsons' ability to achieve the necessary accumulation, based on their available cash flow and the direction of interest rates, Ed might be able to meet his targeted retirement age of 62.

After refinancing their residence and acquiring the recommended insurance, the Martinsons' cash flow for the two accumulation objectives (supplementary retirement income for Ed and Amy and lifetime income stream for Scott) are shown in the table below. As the table illustrates, the Martinsons will comfortably be able to achieve their goals and continue accumulating a surplus.

Table 7-14 Martinsons' Cash Inflow and Outflow to Meet Funding Objectives after Acquiring Insurance and Refinancing Their Residence	
Year	Cash Inflow Minus Cash Outflow
Current Year	$16,029.50
Next Year	$10,294.93
Two Years from Today	$454.20

CASE II

Acquisition of Additional Insurance and Refinancing of the Residence

New Assumptions

1. Beginning in 2011, $11,414 will be spent on the additional insurance.
2. The investable cash flow will earn a before-tax return of 8.35 percent.
3. The residence will be refinanced for a period of 30 years with a fixed interest rate of 7.5 percent with 3 points being paid.

Continuing Assumptions

1. The checking account balance is maintained at $12,000; the account is noninterest bearing.
2. Ed's salary is increased at 5 percent annually.
3. The money market deposit account earns 4.75 percent annually.
4. Investable cash is invested and earns 5 percent annually.
5. Expenditures for food, clothing and cleaning, utilities, phone, vacations, and charitable contributions will increase annually at 3 percent.
6. Expenditures for transportation will increase 4 percent annually.
7. Expenditures for entertainment will increase 5 percent annually.
8. Expenditures for medical insurance and other medical expenses will increase at 6 percent annually.
9. Decreases in the value of furniture have been ignored.
10. Automobiles decrease in value at a rate of 15 percent annually.
11. The value of the home will increase at one percent annually.
12. The common stock portfolio will increase at 9 percent annually.
13. Dividends from the common stock portfolio are currently $3,120, will increase 4 percent annually, and are reinvested in the portfolio.
14. IRAs will earn 8.1 percent annually over the next 4 years.

CHAPTER REVIEW

Review Questions

These questions are intended to help students answer questions about case studies, goals and assumptions. Answers to these questions can be found in the study supplement.

1. What are four criteria used to help determine appropriate investment instruments for a high income executive? [1]

2. Sarah is covered by a group life insurance policy at work with a death benefit if $100,000. The employer owns the insurance policy, Sarah is allowed to pick the beneficiary. She has appointed her daughter. Will this policy be included in her gross estate if she were to die? [2]

3. Sarah stops working at her employer, and purchases the policy for slightly more than its face value. To avoid estate taxes on the death benefit, Sarah transfers ownership of the policy to an irrevocable life insurance trust. The policy has a death benefit of $100,000, cash value of $40,000 and cost basis of 55,000. If Sarah dies today, what value if any is included in her gross estate? [2]

4. What are suggested uses of an UGMA or UTMA account? What are potential negative aspects of using an UGMA or UTMA account? [1]

5. Jim is considering refinancing his mortgage. He owes $200,000 on his current note and pays $1,271.70 a month. Jim can refinance at a 5.0 percent rate and pay total closing costs of 3.0 percent of the loan value. Jim can roll the costs of the loan into the mortgage. Assuming Jim refinances, how many months does he need to live in the home before the mortgage again reaches $200,000? [2]

Learning Objectives

An understanding of the material in this chapter should enable the student to

1. Review planning for the surviving spouse.
2. Discuss insurance fraud and consequences.
3. Review Social Security benefits for a surviving spouse.

Frequently a financial services professional needs to counsel the soon-to-be or already-widowed spouse. Are there unusual Federal income tax and estate tax issues to consider for the first time now that the client will soon be widowed? Are the current insurance policies still appropriate, or must the insurance program be adjusted in accordance with the change in personal status? Is the existing investment picture still viable in light of the new situation? These are but a few of the issues for which the client requires professional advice.

The planner must balance a financial plan of action with the emotional and family issues associated with loss. The spouse must be allowed to grieve while implementing potentially complicated financial decisions. The planner must take a cautious approach, with patience and compassion, in presenting financial recommendations and alternatives.

Clearly the financial planner should allow the client time to adjust to a changed personal situation, but in some cases immediate action must be taken to deal with the impending death of a spouse and to marshal resources to provide for long-term financial needs arising from changes in health or marital status. Widowed status, either actual or impending, means many changes in tax, estate, insurance, and investment planning that require the client to take appropriate steps in these areas in a timely fashion. One factor that may be helpful in motivating the client to act is that the spouse's impending or actual death triggers planning regarding federal estate tax, state inheritance tax, insurance, and investments. Clients may feel that this situation is a learning experience and that failure to consider and develop effective plans harms the family's or the survivors' financial future. The financial planner may find clients in such a situation to be very cooperative.

Often the planner has been only recently sought out, not having previously advised the client. A debilitating illness, a comment of a friend or confidant, or the client's own recognition of the need for advice can lead to using a planner's service.

CASE NARRATIVE

Present Situation

Elizabeth and James Black met with you 5 years ago. They implemented most of your planning recommendations and have been on track saving $500 per month. Three years ago they had twins, William and Richard. William and Richard attend preschool 2 days per week. James has succeeded in his career with Golden Circle systems and is now an assistant sales director. Last year James earned a base salary of $65,000 and commissions of $35,000. He and Elizabeth were looking to a bright future.

During last year's annual meeting, James confided in you that he has been diagnosed with aggressive lung cancer. He has told his family, and they were initially optimistic. After 6 months, however, the certainty of James' mortality had set in. Only Elizabeth attended this year's meeting, and James has about a month left. She asks what steps she can pursue to make sure their affairs in the order.

In the meeting, Elizabeth was upset. She confided that James omitted that he was an occasional smoker on his life insurance policy purchased from you. In fact, he stated he was a nonsmoker when receiving his medical exam. The insurance company completed a medical exam on James and did not discover he smoked occasionally. Elizabeth is terrified that the insurance company will find out about occasional tobacco usage and not pay at James' death.

James and Elizabeth executed simple wills after your initial meeting 5 years ago. They have been receiving disability insurance through James' employer equal to 50 percent of his base salary. James did not purchase any supplemental individual disability coverage. James and Elizabeth have stopped working with James' brother to provide investment advice and have instead purchased no-load S&P 500 Index funds in their Roth IRAs and in a taxable mutual fund account. Their basis in the taxable account is $10,500 and the account is owned jointly with rights of survivorship (JTWROS).

James is covered under his company health insurance program and he met the deductible earlier this year. James is treated by in-network physicians. His employer will pay all costs associated with health care benefits for 6 months to Elizabeth and her children after his death; after that, she will need to access COBRA. James is covered with one times his salary of employer life insurance.

James purchased a $600,000 20-year term life insurance policy at your initial meeting 5 years ago. He has made consistent premium payments. His waiver-of-premium coverage has begun making payments on his behalf over the past 6 months. They paid off all student loans last year. However, James and Elizabeth have accrued $33,000 of credit card debt sustaining living expenses over the past 6 months.

The credit card is jointly owned. Elizabeth has provided you with an updated balance sheet. Elizabeth has left her job and works in the home. She does not want to go back to work until her children are in elementary school (which will be in 2 years) but will if she needs to. Elizabeth wants to stay in her home, which is near her family. Elizabeth discusses her current cash flow with you during the meeting. You make notes of her after-tax expenses; she does not supply you with a formal cash flow statement. James and Elizabeth followed your advice 5 years ago, but their aggregate annual expenses have inflated at a higher rate then they initially projected. James' medical costs have accelerated well beyond either of their expectations. James refinanced the loan on his truck last month. They refinanced to a new 48-month loan on a $8,500 balance at a 4.25 percent interest rate. The first payment on the new loan will be due next month.

Elizabeth was emotionally drained and visibly upset during the meeting. She has asked you to get back with her within the week to outline steps she and James should take. James is heavily medicated but aware and cognizant a few hours every day. James recently entered hospice and is living at home. Elizabeth could reenter the workplace and earn around $3,000 per month before taxes. She is overwhelmed.

During the course of conversation, Elizabeth tells you that James' brother in law (a stock broker) has been calling and has told family members that he will be working with her after James passes away. Elizabeth expressed that she is uncomfortable with this arrangement and would rather continue her relationship with you. She does not know how to broach the issue with James' family.

At the end of the meeting, Elizabeth regained her composure and asked you to forget everything she said about James and the underwriting process. She would like you to call her to discuss next steps.

Agent's Ethical Concern

After meeting with Elizabeth, the agent has to make an important ethical decision. The financial adviser faces a multitude of variables in the decision making process. The obligation to the insurance company must be weighed against obligations to the client. Compensation models may influence adviser actions. Did the adviser sell the insurance policy or meet with the client after the initial policy had been sold? The financial adviser has the following options to consider. Each option has potentially negative consequences in both the short and long term.

Agent Options	Short-Term Outcome	Long-Term Consequences
Inform the insurance company	Elizabeth may become disgruntled and cut off communication with the adviser. Potential Errors & Omissions suit filed by Elizabeth.	Elizabeth will most likely not receive a full death benefit. The adviser may be sued for malpractice.
Take no action	The insurance company may find that James misrepresented himself or lied on the insurance application and ask the adviser for more information.	The insurance company may have failed in the underwriting phase, but the selling agent is contractually obligated to report ethically unsuitable behavior.
Deceive the insurance company	If asked by the insurance company, omitting or lying could cause the representative to lose licenses and face civil penalties.	The adviser takes a risk that has potentially drastic consequences. Elizabeth may receive a full death benefit if smoking is not uncovered.

Balance Sheet: James Terminally Ill

Table 8-1 Balance Sheet James and Elizabeth Black: James Terminally Ill		
Assets		
Home	$165,000	
James 401(k)	$20,850	
Roth IRA balances	$20,000	
Honda Accord	$1,000	
Ford F-250	$8,000	
Personal property	$55,000	
Wedding set	$5,000	
Checking account	$4,500	
Savings account	$5,000	
Mutual fund holdings	$10,250	
Total Assets		$284,350
Liabilities		
Mortgage	$108,000	
Car loan	$8,200	
Credit card debt	$33,000	
Total Liabilities		$149,200
Net Worth		**$135,150**

Schedule of Expenses James Terminally Ill

Table 8-2 James and Elizabeth Black Expense Schedule: James Terminally Ill	
Income tax	$7,500.00
401(k) contribution	$3,900.00
HC premiums	$4,500.00
Payments on mortgage	$8,753.64
Car note	$3,976.00
Student loans	$ 0
Roth contributions	$5,000.00
Living expenses	$36,000.00
Auto insurance	$2,020.00
Homeowners	$1,400.00
Property taxes	$3,180.00
Medical expenses out of pocket	$24,000.00
Life insurance James	Waiver of Premium
Life insurance Elizabeth	$460.00
Preschool costs (2 days/week)	$7,200.00
	$107,889.64

CASE INSTRUCTIONS: JAMES TERMINALLY ILL

Financial planning is a profession that deals with the intersection of people and personal finance. Other cases in the text have focused on the personal finance element of financial planning. This case study requires the student to answer ethical and process model questions.

Students are challenged to answer the following open-ended questions while completing a case study. Instead of assuming a static client process, students need to address current steps over multiple time frames.

- Immediate actions to take while James is living and capable of executing documents.
- Decisions made if James were to lapse into a coma or other non responsive state.
- Actions immediately following James' death.
- Actions 3–6 months after James' death.

The plan needs to be less structured and written compassionately. Realistically client decisions would take place over a series of short meetings and phone calls.

Immediate Actions

Students are encouraged to answer these questions before developing plan documents. Answers to these questions will help shape the planner's course of action and establish how and when to contact James and Elizabeth.

- How should a planner address James' life insurance policy?
- What alternatives are available to the insurance company?
- What additional documents are needed from the Blacks?
- What information do you need about James and Elizabeth's debts?
- Are there any documents James and Elizabeth need to draft expediently?
- Would James or Elizabeth benefit from any additional professional or spiritual guidance?
- How could the planner help them find a network of other professionals?
- How can the planner help with funeral plan arrangements?
- How should the planner effectively address the relationship with James' brother in law?

- What are additional steps the planner can take to help James and Elizabeth?

Actions if James Loses Capacity

- What steps should Elizabeth take if James loses the ability to control his financial assets?
- How can the planner assist Elizabeth if James were to become comatose?
- What documents do Elizabeth need to have executed to act on James' behalf?
- Where does she need to go to execute these documents?
- What type of professionals can Elizabeth benefit from contacting?
- How can the planner assist Elizabeth in this process?

Actions when James Passes Away

- What can the planner do to assist Elizabeth when James passes away?
- To what extent can the planner help with funeral arrangements or send a memorial gift?
- How should Elizabeth pay for funeral costs?
- If the insurance policy pays, what options and time frame are available to Elizabeth?
- If the insurance policy delays payment pending an investigation, what options are available to Elizabeth?
- James' brother in-law suggests Elizabeth not work outside of the family. What strategies are available to help work with the brother in-law?
- What asset allocation decisions should be considered?
- What type of professionals can Elizabeth benefit from contacting?
- How can the planner assist Elizabeth in this process?
- How long can Elizabeth grieve before she looks for work if she does not receive life insurance policy proceeds?
- How long can Elizabeth grieve before she looks for work if she does receive life insurance policy proceeds?
- How can the planner help assist in the job search process?
- How can the planner help Elizabeth look for more affordable child care?

Actions Six Months after James' Death

- How often should Elizabeth be contacted after James' death?
- What boundaries are important to keep in place between the planner and Elizabeth's family or Elizabeth herself?
- If James left money directly to his children at his death, what procedures and type of accounts will need to be established on their behalf?
- How should Elizabeth file her taxes?
- What other type of tax returns might Elizabeth need to file?
- What asset allocation decisions are appropriate following James' death?
- What type of professionals can Elizabeth benefit from contacting?
- How can the planner assist Elizabeth in grieving and the planning process?

WORKING OUTLINE

1. Clients' Objectives

    a. Immediate Actions

        (1) Devise a proper estate plan prior to James's death.

        (2) Help Elizabeth prepare for the emotional aspects of James' passing.

        (3) Discuss and develop a course of action for James' life insurance situation.

        (4) Build a team to assist Elizabeth during this difficult time.

    b. Actions if James loses capacity

        (1) Execute documents and authority over James' financial and health care decisions.

        (2) Finalize James' wishes and family concerns.

        (3) Minimize the costs of settling James' estate and transferring assets to Elizabeth.

        (4) Help Elizabeth manage time and resources.

    c. Actions when James passes away

        (1) Assist Elizabeth in settling James' estate.

> > (2) Help Elizabeth manage grief and assemble a team as needed.
> >
> > (3) Effectively delegate debt payments and communicate with insurance companies.
>
> > d. Actions six months after James' death
> >
> > > (1) Review and develop a budget for Elizabeth.
> > >
> > > (2) Develop a financial plan for Elizabeth.
>
> Personal Planning
>
> > a. Cash flow recommendations
> >
> > > (1) Monitor current spending situations.
> > >
> > > (2) Evaluate Social Security benefits.
> > >
> > > (3) Discuss child care and future retirement planning.
> > >
> > > (4) Determine Elizabeth's income needs.
> >
> > b. Life insurance recommendations
> >
> > > (1) Survivor needs
> > >
> > > (2) Lump sum needs
> > >
> > > (3) Cash flow needs
> >
> > c. Investment recommendations
> >
> > > (1) Retirement accounts
> > >
> > > (2) Investment accounts
> > >
> > > (3) Investment alternatives

IMMEDIATE NEEDS FOR JAMES AND ELIZABETH BLACK

Elizabeth and James need to consider some immediate actions before James passes away.

Communication during a Difficult Time

A financial adviser can rely on communication skills to help Elizabeth and James during their time of need. Financial services professionals must themselves grieve for their deceased clients. At the same time, they must actively listen to the verbal and nonverbal messages from survivors and maintain a professional demeanor.

Financial service professionals may be the only ones capable of playing devil's advocate on financial decisions facing survivors. Financial services professionals must suggest the correct moves financially even if doing so provokes angry confrontation now or in the future. Survivors generally will be able to make better rational evaluations and decisions 6 to 9 months after the death.

Aiding survivors is every bit as demanding as initial sales work. It requires empathy, diplomacy, patience, warmth, genuineness, and persistence. The communication often is highly emotional. Strong negative emotions may be directed at professional advisers.

Consequently, financial services professionals must keep cool and maintain their composure. This may require some advance strategies for disengaging or otherwise calming the emotional fervor of conversations with survivors. This phase of service is the final stage for previously sold products and services, but it may be the initial stage for future product and service sales. Establishing credibility and reliability with survivors can expand potential referrals and thereby be a positive influence on future business. Each death creates the need to terminate an estate, but at the same time it reminds surviving family and friends that they have unfinished business to attend to before their own death. The financial services professional who performs extraordinary service for widows and widowers is enhancing his or her credibility.

Revisit Estate Planning Needs

Meet with an attorney and review James' will and all ancillary planning documents. James urgently needs to exercise durable health-care and financial powers of attorney. Additionally, he needs to ensure his premiums are being paid on his group life insurance policy. James should also write a letter of last instruction, cementing the location of executed testamentary documents, life insurance policies and other important items.

Coordinate hospice care with James' physician. Hospice care does not attempt to cure medical conditions but rather is devoted to easing the physical and psychological pain associated with death. In addition to providing services for the dying patient, a hospice may offer counseling to family members. A hospice may be a separate facility, but this type of care can also be provided on an outpatient basis in the dying person's home.

Social Security Survivor Benefits

James should locate his most recent Social Security statement. James has been working full-time for 5 years and is considered fully insured for the purposes of his family receiving Social Security survivor benefits. The Social Security statement lists the survivor benefit available at James' death. Elizabeth will receive the benefit until the twins turn 18 if they are unmarried and 19 if they are unmarried and attending school full-time.

Elizabeth is entitled to receive 75 percent of James' primary insurance amount (listed on his statement) and each of the children will also receive 75 percent of this amount. However, James' heirs can only receive the maximum family benefit. The maximum family benefit in James' case is around 160 percent of his primary insurance amount. This benefit is limited by a case study approach, but is assumed to be $2,700 and is based on the amount James paid into the social security system over his working years.

The maximum family benefit is distributed equally to each child (William and Richard) and Elizabeth. Each party will receive one third of the benefit and the checks will be made out to Elizabeth until the children reach an age of majority. William and Richard's benefits will not be taxable as they do not have any other income. Up to 85 percent of Elizabeth's benefits may be taxable based on her income after James' death. The case presented makes a conservative estimation that 85 percent of Elizabeth's benefit is taxable.

Elizabeth will continue receiving benefits until her children are 16 unless they become disabled. She can apply for retirement benefits as early as her age 60, though these will be reduced and based on James primary insurance amount. As Elizabeth plans on returning to the workplace, her Social Security benefit may be richer than James' benefit later in life and she may want to take her own benefit in lieu of James'.

If Elizabeth remarries, she will still receive survivor benefits while her children are under age 16. She will not be able to draw survivor retirement benefits from James' primary insurance amount if her new marriage is in place when she turns 60.

At James' death, Elizabeth will need to provide:

- Proof of death—either from a funeral home or death certificate
- Elizabeth's Social Security number, as well as James'
- Elizabeth's birth certificate
- Elizabeth and James' marriage certificate

- William and Richard's Social Security numbers and birth certificates
- James' W-2 forms for the most recent year
- Bank name, routing number and account number

DISCUSSIONS OF SELECTED CASE QUESTIONS

Students are encouraged to answer all of the questions presented in the text and develop case solutions. In this case, the planner is functioning primarily in a problem-solving capacity and less as a salesperson or in a product implementation capacity. Answers to selected questions are presented in the following text.

Life Insurance Misrepresentation

James misled the insurance company and agent upon the issuance of his policy. He occasionally smoked and reported that he was a nonsmoker. This misrepresentation influenced his premium to be cheaper than it would have been, and allowed him to afford more life insurance than he would have otherwise. The misstatement of a material fact, such as smoking, constitutes fraud from the standpoint of the insurance company. If clearly stated in the insurance policy, the insurer could cancel the policy if charges of fraud can be sustained.

Elizabeth would have a fundamentally higher quality of life if she received James' death benefit proceeds. Her children would have a better chance of attending college, receive a higher-quality child care, and Elizabeth would be able to fulfill her dream of staying at home until her children began college. Elizabeth has a driving motivation to collect on James' policy.

The financial planner is in the middle of the discussion, and they face many decisions as a result of James' misstatement. Primarily, should the financial planner tell the insurance company that he or she suspects James misstated a material fact? Elizabeth's statement came when she was under emotional duress and very upset. Does her emotional condition impact financial planner disclosure?

Financial planners do not enjoy any legal privilege similar to a priest or attorney. If compelled by a court to give evidence a financial planner must comply or face contempt charges, which could lead to loss of license and consequentially livelihood. The financial adviser must weigh the obligation to the client against an obligation to the company. As James passes from lung cancer, the insurance company would likely review his medical records for evidence and history of tobacco usage. However, if the company does not suspect any wrongdoing there is a chance the insurer will pay the claim without an in-depth analysis.

If the planner is a contracted agent of the insurer, the ethical obligation carries legal overtones. By contracting with the insurer the agent has made contractual promises to represent the insurer and report material information to the insurer. These contractual promises are binding to the agent and may compel negative recourses if the agent is party to fraud well beyond state defrocking or censure.

While the financial planner in this case study did originally sell the policy and is assumed to be an agent of the insurer, if a planner was not associated with the insurance company, would they have an ethical obligation to report the fraud? Or would their obligation be to protect the client's interest?

By telling the planner about James' misdirection, even in an emotional state, Elizabeth has caused the planner to face an ethical dilemma. If the planner claims a fiduciary duty to the client or favors a product sale, he or she may be motivated to not report the potential fraud. The planner will certainly trigger a postmortem investigation by reporting potential abuse, but without intervention the claim may be paid.

A financial planner should consult with his or her own legal counsel regardless of their decision. Elizabeth may attempt to sue for malpractice if the insurance company is notified, and the insurance company might take action if they learn the planner was involved in a decision to omit material information.

Death Certificates

There are many matters that must be settled after death, and most of them require that a death certificate be submitted. Copies of the death certificate can be obtained from the funeral director or from the local registrar of vital statistics. Settlement of even the simplest estate will often require a dozen copies of the death certificate, and complex estates may need three or four dozen copies of the death certificate.

Misrepresentation in Application

The applicant for a life insurance policy must submit a written application that supplies various types of information, including information about the applicant's past and present health. The applicant may also have to undergo a medical examination, including an interrogation by the medical examiner. It is standard practice for the soliciting agent to fill out the application for the applicant and for the medical examiner to write in the answers to the questions that he or she asks the applicant.

There is always the possibility that the agent or medical examiner may incorrectly record information supplied by the applicant in the application. This may occur inadvertently or by design. Unless there is collusion, the medical examiner has little or no reason to falsify the medical records. The agent, however, because he or she is paid on a commission basis, does have an incentive to falsify information—either with or without the applicant's knowledge—that might adversely affect the application's acceptance.

If there is collusion between the applicant and any agent of the insurer to falsify the application, the insurer loses none of its defenses. If, on the other hand, the agent is acting alone and tells the applicant that an item of information is not being recorded correctly, the agent is likely to imply that the information is immaterial and should not be permitted to complicate home office underwriting officials' consideration of the application. In cases where the applicant's truthful answers have been falsely recorded in the application by the agent (or the medical examiner), it becomes important to determine the legal effect of these misstatements.

It is a well-settled rule that one who signs and accepts a written instrument with the intention of contracting is bound by its terms. However, if the instrument contains false statements, the aggrieved party has the right to avoid the contract. Hence, in accordance with strict contract law, material misstatements in the application should give the insurance company power to avoid the contract, regardless of the circumstances surrounding the statements' falsification. However, the courts, recognizing that a life insurance policy is a contract of adhesion that the insured seldom reads, do not apply strict contract law in these cases. The rule supported by the weight of authority is that if the application is filled out by an agent of the company who—without fraud, collusion, or the applicant's knowledge—falsely records information that the applicant had provided truthfully, the company cannot rely on the falsity of such information in seeking to avoid liability under the contract.[15] According to one court, "To hold otherwise would be to place every

---

15. In New York, the insured is bound by false answers entered by the agent or medical examiner if the insured certifies as to the answers. *Bollard v. New York Life Insurance Co.*, 228 N.Y. 521, 126 N.E. 900 (1920).

simple or uneducated person seeking insurance at the mercy of the insurer who could, through its agent, insert in every application, unknown to the applicant, and over his signature, some false statement which would enable it to avoid all liability while retaining the price paid for supposed insurance."[16]

The key to the rule is that the agent, in filling out the application, is acting for the company, not for the insured. In other words, the soliciting agent is, in a legal sense, the agent of the company, the principal. This finding can support either of two legal theories, both of which have been used by the courts to justify their decisions. The first theory holds that there is no deception of the insurance company since it knew through its agent that the written statement or statements were not true.[17] The second theory, more widely used, recognizes that there is deception but holds that since the company, through the knowledge of its agent, knowingly issued a voidable policy, it is estopped from voiding it. In both theories, the insurer has a right of action against the agent for breach of his or her duty to the principal.

To find an estoppel against the insurer, the courts must permit testimony, usually from the beneficiary, as to the answers the applicant provided to the agent. This would seem to be in violation of the parol evidence rule, but the general holding is that the parol evidence rule does not exclude oral testimony to establish waiver or estoppel.

The courts are likewise inclined to find a waiver or an estoppel when the applicant knows an answer is false but the agent asserts that it is immaterial. The view is that the applicant is entitled to rely on the superior knowledge of the agent or medical examiner, as the case may be. Even a stipulation in the application that oral statements made to the agent will not be binding on the company has been held unenforceable. However, when the applicant knows that the agent or medical examiner is not truthfully reporting obviously material facts to the company, the applicant is guilty of fraud and cannot invoke the doctrine of estoppel, which requires honest reliance. The applicant's behavior in this situation is regarded as collusive.

Emotional Aspects of Death and Dying

Death is a part of every life cycle, but the details of death vary immensely. In some cases, death is almost instantaneous as in some accidents, drowning,

16. *State Insurance Co. of Des Moines v. Taylor*, 14 Colo. 499, 508, 24 Pac. 333, 336 (1890).

17. *Heilig v. Home Security Life Insurance Co.*, 222 N.C. 21, 22 S.E. 2d 429 (1942).

severe heart attacks, and so forth. In other cases dying may take a while or even be very prolonged (for example, Alzheimer's cases).

In our society we do a poor job of preparing for and anticipating death, regardless of how rapidly it occurs. People who die instantaneously have rarely communicated their thoughts and desires about relevant issues to their closest family and friends who will have to handle the finances, property distribution, and ongoing support of dependents.

Ours is basically a death-denying society wherein the topic of death is avoided. We speak in euphemisms about a person's "having expired," "met his maker," or "passed away," rather than address death directly. The discomfort associated with the topic of death prevents many people from ever discussing their own inevitable death or taking positive steps in its anticipation, like making a will. This tendency to avoid preparing for death is so strong in the United States that even persons who are terminally ill continue to procrastinate and suppress their thoughts and feelings about death. Quite often the dying individual will withdraw from relationships and minimize contact with other people in an attempt to avoid dealing with the impending death.

Very often the people closest to a dying person have even stronger tendencies to avoid the topic than the dying person. They may retreat from contact and communication altogether or insist on changing the subject to something more positive if the subject of death emerges in conversation. Death is generally considered negatively and hence is not a welcome topic in our hedonistic society. For these reasons, many friends and close family members cease contact with the dying person even before the dying process restricts his or her mobility or other functions.

In one case with which I am familiar, even the grade-school-age children of a dying father withdrew from close contact and curtailed normal household conversation after becoming aware of their father's terminal cancerous condition. The father felt isolated and became severely depressed in that atmosphere of minimal emotional support. His only supporter was his dear and devoted wife.

In many cases of terminal illness, the spouse who is well is not able to sustain his or her strong emotional support all the way to the end of a trying and prolonged dying process. Sometimes the emotional strain of a prolonged decline even results in divorce prior to death.

There are many forces at work in our dynamic society that increase emotional stress on persons facing imminent death. Medical providers are very uncomfortable with death. They devote their careers to preserving and prolonging life. Many of them see death as an enemy and insist on bringing to bear every possible medical procedure in order to postpone death. What's more, they also have a well-founded fear of liability for negligence if they do not take heroic steps to extend life.

Consequently, medical providers generally will pressure the dying person and his or her family to pursue all avenues of intervention embraced by Western medicine. They are apt to show their distaste for living wills. Some physicians go so far as to cease pain relief medication once a living will is involved and a do-not-resuscitate directive has been issued.

Other societal sources of stress come from our extreme specialization that has resulted in many services being performed impersonally by strangers. Funeral directors, adult day care centers, transport services, nursing homes, hospitals, and emergency medical transport teams now perform functions that were previously furnished by the family, if at all. The services' businesslike manners often leave the customers feeling more like commodities than people. Lynn Caine gives a good example of this in her book *Widow;* she describes the rules that prevented her young children from visiting their hospitalized father during the last 6 months of his life. Furthermore, we have also heard many accounts of inadequate care and hygiene in some nursing homes. Sometimes the deficiencies are so severe that health officials close the institution.

Moreover, the affluence of our economy and the wide geographic dispersal of family members have contributed to the breakdown of multigenerational families. Parents and grandparents almost always live apart, often in different states. This has lessened the frequency and duration of personal contact. Long-distance communication tends to discourage sharing details about day-to-day living and other experiences that strengthen emotional bonds in close-knit families.

Another indication of weaker emotional bonds in our society is the high incidence of divorce among healthy persons. This is concurrent with a weakening of spiritual commitment evidenced by declining support of many religious institutions. Many members of our society, submerged in their materialistic surroundings, are isolating themselves from direct human contact. They travel in a sealed air-conditioned car, and they work at home on their computer, connected to the outside only by a phone line; their entertainment is also computer generated. Will these shifts in society increase or decrease emotional stress? Will they alter the ways in which we react to death?

Grieving

There is an established body of literature dealing with the human emotions surrounding death. There are some universal reactions that survivors have after the death of a close friend, family member, or loved one. In fact, dying persons who are aware of their impending death experience essentially the same emotions (with slight variations) as survivors. These emotions were first identified in the literature by Dr. Elisabeth Kübler-Ross[18] as anger, denial, bargaining, depression, and acceptance. People coping with death often experience periods or stages when one of the five emotions dominates the others. Each of these emotions will be dominant in one or more phases, and there is no established order or duration.

Denial or anger surfaces as the first or an early phase of coping with death. Acceptance is often (but not always) the last phase. Most of these emotions can be experienced simultaneously, and people's conscious thoughts cycle frequently from one emotion to another.

Denial is often the first reaction to death (especially among the young who so often think of themselves as immortal). It is a temporary defense, often linked with magical thinking that, "if I ignore it, maybe it will go away." People often use denial to cope with painful and uncomfortable things in life. Both the physician and the dying patient may be covertly engaging in denial. Among survivors, denial often makes it easier to continue contact and communication during the terminal illness. After death, the survivors usually get over their denial and other grieving emotions within a year. However, in some extreme cases parents may extend the denial phase for years.

Anger is one way of expressing strong emotional trauma. It can be directed (usually without reason) at doctors, advisers, employers, relatives, or friends. Survivors often direct their anger at the deceased for leaving them.

Bargaining is an attempt to postpone the impending death. It is a plea to extend the duration of life another month, season, year, and so forth; in return the bargaining person intends to cease current vices, strengthen his or her commitment to family and loved ones, or increase support to religious or

---

18.   Elisabeth Kübler-Ross is the author of *On Death and Dying* (New York: Macmillan), 1968.

charitable organizations. Bargaining can prompt vigorous bursts of energy and enthusiasm.

Emotions Associated with Grieving
• anger • denial • bargaining • depression • acceptance

Depression may initially be triggered by the limitations of deteriorating physical health. It is also a manifestation of the loss of hope (the death of dreams). It saps the person's energy and often stops him or her from attempting things that he or she is still capable of doing. During times when depression is the predominant emotion of grieving, it is very hard to communicate with the person. Depression prompts individuals to withdraw from other people and focus on their inner thoughts and fears.

Acceptance of death may be short and recurrent. It may or may not be a prevalent emotion at the actual time of death. Acceptance of death is often accompanied by a cessation or reduced intensity of the emotional fight for survival. It is frequently marked by an increased desire and need for sleep. When acceptance is the final stage, death can be somewhat serene and tranquil.

When the dying process is long enough for the person to be cognizant of physical and/or mental deterioration, the dying person is aware of the loss of control of his or her own life and the loss of independence. Even in these impaired conditions there is a strong human need for dignity and self-respect. The dying person deserves humane treatment from those around him or her. Family members are often better at maintaining a warm nurturing environment if they have not already been stretched to their limits and experienced burnout.

Some religious and ethnic groups have developed ceremonies and procedures to accompany death. They are often devoted to extending dignity and humane treatment to those nearing death. They further promote respect for the deceased and support for survivors and their grieving. Survivors often require up to one year to adjust to the death and work through the grief.

During that year their emotions are usually a roller coaster of extreme highs and lows. Survivors also need nurturing.

Surviving spouses are often so distraught that they make major lifestyle changes in hopes of easing their pain. Frequently these decisions are not good ones for the survivor's long-term best interests. Family and friends of survivors can provide some protection from making foolish decisions by playing the role of devil's advocate with the survivor and those who strongly influence him or her. All of us have the capability of making irrational choices. The likelihood of doing so seems to increase while we are grieving over the death of a loved one.

The grieving process is just as important to children as it is to adults. All survivors need to release their ties to the deceased. The stronger those ties were, the more painful the grieving process. Survivors who try to avoid the pain of grieving by not reacting to the death often display one or more of the following reactions: overactivity without a sense of loss, symptoms similar to those of the deceased prior to death, intense hostility toward specific persons, agitated depression, trouble sleeping and nightmares when sleeping, preoccupation with the deceased's image, and a long-term decrease in their level of social interaction.[19]

Death Claims

Among the many considerations for policyowners at the time of a life insurance purchase is the manner in which any death proceeds will be paid. Failure to do so may defeat the very purpose for which the insurance was intended.

When the death benefits of a life insurance policy are being considered for the most appropriate payout options, one special consideration does not apply to other situations: You will be dealing with a beneficiary instead of the insured policyowner who worked with you to design the coverage and keep it in force. When a life insurance death benefit has been paid to a beneficiary, the proceeds are the sole property of the beneficiary. The insurance company gives up control at distribution.

The insurance adviser should offer to help a beneficiary who receives life insurance proceeds. All too often, no effort is made to forge new counseling

---

19. E. Lindeman, "Symptomatology and Management of Acute Grief," *American Journal of Psychiatry*, vol. 2 (1944).

ties with the beneficiary. This can alter the wishes of the insured and can impede the purposes for which the insured purchased the insurance policy.

The loss of a loved one will make current decisions emotionally charged, and immediate concerns may appear to be unrealistically more important than long-term needs at this difficult time. It can be an awkward time to talk about money with some people. Doing nothing may be better than taking action. You must advise your clients carefully. You may be well advised to suggest leaving the cash proceeds with the insurance company at interest for 6 months or so.

Later, after the initial adjustment to the loss of the loved one, you can help suggest a course of action that will assure the proceeds will be used in the most advantageous way to meet long-term goals. You can bring in additional expertise if it seems appropriate. Your influence in the situation will be easier to handle after a period of time. This does not mean that the adviser should ignore beneficiaries and not care about their concerns and interests. Just as the family was of professional concern to the adviser during the years of work with the client, that same interest should continue and intensify through the new bond of common sorrow that has emerged.

Because this may be an emotional time for the beneficiary, you may find yourself offering services that you normally would not. You may have to call the funeral director and help make the arrangements for the funeral. You may have to contact the deceased's other financial advisors or attorney. You may have to help in locating and procuring important papers, such as certified copies of the death certificate or a copy of the most recent will.

Contacts may have to be made with the local veterans' and/or Social Security office and you may have to be the one who starts the process. The beneficiary may be entitled to Civil Service or employer benefits and may not even think about this aspect of the claims process. As the deceased's insurance advisor, you may have to contact several life insurance companies and help the beneficiaries file claims. You may find it helpful to have the following information on hand before contacting the companies involved:

- policy number(s) and face amount(s)
- deceased' Social Security number
- deceased' full legal name and address
- deceased's occupation, last day worked, employer's name, address, and telephone number
- deceased's date and place of birth

- date, place, and cause of death
- beneficiary's name, age, address, and Social Security number
- several certified copies of the death certificate

In any case, you need to be prepared to handle or find a resource for any matter that may cross your path in regard to the deceased. The advisor's job is not complete when death occurs; in many cases it is just beginning.

Always remember that when you help your clients' beneficiaries select the most appropriate payout options for their circumstances, you will be doing the right thing and earning a reputation as a trustworthy professional who sticks with your clients and their families in good times and bad.

Guardians

guardian   A *guardian* is someone appointed by the court who is responsible for caring for another. The individual who requires a guardian is either a minor or a person who is mentally or physically incompetent to care for his or her personal needs or property. The individual for whom the guardian is appointed is known as a ward. In some states, a guardian, unlike a trustee, does not necessarily have legal title to the property administered for the incompetent individual. Guardians are appointed by the court and must be discharged by the court when the term of the guardianship ends. The guardian's source of authority is the statutory and judicial law of the state in which he or she serves. This differs from the trustee, whose authority comes from both state law and from the trust instrument specifying the trustee's powers. Guardianship lasts only for the period of minority or incompetency. In actuality, a guardianship may last for the ward's lifetime. In contrast, a trustee may serve succeeding generations of beneficiaries. Like an executor, a guardian may be required to post a bond. Once the court is satisfied that the guardian is competent to serve, the court issues letters of guardianship as evidence of the guardian's authority to take responsibility for the ward's property as well as to care for the ward personally. A guardian's duties may be as varied as those of a parent.

guardian ad litem   There are several types of guardianships. The most common are the guardian of the person and the guardian of the property. When a guardianship pertains to the care and management of the ward's property, it is purely a business relationship for which the guardian generally receives a fee for services. A guardian of the person usually is given funds from the guardian of the property to take care of the minor or incompetent individual. The guardian of the person might live with the incompetent individual and provide food, clothing, shelter, and education for the minor. Another type of guardian, called a *guardian ad litem*, is appointed by the court for a particular purpose, generally to defend a specific lawsuit or legal proceeding in which the minor is a party. This type of special guardian is discharged by the court when the legal issue is resolved.

testamentary guardian

guardian de son tort

A parent may name a guardian of his or her minor children in a will. Unless there is good reason to override this choice, the court usually honors it and appoints that person, called a *testamentary guardian*. The natural guardians of a child are the parents. However, courts in many states may not name the natural parent as guardian of the property of a minor. If the minor is old enough, a guardian may also be elected by the minor child. In some states, a minor over age 14 or 15 may choose his or her own guardian, who will be appointed unless there are reasons not to do so. Occasionally, a person assumes a guardianship of a minor or incompetent individual without seeking or obtaining court approval. This type of guardian is called a *guardian de son tort* (of his or her own wrong). Because this type of guardian assumes these responsibilities, he or she is held fully responsible for all acts performed as a guardian.

Because a guardian is a fiduciary, he or she is held to the same standards as trustees or executors. One should not accept a position as guardian unless one intends to devote the attention required by the scope of the relationship.

CLIENT SITUATION SIX MONTHS AFTER JAMES' DEATH

Elizabeth meets with you 6 months after James' death. She has found employment and works as an account manager at Golden Circle. Elizabeth is paid a base salary of $36,000 annually. She anticipates receiving $12,000 of commissions this year and has found most of James' old clients are willing to continue working with her. Elizabeth believes she will receive 10–percent raises over the next few years and participates in all the benefits that had previously been available to James. Elizabeth does not work in any self-employed capacity.

Elizabeth is receiving Social Security survivor benefits for herself and her children. The benefits are electronically deposited in her bank account monthly.

An investigation into James' insurance policy is in process, and Elizabeth has initiated arbitration. She does not anticipate receiving more than 6 years of premiums ($12,000) but has contacted an attorney. The attorney has told Elizabeth she may be able to negotiate a settlement based in the insurance company's vague definition of "occasional smoker" as outlined in the policy. A majority of Elizabeth's costs are tied up in child care and debt payments. She used James' group life insurance benefit to pay for funeral costs and living expenses for 6 months. Elizabeth has provided you with a balance sheet. She wants to make sure she has correct insurance in place for herself.

Elizabeth wants to reevaluate her own life insurance coverage. She has lost weight from your first meeting and is now considered preferred from an underwriting perspective. She asks you to help her determine how much insurance to purchase and what type of estate planning documents she needs in place. If she died she would want her most responsible brother Steve to manage the children's assets but would want her fun loving brother Walter to raise the children.

Her family is helping her pay for day care for the boys while she is at work, but she would like to discontinue their assistance as soon as possible. Elizabeth sold James' truck after his death for the loan amount. Her car is beginning to fail and she is looking at buying a $15,000 car. She is concerned about buying the car because of her negative cash flow.

Elizabeth also has asset allocation and investment questions. What should she do with her investment assets, how should she handle her credit card debt, and what types of products would help her guarantee returns moving forward? The credit card debt is at 15.99 percent interest and has minimum payments of 0.1666 percent of the balance along with monthly interest. Elizabeth has consolidated her old savings and checking accounts into one master checking account. Elizabeth is also going to meet with James' brother about her financial situation.

Balance Sheet 6 Months after James' Death

Table 8-3 Balance Sheet Elizabeth Black: 6 Months after James' Death		
Assets		
Home	$165,000	
Elizabeth IRA rollover	$20,850	
Elizabeth Roth IRA	$20,000	
Honda Accord	$500	
Personal property	$55,000	
Wedding set	$5,000	
Checking account	$10,000	
Mutual fund holdings	$10,250	
Total Assets		**$284,350**
Liabilities		
Mortgage	$108,000	
Credit card debt	$33,000	
Total Liabilities		**$149,200**
Net Worth		**$135,150**

Cash Flow 6 Months after James' Death

Table 8-4 Cash Flow 6 Months after James' Death			
Income			
Elizabeth salary	$ 36,000.00		
Elizabeth bonus	$ 12,000.00		
Social Security twins	$ 21,600.00		
Social Security survivor Elizabeth	$ 10,800.00		
		$ 80,400.00	
Gross Income			**$ 80,400.00**
Gifts from Family			**$ 8,000.00**
Expenses			
Payroll taxes			
Soc. Sec. on wages (Does not assume any federal stimulus reduction)	$ (2,976.00)		
Medicare on wages (Does not assume any federal stimulus reduction)	$ (696.00)		
		$ (3,672.00)	
Federal income tax			
Taxes due (4% EFF RT)	$ (2,287.20)		
4% of wages, 4% of 85% of Soc. Sec.		$ (2,287.20)	
Property taxes			
	$ (3,180.00)		
		$ (3,180.00)	
Debt payments			
Payments on mortgage	$ (8,521.68)		
Credit card	$ (6,036.70)		
		$(14,558.38)	
Living expenses			
General expenses	$ (36,000.00)		
Child care	$ (20,000.00)		
Homeowners Insurance	$ (1,400.00)		
Auto insurance	$ (1,500.00)		
Health care premiums	$ (3,500.00)		
		$(62,400.00)	
Voluntary savings			
401(k) contribution	—		
Roth IRA contributions	—		
		—	
Expenses			$(86,097.58)
Net Available Cash Flow			**$ 2,302.42**
Monthly			$ 191.87

PLANNING RECOMMENDATIONS 6 MONTHS AFTER JAMES PASSES AWAY

Elizabeth is concerned about cash flow, survivor needs, estate planning and investment planning. Six months after James' death she has made some steps towards financial independence but is hindered by child care costs, credit card debt and a failing car.

Revised Cash Flow Recommendations

Elizabeth is facing resource allocation decisions. With gifts from her family, she is able to maintain a small monthly surplus ($191). This surplus is artificial and could not continue for a long period of time. Her cash flow does not have any retirement or emergency fund savings in place.

When first introduced to Elizabeth and James, they provided specific information about their personal property. Elizabeth had antique furniture she valued at $40,000. While the furniture has sentimental value, she could sell it and use the proceeds to pay off her credit card debt. Paying off the credit card debt will provide her with an additional $6,000 annually (about 7 percent of current expenses) and allow her to purchase adequate life insurance.

William and Richard will be old enough for public kindergarten in 2 years, which will substantially free up cash flow currently going towards day care expenses. Retirement savings may have to be delayed until child care expenses have decreased.

Elizabeth should critically analyze her budget and try to pair down the $3,000 per month she spends on non-housing living expenses. Any savings can be used to bolster her emergency fund.

If her arbitration with the life insurance company is favorable, the proceeds can be used to purchase a car. If not, she may consider using a portion of her mutual fund holdings along with current car trade-in values. Financial advisers should evaluate leasing and purchasing options with Elizabeth and determine which approach is in her best interest.

Revised Life Insurance Needs for Elizabeth

After selling her furniture and paying off credit card debt, Elizabeth will generate $500 per month in free cash flow. This cash flow can be used to purchase a new life insurance policy that appropriately measures survivor needs at her death.

Revised Lump Sum Needs for Elizabeth

At Elizabeth's death she would have the following lump sum costs.

Lump sum needs include all liabilities.

Table 8-5 Revised Lump Sum Needs at Death		
Liabilities		
Mortgage	$108,000	
Total Liabilities		$108,000

Additionally, her estate will need proceeds to provide funeral costs ($25,000) and costs associated with relocating the children, which could range between $25,000 and $50,000.

Total Lump Sum Needs = $108,000 + $25,000 + $50,000 = $183,000

Revised Cash Flow Needs for Elizabeth

How much will William and Richard need on an ongoing basis if Elizabeth passes away?

They will have child care costs, living expenses, and eventually higher education expenses. These expenses will be offset by Social Security and assets available to Elizabeth. Each expense can be calculated independently and the present value of the results added back together. Financial software could also be used in the process.

Child Care Costs

Child care costs will continue through adolescence. Current costs of $20,000 will continue through the next 2 years (when the children enter public schools) but reduced costs will remain through adolescence. Assume reduced costs of $500 per month ($6,000 per year). Two present value calculations can be used to capture the child care costs. The first will measure costs in excess of $6,000 for years one and two. The second will measure ongoing costs.

Children's Age—3

Full Need—5

Years to Fund—2

PV = Solve

Pmt = -$14,000

FV = 0

N = 2

I = 1.94% (inflation adjusted rate)

The inflation-adjusted interest rate is used because it accounts for inflating payments. Assume an inflation rate of 3.0 percent for child care costs and a universal discount rate of 6.0 percent. PV is calculated at $27,205. This number is the amount of money needed for the next 2 years of child care costs. Remaining years can be funded with $6,000 inflating payments over the next 15 years using an identical methodology. PV for continual payments is $77,442. Child care payments total approximately **$105,000.**

Living Expenses

William and Richard will incur living expenses above child care. Elizabeth's brother, Steve, will be named as custodian on behalf of the children. Trusts managed by Steve will need to be funded for each child. Distributions from the trusts will be made at the request of the guardian (Walter) while the children are younger and by William and Richard themselves as they grow older. Living expense distributions may at times be continuous when the trustee is a different individual than a named guardian. Specific wording of Elizabeth's estate planning documents will help alleviate confusion and stress.

Walter may already have a home that Elizabeth believes is appropriate to house William and Richard. If he does not, Elizabeth will need to leave enough proceeds for her children to be raised commensurately with her wishes. Non-housing living expenses are currently $3,000 per month for Elizabeth and her children; assume this amount will continue if Elizabeth were to pass away. Assume expenses would begin immediately and set your calculator to BGN mode.

Children's Age—3

Full Need—23

Years to Fund—20

PV = Solve

Pmt = -$36,000

FV = 0

N = 20

I = 1.94% (inflation adjusted rate)

The inflation-adjusted interest rate is used because it accounts for inflating payments. Assume an inflation rate of 3.0 percent for living expenses and a universal discount rate of 6.0 percent. PV is calculated at **$603,560.51**. Students may consider using a larger or smaller N, depending on how long they want to model the length of provided living expenses. N =20 will take the children through age 23.

Higher Education Expenses

Elizabeth wants her children to attend college and would like to fund their college education in the event of her death. They are currently 3, and Elizabeth estimates they will begin attending college in fourteen (14) years. The cost of attending college today is estimated at $30,000; and Elizabeth assumes a college inflation rate of 5.5 percent. She assumes her money would be able to earn 6.0 percent in an account for college costs.

Step One: How much will one year of college cost the twins in fourteen years?

PV = −30,000

I = 5.5%

PMT = 0

N = 14

Solve FV = $63,482.75

Step Two: How much will either twin need at the start of college for four years of education?

BGN MODE — Tuition must be paid at the beginning of a semester!!

PMT = –63,482.75

I = 0.4739 (inflation adjusted return considering 6.0% market return and 5.5% inflation)

FV = 0

N =4

Solve PV = 252,140.08. This is the amount needed the day either of the twins start college; to pay tuition annually over four years of college

Step Three: How much would Elizabeth need (as a lump sum) to provide college education costs beginning in fourteen years

(Clear your calculator from the previous equations)

PMT = 0

FV = 252,140.08

N = 14

I = 6.0 (Elizabeth's discount rate)

Solve PV = $111,521.80 per twin; $223,043.60 for both children.

Elizabeth would need to set aside $223,403.60 today and earn 6.0 percent annually over the next fourteen years to provide for four years of college costs for her children.

Total Cash Flow Needs

Total cash flow needs are child care costs ($105,000), Living expenses (603,560.51) and Education Expenses (223,403.60) totalling $931,964.11

Revised Total Insurance Need for Elizabeth

Elizabeth's lump sum needs are $183,000. Her cash flow needs total around $932,000. Elizabeth's total need is $1,115,000. This need is offset by Elizabeth's total assets, any insurance proceeds and the present value of Social Security survivor benefits.

Elizabeth's net worth is $135,000. One times her salary is $36,000. The present value of Richard and William's Social Security benefits can be determined below. Social Security payments begin the month following death, and students should use END mode on their calculators for this equation.

Children's Age—3

Full Need—19

Years of benefits—16

PV = Solve

Pmt = –$21,600*

FV = 0

N = 16

I = 2.19% (inflation-adjusted rate)

The inflation-adjusted interest rate is used because it accounts for inflating payments. Assume a Social Security inflation rate of 3.0 percent and a universal discount rate of 6.0 percent. PV is calculated at **$288,775** and rounds to $289,000. Social Security benefits may be slightly higher. James and William will each receive 75 percent of the higher of James or Elizabeth's primary insurance amount as found on James' Social Security statement. If Elizabeth passes away they will not be subject to the family maximum benefit limit and may receive more than $900 each per month. A $900 monthly benefit provides a conservative assumption for planning purposes.

Elizabeth's total need ($1,115,000) less available resources ($460,000) give Elizabeth a total insurance need at $655,000. Insurance is typically sold in $50,000 lots and Elizabeth should purchase at least $650,000 of coverage, potentially $700,000. Twenty-year term coverage is appropriate considering Elizabeth's cash flow constraints and time horizon. Twenty-year term coverage with a waiver-of-premium benefit for disability will cost Elizabeth between $40 and $80 per month. This amount is well within her budget if she divests herself of antique furniture to pay off her credit card debt.

Revised Investment Recommendations

Elizabeth was named as the primary beneficiary on both James' Roth IRA and 401(k) Plan. As a spousal beneficiary, Elizabeth can make a qualified rollover of James' retirement plan assets directly into her name. Once establishing new accounts Elizabeth should establish the children as primary beneficiaries and consider contingent beneficiaries.

Elizabeth's mutual fund account assets received a step up in basis at James' death. This account can be used as a tool towards retirement or college education funding costs. Elizabeth needs to develop an overall asset allocation taking advantage of the tax status of each of her accounts. The Roth IRA and Traditional IRA accounts can be used to hold dividend and income-producing securities such as bonds and large company value stocks. The taxable mutual fund position should focus on stocks that reinvest capital gains, such as large and medium sized growth stocks. A balanced portfolio can be designed to meet Elizabeth's risk tolerance.

Consider broad-based mutual fund investing or purchasing a variable annuity. Elizabeth might benefit from an age-based lifecycle fund. These funds reallocate annually based on Elizabeth's age and will become more conservative as she nears retirement. A variable annuity may be appropriate for the nonqualified account as it will provide tax deferral and help limit Elizabeth's income tax. Either investment option requires less than a $10,000 account minimum to accommodate the size of the account.

CHAPTER REVIEW

Key Terms and Concepts

guardian	testamentary guardian
guardian ad litem	guardian de son tort

Review Questions

These questions are intended to help students answer questions about case studies, goals and assumptions. Answers to these questions can be found in the study supplement.

1. When a wage earner dies, what documents are necessary to file a Social Security death claim? [3]

2. What is the family maximum benefit surviving beneficiaries can receive from a primary wage earners PIA? [3]

3. Are insurance companies legally bound by the contents of an insurance application? [2]

4. What are the five stages of grief? [1]

5. What is a testamentary guardian? Are individuals named as guardians always appointed? [1]

Learning Objectives

An understanding of the material in this chapter should enable the student to

1. Develop an understanding of advanced financial planning topics.

2. Practice a case study method similar to methods used on the CFP® exam.

3. Review multiple financial planning case studies.

4. Master advanced topics through the application of comprehensive questions.

financial planning case studies

This chapter is comprised of a series of financial planning cases with multiple-choice answers. The cases included in the analysis should be solved as of the planning date at the beginning of each case study. Each case presented focuses on at lease two financial planning topic areas. Topic areas include general principles, ethics, education planning, investment planning, estate planning, insurance planning and integrated concepts. Case studies will be presented followed by closed ended multiple choice questions. The answers and rationale for case study answers will follow the text.

professional designation exams

Professional designation exams, such as the CFP®, CPA and CFA marks often rely on case studies to test a student's ability to apply knowledge. Case studies used in the examination process often revolve around one particular theme, such as risk management or retirement planning. Instead of solving the case study as a comprehensive financial plan, case studies oriented towards exams ask students closed ended questions. Most professional designation exams are timed, and students can develop both their financial planning and test taking strategies by working through practice case studies. Minicase questions are similar to those found on the CFP® exam. The rationale assumes a functional level of financial planning knowledge including terms and definitions.

Students should read-through the mini-case before looking at the questions. After reading through the case, write down key facts about the case. Key facts might include client age, children, objectives, and key financial information. After outlining the case, begin to work on the case questions. Skip any questions that are difficult and come back to those questions after answering easier ones.

MINI-CASE 1: FRANK AND CHARLES

Note

This case focuses on retirement planning and financial planning for same-sex married couples. Students should review retirement planning distributions, taxation, 401(k) plans and same-sex planning techniques before attempting to answer this case. Students should also consider reviewing general estate tax concepts, especially as they pertain to gay and lesbian couples.

Assume a date of 12/31/2011

Frank is a bank executive at Big Brother Bank. He is 55 and has been with the bank full-time for 10 years. Frank earns a base salary of $135,000 annually and will earn a holiday bonus of $10,000 at the end of 2010. Frank is in a relationship with Charles, and they have been together for the past decade. Last year they married when their state approved a same-sex marriage resolution. Charles is 48 and works as a teacher, earning $60,000 annually.

Frank and Charles want to begin travelling at retirement. Frank has amassed $500,000 in his employer 401(k); he is 100 percent vested. Frank has contributed $12,000 into the plan through 2010 and his employer matches $0.25 of every $1.00 he contributes. Frank has checking and savings accounts with a total value of $50,000. Charles is listed as the primary beneficiary of the retirement plan. Frank has life insurance equal to his base salary with Charles listed as the primary beneficiary. Frank would like to retire at 57. Charles does not have any retirement savings but will receive an annual pension of $2,800 per month beginning at age 60. The pension calculation assumes he will continue working through age 60. Charles does not have any employer-provided life insurance.

If either Frank or Charles were to die today, they would want all assets to go to one another. Neither Frank nor Charles has any children. Charles' parents are still living and do not support his relationship with Frank. Charles and Frank live in a condo owned by Frank. Frank owns the condo free and clear of any mortgage, though both Charles and Frank have made property tax and homeowners association dues payments over the past decade. In today's real estate market the condo is worth around $1,000,000. Homeowner association dues are $15,000 annually, insurance costs are $5,000 annually, and utilities cost about $400 per month.

If he dies first, Frank wants to leave Charles enough money to pay for condo expenses into perpetuity, without using any principal or retirement assets. Charles has the same wish for Frank. Both Charles and Frank are comfortable with the risk necessary to earn a 6.0 percent interest rate on long-term investments. Neither Frank nor Charles have any estate planning documents.

Case Questions: Frank and Charles

1. What is the maximum amount Frank can save in an IRA for the 2011 tax year?

   a. $0
   b. $2,250
   c. $5,000
   d. $6,000

2. What is the maximum amount Charles can save in a Roth IRA for the 2011 tax year?

   a. $0
   b. $4,000
   c. $5,000
   d. $6,000

3. Which estate planning measure is least effective in protecting Frank or Charles' interest when planning for either of their deaths?

   a. Change the title on all Frank and Charles' property to joint with rights of survivorship; make taxable lifetime gifts if necessary.
   b. Title all property into living trusts, appointing each other as cotrustees and trust beneficiaries at death.
   c. Create simple wills leaving Frank and Charles' property to one another at death.
   d. Purchase life insurance on one another for the amount of the condo to protect ownership interests.

4. How much life insurance should be purchased on Frank's life to pay condo costs into perpetuity with Charles as the primary beneficiary?

    a. $825,333

    b. $413,333

    c. $278,333

    d. $0

5. How much life insurance should be purchased on Charles' life to pay condo costs into perpetuity with Frank as the primary beneficiary?

    a. $825,333

    b. $413,333

    c. $278,333

    d. $0

6. If Frank died today, which of the following options are available to Charles with regard to Frank's 401(k) plan?

    a. Roll the entire $500,000 into an IRA for Charles. Charles is not forced to begin any distributions at this time and can make future contributions into the IRA.

    b. Leave the $500,000 in the 401(k) and liquidate the position by taking distributions out of the plan over the next 10 years.

    c. Roll the entire $500,000 into a nonspousal beneficiary IRA using a trustee to trustee transfer. Charles is forced to begin taking distributions based on his (Charles) life expectancy.

    d. Roll the entire $500,000 into a nonspousal beneficiary IRA. using a trustee to trustee transfer. Charles must begin taking distributions from the IRA based on Frank's life expectancy.

7. If Frank continues to invest $12,000 annually in his 401(k) plan, how much will be available to him at his retirement? Answer selections are rounded to the nearest thousand.

    a. $593,000

    b. $598,000

    c. $633,000

    d. $643,000

8. What options are available to Charles and Frank when filing 2011 federal income tax returns?

   a. Married Filing Jointly
   b. Married Filing Separately
   c. Single
   d. Head of Household

9. If Frank died today, what is the value of his Gross Estate for the purpose of calculating the Federal Estate Tax?

   a. $0
   b. $1,550,000
   c. $1,635,000
   d. $1,685,000

10. If Frank died today, which of his assets may be subject to state intestate laws?
    I. Frank's 401(k)

    II. Frank's Checking Account

    a. I
    b. II
    c. I and II
    d. None of the above

Case Discussion: Frank and Charles

1. What is the maximum amount Frank can save in a Roth IRA for the 2011 tax year?

   - **d. $6,000** — Frank will be able to make a **non deductible** $5,000 contribution to an IRA as well as a $1,000 catch-up contribution for being over 55. Frank's MAGI ($145,000) is greater than the ROTH phaseout amount for 2011 (prohibiting him from making a ROTH contribution) and Frank is covered under an employer plan. Frank is allowed to make a non deductible contribution.

2. What is the maximum amount Charles can save in a Roth IRA for the 2011 tax year?

   - **c. $5,000** — Charles will be able to make a regular $5,000 contribution to a Roth IRA in 2011. Charles can make a contribution while he is covered by a state retirement plan.

3. Which estate planning measure is least effective in protecting Frank or Charles' interest when planning for either of their deaths?

- **d. Purchase life insurance on one another for the amount of the condo to protect ownership interests**. — This option leaves Charles and Frank without wills or trusts. The case states Frank's parents do not support his relationship with Charles, and they could petition a court to follow potentially unfavorable intestate laws. Wills or Trusts would protect Charles and Frank's condo interest, where life insurance would only provide cash.

4. How much life insurance should be purchased on Frank's life to pay condo costs into perpetuity with Charles as the primary beneficiary?

- **c. $278,333** — Annual condo costs are $15,000 + $5,000 + $4,800 = $24,800. Assuming a 6 percent interest rate, Frank will need total death benefits of $413,333 to fund condo costs. Frank already has a base salary of life insurance coverage ($135,000) reducing his need to $278,333. Frank specifically requested that no retirement assets should be used in calculating a condo endowment.

5. How much life insurance should be purchased on Charles' life to pay condo costs into perpetuity with Frank as the primary beneficiary?

- **b. $413,333** — The same justification applies as in number 4, except that Charles has no existing group life insurance.

6. If Frank died today, which of the following options are available to Charles with regard to Frank's 401(k) plan?

- **c. Roll the entire $500,000 into a non spousal beneficiary IRA using a trustee to trustee transfer.** — Charles can open a non spousal IRA but must begin taking distributions based on his life expectancy. Charles cannot leave the assets in Frank's 401(k) for longer than five years, making b invalid. A is only available for a spouse recognized on a federal level, and currently two men would not be recognized as married through ERISA rules.

7. If Charles continues to invest $12,000 annually in his 401(k) plan, how much will be available at his retirement? Answer selections are rounded to the nearest thousand.

   - **a. $593,000** —Frank has $500,000 in his 401(k) today. He will save $12,000 annually and his employer will match $3,000. Frank will continue saving for 2 more years and his money is projected to earn 6.0 percent.

8. What options are available to Charles and Frank when filing 2010 federal income tax returns?

   - **c. Single** — Frank and Charles may me married under state law, but as of 2010 the federal government and the IRS do not recognize same sex marriages. Charles and Frank would have to file single federal returns even if they could file married state tax returns.

9. If Frank died today, what is the value of his Gross Estate for the purpose of calculating the Federal Estate Tax?

   - **d. $1,685,000** — Frank's gross estate consists of his life insurance through work ($135,000), Condo ($1,000,000), 401(k) ($500,000) and savings account ($50,000).

10. If Frank died today, which of his assets may be subject to state intestate laws?

    - **b. II** — Frank's 401(k) would pass to Charles through beneficiary designation. His checking account may be subject to intestate laws.

MINI-CASE 2: ANNE AND MARK

Note

This case focuses on retirement plan selection and education planning. Review retirement plan types and contribution methods before continuing on with this case study. Students are encouraged to review 529 and UGMA rules as well.

Anne is a dentist living in a community property state. Anne is the 100 percent owner of her practice, operating as an S corporation. Her practice focuses on dental services for the entire family, including children, and she has been in business for 20 years. Anne is married to Mark who works as an engineer. Anne is 51 and Mark is 53; they have two children, Karen (13) and Michael (17). Both Karen and Michael intend to begin college at age 18.

Assume a date of 12/31/2011

Anne has supplied you with an active employee census. Mark, Karen and Michael do not participate in Anne's business.

Table 9-1 Employee Census for Anne's Business					
Employee Name	Title	Age	Years at Practice	Annual Wages	Hours Worked per Year
Anne	Dentist	51	20	$150,000	2,000
Deborah	Hygienist	50	9	$50,000	2,000
Steve	Hygienist	28	2	$35,000	1,200
Joseph	Assistant	23	3	$15,000	800

Anne's practice has generated a substantial cash flow surplus for 2011. After paying all expenses and wages she has a surplus cash flow of $50,000 in her corporate checking account. Anne expects to earn at least this much in future years and is considering implementing a retirement plan for her business.

She and Mark are also saving towards their children's college. Michael will begin college next year, and Karen will begin when she turns 18. Anne and Mark have provided a statement of current college savings.

Michael

- Unified Gift to Minors Account (UGMA)
    - $8,000 Money Market Account
    - $8,000 High Yield Bond Fund

- 529 Plan
    - $8,000 Domestic Large Cap Growth Fund
    - $6,000 Domestic Large Cap Value Fund

Karen

- Unified Gift to Minors Account (UGMA)
    - $25,000—Money market Account

Mark and Anne estimate college expenses to be $15,000 annually today and will inflate at 6.0 percent. Mark and Anne believe they can achieve an 8.0 percent rate of return for education and retirement needs.

Case Questions: Anne and Mark

1. If Anne adopted a Money Purchase Pension plan, how much of Steve's salary can he elect to defer into the plan this year?
    a. $0
    b. $16,500
    c. $22,000
    d. $49,500

2. What type of contribution formula and retirement plan would provide Anne with the largest percentage of total contribution?
    a. Cross testing profit sharing plan
    b. Profit sharing plan integrated with Social Security
    c. Safe harbor 401(k) plan with a 2.0 percent match for all employees
    d. SIMPLE

3. Anne adopts a profit sharing plan covering employees who work at least 1,000 hours per year. She makes a contribution of her entire cash surplus, and allocates the contributions to participant accounts by the ratio that the compensation of each participant bears to the aggregate compensation of all participants. How much will Steve's contribution be this year?
    a. $0

    b. $3,733

    c. $7,000

    d. $7,445

4. Anne adopts a 401(k) profit sharing plan. How much can Anne defer from her salary into the plan?

    a. $16,500

    b. $22,000

    c. $49,000

    d. $50,000

5. All employees have indicated they are not interested in participating in the retirement plan. What is Anne's most cost-effective technique to minimize employer contributions to the plan but ensure compliance with 401(k) safe harbor provisions?

    a. Make a nonelective contribution of 2.0 percent of employee compensation.

    b. Make a nonelective contribution of 3.0 percent of employee compensation.

    c. Match employee contributions dollar for dollar for the first 2.0 percent of the employee's compensation and $0.50 on the dollar for any additional contributions.

    d. Match employee contributions dollar for dollar for the first 3.0 percent of the employee's compensation and $0.50 on the dollar for any additional contributions.

6. How much is a year of college projected to cost when Karen turns 18?

    a. $15,852

    b. $17,865

    c. $20,073

    d. $26,435

7. What change to Michael's asset allocation would reduce interest income?

    a. Sell all his positions and invest in corporate bonds.

    b. Hold bond positions in Michael's 529 college savings plan and value-oriented equity positions in his UGMA account.

    c. Hold bond positions in Michael's 529 college savings plan and growth-oriented equity positions in his UGMA account.

    d. Add dollars only to Michael's UGMA account.

8. Anne is the owner of Michael's 529 plan and is also listed on his UGMA account. If Michael decided not to attend college, what are Anne's options?

    a. Anne can withhold Michael's 529 plan proceeds and UGMA account from him and give them to Karen.

    b. Michael will have full access to his UGMA account when he reaches an age of majority, but Anne can change the beneficiary of the 529 plan to Karen.

    c. Michael will have full access to his 529 plan account when he reaches an age of majority, but Anne can give his UGMA account to Karen.

    d. Anne cannot make any changes to Michael's UGMA or 529 plan.

9. If Anne and Mark meet their target savings rate, how much money will Michael have available for college next year?

    a. $31,800

    b. $32,400

    c. $33,000

    d. $33,850

10. What is an appropriate inflation-adjusted rate of return to use for college funding calculations with an annuity element?

    a. 1.35%

    b. 1.50%

    c. 1.88%

    d. 2.00%

Case Discussion: Anne and Mark

1. If Anne adopted a money purchase pension plan, how much of Steve's salary can he elect to defer into the plan this year?

    • **a. $0** — Steve is unable to defer his salary into a profit-sharing plan unless the plan has 401(k) provisions.

2. What type of contribution formula and retirement plan would provide Anne with the largest percentage of total contribution?

    • **b. Profit-sharing plan integrated with Social Security** — Because Anne is the only employee earning above the Social Security wage base and she has an employee on staff who is older, an integrated profit-sharing plan will allow her to maximize the contribution in her favor.

3. Anne adopts a profit-sharing plan covering employees who work at least 1,000 hours per year. She makes a contribution of her entire cash surplus and allocates the contributions to participant accounts by the ratio that the compensation of each participant bears to the aggregate compensation of all participants. How much will Steve's contribution be this year?

    - **d. $7,445** — Steve's salary consists of 14 percent of the wage base after excluding Joseph's wages (Joseph works under 1,000 hours per year). Steve would have to be covered under a profit sharing plan after working with Anne for 2 years. 14.89 percent of the wage base times $50,000 contribution would provide Steve with a $7,445 contribution.

4. Anne adopts a 401(k) profit-sharing plan. How much can Anne defer from her salary into the plan?

    - **b. $22,000** — Anne could defer $16,500 of her salary into a Roth (or regular) 401(k) plan. She can make a catch-up contribution of $5,500 based on her age IRS publication 560 contains useful information about retirement plans, students are suggested to reference this publication if they need more information.

5. All employees have indicated they are not interested in participating in the retirement plan. What is Anne's most cost effective technique to minimize employer contributions to the plan but ensure compliance with 401(k) safe harbor provisions?

    - **d. Match employee contributions dollar for dollar for the first 3.0 percent of the employee's compensation and $0.50 on the dollar for any additional contributions.**—This will satisfy safe harbor requirements and potentially minimize Anne's contributions. If employees begin participating in the plan she can amend the plan.

6. How much is one year of college projected to cost when Karen turns 18?

    - **c. $20,073**—Karen will begin college in 5 years when she turns 18. The current cost of college is $15,000 annually and inflation is expected to be 6.0 percent. PV = $15,000; N=5; I = 6.0%; No PMT; Solve for FV

7. What change to Michael's asset allocation would reduce interest income?

   - **c. Hold bond positions in Michael's 529 college savings plan and growth-oriented equity positions in his UGMA account.** This is the only option that would help reduce interest income. Growth stocks tend to not pay dividends, which would minimize any income generated from the UGMA account.

8. Anne is the owner of Michael's 529 plan and is also listed on his UGMA account. If Michael decided not to attend college, what are Anne's options?

   - **b. Michael will have full access to his UGMA account when he reaches an age of majority, but Anne can change the beneficiary of the 529 plan to Karen.** Michael will have full use and access to proceeds in his UGMA account when he turns 18 or 21 (depending on the state age of majority) regardless of his college status. Anne can change the beneficiary of Michael's 529 account at any time.

9. If Anne and Mark meet their target savings rate how much money will Michael have available for college next year?

   - **b. $32,400**—Michael has $30,000 available today. One year of growth at 8 percent would be $32,400. $30,000 × (1.08) = $32,400.

10. What is an appropriate inflation-adjusted rate of return to use for college funding calculations with an annuity element?

    - **c. 1.88%**—An inflation-adjusted rate is found by dividing (1 + growth rate) / (1 + inflation rate) and subtracting one from the product. In this case the growth rate is 8 percent and inflation rate is 6 percent.

MINI-CASE 3: MICHAEL BLUE

Note

This case focuses on health insurance, retirement distribution options and comprehensive financial planning. Students should review rules surrounding high deductible health care plans and health care savings accounts before working through the case. This case is an example of divorce planning when adult children are present. NOTE — Health Care reform of 2011 eliminated lifetime caps on health care coverage for new policies issued after reform took effect. This case retains lifetime caps, as planners may encounter them on older policies or if health care reform changes in the next election cycle.

Assume a current date of 1/1/2011.

Michael Blue, 57 years old, is a retired executive from General Electric. Today is Michael's birthday. Over his 30 years at GE he worked his way from engineer to vice president of product development for North America. Michael retired last month and is looking for help with some difficult retirement decisions. He wants to travel the world and wants to develop a comprehensive retirement plan to help him sustain an active retirement. Michael participated in the GE pension plan. He is not sure if he should roll dollars out of the plan into an IRA or take one of the plan annuity options. Michael has continued benefits through his employer health plan as a retiree, but in a measure to cut costs, GE does not provide any match for retired executives to continue participating in the group health plan. GE allows Michael to choose between a traditional medical expense plan and a PPO until he is eligible for Medicare.

Michael is recently divorced and has one adult child, Julie. Julie is successful and following her father's path at GE. Michael has over $1,000,000 in investment assets, cash, and savings accounts. He intends on leaving these assets to Julie at his death.

Michael can choose between the following two plans at his retirement.

High Deductible Health Plan

The traditional medical plan has a high deductible ($3,500) and pays 90 percent of all approved costs after the deductible is met up to a maximum out-of-pocket limit of $10,000. The plan has a lifetime maximum of

$2,000,000. Michael has spent $190,000 of that maximum over his career with GE. These costs were incurred when he fell off a ladder 10 years ago. The traditional medical plan has a monthly premium of $200 and the premium has inflated at 10 percent annually over the last 5 years.

This health care plan has a prescription carve-out that gives Michael $30 per month of copays on generic drugs, $50 per month on listed medications, and $100 per month on non-listed medications after satisfying the annual deductible. Michael takes a blood pressure and an anti-depression medication; both are listed as approved plan medications.

PPO Supplemental Plan

The PPO limits providers to Michael's hometown. Michael pays $50 to see any listed provider. The provider list is comprehensive and includes specialists as well as general practitioners. Michael's general practice doctor and psychiatrist are on the list of preferred providers. The plan will provide 70 percent of approved costs if Michael saw an out-of-network provider, after a $2,000 out-of-network deductible. Maximum lifetime medical costs are limited to $1,000,000. The PPO has a monthly premium of $325 and the premium has inflated at 5 percent annually over the last 5 years. This plan offers $20 per month of copays on generic drugs, $40 per month on listed medications, and $75 per month on non-listed medications.

Pension Plan

Michael's GE Pension plan offers him three options. He must make an irrevocable decision within 90 days of leaving GE. If Michael does not act within the 90-day period, the plan will annuitize and begin monthly payments. Michael's options include:

- Roll a lump-sum payout of $604,000 into cash or directly to an IRA.
- Take a life annuity (without inflation protection) of $2,862 per month. The annuity payments would begin immediately.
- Take a life-with-10-year-certain annuity paying $2,450 per month. Annuity payments would begin immediately.

Case Questions: Michael Blue

1. If Michael selects the high deductible plan, how much can he contribute pre-tax in a health care savings account this year?

   a. $3,050
   b. $3,550
   c. $4,050
   d. $6,550

2. If Michael selects the high-deductible traditional medical plan, he can make qualified distributions out of his health care savings accounts for

   - I. Long Term Care Insurance Premiums
   - II. Blood Pressure Medication

   a. I
   b. II only
   c. I and II
   d. None of the above

3. Michael selects the PPO plan. If he has an illness next year while on vacation and incurs a bill of $12,500 from an out-of-network provider, what will be his total out of pocket costs?

   a. $2,000
   b. $3,200
   c. $5,150
   d. $8,200

4. If Michael develops aggressive lung cancer and needs to see specialists, some of which are listed on the PPO plan and some not, which health care plan would be most appropriate for Michael and why?

   a. The high deductible plan because it has $2,000,000 of lifetime maximum benefits when contrasted to the PPO plan.
   b. The high deductible plan because it has lower monthly premiums when contrasted to the PPO plan.
   c. The PPO plan because it provides out of network coverage and the high deductible plan limits doctor options.

    d. The PPO plan because it provides lower pharmacy deductibles which would lower the cost of Michael's chemotherapy.

5. Michael is in great health and is confident of Julie's continued success. If he can confidently achieve a 2.0 percent risk-free rate of return and has no bequest motive, which annuity option should he choose?

    a. Take a lump sum distribution and invest the IRA rollover on his own.

    b. Take a lump sum distribution and make annual gifts to Julie.

    c. Select the life-annuity-with-10-year-certain option.

    d. Select the life annuity option.

6. Assume Michael is making a decision to annuitize or not annuitize based on a life expectancy of 90. What minimum risk-free rate of return would Michael have to earn to consider taking the lump sum option?

    a. 2.51 percent

    b. 2.98 percent

    c. 3.92 percent

    d. 4.24 percent

7. Michael selects a life annuity pension option. He dies in 3 years at age 60. The Federal midterm rate is 5.2 percent in the year of his death. What is the residual pension value used to calculate his gross estate?

    a. $0

    b. $172,194.74

    c. $515,800.00

    d. $604,000.00

8. Michael begins taking early Social Security at age 62. Assuming he is not disabled or suffering from kidney trouble, when will he become eligible for Medicare part B?

    a. 62

    b. 64

    c. 65

    d. 67

9. Michael elects to take the 10-year-certain annuity and promptly dies the next year. Julie is listed as his beneficiary. Which of the following statements is true?

   a. Annuity benefits will not be taxable to Julie because of the step up in cost basis that occurs at Michael's death.

   b. Michael's estate will pay income taxes on the residual value of the annuity due at his death.

   c. Julie will owe estate taxes on the residual value of the annuity in the year of Michael's death.

   d. The residual value of the annuity will be included in Michael's gross estate.

10. If General Electric declared bankruptcy before Michael's annuitization decision, which government institution would help protect Michael's retirement?

    a. Federal Deposit Insurance Corporation

    b. Securities Investor Protection Corporation

    c. Pension Benefit Guaranty Corporation

    d. National Association of Insurance and Annuity Companies

Case Discussion: Michael Blue

1. If Michael selects the high deductible plan, how much can he contribute pre-tax in a health care savings account this year?

   • **c. $4,050**—Michael is limited by a $3,050 maximum contribution for 2011. He can make an additional $1,000 step-up contribution as long as he is not enrolled in Medicare. IRS publication 969 contains additional information about Health Care Savings Accounts and other tax qualified plans.

2. If Michael selects the high-deductible traditional medical plan, he can make qualified distributions out of his health care savings accounts for which of the following?

   • **c.** — Michael can use HSA dollars for LTC premiums and medical costs.

3. Michael selects the PPO plan. If he has an illness next year while on vacation and incurs a bill of $12,500 from an out of network provider, what will his total out of pocket costs be?

   • **c. $5,150**—Michael will be out of pocket an initial deductible of $2,000. After that deductible, he will have to pay 30 percent of the remaining claim ($10,500) or $3,150.

4. If Michael develops aggressive lung cancer and needs to see specialists, some of which are listed on the PPO plan and some are not, which health care plan would be more appropriate for Michael and why?

   - **a. The high deductible plan** because of a higher lifetime maximum benefit. Cancer costs can escalate rapidly and providing him with inadequate health coverage could destroy his financial situation.

5. Michael is in great health and is confident of Julie's continued success. If he can confidently achieve a 2.0 percent risk-free rate of return and has no bequest motive, which annuity option should he choose?

   - **d. Select the life annuity option**—Michael is in good health and has not expressed any need to take the 10-year certain option. Michael indicates he is in great health, and if he lives to be 90, 95, or 100 he will have maximized his utility taking the life annuity option. At a 2.0 percent fixed rate of return, he will realize more utility from taking the income stream than the lump sum.

6. Assume Michael is making a decision to annuitize or not annuitize based on a life expectancy of 90. What minimum risk-free rate of return would Michael have to earn to consider taking the lump sum option?

   - **d. 4.24 percent**—Michael needs to find the minimum interest rate assuming a 33-year life expectancy (N), $33,344 (annualized payments) (PMT) with a balance of $604,000 (PV). Using a time value of money function, students should solve for N; either PV or PMT must be negative in the equation. Solve for interest rate. Michael needs to be able to secure a risk-free rate of at least 4.24 percent before he should mathematically consider taking the lump sum. Calculator strokes are as follows: PV = —$604,000; PMT = $33,344; N=–33; FV = $0 Solve for I.

7. Michael selects a life annuity pension option. He dies in 3 years at age 60. The Federal Midterm rate is 5.2 percent in the year of his death. What is the residual pension value of used to calculate his gross estate?

- **a. $0**—If Michael selects a life annuity option, payments will stop upon his death. His estate will have no residual value.

8. Michael begins taking early social security at his age 62. Assuming he is not disabled or suffering from kidney trouble, when will he become eligible for Medicare part B?

    - **c. 65**—Michael can begin receiving medicare three months before he turns 65, regardless of when he begins receiving Social Security.

9. Michael elects to take the 10-year-certain annuity and promptly dies the next year. Julie is listed as his beneficiary. Which of the following statements is true?

    - **d. The residual value of the annuity will be included in Michael's gross estate.** Michael's gross estate will include the residual value of the annuity. The other statements are false.

10. If General Electric declared bankruptcy before Michael's annuitization decision, which government institution would help protect Michael's retirement?

    - **c. Pension Benefit Guaranty Corporation**—General Electric is a large, publicly traded company with an ERISA retirement plan. Michael's pension would be protected by the PBGC.

MINI-CASE 4: TONY AND MARIA LOPEZ

Note

This case focuses on property casualty insurance and general financial planning principles. Students should review homeowners, umbrella, and mortgage rules before completing this case study.

Assume a case date of 01/01/2011

homeowners coverage

Tony and Maria Lopez are considering selling their home and moving into a smaller condo. The condo is located in an upscale part of town with significant new construction and renovation in progress. The condo is listed at $500,000 and is located close to the hospital where Tony, who just turned 60, works as a cardiologist. Tony is an independent contractor and does not have access to any employer benefits or group insurance coverage.

net worth statement

Maria is 55 and works as a schoolteacher in a nearby suburban school district. She is 5 years away from retirement. Tony and Maria have provided an inventory of their assets and liabilities:

Table 9-2 Assets and Liabilities for Tony and Maria Lopez		
Assets	**Value**	**Notes**
Home	$450,000	The home was purchased for $500,000 three years ago.
Brokerage account JTWROS	$250,000	Cost basis of $400,000. No contributions or reinvestments were made in 2008.
Tony's 403(b)	$350,000	Tony has made $200,000 pre-tax contributions over the years. His employer made contributions of $50,000.
Savings account	$10,000	
Home furnishings	$40,000	
Maria's wedding ring	$35,000	
Liabilities		
Mortgage	($352,000)	
HELOC	($30,000)	
Credit card debt	($25,000)	

The Lopezes currently have an HO-3 policy on their home with a deductible equal to 1 percent of the insured value. The policy lists the replacement value of the home at $490,000. Tony and Maria have an umbrella insurance policy with $2,000,000 of liability coverage protection.

Tony and Maria have great credit and qualify for a 15-year conventional mortgage with a 5.0 percent rate. Tony and Marie plan on putting 20 percent down on their home.

Case Questions: Tony and Maria Lopez

1. What property insurance form coverage do Tony and Maria need to purchase for their new condo?

   a. HO-1

   b. HO-3

   c. HO-4

   d. HO-6

2. A dinner guest carelessly set a lit cigarette next to a lace curtain and the home burned down, a total loss. How much will Tony and Maria's insurance company pay out in total claims?

   a. $485,100

   b. $525,100

   c. $690,000

   d. $703,100

3. Tony and Maria decide to move to an apartment in the city for a year while upgrading and renovating their home. After packing up the moving truck, all of their home furnishings are destroyed in a car accident. Tony was driving the moving truck. How much will Tony and Maria receive from their homeowners insurance company?

   a. $0

   b. $40,000

   c. $36,000

   d. $35,100

4. Maria loses her wedding ring in the move. Maria does not have any special riders or endorsements on the policy. How much will Maria receive from her homeowners policy?

   a. $0

   b. $1,500

      c. $2,500

      d. $30,100

5. Tony and Maria purchase and move into their condo before selling their home. Which of the following options provide them with appropriate coverage?

      a. Notify the insurance company of the move, maintain coverage on their home and purchase additional property insurance for their condominium.

      b. Change their coverage on their unoccupied home to form HO-4 coverage and purchase additional property insurance for their condominium.

      c. Drop all coverage on the home and purchase property insurance for their condominium.

      d. They do not need to purchase additional coverage on the condominium.

6. Which of these situations is covered under the Lopezes' personal umbrella policy?

      a. Tony is listed by name in a lawsuit brought against the hospital where he works.

      b. Tony is sued for $2,000,000 in a malpractice claim by a hospital patient.

      c. Maria is involved in an accident with a school bus and her personal liability exceeds her automobile limit. Maria was arrested for driving under the influence of alcohol at the time of the accident.

      d. Tony backs over a coworker at the hospital on his way home from work. The coworker sustains over $1,000,000 of medical bills and lost wages.

7. What strategy would offer Tony and Maria more creditor protection than they have today?

      a. Sell brokerage assets and purchase a 6-month CD.

      b. Take out a home equity loan and invest the proceeds in an offshore savings account.

      c. Gift brokerage account assets in-kind into a revocable living trust with Tony as the trustee.

      d. Use a portion of brokerage account assets to fund a cash-value life insurance policy.

8. Tony and Maria decide to sell everything and tour the country in an RV. What are the tax consequences of Tony and Maria liquidating their home, brokerage account, and taking a lump-sum distribution of their 403(b)?

    a. $200,000 long–term capital loss; $100,000 unearned ordinary income

    b. $100,000 long–term capital loss; $0 unearned income

    c. $200,000 long–term capital loss; $350,000 unearned ordinary income

    d. $150,000 long–term capital loss; $350,000 unearned ordinary income

9. What is Tony and Maria's net worth?

    a. $768,000

    b. $728,000

    c. $808,000

    d. $628,000

10. Assume Tony and Maria purchase the condo for its list price, pay all closing costs out of pocket, and make a 20 percent down payment. Tony and Maria do not escrow taxes and insurance. What will their monthly payments be on a 15-year conventional note with a 5.0 percent interest rate?

    a. $3,163

    b. $3,953

    c. $2,684

    d. $2,147

11. Tony and Maria purchase the condo using a 30-year conventional note and qualify for special 5.0 percent promotional financing. They pay 20 percent down. Assuming the condo price is unchanged, how much equity will they have in the condo after one year?

    a. $100,000

    b. $105,901

    c. $107,377

    d. $118,375

12. What is Tony and Maria's solvency ratio?

    a. 0.64

    b. 0.56

    c. 1.56

    d. 1.64

13. What action would increase their solvency ratio?

    a. Pay off credit cards and HELOC by selling mutual funds.

    b. Take an additional HELOC and save the proceeds.

    c. Sell Maria's wedding ring and purchase mutual funds with the proceeds.

    d. Sell Maria's wedding ring and purchase a deferred fixed annuity with the proceeds.

14. Tony and Maria close on their condo before selling their home. The housing market continues to decline, and the value of their home drops to $200,000. Tony is forced to take a salary cut at work. Which option would have the most favorable outcome on Tony and Maria's credit score?

    a. Walk away from the home and allow it to enter foreclosure.

    b. File Chapter 13 bankruptcy and restructure note payments on the condo and home.

    c. File Chapter 7 bankruptcy.

    d. Negotiate with the bank to write off a portion of the HELOC loan and restructure the mortgage to an interest-only loan with higher interest but lower payments.

15. Which financial planning recommendation has the highest priority for Tony and Maria?

    a. Pay off credit card balances.

    b. Make additional premium payments on the mortgage.

    c. Purchase a personal article floater for Maria's wedding ring.

    d. Purchase disability insurance for Tony.

Case Discussion: Tony and Maria Lopez

1. What form of property insurance coverage do Tony and Maria need to purchase for their new condo?

    • **d. HO-6** —HO-6 coverage is homeowners coverage for condominiums owners and shared dwelling spaces. HO-4 would be appropriate if the Lopezes were renting a condo; HO-3 is for traditional homes. HO-1 is not an appropriate answer.

2. A dinner guest carelessly set a lit cigarette next to a lace curtain and the home burned down, a total loss. How much will Tony and Maria's insurance company pay out in total claims?

    •   **b. $525,100**—The homeowners policy will pay for replacement on the home and furnishings, subject to a 1 percent deductible. $490,000 replacement value + $40,000 of personal property less ($4,900) deductible = $525,100.

3. Tony and Maria decide to move to an apartment in the city for a year while upgrading and renovating their home. After packing up the moving truck, all of their home furnishings are destroyed in a car accident. Tony was driving the moving truck. How much will Tony and Maria receive from their homeowners insurance company?

    •   **d. $35,100**—The homeowners policy will pay for personal property less deductible, even if it is destroyed in an automobile accident. The policy would not pay for any auto damage. $40,000 less $4,900 = $35,100.

4. Maria loses her wedding ring in the move. Maria does not have any special riders or endorsements on the policy. How much will Maria receive from her homeowners policy?

    •   **a. $0**—The policy will pay for stolen or damaged items up to a sublimit. The policy will not pay for lost items without a rider or endorsement.

5. Tony and Maria purchase and move into their condo before selling their home. Which of the following options provide them with appropriate coverage?

    •   **a. Notify the insurance company of the move, maintain coverage on their home and purchase additional property insurance for their condominium.**— Tony and Maria need insurance on all real estate they own in order to finance any purchases. HO-2 or HO-3 coverage may be needed to adequately insure the home and HO-6 coverage on the condo.

6. Which of these situations is covered under the Lopezes' personal umbrella policy?

    •   **d. Tony backs over a coworker at the hospital on his way home from work.**—The other options would not be covered under a personal policy. Maria's accident while intoxicated would most likely be excluded from coverage under the terms of her contract.

7. What strategy would offer Tony and Maria more creditor protection than they have today?

   - **d. Use a portion of brokerage account assets to fund a cash value life insurance policy.**—The cash value element of life insurance is protected from creditors. Even if Tony were sued professionally his cash value elements could not be collected. Mutual funds or CDs not in an ERISA plan could be seized to pay a claim, and a revocable trust with no restrictions may also be seized by creditors.

8. Tony and Maria decide to sell everything and tour the country in an RV. What are the tax consequences of Tony and Maria liquidating their home, brokerage account, and taking a lump sum distribution of their 403(b)?

   - **d. $150,000 long-term capital loss; $350,000 unearned income**—Tony and Maria would realize $150,000 of long term capital losses from the sale of their brokerage account. The loss on their principle residence is not deductible. They would also realize $350,000 of taxable income from a lump sum distribution of their 403(b). Gains and losses in the 403(b) are immaterial in considering the income tax consequences of a lump sum distribution.

9. What is Tony and Maria's net worth?

   - **b. $728,000**—Asset values are added and total $1,135,000. The value of the home should be $450,000, which is the market value of their property. Liabilities total $407,000.

10. Assume Tony and Maria purchase the condo for its list price, pay all closing costs out of pocket, and make a 20 percent down payment. Tony and Maria do not escrow taxes and insurance. What will their monthly payments be on a 15-year conventional note with a 5.0 percent interest rate?

    - **a. $3,163**—Using a financial calculator, find the payments on $400,000 financed over 180 periods (15 years) with an annual interest rate of 5.0 percent.

11. Tony and Maria purchase the condo using a 30-year conventional note and qualify for special 5.0 percent promotional financing. They pay 20 percent down. Assuming the condo price is unchanged, how much equity will they have in the condo after one year?

   - **b. $105,901**—PV=$400,000 ($500,000 less $100,000). N=360; I/yr = 5.0%; FV=$0; Solve PMT = $2,147.29. 1 INPUT, 12 AMORT. Display principle =$5,901.46. Add $100,000 to $5,901.46 to find $105,901.

12. What is Tony and Maria's solvency ratio?

   - **a. 0.64**—The solvency ratio is net worth divided by total assets. A solvency ratio measures how much an individual is leveraged. $728,000/$1,135,000. A solvency ratio of 1 indicates no debt, while a solvency ratio near 0 indicates a high level of personal debt.

13. What action would increase their solvency ratio?

   - **a. Pay off credit cards and HELOC by selling mutual funds.**—This option would not have an impact on net worth, but would increase assets in proportion to liabilities, which would in make the client less leveraged and increase the solvency ratio.

14. Tony and Maria close on their condo before selling their home. The housing market continues to decline, and the value of their home drops to $200,000. Tony is forced to take a salary cut at work. Which option would have the most favorable outcome on Tony and Marie's credit score?

   - **d. Negotiate with the bank to write off a portion of the HELOC loan and restructure the mortgage to an interest-only loan with higher interest but lower payments.**—Tony and Maria would have less negative impact with a write-down on $30,000 than walking away from a $352,000 note or filing bankruptcy.

15. Which financial planning recommendation has the highest priority for Tony and Maria?

   - **d. Purchase disability insurance for Tony.**—Without proper disability protection in place, the entire financial plan is likely to crumble and become ineffective if Tony is disabled. Their level of living and other long-term goals could not be met today in the event of a catastrophic disability.

MINI-CASE 5: ALLISON AND TRAVIS

Note

This case addresses financial planning issues less frequently experienced by affluent clients, but very important to a large segment of Americans. Consumer Credit issues such as child support, debt management, bankruptcy and consumer protections are critical elements of financial planning and give financial service professionals an opportunity to make an impact in their clients' lives. This case also addresses financial planner confidentiality and ethical considerations.

Assume a date of 12/30/2011

Allison has been referred to you from one of your most successful clients, Richard. Allison is new to the sales force at Richard's company and he believes that she has the potential for a great career. Her assets and income are well under that of a typical client in your firm. You agree to meet with her on a pro bono basis to help her get on the right track. Allison is 32 and recently divorced. She has full custody of her son, Travis, who is 5. Travis currently receives day care at a church. Allison spends a significant portion of her income on child care and tutoring, and is worried about her son's future. Her ex-husband provides state-mandated child support payments of $1,200 per month. Allison does not receive any alimony. His payments arrive on the first of the month about 80 percent of the time. Allison occasionally has to call and remind him to send payments.

Allison is hesitant to meet with you, but does with Richard's encouragement. Allison has significant consumer and medical debt and is worried that her long-term job security could be jeopardized if her financial situation were made public. You ensure Allison that you will keep her information confidential and secure through the planning process. Allison is afraid of using bank accounts because she heard they can be directly accessed by creditors. Allison operates on a cash only basis. Allison began receiving phone calls from creditors at all hours of the day and disconnected her home phone. She has about $4,000 of cash hidden in her apartment and a 20-year-old car that she owns outright. Her car has no measurable value on a balance sheet.

Richard told you that Allison earns $50,000 annually and will receive a year-end bonus of around $5,000. She provided you with the following monthly budget:

Table 9-3 Allison's Monthly Cash Flow	
Cash inflow	
Wages	$3,500
Child support	$1,200
Non-debt expenses	
Rent	($2,000)
Day care and tutoring	($1,800)
Food, auto and entertainment	($1,200)

Allison has also supplied you with a list of her debts:

Table 9-4 Allison's Debt Schedule				
Name	**Balance**	**APR**	**Monthly Payment**	**Notes**
Local department store credit card	$3,000	16.99%	$110	$4,000 limit. Allison is in good standing.
National Credit Card	$9,000	19.99% default	$538 due next month	Allison has been delinquent for one month and is over the limit. Her credit limit is $8,000 for this card. It has a $75 monthly over-limit fee and $100 monthly late fee. Interest accrues on the previous month's balance. Fees are added to the balance on the 31st of each month.
Consolidated federal student loans	$22,500	18.99% default	$430	Student loans are in default. Allison has missed her last five payments. She initially borrowed $18,000.
Unsecured debt consolidation loan	$18,000	24.99% default	$373	Delinquent by two months
Outstanding hospital bill	$36,800	not provided	not provided	$24,000 initial bill from her son's birth. Allison has never made a payment on the bill.

Case Questions: Allison and Travis

1. What is Allison's net worth?

   a. ($82,000)

   b. ($84,300)

   c. ($85,300)

   d. ($101,000)

2. How much does Allison have available at the end of each month to pay her debts?

     a. $0
     b. $900
     c. $2,300
     d. $2,800

3. If Allison does not make her monthly payment to National Credit Card this month, what will her balance grow to next month?

     a. $9,285
     b. $9,327
     c. $13,001
     d. $10,050

4. Which of the following activities by Allison's debt collectors violates the Fair Debt Collection Practices Act?

     a. A debt collector calls Allison at 8:00 p.m. for more than two days in a row.
     b. A creditor continues calling Allison at home after she has verbally asked the creditor to stop on multiple occasions.
     c. A debt collector threatens to sue Allison in writing and over the phone for the amount she owes plus attorney's fees and interest.
     d. A debt collector calls Allison at work after she has informed the creditor that her employer does not allow personal phone calls in the workplace.

5. You are legally compelled to testify in Allison's bankruptcy proceedings. When asked if you know about any assets Allison may have hidden at her apartment, which of the following is true?

     a. You do not have to answer any questions; your relationship with Allison is protected under agent-client privilege.
     b. You do not have to answer any questions; your relationship with Allison is protected under planner-client privilege.
     c. You must disclose what Allison told you about her cash savings.
     d. You must disclose what Allison told you about her cash savings; but would not if she had paid you a planning fee.

6. Which of the following options is least likely to lower Allison's FICO score?

   a. File and successfully complete the terms of Chapter 13 bankruptcy.
   b. File and successfully complete the terms of Chapter 7 bankruptcy.
   c. Call creditors and ask them to write down portions of Allison's debt.
   d. Call creditors and attempt to negotiate more favorable interest rates.

7. After meeting with Allison, Richard calls you and asks if she is in any sort of trouble. What can you tell Richard about Allison?

   a. Confirm that Allison is in trouble but give no material facts.
   b. Tell Richard that Allison is considering filing bankruptcy.
   c. Tell Richard that you can not talk about Allison's financial situation with him without her consent.
   d. Because this is a pro bono relationship Allison is not considered your client. You can tell Richard general case facts.

8. Allison files for and receives a Chapter 7 discharge of her debts and is required to surrender her $4,000. Allison is not required to sell her car during the proceedings. What will her net worth be after this discharge?

   a. ($22,500)
   b. ($18,500)
   c. $0
   d. $4,000

9. If Allison receives a Chapter 13 discharge of her debts, how long will the bankruptcy remain on her credit report?

   a. 5 years
   b. 7 years
   c. 10 years
   d. 13 years

10. If Allison receives a $5,000 bonus at the end of the year, what will her adjusted gross income be for 2008?

    a. $50,000

    b. $55,000

    c. $64.400

    d. $69,400

Case Discussion: Allison and Travis

1. What is Allison's net worth?

    • **c. $(85,300)**—Allison's net worth is negative. Her current debt balances ($89,300) minus her cash on hand ($4,000) = $85,300. Allison's cash at home is considered an asset. This cash also creates incentive for a burglary. If no liens are presently against her, Allison can open a savings account without worrying about her money being seized by creditors.

2. How much does Allison have available at the end of each month to pay her debts?

    • **a. $0. Allison does not have any money available to pay her debts. In fact, Allison is spending more money than she earns on a monthly basis and keeps digging herself into debt. Allison desperately needs to revisit her spending and renegotiate her debt terms.**

3. If Allison does not make her monthly payment to National Credit Card this month, what will her balance grow to next month?

    • **b. $9,327**—If Allison misses her payment she will incur a $75 late fee and $100 over-limit fee, causing her balance to grow from $9,000 to $9,175. One month of interest is then applied (post fees) at her default rate (19.99%/12). The interest comes to $152.15. Add interest to the balance and her account will grow to $9,327. Her credit card is noted and charges interest on the monthly balance at the end of the month. Once in default, cardholder agreements become less favorable to the cardholder.

4. Which of the following activities by Allison's debt collectors violates the Fair Debt Collection Practices Act?

    • **d. A debt collector calls Allison at work**—The Fair Debt Collection Practices Act protects consumers from intimidation, but does not provide complete relief against debt collectors. Debt collectors can call between 8:00 a.m. and 9:00 p.m. on multiple days, so long as the calls are not threatening or make false claims. Creditors only have to stop contacting an individual if they are contacted in writing. A debt collector can threaten to sue in writing so long as they actually intend to follow through with the threat. A debt collector cannot call a place of work if they have been informed the employer does not allow personal phone calls.

5. You are legally compelled to testify in Allison's bankruptcy proceedings. When asked if you know about any assets Allison may have hidden at her apartment, which of the following is true?

   • **c. You must disclose what Allison told you about her cash savings.**—Financial planners do not have any type of confidentially privilege that prevents them from incriminating a client unless they are an attorney, accountant, or member of the clergy and planning is ancillary to other professional counseling services. Allison's pro bono status is immaterial.

6. Which of the following options is least likely to impact Allison's FICO score?

   • **d. Call creditors and attempt to negotiate more favorable interest rates.**—Even with lower interest rates the amount Allison owes will remain unchanged and her delinquencies will remain open. Bankruptcy may help Allison's long-term credit situation.

7. After meeting with Allison, Richard calls you and asks if she is in any sort of trouble. What can you tell Richard about Allison?

   • **c. Tell Richard that you can not talk about Allison's financial situation with him without her consent.**—While a financial planner may be legally compelled to discuss information about a client, agents, brokers and investment advisers violate a client's confidentiality by disclosing information to another individual without consent.

8. Allison files for and receives a Chapter 7 discharge of her debts. Allison is not required to sell her car during the proceedings. What will her net worth be after this discharge?

   • **a. ($22,500)**—Allison will not be able to discharge her federal student aid. Her balance of that loan is $22,500. Allison will most likely have to forfeit her $4,000 cash during the proceedings and could face criminal charges if she hid her cash.

9. If Allison receives Chapter 13 discharge of her debts, how long will the bankruptcy remain on her credit report?

- **b. 7 years.**—A Chapter 13 discharge remains on credit reports for 7 years, and a chapter 7 remains on a credit report for 10 years.

10. If Allison receives a $5,000 bonus at the end of the year, what will her adjusted gross income be for 2008?

- **b. $55,000**—Allison's AGI does not reflect child support payments, but would reflect alimony payments.

MINI-CASE 6: KELLY'S INVESTMENTS

Assume a case date of 1/2/2012

investment planning

This case study focuses exclusively on investment planning. Students are encouraged to review calculating security returns, standard deviation, dividend growth models, CAPM Model, and value at risk before solving the case. Kelly is typical of an affluent investor who has become dissatisfied with her broker in an era of poor market performance and a depressed economy. This case study is the most technical presented in the text, and gives students a chance to exhibit knowledge of investment planning topics.

Kelly has two portfolios. The first is an IRA managed by a competing broker and the second is a nonqualified brokerage account titled in her name. Kelly manages her own brokerage account and has some specific questions about her recent performance.

Kelly's IRA consists of the following assets:

Table 9-5 Kelly's IRA	
General Electric (GE) stock	1,250 Shares
Citigroup (C) stock	1,000 Shares
Ford (F) stock	2,000 Shares

Kelly's nonqualified brokerage account (titled in her name) consists of the following assets and account values:

Table 9-6 Kelly's Nonqualified Brokerage Account	
IVV (S&P 500 Index ETF)	$25,000
EFA (MCSI EAFE Index ETF)	$20,500
Cash ($1.00 per share money market account)	$3,000

The following table uses share prices on 1/2/2012:

Table 9-7 Share Prices on January 2nd, 2012	
GE	$16.00
C	$7.00
F	$2.61
IVV	$88.34
EFA	$43.09

You have pulled a table showing annual performance. The annual performance listed below includes reinvested dividends. It also provides Kelly's initial purchase price for each security on 1/3/2009.

Table 9-8 Historical Performance and Share Prices from 2009–2011				
Security Name	2009	2010	2011	1/2/2009 Historical Price
GE	(56.81%)	(0.38%)	6.16%	$35.50
C	(76.98%)	(47.14%)	14.76%	$48.50
F	(61.71%)	(10.39%)	(2.72%)	$8.50
Cash	3.20%	2.50%	2.00%	$1.00
IVV	(40.00%)	3.33%	13.90%	$128.00
EFA	(45.34%)	7.20%	23.19%	$62.50

Kelly has a series of questions about her portfolio.

Case Questions: Kelly's Investments

1. What was the arithmetic average return for GE over the past three years?

    a. (10.22%)
    b. (14.85%)
    c. (17.01%)
    d. (21.12%)

2. What was the geometric average return for GE over the past three years?

    a. (5.10%)
    b. (14.83%)
    c. (17.01%)

    d. (22.98%)

3. Which statement(s) are true regarding the differences between GE's arithmetic average and geometric average returns?
I. The geometric return adjusts for variances in return.

    II. The geometric return will always be less than the arithmetic return for an equity if returns are not constant.

    a. I
    b. I and II
    c. II
    d. None of the above

4. What is the standard deviation of GE over the last three years?

    a. (5.20%)
    b. (2.52%)
    c. 11.99%
    d. 34.62%

5. Assume Kelly has the same number of shares in GE, Citigroup and Ford that she did three years ago. What is the holding-period return (HPR) of Kelly's IRA over the past 3 years?

    a. (70.68%)
    b. (30.93%)
    c. (24.43%)
    d. (17.42%)

6. What was the initial value of Kelly's IRA?

    a. $36,610
    b. $149,875
    c. $119,304
    d. $172,832

7. What is the minimum annualized rate of return Kelly needs to earn on her nonqualified portfolio (assuming no future contributions) over the next five years to grow the portfolio to $75,000?

    a. 5.32%
    b. 9.11%
    c. 11.77%
    d. 12.76%

8. Kelly believes GE will continue paying a quarterly dividend of $0.40 per share indefinitely. She requires GE to provide her with at least an 8.0 percent return. Should Kelly continue holding GE?

   a. Yes—the intrinsic value of GE to Kelly is lower than the market price.

   b. Yes—the intrinsic value of GE to Kelly is higher than the market price.

   c. No—the intrinsic value of GE to Kelly is lower than the market price.

   d. No—the intrinsic value of GE to Kelly is higher than the market price.

9. Kelly expects Ford to pay a 0.10 quarterly dividend in 2012. She expects this dividend to grow by 5 percent per year beginning in 2013 and continue growing indefinitely. Kelly requires at least a 10.0 percent return to hold Ford stock. Should Kelly continue holding Ford stock?

   a. Yes—the intrinsic value of Ford to Kelly is lower than the market price.

   b. Yes—the intrinsic value of Ford to Kelly is higher than the market price.

   c. No—the intrinsic value of Ford to Kelly is lower than the market price.

   d. No—the intrinsic value of Ford to Kelly is higher than the market price.

10. The one-week value at risk (VAR) for Kelly's portfolio is $5,000 at a 0.05 confidence level and $10,000 at a 0.01 confidence level. How would you best explain this to Kelly?

   a. Kelly's portfolio has a 95 percent chance of being worth more than $10,000 and a 99 percent chance of being worth more than $5,000 at the end of the week.

   b. Kelly's portfolio has a 5 percent chance of losing as much as $5,000 and a 1 percent chance of losing as much as $10,000 in a one-week period.

   c. Kelly's portfolio has a 5 percent chance of growing by $5,000 and a 1 percent chance of growing by $10,000 in one week.

   d. Kelly's portfolio has a 50 percent chance of growing by $5,000 and a 10 percent chance of losing $10,000 in one week.

Case Discussion: Kelly's Investments

1. What was the arithmetic average return for GE over the past three years?

   - **c. (17.01%)**—The arithmetic mean is calculated as follows:

   $$ArithmeticAvg = ((-56.81\,\%) + (-0.38\,\%) + (6.16\,\%)) / 3$$

2. What was the geometric average return for GE over the past three years?

   - **d. (22.98%)**—The Geometric mean accounts for variance. The result will always produce a lower number than the arithmetic mean. The difference will be larger in proportion to the variance of returns.

   $$\sqrt[3]{(1 - .5681) * (1 - .0038) * (1 + .0616)} - 1$$

3. Which statement(s) are true regarding the differences between GE's arithmetic average and geometric average returns? I. The geometric return adjusts for variances in return.

   II. The geometric return will always be less than the arithmetic return for an equity if returns are not constant.

   - **b. I and II**—Both statements are true.

4. What is the Standard Deviation of GE over the last three years?

   - **d. 34.62%**—Standard deviation is the square root of the variance. Using the arithmetic mean as an average, standard deviation can be solved on a financial calculator that allows data points, or by applying the following formula.

   $$\sqrt{\frac{\sum_{i=1}^{N}(X_i - \bar{X})^2}{N}}$$

5. Assume Kelly has the same number of shares in GE, Citigroup and Ford that she did three years ago. What is the holding period return (HPR) of Kelly's IRA over the past 3 years?

   - **a. (70.68%)**—Kelly's IRA has experienced an abysmal performance over the last 3-year period. Her holding period return is calculated by taking today's balance and subtracting the beginning balance, then dividing the total by the beginning balance. Total Balance in IRA as of today is $32,220. The total balance in IRA assets at the beginning was $109,875. ($32,220 — $109,875)/$109,875 = (70.68%)

6. What was the initial value of Kelly's IRA?

   - **c. $119,304.**—Find the value of each stock on the date of Kelly's purchase. Then apply the growth rate to each initial value and add them together. GE = $44,357 x (1 + 0.0616) = $47,108.50. Repeat the process for Citigroup ($55,658) and Ford ($16,537).

7. What is the minimum annualized rate of return Kelly needs to earn on her nonqualified portfolio (assuming no future contributions) over the next five years to grow the portfolio to $75,000?

   - **b. 9.11%**—This problem asks to solve interest rate in a time value of money scenario. PV is the current value of Kelly's nonqualified portfolio ($48,500). FV is $75,000. N is 5 years. PMT is 0. Solve for I.

8. Kelly believes GE will continue paying a quarterly dividend of $0.40 per share indefinitely. She requires GE to provide her with at least an 8.0 percent return. Should Kelly continue holding GE?

   - **b. Yes—the intrinsic value of GE to Kelly is higher than the market price.**—Using the constant-dividend growth model, Kelly finds that the intrinsic value of GE is ($1.60/(0.08–0.0)) or $20.00. The intrinsic value ($20) of GE is higher than the current market price ($16). GE is undervalued by the market, and Kelly should maintain a position expecting the value to appreciate.

9. Kelly expects Ford to pay a 0.10 quarterly dividend in 2012. She expects this dividend to grow by 5 percent per year beginning in 2013 and continue growing indefinitely. Kelly requires at least a 10.0 percent return to hold Ford stock. Should Kelly continue holding Ford stock?

   - **b. Yes—the intrinsic value of Ford to Kelly is higher than the market price.**—Using the constant-dividend growth model, Kelly finds that the intrinsic value of Ford is ($0.40/(0.10 – 0.05)) = $8.00. The current price of Ford ($2.61) is less than its intrinsic value ($8.00) which is the price Kelly should require to take the risk of owning Ford. Ford is undervalued by the market, and Kelly should maintain a position expecting the value to appreciate.

10. The one-week value at risk (VAR) for Kelly's portfolio is $5,000 at a 0.05 confidence level and $10,000 at a 0.01 confidence level. How would you best explain this to Kelly?

    - **b. Kelly's portfolio has a 5 percent chance of losing as much as $5,000 and a 1 percent chance of losing as much as $10,000 in a one-week period.**—Value at risk measures the chance of loss at a stated confidence interval over a given time period. The VAR is an alternative method of explaining portfolio risk to a client.

APPENDIX A: BIBLIOGRAPHY AND RECOMMENDED IN-DEPTH READINGS

McFadden, John J. *Employee Benefits*. 7th ed. Chicago: Dearborn Financial Publishing, Inc., 2004.

Canan, Michael J. *Qualified Retirement and Other Employee Benefit Plans* (West's Handbook Series). St. Paul: West Publishing Co., 2003.

Dalton, Michael A, Langdon, Thomas P., ed. *Estate Planning for Financial Planners*. 3d ed. Kenner, LA: Money Education, 2009.

Graves, Edward E., ed. *McGill's Life Insurance*. 7th ed. Bryn Mawr: The American College, 2009.

Lehmann, Michael B. *The Business One Irwin Guide to Using The Wall Street Journal*. 6th ed. Homewood, Illinois: Business One Irwin, 2000.

Tacchino, Kenn Beam, and Littell, David A. *Planning for Retirement Needs*. 10th ed. Bryn Mawr: The American College, 2009.

McFadden, John J., ed. *Financial Planning—The New Century: The American College's Guide to the State of the Art for Financial Services Professionals*. Bryn Mawr: The American College, 2001.

Stephens, Richard B.; Maxfield, Guy B.; Lind, Stephen A.; and Calfee, Dennis A. *Federal Estate and Gift Taxation*. 8th ed. RIA Group, 2002 (with supplements).

Tax Management United States Income Series. Tax Management, Inc., a division of The Bureau of National Affairs, Inc. Washington, D.C.

Tax Management Estate, Gifts and Trust Series. Tax Management, Inc., a division of The Bureau of National Affairs, Inc. Washington, D.C.

The statute and the regulations thereunder are available as the Complete Internal Revenue Code of 1986 (as amended), the Income Tax Regulations (as amended), and the Estate and Gift Tax Regulations (as amended) from various legal publishers, such as Prentice-Hall, Inc., Commerce Clearing House, Inc., and others.